T0326312

PEOPLE, MARKETS, GOODS:
ECONOMIES AND SOCIETIES IN HISTORY
Volume 21

Labour Laws in Preindustrial Europe

PEOPLE, MARKETS, GOODS:
ECONOMIES AND SOCIETIES IN HISTORY

ISSN: 2051–7467

Series editors
Marguerite Dupree – University of Glasgow
Steve Hindle – Washington University in St Louis
Jane Humphries – University of Oxford, London School of Economics
Willem M. Jongman – University of Groningen
John Turner – Queen's University Belfast
Jane Whittle – University of Exeter
Nuala Zahedieh – University of Cambridge

The interactions of economy and society, people and goods, and transactions and actions are at the root of most human behaviours. Economic and social historians are participants in the same conversation about how markets have developed historically and how they have been constituted by economic actors and agencies in various social, institutional and geographical contexts. New debates now underpin much research in economic, social, cultural, demographic, urban and political history. Their themes have enduring resonance – financial stability and instability, the costs of health and welfare, the implications of poverty and riches, flows of trade and the centrality of communications. This paperback series aims to attract historians interested in economics and economists with an interest in history by publishing high-quality, cutting-edge academic research in the broad field of economic and social history from the late medieval/early modern period to the present day. It encourages the interaction of qualitative and quantitative methods through excellent monographs and collections offering path-breaking overviews of key research concerns. Taking as its benchmark international relevance and excellence, it is open to scholars and subjects of any geographical area, from the case study to the multi-nation comparison.

PREVIOUSLY PUBLISHED TITLES IN THE SERIES ARE
LISTED AT THE BACK OF THIS VOLUME

Labour Laws in Preindustrial Europe

The Coercion and Regulation of Wage Labour, c.1350–1850

Edited by Jane Whittle and Thijs Lambrecht

THE BOYDELL PRESS

First published 2023
The Boydell Press, Woodbridge

ISBN 978–1-78327–768–1

The Boydell Press is an imprint of Boydell & Brewer Ltd
PO Box 9, Woodbridge, Suffolk IP12 3DF, UK
and of Boydell & Brewer Inc.
668 Mt Hope Avenue, Rochester, NY 14620–2731, USA
website: www.boydellandbrewer.com

A catalogue record for this book is available
from the British Library

The publisher has no responsibility for the continued existence or accuracy of URLs for
external or third-party internet websites referred to in this book, and does not guarantee
that any content on such websites is, or will remain, accurate or appropriate

This publication is printed on acid-free paper

Dedicated to the memory of
Theresa Johnsson
1969–2022

Contents

Illustrations

Figures

Tables

Map

Full credit details are provided in the captions to the images in the text. The editors, contributors and publisher are grateful to all the institutions and persons for permission to reproduce the materials in which they hold copyright. Every effort has been made to trace the copyright holders; apologies are offered for any omission, and the publisher will be pleased to add any necessary acknowledgement in subsequent editions.

Contributors

Professor emerita Francine Michaud, University of Calgary, Canada, is the author of *Earning Dignity: Labour Conditions and Relations during the Century of the Black Death in Marseille* (Brepols, 2016). Her work on labour strategies emphasises vulnerable labourers' access to income resources.

Dr Davide Cristoferi, University of Ghent, Belgium, is a FWO postdoctoral researcher. He studies the relationship between economic inequality, fiscal and labour policies and agrarian systems such as sharecropping and transhumance in late medieval Tuscany. He has published several articles on this topic, a book and an edition of sources.

Dr Thijs Lambrecht, University of Ghent, is a Senior Lecturer in Rural History. He has published on the history of labour relations, economic inequality and poor relief in the Low Countries during the late medieval and early modern period.

Professor Raffaella Sarti, Università di Urbino Carlo Bo, Italy, is author of *Europe at Home: Family and Material Culture 1500–1800* (Yale University Press, 2002) and editor of *What is Work? Gender at the Crossroads of Home, Family, and Business from the Early Modern Era to the Present* (Berghahn, 2018).

Dr Charmian Mansell, University of Cambridge, holds a British Academy postdoctoral fellowship to research 'Everyday Travel and Communities in Early Modern England'. She has several publications on female servants in early modern England, and a digital edition of court records.

Dr Hanne Østhus, Norwegian University of Science and Technology, Trondheim, Norway, is currently engaged on a research project 'Servants and Slaves', examining the lives of non-European servants and slaves who were transported to seventeenth- and eighteenth-century Scandinavia.

Dr Carolina Uppenberg, Stockholm University, Sweden, studies agrarian social relations with a gender perspective and is currently leading a research project titled 'Challenging the domestic. Gender division of labour and economic change studied through 19th century crofters' households'.

Dr Theresa Johnsson, Uppsala University, Sweden, was a postdoctoral fellow in the Hugo Valentin Centre, where her research focused on class and social, economic and legal inequality and how these variables shaped people's lives, c.1780–1850.

Dr Vilhelm Vilhelmsson, University of Iceland, Iceland, is director of the University of Iceland Research Centre North-West. His book *Sjálfstætt fólk: Vistarband og íslenskt samfélag á 19. öld* [Independent People: Compulsory Service and Icelandic Society in the 19th Century] (Sögufélag, 2017) was short-listed for the Icelandic Literature Price.

Professor Jane Whittle, University of Exeter, is editor of *Servants in Rural Europe c.1400–c.1900* (Boydell Press, 2017) and co-author of *The Experience of Work in Early Modern England* (Cambridge University Press, forthcoming), as well as many other publications.

Acknowledgements

This book began as a workshop at Ghent University in June 2018 funded by the FWO Comparative Rural History Network (CORN) and was developed in a set of parallel sessions at the European Rural History (EURHO) Conference in Paris in 2019. Chapter drafts were discussed at workshop organised as part of Jane Whittle's European Research Council Advanced grant 'Forms of Labour' originally planned for Exeter in May 2020 but held online due to the pandemic. We would like to thank all the participants of those workshops and conference panels, along with the anonymous reviewers for Boydell Press, for their enthusiastic and critical comments. Open Access publication has been made possible by funding from the European Research Council, the Research Foundation Flanders, and the University of Iceland. Tragically, one of the original members of our group, Theresa Johnsson, died from a long-term illness in February 2022. We dedicate the book to her memory.

Abbreviations

ADBRM	Archives départementales des Bouches-du Rhône, Marseille
AMM	Archives Municipales Marseille
ASFi	Archive of Florence
DHC	Devon Heritage Centre
DL	The Danish Law of 1683
GA	Gloucestershire Archives
HARC	Herefordshire Archive and Records Centre
JP	Justice of the Peace
NAI	National Archives of Iceland
NL	The Norwegian Law of 1687
P. R.	*Parliament Rolls of Medieval England*, https://www.british-history.ac.uk/no-series/parliament-rolls-medieval [accessed 17 March 2020]
RA	The National Archive of Norway
SAB	State Archives, Bruges
SAO	Regional State Archive, Oslo
SFS	Svensk författningssamling
SHC	Somerset Heritage Centre
S. R.	*Statutes of the Realm* Vol 1–4, available on HeinOnline: https://heinonline-org.uoelibrary.idm.oclc.org/HOL/Welcome [accessed 23 June 2020]
ULA	Uppsala State Archives

Introduction: Towards a Comparative History of Europe's Labour Laws, c.1350–1850

THIJS LAMBRECHT AND JANE WHITTLE

Approaches to wage labour

In his pioneering study from 1886 on living standards in the past, the economic historian James Thorold Rogers delivered a harsh verdict on the labour laws that governed employer–worker relations in England between 1563 and 1824. Rogers described this body of labour legislation as nothing less than a 'conspiracy' aiming 'to cheat the English workman of his wages, to tie him to the soil, to deprive him of hope, and to degrade him into irremediable poverty'.[1] This characterisation of English labour legislation as a socially selective and oppressive body of law that resulted in low wages, immobility and poverty was informed by Rogers' liberal ideological stance. In their design, the English labour laws were indeed completely antithetical to the principles of free trade that Rogers advocated as a politician. Of most significance here, however, is that the quotation illustrates that the founders of economic history paid ample attention to the legal framework in which labour was mobilised, supervised and remunerated. The material realities of work and wages that Rogers sought to reconstruct could not be dissociated from the legislative framework of work and wages that characterised English society between the late Middle Ages and the early nineteenth century. Other pioneers of English economic history followed in Rogers' footsteps. On the eve of the First World War, Richard Tawney published a lengthy article on the periodic assessment of wages by Justices of the Peace – one of the key elements of early modern English labour laws.[2] This interest in the history of pre-industrial economic relations would expand beyond England. In his opus magnum on the history of economic development in Europe, the Russian historian Maxim Kowalewsky devoted more than 200 pages to the early history of labour laws in late medieval Europe.[3] In

---

1 J. T. Rogers, *Six Centuries of Work and Wages: The History of English Labour* (London, 1884), p. 398.
2 R. H. Tawney, 'The Assessment of Wages in England by the Justices of the Peace', *Vierteljahrschrift fur Sozial- und Wirtschaftsgeschichte*, 11 (1914), 307–37, 533–64.
3 M. Kowalewsky, *Die ökonomische Entwicklung Europas bis zum Beginn der kapitalistischen Wirtschaftsform*, vol. 5 (Berlin, 1911), pp. 208–445; M. Kowalewsky, 'La législation

his view, late medieval labour legislation was an elite response to the breakdown and demise of serfdom in many parts of Europe. Kowalewsky identified labour laws as a characteristic feature of the transition from feudalism to capitalism in late medieval Europe. Nor was this interest in the history of labour legislation restricted to economic historians. In Germany in particular the history of the legal status of servants attracted much attention. During the late nineteenth and early twentieth centuries numerous – and sometimes lengthy – studies were published that retraced and reconstructed the vast regional bodies of labour laws that governed master–servant and employer–worker relations in the past.[4] All these historians shared the belief that labour laws were more than a footnote in the economic history of Europe; in their design, operation and enforcement, labour laws exposed the social, economic and legal realities and hierarchies of work in the pre-industrial past.

In the second half of the twentieth century, this perspective was gradually abandoned. Economic historians produced a wealth of new data on wages and earnings in the past, but the potential impact of legal labour regimes on the operation of the labour market was rarely researched or acknowledged. In contrast, it was social historians who from the 1970s onwards stressed the fundamental role of labour, poor and vagrancy laws in creating a disciplinary environment for the different categories of pre-industrial workers.[5] With particular reference to England, economic historians sketched a narrative of labour markets that were seemingly immune to the impact of labour laws. This was due to the focus on the settled male day labourer as the preferred unit of analysis, combined with a relative neglect of different forms of labour organisation, such as service or migrant labour. Yet, work performed by living-in servants still accounted for the majority of waged work in the agricultural sector in England until the 1770s.[6] The privileged attention of economic historians on male day labourers produced a skewed and incomplete picture of the lived realities of waged labour in the pre-industrial countryside. Arguably, immobile married adult male labourers were the category of workers that were the least affected by labour, poor and vagrancy laws. The vast body of labour laws predominantly targeted other categories of workers: the young, the unmarried,

---

ouvrière aux XIIIe et XIVe siècles', *Annales Internationales d'Histoire* (1900), 173–212.

4   For example, R. Wuttke, *Gesindeordnungen und Gesindezwangsdienst in Sachsen bis zum Jahre 1835* (Leipzig, 1893); H. Platzer, *Geschichte der ländlichen Arbeitsverhältnisse in Bayern* (Munich, 1904); E. Lennhoff, *Das ländliche Gesindewesen in der Kurmak Brandenburg vom 16. bis 19. Jahrhundert* (Breslau, 1906); O. Könnecke, *Rechtsgeschichte des Gesindes in West- und Suddeutschland* (Marburg, 1912).

5   See, for example, C. Lis and H. Soly, *Poverty and Capitalism in Pre-Industrial Europe* (New Jersey, 1979) and A. Beier, *Masterless Men: The Vagrancy Problem in England 1560–1640* (London, 1985).

6   C. Muldrew, *Food, Energy and the Creation of Industriousness. Work and Material Culture in Agrarian England, 1550–1780* (Cambridge, 2011), pp. 223–4.

the mobile and the property-less. Also, recent research on England has shown that young women were disproportionally affected by late medieval and early modern labour laws. Late medieval compulsory service, for example, targeted women in particular.[7] The reconstruction of women's wages in the long run by Humphries and Weisdorf indicates that legal wage ceilings imposed by the labour laws effectively held down the earnings of women employed on annual contracts.[8] Importantly, the relative lack of information and detailed studies on these categories of workers compared with male day labourers produces an unrealistic picture of the impact of labour laws in pre-industrial England and other parts of Europe. As we show, numerous studies have unearthed a substantial body of late medieval and early modern labour legislation that actively shaped labour markets and had a direct impact on substantial parts of the pre-industrial rural workforce.

From 1349 onwards, in the aftermath of the Black Death, laws to control waged work multiplied across Europe. Some were local by-laws, others national statutes; some sought to regulate wages and contracts, others sought to control mobility and force potential workers into employment. What these laws demonstrate is a shared belief that hired workers could not be left unregulated. Thus, although waged work became a common form of labour across much of the continent during the late medieval and early modern period, this wage labour was not necessarily 'free'. That is to say, receiving payment in return for work does not necessarily mean that a free labour market existed, where workers and employers met on equal terms and bargained to create a labour contract. Instead, governments and local elites sought to control those social groups that provided wage labour – particularly the young, the relatively poor, and the mobile – and create terms of employment that favoured the employer. In many regions, service was preferred over day labouring as a means of exercising greater control over wage workers. Many laws contained provisions for unemployed or casually employed people to be forced into compulsory service. What we observe, in many parts of Europe, is a selectivity in how labour markets were organised resulting in the restriction of freedom for some categories of workers. The timing, nature and enforcement of such restrictions on the operation of a 'free' labour were subject to important variations. However, as the chapters in this book indicate, labour laws cannot be isolated from underlying economic, social, political and cultural structures.

This book is largely concerned with rural workers, the most common form of wage labour in late medieval and early modern Europe. It concentrates on Western Europe, the region where free wage labour is imagined to have

---

7   J. M. Bennett, 'Compulsory Service in Late Medieval England', *Past and Present*, 209 (2010), 7–51.
8   J. Humphries and J. Weisdorf, 'The Wages of Women in England, 1260–1850', *Journal of Economic History*, 75 (2015), 423–4.

developed. While recent histories have rightly characterised the late medieval and early modern economies of many European regions as dynamic and highly commercialised, this does not mean that free labour markets necessarily existed. The book explores the variety of legal and regulatory regimes that existed to control labour and how workers experienced those controls. As such, it views labour not just as a relationship between worker and employer but as one between worker, employer and the state. The rest of this section briefly explores the wider implications of wage labour and its regulation for our understanding of this period. Part two of the introduction provides an overview of the context and motivations of labour regulation in different regions, while part three summarises the laws enforced. The final section explains the structure of the book.

Building on the ground-breaking articles of Samuel Cohn and Catharina Lis and Hugo Soly, this book aims to place the development of Europe's labour laws in comparative perspective.[9] Viewing labour regulation comparatively across geographical regions demonstrates both the range of ways labour was organised and the variety of means used to control hired workers. While there were many similarities across regions – for instance, the division of the hired workforce into three main groups, servants employed on annual contracts, day labourers and skilled craftsmen – there were also important differences. Robert Brenner's description of rural economic development in medieval and early modern Europe envisaged workers either as subject to serfdom or as free peasants or wage workers.[10] Yet wage labour did not necessarily entail freedom of action for workers within labour markets. Instead labour was controlled in a variety of ways: sometimes by types of taxation and forms of tenancy (late medieval Italy),[11] sometimes by guild regulations (Germanic regions),[12] sometimes using by-laws created by local elites (southern Low Countries),[13] and sometimes by national and regional laws (England and Scandinavia).[14] These regulations could be all-encompassing and tightly enforced (as in eighteenth-century Sweden, nineteenth-century Iceland and parts of early modern

---

9   S. Cohn, 'After the Black Death: Labour Legislation and Attitudes towards Labour in Late Medieval Western Europe', *Economic History Review*, 60 (2007), 457–85; C. Lis and H. Soly, 'Labor Laws in Western Europe, 13th–16th Centuries: Patterns of Political and Socio-Economic Rationality', in M. van der Linden and L. Lucassen (eds), *Working on Labor: Essays in Honor of Jan Lucassen* (Leiden, 2012), pp. 297–321.

10   R. Brenner, 'The Agrarian Roots of European Capitalism', *Past and Present*, 97 (1982), 16–113.

11   See the chapter of Cristoferi in this volume.

12   S. Ogilvie, *State Corporatism and Proto-Industry: the Württemberg Black Forest, 1580–1797* (Cambridge, 1997).

13   See Lambrecht in this volume.

14   See Whittle, Østhus and Uppenberg in this volume.

Germany),[15] or unevenly enforced (early modern England).[16] But, wherever they existed, they demonstrate that the holders of political power conceived of wage workers not as 'free' but as subservient and in need of control – economic, social and moral. Workers were seen not as choosing to labour but instead as having a duty to work, and to work in a particular way.

Wage labour is an important aspect of how historians envisage economic change in late medieval and early modern Western Europe. Large farms worked by wage labourers are seen as characterising agrarian capitalism and as more economically advanced than large farms worked by labour services under serfdom, or small farms that relied predominantly on family labour.[17] Similarly, the proportion of the population who were wage earners is seen as a measure of overall economic development and dynamism.[18] Yet, typically, these schema leave unexplored the range of types of wage labour and the nature of markets in which labour was offered for wages. This not only overlooks the human experience of work but risks misrepresenting the context of economic change. We imagine labour markets emerging 'naturally' and operating smoothly according to supply and demand. Yet both Karl Marx and Adam Smith recognised that worker and employer did not meet as equals in the labour market: the employer benefited not only from ownership of capital but also from the support of legislation.[19]

Historians of labour regulation have developed a parallel account of the development of wage labour in Western Europe that draws very different conclusions. Historians including Robert Steinfeld, Douglas Hay and Paul Craven, and Alessandro Stanziani argue that wage labour was not 'free' until reforms in master–servant laws in the second half of the nineteenth century.[20] Before that time laws and litigators conceived of wage workers not as free agents

15   See Uppenberg and Vilhemsson in this volume. For Germany: S. Ogilvie, 'Married Women, Work and the Law: Evidence from Early Modern Germany', in C. Beattie and M. Stevens (eds), *Married Women and the Law in Northern Europe c.1200–1800* (Woodbridge, 2013), pp. 213–39.
16   See Mansell in this volume.
17   L. Shaw-Taylor, 'The Rise of Agrarian Capitalism and the Decline of Family Farming in England', *Economic History Review*, 65 (2012), 26–60.
18   T. de Moor and J. L. van Zanden, 'Girl Power: the European Marriage Pattern and Labour Markets in the North Sea Region in the Late Medieval and Early Modern Period', *Economic History Review*, 63 (2010), 12–13.
19   A. Smith, *Wealth of Nations*, vol. 1 (London, 1776), pp. 97–9; K. Marx, *Capital*, vol. 1 (London, 1887), chapter 28.
20   R. J. Steinfeld, *The Invention of Free Labor: The Employment Relation in English and American Law and Culture, 1350–1870* (Chapel Hill, 1991); D. Hay and P. Craven (eds), *Masters, Servants and Magistrates in Britain and the Empire, 1562–1955* (Chapel Hill, 2004); A. Stanziani, *Bondage: Labor and Rights in Eurasia from the Sixteenth to the Early Twentieth Centuries* (New York, 2014).

entering into contracts as equals but as servants and as subservient.[21] Not only were servants (workers employed on longer contracts, often living with their employer) numerically dominant, they were also the normative conception of a wage worker and were assumed to be subservient – that is, of inferior social status and possessing inferior legal rights. In this conception, the late medieval and early modern period was not one of free wage labour markets, but instead was characterised by varied forms of wage labour, typically dominated by live-in service and heavily regulated by laws. Most of these forms of labour were less than free.

Implicit in this 'less than free' wage labour approach is another important observation. Wage labour is not a self-evident concept; instead, like slavery and serfdom, it consists of a bundle of rights that might or might not be extended to different workers and types of worker. For instance, Marcel van der Linden argues for an approach to all forms of labour that examines the entry, conduct and exit from employment arrangements separately in order to discern the degree of freedom allowed to the worker.[22] Lists of possible freedoms or rights, used in comparative histories of slavery, can also be applied to wage workers.[23] The argument here is not that wage labour was equivalent to slavery or serfdom but rather than each form of labour is made up of characteristics that varied and need to be identified and considered in each particular case. As a consequence, it is helpful to think of many varieties of late medieval and early modern wage labour as 'less than free' rather than 'free' or 'unfree'.

The integration of the 'less than free' wage labour perspective into interpretations of economic and social change in Western Europe (and elsewhere) has a number of important implications. The first is that the development of capitalism (or highly commercial and market-orientated societies) does not depend on the dominance of free wage labour. This point has been made repeatedly by historians of early modern slavery,[24] and is implicit in the continued existence of slavery and other forms of coercion in the modern world.[25] But it is also true that the development of capitalism between the fourteenth and eighteenth century, and during the Industrial Revolution, often depended on 'less than free' labour within Western Europe. Thus the second important implication is that

21   This issue is explored in Sarti, this volume.

22   M. van der Linden, 'Dissecting Coerced Labor', in M. van der Linden and M. Rodríguez García (eds), *On Coerced Labor: Work and Compulsion after Chattel Slavery* (Leiden, 2016), pp. 293–322.

23   For example, R. E. Wright, *The Poverty of Slavery: How Unfree Labor Pollutes the Economy* (London, 2017), pp. 25–7.

24   See, for example, B. L. Solow, 'Capitalism and Slavery in the Exceedingly Long Run', in B. L. Solow and S. L. Engerman (eds), *British Capitalism and Caribbean Slavery: The Legacy of Eric Williams* (Cambridge, 1988), pp. 51–78.

25   D. Eltis *et al.* (eds), *The Cambridge World History of Slavery. Vol. 4: 1804–2016* (Cambridge, 2017).

the presence of markets in labour indicate neither the presence of capitalism nor the absence of unfree labour. Markets and capitalism are not synonymous, and the absence of serfdom or slavery does not imply freedom for all workers.

The third point, following from this, is that wage rates do not necessarily reflect market forces (i.e. supply of and demand for labour or the productivity of the worker), but may reflect the freedom of workers to negotiate contracts and the balance of power within wider society. Workers' freedoms could be constricted not only by laws that sought to set wages but also regulations that impeded mobility, created harsh punishments for breaking contracts and forced the unemployed into work. Lack of social status and political power reduced the ability to demand higher wages, as studies of women's work demonstrate.[26] This leads to the fourth point: to understand restrictions to workers' freedoms we need to look beyond the regulation of wages to not only other aspects of labour legislation but also vagrancy laws and the poor laws, to which the labour laws were closely related. Vagrancy laws constricted mobility and punished unemployment. Poor laws could force the able-bodied into work, but, perhaps more significantly, they also sanctioned moral and social interference by economic and political elites in the lives of the relatively poor, undermining freedom in other ways.[27] A final, perhaps rather obvious, point is that the labour laws make it very clear that the legal system was not socially or politically neutral. While laws occasionally offered rights to workers, for instance to reclaim unpaid wages or challenge broken contracts, they were predominantly used to empower employers and enforce workers' subservience. In that sense, labour laws created, reproduced and amplified social and economic inequalities in pre-industrial Europe.

Motives and context

A large number of European studies have exposed the emergence and existence of various legal measures and mechanisms that intervened in the operation of rural labour markets in pre-industrial Europe. In general terms, these legal interventions – commonly referred to as labour laws – were a reaction to the 'problem of labour'. This problem – real or perceived – manifested itself through anxieties and concerns about the labour supply, wage levels and worker subservience.[28] As this section will show, these challenges often prompted different and divergent responses from those who sought to address the problem of labour.

---

26   E.g. Humphries and Weisdorf, 'The Wages of Women', 419–30.
27   S. Hindle, *On the Parish? The Micro-Politics of Poor Relief in Rural England c.1550–1750* (Oxford, 2004); see also Johnsson and Vilhelmsson, this volume below.
28   C. Lis and H. Soly, 'Policing the Early Modern Proletariat, 1450–1850', in D. Levine (ed.), *Proletarianization and Family History* (Orlando, 1984), pp. 163–228.

Existing research illustrates that European elites resorted to an impressive and varied arsenal of formal legal measures to bring labour under their control. Labour laws were a pan-European phenomenon during most of the medieval and early modern period, but were equally characterised by substantial differences in the nature of the measures that were adopted.

The variety of responses recorded in pre-industrial labour laws defies any logic at first sight. With respect to the timing, institutions, targeted worker populations and disciplinary measures, the European countryside displays significant differences. Following the outbreak of the Black Death, many regions throughout Europe resorted to some kind of labour control.[29] In some regions these interventions were either short-lived or failed to produce the desired effects. For example, historians have been sceptical about the effects of the labour laws introduced in the region of Paris and the county of Hainaut to combat the mid- fourteenth-century inflation of wages and labour costs.[30] In other regions the measures introduced during the 1350s proved more resilient and marked the starting point of centuries of labour and wage control. For example, in England, northern Italy and some German regions labour laws following the demographic catastrophe of the late 1340s and 1350s initiated interventions in the labour market in the longer term. In contrast, some regions remained untouched by top-down labour market intervention following the Black Death. In the Low Countries most rural regions did not introduce labour legislation in the fourteenth century. Here, the second half of the sixteenth century witnessed an upsurge in local and regional initiatives to deal with the 'problem of labour' following a number of mortality crises.[31] Other regions did not introduce labour laws until the seventeenth century. In large parts of Central and Eastern Europe the demographic downturn triggered by the Thirty Years War (1618–48) marked a new starting point of decades of active labour market intervention.[32]

There was more uniformity with respect to the demise of efforts to control the rural labour market via legal means. In the course of the nineteenth century

---

29   For an overview of post-Black Death interventions in European rural labour markets see R. Schröder, *Zur Arbeitsverfassung des Spätmittelalters. Eine Darstellung mittelalterlichen Arbeitsrecht aus der Zeit nach der grossen Pest* (Berlin, 1984), pp. 74–104 and R. Braid, 'Et non ultra: politiques royales du travail en Europe occidentale au XIVe siècle', *Bibliothèque de l'Ecole des Chartes*, 161 (2003), 437–91.

30   G. Fourquin, *Les campagnes de la région parisienne à la fin du Moyen Age* (Paris, 1964), p. 258 and G. Sivery, *Structures agraires et vie rurale dans le Hainaut à la fin du Moyen Age*, vol. 2 (Lille, 1980), pp. 429–30.

31   C. Verlinden and J. Craeybeckx, *Prijzen- en lonenpolitiek in de Nederlanden in 1561 en 1588–1589. Onuitgegeven adviezen, ontwerpen en ordonnanties* (Brussels, 1962).

32   W. Abel, *Agrarkrisen und Agrarkonjunktur. Eine Geschichte der Land- und Ernährungswirtschaft Mitteleuropas seit dem hohen Mittelalter* (Hamburg–Berlin, 1978), pp. 160–1; S. Simon, *Die Tagelöhner und ihr Recht im 18 Jahrhundert* (Berlin, 1995), p. 258.

rural labour laws were either abolished, simplified or reformed to bring workers and employers onto an equal legal footing. Labour market intervention in England remained in force until the third quarter of the nineteenth century but after the 1720s targeted the industrial sector in particular. In contrast to previous centuries, the impact of labour laws in eighteenth-century rural England was limited.[33] In France, the revolutionary period marked the end of Old Regime rural labour laws. Although there were temporary measures to deal with rural labour shortages and wage inflation during the Revolution (see below), legal measures during the nineteenth century were restricted to the prevention of worker coalitions (to obtain higher wages) and breach of contract.[34] There is an overall impression of a gradual relaxation of legal means to control the rural workforce during the second half of the nineteenth century. Labour laws were increasingly undermined by the growth of industry and rapid urbanisation in the nineteenth century as large sections of the rural population were offered an alternative to agricultural employment. Liberal governments throughout Europe deliberately deregulated rural labour markets to facilitate internal migration and inter-sectoral mobility.[35] However, the disappearance of labour laws did not necessarily imply that rural elites lost their overall grip on the local labour market. In England, for example, the (old and new) poor laws offered ample opportunities for employers to gain formal and informal control over the working lives of the labouring population. Poor laws and labour laws had worked for centuries in tandem to discipline and control England's rural workforce.[36] The growing poverty of the rural workforce from the middle of

---

33   W. E. Minchinton, 'Wage Regulation in Pre-Industrial England', in W. E. Minchinton (ed.), *Wage Regulation in Pre-Industrial England* (Newton Abbot, 1972), pp. 10–36; M. Roberts, 'Wages and Wage-Earners in England: the Evidence of the Wage Assessments, 1563–1725', unpublished PhD dissertation (University of Oxford, 1981); J. Innes, 'Regulating Wages in Eighteenth and Early Nineteenth-Century England: Arguments in Context', in P. Gauci (ed.), *Regulating the British Economy, 1660–1850* (Farnham, 2011), pp. 195–216.

34   Y. Crebouw, 'Les salariés agricoles face au maximum des salaires', in *La Révolution française et le monde rural* (Paris, 1989), pp. 113–22; Y. Crebouw, 'Droits et obligations des journaliers et des domestiques, droits et obligations des maîtres', in R. Hubschner and J.-C. Farcy (eds), *La moisson des autres. Les salariés agricoles aux XIXe et XXe siècles* (Ivry-sur-Seine, 1996), pp. 181–98. Crebouw notes that – at least in theory – French law placed farmers and their workers on an equal legal footing.

35   See the case of German territories in T. Keiser, 'Between Status and Contract? Coercion in Contractual Labour Relationships in Germany from the 16th to the 20th century', *Journal of the Max Planck Institute for European Legal History*, 21 (2013), 32–47.

36   See the examples in A. L. Beier, 'A New Serfdom. Labor Laws, Vagrancy Statutes and Labor Discipline in England, 1350–1800', in A. L. Beier and P. Ocobock (eds), *Cast Out. Vagrancy and Homelessness in Global and Historical Perspective* (Athens, 2014), pp. 55–6; T. Wales, 'Living at Their Own Hands: Policing Poor Households and the Young in Early Modern Rural England', *Agricultural History Review*, 61 (2013), 33.

the eighteenth century onwards made the poor laws a more effective tool of labour market control for rural elites.[37] The impact and use of labour laws might have receded, but rural elites found other ways to gain control over the local labour market.

In addition to differences in timing, European labour laws also tended to target different categories of workers. As noted, there was an important element of selectivity in labour laws. In most Scandinavian countries, for example, labour laws targeted unmarried adolescents who were brought under the control of employers through the institution of service. Swedish, Norwegian and Icelandic labour laws were a response to the low population densities that characterised these countries. Service became the favoured strategy to hire workers because it assured the employers of year-round access to labour.[38] In late medieval and early modern France labour laws were primarily designed to facilitate the recruitment and supply of day-labourers. These laws were mainly constructed to avoid labour shortages during peak agricultural periods. The grain and grape harvests in particular were at stake and these required the availability of labourers that could be hired for shorter periods. These differences can also be observed within countries. As the examples of England and the Low Countries indicate, labour laws – in either their design or their enforcement – targeted workers selectively. The specific nature of agricultural production and the associated logic of labour deployment (servants, day labourers and/or migrant workers) largely determined the type of labour that was targeted through the labour laws. Labour laws, therefore, clearly built on pre-existing patterns of labour demand and targeted those categories of workers that were essential to agricultural operations. Labour laws largely mirrored the specific demographic and agricultural characteristics of a region and were not designed with the aim of introducing radical changes in either the supply or the recruitment of labour.

Thirdly, there are also substantial differences in the institutions that enacted labour laws, which could range from national parliaments to local lords. National labour laws that were enacted in a uniform manner throughout a large territory flourished in particular in regions characterised by early forms of political and territorial centralisation. Late medieval and early modern England is the best example of this situation. Here, national labour laws were enacted by parliament from 1351 onwards and – in theory – a set of identical labour laws

37   K. Snell, *Annals of the Labouring Poor. Social Change and Agrarian England, 1660–1900* (Cambridge, 1985), p. 124. For examples from the Low Countries, see Lambrecht in this volume.
38   See the overview in A. Imhof, 'Der Arbeitszwang für das landwirtschaftliche Dienstvolk in den nordischen Ländern im 18 Jahrhundert', *Zeitschrift für Agrargschichte und Agrarsoziologie*, 22 (1974), 59–74 and Østhus, Uppenberg, Johnsson and Vilhelmsson in this volume.

applied to all English regions and villages. The English case, however, is exceptional in late medieval Europe. Although in many other European countries and principalities some form of 'national' labour law can be encountered, these national initiatives often operated in tandem with legislation enacted by other political entities.[39] In early modern France, for example, there was national labour legislation concerning work during the harvest period, but local and regional authorities could supplement these laws with additional measures. For example, the provost of Paris introduced maximum wages in 1601 for the Parisian countryside, including harvest work. Whereas the national labour laws of the sixteenth century stated only that able-bodied rural dwellers should hire themselves for 'reasonable' wages during harvest, local and regional magistrates could complement this labour legislation by setting maximum wages for harvest operations. The body of labour laws that controlled harvest work in early modern France was thus the result of a dialogue between the national and local level.[40] This can also be witnessed in the case of work regulation in the production of wine. During the fourteenth and fifteenth centuries the French monarchy did not issue any top-down labour regulations for this important rural sector, but endorsed and ratified labour regulations solicited and enacted by local and regional authorities.[41] Such a pattern can also be observed in the German principalities. In the sixteenth century the so-called *Reichspolizeiordnungen* of the Holy Roman Empire instructed the different territories to draft labour legislation to halt the inflation of wages and introduce measures to control the mobility of servants, but was silent on how this should be achieved in practice. It was up to the states and regions to design tailor-made labour laws suited to their specific social and economic contexts. As the *Reichspolizeiordnungen* explicitly acknowledged, labour market conditions within the Holy Roman Empire were too diverse to be captured by a uniform set of labour laws.[42]

Finally, labour laws also differed with respect to the economic interests they served. Although many labour laws frequently invoked the 'common good' to justify measures, in most preambles of labour laws a rhetorical strategy hides the true beneficiaries of these policies. In the case of northern Italy, numerous studies have shown that the urban interest was the primary driver of labour legislation. Labour laws for rural workers were the logical complement of an

---

39   See the case of the Danish state in Østhus, this volume.

40   J. Jacquart, *La crise rurale en Île-de-France, 1550–1670* (Paris, 1974), pp. 266–7; H. Heller, *Labour, Science and Technology in France, 1500–1620* (Cambridge, 1996), pp. 50–1, 186.

41   M. Delafosse, 'Notes d'histoire sociale. Les vignerons d'Auxerrois, XIVe–XVIe siècles', *Annales de Bourgogne*, 20 (1948), 22–34; D. Stella, 'Un conflit du travail dans les vignes d'Auxerre aux XIVe et XVe siècles', *Histoire et Sociétés Rurales*, 5 (1996), 221–51.

42   M. Weber, *Die Reichspolizeiordnungen von 1530, 1548 und 1577. Historische Einführung und Edition* (Frankfurt am Main, 2002), pp. 152, 159, 200–1, 255.

economic policy that was aimed at political domination and economic exploitation of the countryside by urban elites. Although some late medieval labour laws in German regions also partly served the urban interest, this was nowhere as explicit and dominant as in northern Italy.[43] Here, it was in the interest of urban landowners to have access to large, cheap and docile reservoirs of rural labour to work their estates in the hinterland of large cities.[44] There is marked contrast with other highly urbanised areas in Europe, where large cities did not seek to expand their control over the surrounding countryside by way of stringent labour laws.[45] Urban dwellers in the Low Countries, for example, primarily resorted to commercial leasehold to exploit their rural estates. In contrast to sharecropping or direct management, this did not necessitate direct interference in the rural labour market.

In England, on the other hand, late medieval labour laws were crafted with other stakeholders in mind. Here, labour laws served the interests of both manorial lords and tenants with holdings that depended on wage labour. In the mid-fourteenth century many manorial demesnes still depended partly on the supply of cheap labour provided by unfree tenants through a range of labour services.[46] The demographic haemorrhage of the Black Death resulted in labour shortages that threatened the supply of both labour services and waged labour on these demesnes. The English labour laws of the fourteenth century contained provisions that directly benefited manorial lords. For example, lords enjoyed a preferential right to hire workers within their manors.[47] The gradual demise of the demesne sector in fifteenth-century England meant that other actors became the main beneficiaries and the labour laws facilitated the recruitment of workers to medium-sized and large farms that depended heavily on wage labour. This benefited the lesser gentlemen, yeomen and tenants farmers who ran large farms.[48] In late medieval and early modern France these groups were the exclusive beneficiaries of royal and local intervention from the onset. In many regions, labour services had been either abolished or severely restricted

43   For example, in 1423 the nobility and some twenty cities in Westphalia issued labour laws for rural servants and labourers. See E. Kelter, 'Das deutsche Wirtschaftsleben des 14. und 15. Jahrhunderts im Schatten der Pestepidemien', *Jahurbücher für Nationalökonomie und Statistik*, 165 (1953), 168.

44   G. Piccinni, 'La politica agraria delle cita', in R. Mucciarelli, G. Piccinni and G. Pinto (eds), *La costruzione del dominio cittadino sulle campagne. Italia centro-settentrionale, secoli, XII–XIV* (Siena, 2009), pp. 601–25. See also Cristoferi in this volume.

45   See the case of Marseille explored by Michaud in this volume.

46   See the recent overview in M. Bailey, *The Decline of Serfdom in Late Medieval England. From Bondage to Freedom* (Woodbridge, 2014).

47   B. Putnam, *The Enforcement of the Statutes of Labourers During the First Decade After the Black Death, 1349–1359* (New York, 1908), p. 71.

48   J. Whittle, 'Land and People', in K. Wrightson (ed.), *A Social History of England 1500–1750* (Cambridge, 2017), pp. 156–65. See also Whittle in this volume.

in the twelfth and thirteenth centuries. Some lords could claim labour services within their seigneuries until the end of the eighteenth century, but these so-called *corvées* were severely restricted by both custom and the intervention of royal courts.[49] In addition, because most lords had resorted to leasing their demesne farms in the later Middle Ages, their direct interests were not the object of labour legislation. Rather, labour laws in late medieval and early modern France met the needs of arable farmers with large holdings in particular.[50] This focus on the interests of larger farms was also the main characteristic of labour legislation in the Low Countries. Legal interventions in the labour market emerged only where large holdings occupied the majority of the land. In regions dominated by peasant agriculture that relied predominantly on unpaid family labour, local officials saw no need to intervene in the operation of labour markets.[51] In addition to the different groups sketched above, the state itself could also benefit directly from labour market intervention. In regions where territorial princes or states exploited substantial demesne farms, it was in their direct interest to control labour through the machinery of law. For example, the labour laws of Hainaut from 1354 benefited the count directly, as he was still employing large numbers of agricultural workers on his rural estates during the fourteenth century.[52] In a similar way, the sixteenth-century Swedish labour laws would also have benefited the more than one hundred royal demesnes that were largely dependent on wage labour.[53]

Although the myriad local, regional and national interventions in labour markets defies any pan-European logic, they nevertheless share a common characteristic. Most fundamentally, the overwhelming majority of labour laws in pre-industrial Europe favoured employers. Although labour and contract law undoubtedly offered labourers some protection against abuse and fraud

---

49 For a survey of these restrictions see M. Gransagne, *Les corvées sous l'Ancien Régime* (Saarbrucken, 2015).

50 L. Vardi, 'Construing the Harvest: Gleaners, Farmers and Officials in Early Modern France', *American Historical Review*, 98 (1993), 1424–47; T. Lambrecht, 'Harvest Work and Labor Market Regulation in Old Regime Northern France', in T. M. Safley (ed.), *Labor Before the Industrial Revolution. Work, Technology and Their Ecologies in an Age of Early Capitalism* (Abingdon, 2019), pp. 113–31.

51 T. Lambrecht, 'The Institution of Service in Rural Flanders in the Sixteenth Century: A Regional Perspective', in J. Whittle (ed.), *Servants in Rural Europe, 1400–1900* (Woodbridge, 2017), pp. 50–4.

52 G. Sivery, 'Le Hainaut et la peste noire', *Mémoires et Publications de la Société des Sciences, des Arts et des Lettres du Hainaut*, 79 (1965), 441–3.

53 On labour organisation of the Swedish Crown estates see C. Pihl, 'Gender, Labour, and State Formation in Sixteenth-Century Sweden', *Historical Journal*, 58 (2015), 685–710. On sixteenth-century Swedish labour laws see T. Kotkas, *Royal Police Ordinances in Early Modern Sweden. The Emergence of Voluntaristic Understanding of Law* (Leiden–Boston, 2014), pp. 43–4, 62.

by employers (for example, in the case of premature dismissal or refusal to pay wages), interventions in the labour market during this period cannot be characterised as precursors of worker protection. Indeed, what most labour laws have in common is an implicit or explicit bias towards the interests of those who employed workers, whether these were manorial lords, urban landowners, large farmers or states. Labour laws shaped this inequality in the face of the law by creating a deliberate asymmetrical relationship between employers and various categories of workers. As illustrated below, this asymmetrical relationship was expressed through a wide range of legal norms and rules. These measures share a common feature: they shaped and defined the boundaries of the bargaining arena for labourers and in doing so constrained the choices and freedom of some workers in offering their labour to the market. Labour laws forced large sections of the rural population into an unequal bargaining position. Admittedly, some aspects of labour law targeted employers as well. For example, employers who paid wages to labourers and servants in excess of those provided by statutes risked and faced prosecution. In addition, employers could be fined and punished if they failed to honour their contractual obliga-tions. Although labourers and employers were treated equally by some parts of the law, the complete body of law governing relations between workers and employers gravitated unequivocally towards the interests of the latter. Taken as a whole, legal provisions concerning rural labour were far from balanced between interested parties.

Of course, the existence of such unequal legal provisions does not imply that all workers were subject to the effects of labour laws all the time. As the case of England has shown, there were marked chronological and geographical differences in levels of enforcement throughout the medieval and early modern period. The enforcement of labour laws was contingent upon a number of factors. The English case shows that rural elites enforced the labour laws when a real or perceived need presented itself. The option to enforce labour laws consti-tuted a powerful tool in the hands of these elites to control large sections of the rural population. As long as rural populations were periodically reminded of this option – either through formal prosecution or face to face with an employer – labour laws would have a direct impact on the outcome of the bargaining process. Formal constraints influence individual and group behaviour because they raise the costs and involve risk.[54] In the case of labour laws, it can be argued that their very existence raised the cost of some actions (through fines or other forms of punishment) and consequently might have deterred some people from pursuing these actions altogether.

---

54   S. Ogilvie, 'Choices and Constraints in the Pre-Industrial Countryside', in C. Briggs, P. M. Kitson and S. J. Thompson (eds), *Population, Welfare and Economic Change in Britain, 1290–1834* (Woodbridge, 2014), p. 298; Humphries and Weisdorf, 'The Wages of Women', 422.

Contents of labour law

The vast body of labour laws and regulations in the countryside also displays significant variation with respect to the specific measures adopted by rural elites to bring the workforce under their control. In many cases a number of elements dominate these laws and regulations, the most common of which were provisions about maximum wages, breach of contract and compulsory work. Although these three elements are important ingredients of pre-industrial labour laws, they do not cover the complete gamut of labour policing efforts. To the extent that poor and vagrancy laws had an impact on the labour supply choices of individual rural workers, they can also be considered labour legislation. Although the vast number of poor and vagrancy acts are rarely exclusively concerned with labour and labour relations, in practice they often operated in tandem with the formal labour laws. As the next section shows, labour laws and poor laws either mutually enforced or supplemented each other. Additionally, demographic policies were often linked to efforts to control the labour market and people without property. In parts of southern Germany, for example, adolescents had to obtain community consent to enter marriage. Although there were many facets to this type of marriage legislation, it also served as a strategy to maintain a large reservoir of unmarried servants within the community.[55]

Controlling wages

The earliest statutory interventions in the operation of 'free' labour markets in the countryside concern wage levels. Already from the twelfth century cities and states tried to regulate the wages of the rural workforce. The oldest examples of such policies can be traced to northern Italy. An undated twelfth-century statute from the city of Pistoia, for example, imposes maximum wages for the rural workforce ('laboratores terrarum') in neighbouring villages. Maximum wages are listed for different types of rural activity and for the summer and winter months. The statute also contains penal sanctions for employers who paid wages in excess of the rates provided by the statute. The aim of this statutory intervention was to halt the rise of wages and inflation in labour costs.[56] In the course of the thirteenth century an increasing number of rural and urban communities included wage regulation in their statutes. Maximum wage rates were not only restricted to agricultural work but also included other activities.

---

55   On marriage prohibitions and labour market policies in early modern Germany see J. Nipperdey, *Die Erfindung der Bevölkerungspolitik: Staat, politische Theorie und Population in der Frühen Neuzeit* (Göttingen, 2012), pp. 441–64.
56   M. Ascheri, *The Laws of Late Medieval Italy (1000–1500). Foundations for an European Legal System* (Leiden, 2013), pp. 150–1.

In particular, large infrastructural works (canals and ports) and maintenance of fortifications and defensive city walls in northern Italy were subject to rural wage control.[57] These interventions in the rural economy paralleled the penetration of urban capital in the countryside. As urban citizens expanded their landed estates in the rural hinterland, they also used their political power to exert economic control over the rural workforce. In this part of Europe, urban economic and political interests were the main driver of wage (and labour) regulation in the countryside.[58]

This context is markedly different from that of other European countries. In the English countryside wage regulation does not appear until the mid-fourteenth-century. English harvest bylaws from the thirteenth century already contain indications about the remuneration of harvest workers, but these bylaws cannot be equated to early forms of wage control because they do not set maximum wages. Importantly, the Ordinance of June 1349 did not introduce wage uniformity throughout the territory, as it instructed only that wages should be reduced to their pre-Black Death level. After 1388 England predominantly switched to a policy of national wage rates, but with the Statute of Artificers (1563) English wage policy reverted to the regional level:[59] English magistrates set wages periodically taking into account the local demographic and economic context. As a result, maximum wages could differ substantially between regions in early modern England. The range of occupations and tasks targeted by these wage assessments was impressive and illustrates an ambition to subject large sections of the labouring population to wage control. In the early seventeenth century, for example, English wage assessments regulated the remuneration of some sixty different occupations and tasks.[60]

The same principles guided German wage assessments (called *Lohntaxen*). The *Reichstagordnung* of 1530 instructed local and regional authorities (or so-called *Obrigkeiten*) to actively police the workforce in their jurisdictions. An important part of this policing consisted of curtailing labour costs through the setting of maximum wages. These top-down instructions were reissued in 1548 and 1577 and would become one of the institutional backbones of early

57   For an exploration of local labour legislation in the exceptionally rich Italian sources see P. Toubert, 'Législation du travail et salariat agricole dans les statuts communaux italiens (XIIIe–XIVe siècles)', in A. Mazzon (ed.), *Raccolta di studo offerti a Isa Lori Sanfilippo* (Rome, 2008), pp. 849–57. See also G. Pinto, *I lavoro, la povertà, l'assistenza* (Rome, 2008), pp. 19–20.

58   On labour legislation as part of the agrarian policies of late medieval Italian city states see Piccinni, 'La politica agraria', pp. 601–25. On the legal domination of hinterlands by north Italian cities see the many examples in M. Knapton, 'Land and Economic Policy in Later Fifteenth-Century Padua', in M. Knapton, J. E. Law and A. Smith (eds), *Venice and the Veneto during the Renaissance: the Legacy of Benjamin Kohl* (Florence, 2014), pp. 197–258.

59   See Whittle in this volume.

60   Roberts, 'Wages and Wage-Earners', p. 107.

modern labour law in German territories.[61] Wage assessments were also issued periodically by states and regions and adjusted wages to new demographic and economic realities. During the seventeenth century in particular local magistrates issued numerous *Lohntaxen* as a response to the labour shortages during and after the Thirty Years War. The many and frequent complaints of farmers about the excessive wages demanded by servants in particular resulted in intensive wage supervision and control during the first half of the seventeenth century.[62] As in England, German wage legislation targeted both servants and day labourers and introduced maximum wages for a range of rural occupations and tasks.

In contrast to England and German territories, French magistrates were not required to assess the wages of rural labourers in any structural and permanent way. In the early seventeenth century employers from the region of Troyes petitioned for the periodic setting of maximum wages by local magistrates, as was the case in English counties, but these demands were ultimately not met.[63] During the first decades of the eighteenth century there were numerous complaints about labour shortages in the countryside and the 'excessive' wages demanded by rural labourers, but these did not translate into a policy of maximum wages.[64] Only when discord between labourers and farmers resulted in violence and social upheaval did regional and national authorities step in to regulate wages. For example, during the eighteenth century magistrates intervened in northern France to set the wages of itinerant harvest workers following repeated conflicts and tensions between local labourers and employers.[65] The only region where wage assessments were issued in a more or less systematic way was Alsace. This region had inherited a labour policy inspired by the German tradition of *Lohntaxen* and continued this practice

---

61   Weber, *Die Reichspolizeiordnungen*, p. 152, 159, 201 and 255.

62   Shortages of servants are frequently recorded in mid-seventeenth-century German farmers' diaries and memorandum books. See the examples in J. Peters, 'Dahingeflossen ins Meer der Zeiten. Über frühmoderne Zeitverständnis der Bauern', in R. Vierhaus (ed.), *Frühe Neuzeit-Frühe Moderne? Forschungen zur Vielsichtigkeit von Übergangsprozessen* (Göttingen, 2012), p. 187; B. von Krusenstjern, 'Der teure Frieden. Aus den Aufzeichnungen eines hessichen Bauern nach dem Dreissigjährigen Krieg, 1648–1651', *Sozialwissenschaftliche Information*, 28 (1999), 253.

63   Y. Durand, *Cahiers de doléances des paroisses du bailliage de Troyes pour les Etats Généraux de 1614* (Paris, 1966), p. 63.

64   M. Marion, 'Un essai de politique sociale en 1724', *Revue Du Dix-Huitième Siècle*, 1 (1913), 31–2; J. Meuvret, *Le problème des subsistances à l'époque Louis XIV. La production des céréales dans la France du XVIIe et du XVIIIe siècle* (Paris, 1977), pp. 180–1.

65   J.-M. Moriceau, 'Les "Baccanals" ou grèves de moissonneurs en pays de France (seconde moitié du XVIIIe siècle)', in J. Nicolas (ed.), *Mouvements populaires et conscience sociale, XVIe–XIXe siècles* (Paris, 1985), pp. 421–34; J. Bernet, 'Les grèves de moissonneurs ou "bacchanals" dans les campagnes d'Ile-de-France et de Picardie au XVIIIe siècle', *Histoire et Sociétés Rurales*, 11 (1999), pp. 153–86.

after incorporation into France in 1648.[66] Only at the end of the eighteenth century was nationwide wage control introduced in France to deal with galloping inflation and labour shortages (as a result of conscription) in the early 1790s. Throughout France, all districts were required to introduce maximum wages that also targeted rural labourers and servants. This nationwide wage control, however, was the result of exceptional circumstances and remained in effect for only a short period. This pattern was also characteristic for the early modern Low Countries. Following instructions from the central government in 1588, regional magistrates were ordered to introduce maximum wages in their territories to halt wage inflation and dampen labour costs. Some rural districts took action and drafted ordinances containing maximum wages for servants and labourers, but this did not lead to structural or long-term government intervention in assessing wage rates.[67]

With the exception of England and German states structural wage control in the long term was rare in Europe. To some extent this can probably be explained by the state of the labour market. In regions where labour was allocated through other systems than the market, there was no need to intervene. In northern Italy, for example, wage control was gradually abandoned in the course of the fifteenth and sixteenth centuries as sharecropping expanded. As most farms in northern Italy ran almost exclusively on family labour, there was simply no market for waged work. In many sharecropping contracts, waged work by sharecroppers was explicitly forbidden.[68] Landlords calibrated the size of the family group with farm size so there were no labour shortages or surpluses at the level of the holding. In such a context, wage control was simply redundant.[69] The absence of wage control cannot only be explained by the relative weakness of competitive labour markets, however. Regions that were highly dependent on wage labour were also characterised by the absence of market interventions. For example, in the Low Countries the coastal regions opposed wage control. The coastal provinces relied heavily on seasonal migrant workers that were recruited from more distant inland regions.[70] Traditionally, these regions attracted workers by offering high wages to meet peak labour demands.

---

66   G. Livet, *L'intendance d'Alsace sous Louis XIV, 1648–1715* (Strasbourg, 1956), pp. 321–5.

67   C. Verlinden, 'Economic Fluctuations and Government Policy in the Netherlands in the Late XVIth Century', *Journal of European Economic History*, 10 (1981), pp. 201–6.

68   See the examples in P. Jones, 'From Manor to Mezzadria: a Tuscan Case-Study in the Medieval Origins of Modern Agrarian Society', in N. Rubinstein (ed.), *Florentine Studies: Politics and Society in Renaissance Florence* (London, 1966), pp. 193–241; F. McArdle, *Altopascio. A Study in Tuscan Rural Society* (Cambridge, 1978), pp. 72, 111; J. Laurent, 'Patterns of Agrarian Control in Fourteenth-Century Ferrara', *Peasant Studies*, 9 (1982), 190.

69   R. J. Emigh, 'Labor Use and Landlord Control: Sharecropping and Household Structure in Fifteenth-Century Tuscany', *Journal of Historical Sociology*, 11 (1998), 37–73.

70   J. Lucassen, *Migrant Labour in Europe, 1600–1900* (London, 1987), pp. 131–70.

Employers in the coastal regions opposed the introduction of maximum wages in the Low Countries because it would harm their economic interests.[71] As in northern Italy, the specific dynamics of labour recruitment explain why the Low Countries did not resort to wage control.

Comparisons between the maximum wages prescribed by wage ordinances and actual wages paid to servants and labourers indicate that employers frequently paid wages in excess of what the statutes ordered. On the estates of the count of Hainaut, higher wages were paid than the maximum wages set by the ordinance from 1354.[72] Evidence for early modern England also shows that employers sometimes paid wages in excess of the official maximum national and regional rates.[73] Moreover, there were ample opportunities to circumvent official wage rates. Most wage ordinances focused on the cash wages only and were silent about any additional recompenses for labourers. These could take different forms, from food and drink to clothing allowances and crops. Indeed, as the Statute of Artificers stated, it was not unlikely that employers and workers concocted 'secret ways and meanes' to pay and receive wages above the official rates.[74] In theory, there were opportunities to navigate official maximum wage rates through various payments in kind that raised the overall compensation of workers. However, infringements and evasion of statutory wages should not be taken as firm evidence for the failure of wage assessments. To the extent that wage control managed to slow down and dampen wage inflation and rising labour costs they can be labelled successful from the viewpoint of the legislator and employers.

Breach of contract

A second common and widespread characteristic of European labour laws was the so-called contract clause. This particular element of labour legislation sought to enforce the contractual agreements between employers and workers. The contract clause was multifaceted. It not only specified the conditions of entry and exit of the work relationship but also contained penalties for employers and workers for breach of contract. The contract clause contained

---

71 Verlinden and Craeybeckx, *Prijzen- en lonenpolitiek*, pp. 101–2. See also B. J. P. van Bavel, 'Rural wage labour in the sixteenth-century Low Countries: an assessment of the importance and nature of wage labour in the countryside of Holland, Guelders and Flanders', *Continuity and Change*, 21 (2006), 37–72.

72 Sivery, *Structures agraires*, p. 430.

73 Tawney, 'The Assessment', p. 564; R. K. Kelsall, 'Wage regulations under the Statutes of Artificers', in W. Minchinton (ed.), *Wage Regulation in Pre-Industrial England* (Newton Abbot, 1972), pp. 116–17; A. Kussmaul, *Servants in Husbanry in Early Modern England* (Cambridge, 1981), p. 36; J. Whittle, 'A Different Pattern of Employment: Servants in Rural England *c*.1500–1660', in Whittle (ed.), *Servants in Rural Europe*, pp. 71–3.

74 Roberts, 'Wages and Wage-Earners', p. 225.

specific measures to deal with premature departure and dismissal of servants and the non-execution of work by labourers. An analysis of the treatment of breach of contract in labour legislation is particularly instructive because it illustrates how labour laws deliberately and progressively transformed a private conflict into a public and punishable offence. Moreover, the selective penalisation of contract breach was one of the main characteristics of most late medieval and early modern labour laws. In essence and originally, breach of contract was a private labour dispute. When servants or labourers reneged on their contractual obligations and left employment before the end of their term or before the contracted work was completed, the wronged employer could claim damages through a civil court procedure. And, vice versa, the premature dismissal of a servant or labourer could expose the employer to court proceedings where workers could claim compensation for the loss of income they had sustained.[75]

In contrast to maximum wage clauses, legal provisions about breach of contract were not necessarily detrimental to the interests of those working for wages. On the contrary, contract clauses could offer both workers and employers legal protection. Clauses on breach of contract protected employers against premature departure by workers or non-execution of work. If this breach of contract resulted in economic or financial damage, the employer could sue for damages in court. Equally, such clauses could safeguard workers against non-compliance by employers. In the case of labourers and servants, premature dismissal could result in loss of income, unemployment and in some cases even temporary homelessness. In regions where a large part of the work was executed by free wage labourers and based on contractual agreements, contract clauses were probably instrumental to guarantee the smooth operation of the labour market. However, as we will illustrate below, contract clauses in European labour laws were frequently skewed towards the interests of the employers. Importantly, laws did not consider all forms of contract breach as problematic. In many regions marriage constituted a valid reason to end service prematurely.[76] Also, unjust treatment by the employer (for example the withholding of food) or the 'scandalous' lifestyle of the employer justified the premature rupture of the contact by the worker. Employers could sometimes invoke insubordination, sickness and lack of skills to justify the premature dismissal of a worker.

The labour laws that emerged throughout Europe from the second half of the fourteenth century introduced two important and significant changes

---

75   For English examples see A. Musson, 'Reconstructing English Labor Laws: A Medieval Perspective', in K. Robertson and M. Übel (eds), *The Middle Ages at Work: Practicing Labor in Late Medieval England* (New York, 2004), pp. 121–2.

76   This was the case in the Low Countries and Germany. See Lambrecht, 'The Institution', p. 51 and Könnecke, *Rechtsgeschichte*, pp. 751–5.

in how rural societies dealt with breach of contract. First, breach of contract was no longer treated exclusively as a private dispute. Employers and workers could still claim damages and compensation in court, but those who reneged on their contractual obligations were also exposed to public prosecution. The penalisation of breach of contract from the late medieval periods onwards is illustrative of the growing interventions of European legislators in labour relations. What was considered a private conflict before the labour shortages of the fourteenth century was thereafter increasingly treated as an offence that could undermine the 'orderly' operation of the labour market and which required state intervention. The penalisation of breach of contract, however, was far from uniform throughout Europe. In the early modern Low Countries, for example, breach of contract was in most regions actively discouraged through fines.[77] In England and large parts of Germany sanctions for breach of contract included harsher punishment such as imprisonment.[78] In these latter labour laws, breach of contract was most radically transformed from a private conflict to a criminal offence.

Second, the contract clauses of labour legislation also introduced an important asymmetry in labour relations. As examples throughout Europe amply illustrate, workers in particular were subject to punishment in the case of contract breach. The English late medieval and early modern labour statutes punished unlawful and premature departure of servants and labourers with imprisonment. In contrast, English employers who laid off their workers before the end of their term risked only a fine of forty shillings at most.[79] These distinct and deliberate inequalities between employers and workers in the punishment of contract breach are also encountered in other European countries. In many German regions, workers found guilty of contract breach not only forfeited their wages but could also be imprisoned or subjected to corporal punishment. In some regions workers – servants in particular – could also be temporarily excluded from the labour market when found guilty of contract breach. In this particular case, local magistrates could order employers not to hire workers that had been found guilty of contract breach. Employers, by contrast, did not suffer such harsh punishment for breach of contract in German law. In most cases they were ordered to pay full (or partial) wages, but did not suffer any additional corrective measures.[80] The unequal position occupied by employers and workers with respect to the punishment of contract breach indicates that labour laws were designed with the interests of employers in mind. Regions

77   J. W. Bosch, 'Rechtshistorische aanteekeningen betreffende de overeenkomst tot het huren van dienstpersoneel', *Themis*, 92 (1931), 405–9.
78   Könnecke, *Rechtsgeschichte*, p. 770.
79   J. Whittle, *The Development of Agrarian Capitalism. Land and Labour in Norfolk 1440–1580* (Oxford, 2000), p. 280; Kelsall, 'Wage Regulations', p. 132.
80   Könnecke, *Rechtsgeschichte*, pp. 769–805, 814–32.

where contract clauses tended to treat workers and employers on an equal footing – such as parts of the late medieval Low Countries – were exceptional.

In many European countries, therefore, rules and regulations concerning breach of contract actively discouraged workers from reneging on their contractual obligations and leaving employment in search for higher wages or better remuneration. The penalisation, and in some cases criminalisation, of such behaviour would probably have deterred workers from breaching their contract. The asymmetric character of the penalties, however, indicates that these regulations were far from neutral labour market instruments. On the contrary, the penalties for employers who breached contract were low. This privileged position allowed employers to dismiss workers without great costs or consequences. For workers, the implications of breach of contract were often far more substantial, both in absolute and relative terms. The level of asymmetry and inequality in clauses concerning breach of contract, therefore, can reveal in a very direct way whose interests legislators had in mind when drafting such legislation.

However, the absence of specific regulations concerning the breach of contract in labour laws does not mean that employers were powerless when confronted with servants and workers who left – or threatened to leave – employment before the end of their contractual term. In early modern France control over the unwanted mobility of workers was achieved through work certificates. From 1565, servants – both in town and countryside – were expected to carry written documentation detailing their employment history. The legislation was enacted to prevent servants and workers leaving employment before the end of the contract and without the consent of the employer. Only a written and signed declaration of the employer could release them from their contractual obligations. Servants and workers that could not produce such written details about their employment history could also not be hired by new employers. Importantly, servants who failed to produce such documentation were considered vagabonds and were subsequently punished under the harsh vagabond laws.[81] The certificate system, therefore, was intended to empower employers and weaken the legal and economic position of workers.[82]

81   J. P. Gutton, *Domestiques et serviteurs dan la France de l'ancien regime* (Paris, 1981), pp. 136–7 and Heller, *Labour*, p. 151. The national regulations concerning work and employment certificates were integrated in local and regional labour laws. See the wage ordinance of the provost of Paris from 1601 in A. Miron de l'Espinay, *François Miron et l'administration municipale de Paris sous Henri IV* (Paris, 1885), p. 355.
82   Rural elites were aware of the power the certificate system gave them to control the unwanted mobility of their workers. See Durand, *Les cahiers*, pp. 107, 144.

Compulsory work

Compulsion could be a temporary measure to deal with peak demands for labour. For example, in small urban textile centres French magistrates devised strategies to ensure the labour supply during the harvest period. The harvest by-laws of the small city of Guines from 1341 stated that wage labour in the textile sector was to be suspended during the harvest season.[83] Although there was no formal obligation to hire oneself to work as a harvest labourer, the high fines imposed on non-compliance with this statute suggest that the magistrates of Guines expected textile labourers to temporarily seek employment in the agricultural sector. These strategies continued to exist after the Black Death, sometimes with a more compelling character. In Normandy, for example, the city of Falaise temporarily ordered the suspension of work in the textile sector in the summer months of 1369 to ensure sufficient labourers were available to bring in the harvest. The textile workers were constrained to hire themselves to farmers for 'reasonable' wages.[84] The late medieval customs of Poitou contain similar provisions. Those who did not abandon their non-agricultural activities between mid-July and the end of the harvest period risked a hefty fine.[85] These local and regional measures aimed at ensuring sufficient hands during the harvest period would ultimately also influence the royal ordinance on gleaning from 1554. This ordinance contained the provision that all able-bodied labourers were forced to hire themselves during the harvest period against reasonable wages.[86] The English labour laws contain a similar clause that compelled rural craftsmen to work in the harvest from the late fourteenth century onwards.[87]

Whereas compulsion was largely restricted to harvest work and casual labour in late medieval and early modern France, compulsory work could take different forms in other parts of Europe. The labour laws of late medieval and early modern England most notably contain specific provisions on compulsory service. The labour statute of 1349 compelled unemployed and able-bodied individuals under the age of sixty to find employment as a servant. These measures were largely repeated in the Statute of Artificers of 1563. The

---

83   G. Espinas, *Le droit économique et social d'une petite ville artésienne à la fin du moyen-âge: Guines* (Lille–Paris, 1949), p. 35.

84   M. Arnoux, 'Les effets de la peste de 1348 sur la société normande: à propos d'un jugement de l'Echiquier de 1395', in E. Lalou, B. Lepeuple and J.-L. Roch (eds), *Des châteaux et des sources; Archéologie et histoire dans la Normandie médiévale. Mélanges en l'honneur d'Anne-Marie Flambard Héricher* (Rouen, 2008), pp. 79–80.

85   R. Filhol, *Le vieux coustumier de Poictou* (Bourges, 1986), pp. 245–6 (art. 732). The customs of Poitou are not dated, but were compiled during the middle of the fifteenth century.

86   Vardi, 'Construing the Harvest', 1432–4; Heller, *Labour*, pp. 50–1.

87   E.g. Statute of Cambridge 1388 and Statute of Artificers 1563.

Elizabethan statute enabled magistrates to compel single persons between the age of twelve and sixty to serve in agriculture. These measures targeted the poorer sections of the population in particular, as they excluded those with property and work in trades. Importantly, those who were compelled to serve were entitled to compensation for their work. Research shows that these clauses did not remain dead letter. In the direct aftermath of the Black Death and during the sixteenth and seventeenth centuries employers and magistrates actively used the law to coerce young unmarried people into service.[88] In particular, during periods characterized by mortality crises and slow population growth magistrates activated the compulsory service clauses of the English labour laws. Once population growth accelerated in the eighteenth century compulsory service gradually disappeared from the rural elite's portfolio of disciplinary measures. Instead, the rural elite threatened to withhold welfare payments to parents whose children were deemed fit to serve.[89] Although the means differed, the effect was the same: children of poor and non-propertied parents in particular could still be coerced into service.

The English measures concerning compulsory service bear a number of similarities with the so-called *Gesindezwangsdienst* that characterised large parts of eastern Europe.[90] However, in contrast to Eastern Europe, early modern English labour laws were not designed within the context of a demesne economy but to meet the labour demands of farmers. This pattern is comparable to some parts of the Low Countries. Here, too, young people from humble backgrounds could be compelled to serve from the middle of the sixteenth century onwards.[91] With the exception of Scandinavia, coercive measures elaborated through labour laws were scarce in other parts of early modern Europe. This does not mean that employers and rural elites lacked the instruments to compel young people in service. Throughout the German territories there was an obligation to serve included in the poor and vagrancy laws. Moreover, young people could be pressured into service through targeted fiscal strategies. Young people living outside service were liable to either weekly or monthly taxes that substantially reduced their net earnings. German servant ordinances were quite explicit about the aims of such taxes: fiscal pressure was exerted to discourage young people from living on their own and to ultimately force them into service.[92]

88   Bennett, 'Compulsory Service'; Whittle, *Development of Agrarian Capitalism*, pp. 280–1; Wales, 'Living', 19–39.
89   Wales, 'Living', 33.
90   See, for example, W. Hagen, *Ordinary Prussians. Brandenburg Junkers and Villagers, 1500–1840* (Cambridge, 2002), pp. 399–408.
91   Lambrecht, 'The Institution', pp. 52–3.
92   See the examples in Simon, *Die Tagelöhner und ihr Recht*, pp. 131–2; R. Dürr, 'Der Dienstbothe ist kein Tagelöhner. Zum Gesinderecht, 16 bis 19 Jahrhundert', in U. Gerard

Whereas compulsory service in England waned after c.1700, coercive measures were still a signature mark of labour legislation in Scandinavian countries until the early nineteenth century.[93] Although compulsory service has its origins in earlier periods, coercion became the preferred instrument of a number of Scandinavian regions between the seventeenth and nineteenth centuries. In Sweden and Finland, for example, servant ordinances from 1686, 1723 and 1739 contained measures that pressured young people into service. Young able-bodied men, for example, could be prosecuted and punished as vagrants if they did not enter service. Young able-bodied women outside service risked imprisonment if they failed to produce evidence that they were actively searching for employment as a servant. In Iceland, Norway and Denmark, too, young unmarried people were equally targeted by the law when they were living outside service and authorities resorted to various legal and penal measures to bring these adolescents under the control and authority of a head of a household. The primary motives to resort to compulsory service varied regionally. In some cases, these were designed to deal with structural labour shortages in the countryside resulting from rural–urban migration and international emigration. In other regions compulsory service was viewed as an instrument to ensure an adequate distribution of surplus family labour throughout the sparsely populated territories. As this section indicates, compulsory service and coercion in labour relations were not unfamiliar to western and northern European labour regimes. These examples from England, France, Germany, the Low Countries and Scandinavia challenge the traditional narrative on agrarian dualism in pre-industrial Europe. Both east and west of the river Elbe rural elites resorted to formal and informal coercion of labour.

As the previous sections have illustrated, many European regions resorted to some form of legal control over the lives of rural workers in pre-industrial times. Our overview has shown that there were actually few regions in Europe where elites and employers could not resort to labour, poor or vagrancy laws to bring labour under their control. Indeed, the absence of formal legal measures to control, discipline or coerce rural workers seems to be the anomaly. Labour, poor and vagrancy laws were part of the standard institutional toolkit of elites and employers throughout pre-industrial Europe and were also interlocked. These tools allowed elites to control and dominate a subservient workforce.[94]

(ed.), *Frauen in der Geschichte des Rechts: von der frühen Neuzeit bis zur Gegenwart* (Munich, 1997), p. 127.

93   See the detailed and extensive discussion of compulsory service in Østhus, Uppenberg, Johnsson and Vilhelmsson in this volume.

94   As one historian observed: 'it was the laws against vagrancy which gave much of the labour legislation its teeth'. C. Given-Wilson, 'The Problem of Labour in the Context of English Government, c. 1350–1450', in J. Bothwell, P. J. P. Goldberg and M. W. Ormrod (eds), *The Problem of Labour in Fourteenth-Century England* (York, 2000), p. 88.

However, although legal labour regimes throughout Europe contained similar ingredients, their specific configuration and dynamics were always shaped by existing political, social, economic, demographic and agrarian structures.[95] There were significant national, regional and local differences in the solutions and responses to the – real or perceived – problems of labour shortages, excessive wage demands, unwanted mobility or work refusal of the rural workforce. Labour laws throughout Europe targeted different categories of workers, but in most cases, young, unmarried and unpropertied individuals were singled out as preferred targets of disciplinary actions.[96] Labour laws were also far from gender neutral. Although in theory they targeted both men and women, in practice unmarried women were disproportionately exposed to compulsory service, strict wage control and disciplinary action. Our overview has also shown that labour laws – in their design and enforcement – were not static but were characterised by dynamism in addressing the unwanted consequences of changing economic and social realities. Finally, although the existing historiography has certainly allowed us to identify a number of commonalities and differences in pre-industrial European labour laws and legal regimes, more research is required to expose and understand the actions and reactions of employers and workers to the 'problem of labour' in pre-industrial rural Europe.

Structure of the book

This collection does not aim to comprehensively cover the history of labour regulation in Europe over more than 500 years, which would not be possible in a single volume. As a consequence, topics, time periods and European regions are not evenly covered. Instead the aim is to offer fresh perspectives and intensify discussion about the nature of wage labour across Europe between the late medieval period and the nineteenth century based on new research. The chapters of the book are divided into three sections. Part one examines different strategies of labour regulation created in the aftermath of the Black Death between the late fourteenth and sixteenth centuries. It shows that, depending on the structures of government and varying local circumstances, different parts of Europe chose very different paths. As Jane Whittle demonstrates, in England a centralised government dominated by the interests of the landed gentry and aristocracy led to the early and active use of national legislation to regulate labour. While laws were not always effectively enforced, the government never lost interest in finding more effective ways to regulate and discipline the

---

95   See also Lis and Soly, 'Labor Laws', pp. 319–21.
96   With particular reference to German labour laws see Keiser, 'Between Status and Contract', 44.

relatively poor and landless to provide a subservient workforce. In southern France, Marseille adopted a strategy close to a free-market solution to obtain an agricultural workforce, as Francine Michaud shows. On the one hand, it seems that the high status of Marseille's existing guild of ploughman mitigated against the harsh regulation of agricultural workers, while, on the other, the unregulated in-migration of workers from surrounding regions eventually undermined the Marseille ploughmen's high wages. Marseille benefited from being a prosperous and relatively peaceful enclave surrounded by regions that offered less favourable employment conditions.

The Italian city states of Tuscany also had to contend with the push and pull between neighbouring polities as well as regulation within them. Davide Cristoferi explores the similarities and differences between the strategies pursued by Florence and Siena. In both states, protecting the interests of wealthy citizens who had invested in landed property let on sharecropping agreements was paramount. Here taxation was the favoured form of regulation. By taxing wage earners and independent peasant farmers more heavily than sharecroppers, they both encouraged and protected sharecroppers, creating a market in which city dwellers could accumulate more land and lease it on favourable terms. By their nature, sharecropping contracts provided an agricultural labour force for tenancies. In the long term, the removal of alternatives allowed urban landowners to squeeze sharecroppers harder and bind them to the land. In late medieval England and Tuscany, the profitability of land for rentier owners was maintained using political power to undermine workers' economic advantage. Only in Marseilles, where conditions proved generally favourable to landowners, was increased regulation largely avoided.

Part two of the book turns to the development of labour laws and the classification of labour in the early modern period. Labour laws and other legal structures not only regulated workers but also described and classified different forms of labour relations – these classifications in turn shaping future regulations. Raffaella Sarti compares how slavery, service and other forms of dependent labour such as apprenticeship were understood by early modern commentators. She demonstrates how workers were seen as implicitly dependent and subservient, whether or not they were paid wages or coerced into providing labour. While historians draw sharp distinctions between service (as a form of voluntary wage work) and slavery (as a highly coercive removal of personal freedom), early modern jurists and other writers saw them as very similar types of labour: these views were found across Europe in Italy, France and England. Hanne Østhus, focusing on the Danish Empire, looks more specifically at the state as a vehicle for regulation and classification. The early modern Danish state ruled an empire that included Denmark, Norway, Iceland and a range of other territories stretching from northern Germany to the Caribbean and south-east Asia. Everywhere the large numbers of statutes attest to the importance with which labour regulation was regarded by the state.

As elsewhere, labour laws were intertwined with the regulation of vagrancy and provision for the poor, and it was taken for granted that the 'idle' who were not appropriately employed should be forced into work. Yet, despite an increasingly absolutist state, labour regulations remained local, shaped by local elites and tailored to particular circumstances.

In this sense, the Danish empire stood somewhere between the southern Low Countries and Sweden in its approach. Thijs Lambrecht shows that in Flanders national and regional labour legislation was absent but local by-laws concerned with labour were common. Unlike England, these showed little concern for wage rates and instead concentrated on the servant labour force by regulating service contracts and mobility. Regional differences are evident: areas of large commercial farms sought to force workers into compulsory service, while areas of peasant farming were more concerned with regulating contracts. In Sweden, Carolina Uppenberg demonstrates that successive national statutes built a system that aimed for near-total control of the rural labour force. The laws not only regulated workers, telling people what work to do and ensuring they did that work, but also controlled employers by proscribing how many workers farmers could employ. These regulations stretched into the family: the children of peasant householders could be forced into service as a consequence of parents being allowed to keep only a certain number of working children at home.

The final part of the book explores how labour regulation was experienced by those affected. Lack of evidence makes the experience of law enforcement hard to uncover before the nineteenth century. Charmian Mansell uses an ingenious approach to weigh popular attitudes to labour legislation in England from 1564 to 1641. Young people, seen as prone to idleness and possessing a duty of subservience, were the prime target of the laws. Evidence from 'exceptions' to the character of witnesses in the church courts allows attitudes towards young people to be tweezed from the documents. This shows that, while neighbours were concerned about the poverty and vagrancy of young people, they did not necessarily see entering service, as proscribed by the labour laws, as the solution to these problems. Theresa Johnsson examines the administration of vagrancy legislation, an essential element of the Swedish labour laws, in the early nineteenth century. She demonstrates how, despite an excessively controlling state, imprecision in the legislation and variations in enforcement created a state of uncertainty for the labouring poor. Her analysis of how people were caught up in a capricious system of state monitoring of livelihoods offers a critique to those who would place too much emphasis on the agency of those who were deliberately denied power by the legal system and its enforcers. Vilhelm Vilhelmsson offers another perspective, looking carefully at the unruly behaviour of servants as evidence of resistance rather than a rhetorical trope. In mid-nineteenth-century Iceland service was compulsory for young unmarried people and courts sought to control many aspects of their lives, yet also provided arbitration in disputes between servants and employers. Cases in these courts demonstrate both the mistreatment of servants and servants' misbehaviour. Yet they also indicate that some servants used the courts and 'weapons of the weak' to renegotiate unsatisfactory situations.

Too often discussions of preindustrial European labour laws have remained restricted to particular national historiographies. Bringing these studies together illuminates three important propositions. First, legal interventions in the operation of labour markets can be witnessed across many different regions of Europe. Second, the combination of the importance of wage labour and a multitude of regulations that sought to ensure the subservience and control of wage workers were a distinctive characteristic of this period. Finally, the most common forms of wage labour in the countryside in this period cannot be considered fully free. Thus, neither the end of serfdom nor the appearance of large numbers of wage workers necessarily resulted in the rise of labour markets in which workers were free to negotiate contracts that suited them. It was not until the nineteenth century that political authorities across Europe, from the village to the nation state, abandoned the assumption that the interests of wage workers should be subordinated to the owners of property.

PART I

REGULATING AGRICULTURAL WORKERS
c.1350–1600

Attitudes to Wage Labour in English Legislation, 1349–1601

JANE WHITTLE

In the midst of the Black Death the English government made the significant decision not to strengthen the institution of serfdom but instead to regulate wage labour with the Ordinance of Labourers of 1349. Its first clause set out the priority for all able-bodied people without significant property not only to work but to 'serve':

> That every man and woman of our realm of England, of whatever condition, free or bond, able in body and within the age of 60 years, not living in merchandizing, nor exercising any craft, nor having his own whereof he may live, nor proper land, about whose tillage he may himself occupy, nor serving any other, if he in convenient service, his estate considered, be required to serve, he shall be bound to serve him which so shall him require, and take only the wages ... which are accustomed.

By prioritising wage labour over serfdom at this point of crisis, those in power recognised the advantages of wage labour as a means of providing a labour force, but at the same time did not envisage this labour as 'free', in the sense of operating in a free market according to personal choice. Among other things, the laws sought to criminalise unemployment, to undermine the power of workers to negotiate contracts and to force men, women and children into compulsory service.

Over the next 250 years, principles of the Ordinance were repeatedly reinforced. Serfdom was left to wither away,[1] but statutes concerned with regulating labour, vagrancy and the able-bodied poor multiplied and became increasingly complex. This chapter revisits those laws and asks what they

---

[1] Mark Bailey, *The Decline of Serfdom in Late Medieval England: From Bondage to Freedom* (Woodbridge, 2014).

reveal about attitudes to wage labour in late medieval and sixteenth-century England. It does so through three lines of inquiry. First, it considers the wider social divisions implied by the laws, by examining who created and enforced them. The laws were created by parliament, so a consideration of who sat in parliament and how they generated legislation is needed, emphasising the dual role of the ruling elite as members of parliament and employers. It is also important to consider who enforced the laws, as enforcement demonstrates support for the labour laws from a much wider social group of less elite employers. Secondly, the chapter examines how workers were classified by the legislation. There was a tripartite division of wage workers into servants, casual labourers and artificers, with those who refused to conform being labelled as vagrants. The categories into which workers and potential workers were placed by the labour laws demonstrates a well-developed understanding of different types of wage labour by 1349. The laws reinforced these categories both through repeated usage and by policing their boundaries. This indicates a conscious ordering of the most mobile and, from an elite perspective, unruly sections of society. Thirdly, the chapter investigates the compulsion to work and the unequal power relations between employer and worker that the laws sought to strengthen. Compulsory work was neither serfdom nor slavery, as it was not inherited or perpetual. However, it did restrict personal freedoms in ways that are often overlooked. The laws were thus contradictory in their approach to wage labour. They implicitly recognised the benefits of wage labour in providing a motivated and well-ordered workforce, while at the same time demonstrating an active hostility to a free labour market.[2]

The chapter crosses a number of traditional boundaries in terms of chronology and subject matter. There are many studies of England's late medieval labour laws. Pioneering research on the widespread enforcement of the medieval laws was undertaken by Bertha Putnam and Nora Ritchie.[3] These findings have been reinforced by more recent research by Judith Bennett, Simon Penn and Chris Dyer, L. R. Poos and Elaine Clark.[4] Chris Given-Wilson has perhaps done most to think about the wider social and political implications of the laws, in terms

2   Robert J. Steinfeld, *The Invention of Free Labor: The Employment Relation in English and American Law and Culture 1350–1870* (Chapel Hill, 1991), especially chapters 2–4.
3   N. Ritchie née Kenyon, 'Labour Conditions in Essex in the Reign of Richard II', in E. M. Carus-Wilson (ed.), *Essays in Economic History*, vol. 2 (London, 1962), pp. 91–111; Bertha H. Putnam, *Proceedings before the Justices of the Peace in the Fourteenth and Fifteenth Centuries: Edward III to Richard III* (London, 1938); Bertha H. Putnam, *The Enforcement of the Statutes of Labourers during the First Decade after the Black Death* (New York, 1908).
4   Judith M. Bennett, 'Compulsory Service and Late Medieval England', *Past and Present*, 209 (2010), 7–51; Simon A. C. Penn and Christopher Dyer, 'Wages and Earnings in Late Medieval England: Evidence from the Enforcement of the Labour Laws', *Economic History Review*, 43 (1990), 356–76; L. R. Poos, 'The Social Context of Statute of Labourers

of both how they were created and how they were intended to be enforced.[5] Yet the medieval laws continue to be studied separately from those of the sixteenth century. S. T. Bindoff and Donald Woodward undertook detailed research into the creation of the 1563 Statute, the most important sixteenth-century law; yet both saw it as new, prefigured only by some stray wage assessments in the early 1560s.[6] In this chapter it is considered as a continuation of the medieval statutes. Studies of the enforcement of the 1563 Statute are relatively limited in comparison to those of the late medieval period. Classic studies by Keith Kelsall, Margaret Davies and F. G. Emmison have recently been supplemented by the research of Douglas Hay and Tim Wales.[7] The sixteenth-century poor laws[8] and the vagrancy laws[9] have a scholarship largely separate from that of the regulation of labour, despite their close relationship.

Enforcement', *Law and History Review*, 1 (1983), 27–52; Elaine Clark, 'Medieval Labor Law and English Local Courts', *American Journal of Legal History*, 27 (1983), 330–53.

5   Christopher Given-Wilson, 'The Problem of Labour in the Context of English Government, c.1350–1450', in James Bothwell, P. J. P. Goldberg and W. M. Ormrod (eds), *The Problem of Labour in Fourteenth-Century England* (York, 2000), pp. 85–100; Christopher Given-Wilson, 'Service, Serfdom and English Labour Legislation: 1350–1500', in Anne Curry and Elizabeth Matthew (eds), *Concepts and Patterns of Service in the Later Middle Ages* (Woodbridge, 2000). But see also Alan Harding, 'The Revolt Against the Justices', in R. H. Hilton and T. H. Aston (eds), *The English Rising of 1381* (Cambridge, 1984), pp. 165–93; Samuel Cohn, 'After the Black Death: Labour Legislation and Attitudes Towards Labour in Late Medieval Western Europe', *Economic History Review*, 60 (2007), 457–85.

6   S. T. Bindoff, 'The Making of the Statute of Artificers', in S. T. Bindoff *et al.* (eds), *Elizabethan Government and Society: Essays Presented to Sir John Neale* (London, 1961), pp. 56–94; Donald Woodward, 'The Background to the Statute of Artificers: The Genesis of Labour Policy 1558–63', *Economic History Review*, 33 (1980), 32–44. See also Bertha H. Putnam, 'Northamptonshire Wage Assessments of 1560 and 1667', *Economic History Review*, 1 (1927), 124–34.

7   R. Keith Kelsall, *Wage Regulation under the Statute of Artificers* (London, 1938); Margaret G. Davies, *The Enforcement of English Apprenticeship: A Study in Applied Mercantilism,1563–1642* (Cambridge, MA, 1956); F. G. Emmison, *Elizabethan Life: Home, Work and Land* (Chelmsford, 1976), pp. 146–74; Douglas Hay, 'England, 1562–1875: the Law and Its Uses', in Douglas Hay and Paul Craven (eds), *Masters, Servants and Magistrates in Britain and the Empire, 1562–1955* (Chapel Hill, 2004), pp. 59–116; Tim Wales, '"Living at their own hands": policing poor households and the young in early modern rural England', *Agricultural History Review*, 61 (2013), 19–39.

8   Paul Slack, *Poverty in Tudor and Stuart England* (London, 1988); Steve Hindle, *On the Parish? The Micropolitics of Poor Relief in Rural England c.1550–1750* (Oxford, 2004); Marjorie K. McIntosh, *Poor Relief in England 1350–1600* (Cambridge, 2012); Marjorie K. McIntosh, *Poor Relief and Community in Hadleigh, Suffolk, 1547–1600* (Hatfield, 2013).

9   C. S. L. Davies, 'Slavery and Protector Somerset: the Vagrancy Act of 1547', *Economic History Review*, 19 (1966) 533–49; J. F. Pound, *Poverty and Vagrancy in Tudor England* (London, 1971); A. L. Beier, 'Vagrants and the Social Order in Elizabethan England', *Past and Present*, 64 (1974), 3–29; A. L. Beier, *Masterless Men: The Vagrancy Problem in England*

Recent research increasingly challenges this fragmented approach. Robert Steinfeld's sweeping survey *The Invention of Free Labor* emphasises the long-term development and wider impact of the labour laws between the fourteenth and nineteenth centuries.[10] A. L. Beier draws important connections between labour, vagrancy and poverty legislation in an essay that nonetheless fails to consider the period before 1500 in any detail.[11] The gap in knowledge about the period between the active enforcement of new legislation in the late fourteenth century and the creation of the Statute of Artificers in 1563 has now been partly filled. Marjorie McIntosh demonstrates the increasing concern of communities across the country regarding measures of social control from the late fourteenth century onwards – measures that included punishment of vagrants and the unemployed.[12] Given-Wilson draws attention to parliament's concern for regulating labour during the fifteenth century,[13] while Paul Cavill has shown that parliament's attempts to reinstitute wage regulation in 1495 caused rebellion in Kent.[14] Jane Whittle has demonstrated that the medieval labour laws, including compulsory service for the unemployed, were being actively enforced in mid-sixteenth-century Norfolk.[15] New digital resources make it far easier to track the development of the laws in parliament.[16] As a consequence, the time is ripe for a reassessment of the laws and their full implications for the development of wage labour.

1560–1640 (London, 1985); Patricia Fumerton, *Unsettled: The Culture of Mobility and the Working Poor in Early Modern England* (Chicago, 2006).

10   Steinfeld, *Invention of Free Labor*.

11   A. L. Beier, '"A New Serfdom": Labour Laws, Vagrancy Statutes, and Labor Discipline in England, 1350–1800', in A. L. Beier and Paul Ocobock (eds), *Cast Out: Vagrancy and Homelessness in Global and Historical Perspective* (Athens, GA, 2008), pp. 35–63.

12   Marjorie K. McIntosh, *Controlling Misbehaviour in England, 1370–1600* (Cambridge, 1998).

13   Given-Wilson, 'Service, Serfdom'; Given-Wilson, 'Problem of Labour'.

14   Paul Cavill, 'The Problem of Labour and the Parliament of 1495', in Linda Clark (ed.), *Of Mice and Men: Image, Belief and Regulation in Late Medieval England* (Woodbridge, 2005), pp. 147–50.

15   Jane Whittle, *The Development of Agrarian Capitalism: Land and Labour in Norfolk 1440–1580* (Oxford, 2000), pp. 275–301.

16   *Parliament Rolls of Medieval England* [PR], https://www.british-history.ac.uk/no-series/parliament-rolls-medieval [accessed 17 March 2020]; *Journal of the House of Lords*: Vol. 1: 1509–1577: https://www.british-history.ac.uk/lords-jrnl/vol1 [accessed 17 March 2020] (the run is not complete for the early sixteenth century); *Journal of the House of Commons*: Vol. 1: 1547–1629: https://www.british-history.ac.uk/commons-jrnl/vol1 [accessed 17 March 2020]; *Statutes of the Realm* [SR] Vols 1–4, available on HeinOnline: https://heinonline-org.uoelibrary.idm.oclc.org/HOL/Welcome [accessed 23 June 2020].

Social divisions and the creation and enforcement of labour legislation

In the aftermath of the Black Death, J. R. Maddicott notes, 'the [House of] Commons largely ceased to speak for "the people" and, instead, began to speak vociferously against them'.[17] This transformation was most evident in the labour laws. With the exception of the Ordinance of Labourers, which was issued as an emergency measure by the king and royal council in June 1349 during the first outbreak of plague,[18] the labour laws were created by parliament. An understanding of whose attitudes the laws expressed requires investigation into how they were created and the mechanisms of enforcement.

During the thirteenth and fourteenth centuries England's parliament developed as a significant part of government.[19] The medieval parliament was (as it still is) composed of two houses, the Lords and the Commons. The Lords was a forum of the most powerful men: magnates and senior churchmen. It was effectively a wider extension of the king's council, and its members were each invited to attend parliament by the monarch. In contrast, the Commons were partly representative. Each county selected two knights of the shire, and towns were represented by two burgesses. As a consequence, the parliamentary electorate in the 1430s consisted of an estimated 15,000 people out of a population of around 2 million.[20] MPs sitting in the Commons were an elite, but quite a broad elite that included a mixture of gentlemen, lawyers (who tended to come from the gentry) and wealthy townsmen. Over time townsmen were increasingly replaced by gentlemen, so that by the end of the sixteenth century gentry MPs outnumbered non-gentry townsmen by four to one.[21]

In the fourteenth century most members of both parliamentary houses would have been manorial lords with servile tenants. Bruce Campbell calculates that half of all tenanted land was subject to serfdom in the fourteenth century.[22] So some support for the institution of serfdom might have been expected. However, all MPs were employers of wage labour. It was impossible for a wealthy man to live during this period without servants, or without craftsmen to build and fix houses, shoe horses and create clothing and saddlery. Many of

---

17 J. R. Maddicott, 'Parliament and the People in Medieval England', *Parliamentary History*, 35 (2015), 345.
18 Given-Wilson, 'Problem of Labour', p. 86.
19 Maddicott, 'Parliament and the People'.
20 Or 0.75 per cent of the population. Maddicott, 'Parliament and the People', 339–41, 348–9.
21 G. R. Elton, *"The Body of the Whole Realm": Parliament and Representation in Medieval and Tudor England* (Charlottesville, 1969), pp. 31, 34.
22 Bruce M. S. Campbell, 'The Agrarian Problem in the Early Fourteenth Century', *Past and Present*, 188 (2005), 37–8.

those who owned land relied on casual labour to bring in the harvest. Thus, while Maddicott notes that, in the early fourteenth century, the Commons supported wider popular interests against the monarchy by seeking to curtail taxation and purveyancing,[23] after 1349 they were united as employers against the large section of the population who earned wages.[24]

New laws or statutes had to be agreed by both houses of parliament and the crown before they could become law, and could originate from any of these bodies.[25] Proposed legislation took the form of petitions in the medieval period, which were known as bills in the sixteenth century. Many petitions and bills were discussed but failed to become statutes. Bindoff's study of the creation of the 1563 Statute of Artificers provides an example of how new legislation was formulated. He traces its origins to a committee of senior lawyers appointed by the newly crowned Elizabeth I's Privy Council in December 1558 'for consideration of all things necessary for the Parliament'. This produced a document that listed twenty-three proposals, including a revival of locally set wage rates and restrictions on apprenticeship. These measures were put to parliament in early 1559, but remained at the discussion stage and were not passed. They were reintroduced at the next parliament in 1563, and after five readings and two 'committals' (when measures were referred back to a committee for further amendments) by the House of Commons over a period of three months, the Statute of Artificers became law.[26] The 1563 Statute repealed all previous labour laws and included a mixture of new and existing measures. Its diverse origins are demonstrated by its size and by the fact that some of its clauses overlap and partially contradict one another.[27] Its creation resulted from the combined concerns of royal government, senior legal advisors, and MPs in the Commons, with support from the Lords.

The level of parliamentary concern is indicated by the sheer quantity of legislation relating to labour and the poor discussed and enacted between 1349 and the end of the sixteenth century. Parliaments were not held every year. Sixteenth-century parliaments were less frequent but stayed in session longer and passed more complex laws than those of the fourteenth and fifteenth centuries. Table 1.1 summarises the frequency of parliaments, proposals for new legal measures relating to labour, vagrancy and the able-bodied poor, and the number of relevant statutes actually passed. It demonstrates that labour legislation and related measures was never far from being a topic of concern. The longest period in which no measures were discussed was the

---

23 Maddicott, 'Parliament and the People', 343–5.
24 Penn and Dyer suggest 'at least one third of the population' gained all or part of their livelihood from wages: 'Wages and Earnings', p. 356. See also Poos, 'Social Context', 28.
25 Paul Cavill, *The English Parliaments of Henry VII 1485–1504* (Oxford, 2009), chapter 5.
26 Bindoff, 'Making of the Statute', pp. 70–1, 80–91.
27 Bindoff, 'Making of the Statute', pp. 59–60.

twenty-six years from 1446 to 1472; this was broken by a request from the Commons for various existing statutes to be enforced, including 'statutes of labourers and artisans'.[28]

Table 1.1. Numbers of parliaments and statutes passed or discussed relating to labour.

Years	Parliaments held	Statutes passed	Proposals discussed but not passed	Parliaments in which laws discussed	% discussing labour laws
1351–1400	45	9	6	15	33
1401–1450	37	7	2	9	24
1451–1500	18	3	2	4	22
1501–1550	25	10	3	12	48
1551–1601	20	9	6	12	60

Sources: PR (1445–1495); *Journal of the House of Lords*: vol. 1 (1510, 1512, 1515, 1534–45); *Journal of the House of Commons*: vol. 1 (1547–1601); SR vol. 1–4 (1349–1601); Given-Wilson, 'Service, Serfdom', p. 37 (1349–1430). Note: Only statutes and proposals related to the regulation of labour, vagrancy and the able-bodied poor are recorded in the table. Some parliaments discussed or passed more than one relevant statute.

The labour laws were unusual in creating a new system for enforcement as well as a set of regulations. In the 1350s special Justices of Labourers were commissioned to hear infringements. After 1360 their duties were fused with those of keeping the peace to create quarter sessions courts presided over by Justices of the Peace (JPs), held four times a year at county level to hear cases relating to the labour laws and other breaches of law and order.[29] These courts endured until 1971. Detecting and reporting infringements at a local level, including enforcing the compulsory service clause, was the responsibility of village sub-constables and similar officials in towns.[30] While JPs were drawn from the gentry,[31] constables were of middling social status and were selected from among the village elite. Like JPs, however, they would typically have been

28 *PR 1472.*
29 These developments were complex, as outlined in Putnam, *Enforcement*, pp. 10–26; Putnam, *Proceedings*, pp. xxiii–xxv. See also Poos, 'Social Context', 30; Anthony Musson and W. M. Ormrod, *The Evolution of English Justice: Law, Politics and Society in the Fourteenth Century* (Basingstoke, 1999), pp. 52–3.
30 Poos, 'Social Context', 31.
31 Musson and Ormrod, *Evolution*, pp. 56–7.

employers of labour and not waged workers themselves.[32] The statutes required workers to be hired in public and servants sworn twice a year to uphold the legislation. This took place at petty sessions held within each community and presided over by constables.[33] This system of enforcement functioned in the late fourteenth century and was active in mid-sixteenth-century Norfolk and across the country after 1563.[34]

There was also a gender dimension to the labour laws and their enforcement. The laws themselves were remarkably egalitarian: the first clause, cited above, explicitly stated that women as well as men had a duty to work for wages. Yet those who created and enforced the laws were exclusively men. A number of historians have argued that women were particularly likely to be targeted for infringements, particularly for failing to enter service and 'living at their own hands', because patriarchal norms classified such behaviour as immoral.[35]

Alan Harding notes that as JPs 'the country gentry became the moral arbiters of society, enforcing their values in the courts'.[36] The same could be said of constables in the regulation of their communities. McIntosh found that, in the fifteenth century, when royal government was weaker, local officials became increasingly engaged in regulating social and moral order.[37] So, while before the Black Death parliament represented the interests of the populace against the monarchy by curbing taxation, after the Black Death the labour legislation demonstrates that it increasingly represented the interests of employers against those of workers. Mechanisms of enforcing the labour laws drew on the support of wider social group of less wealthy employers and for the first time divided English society into two opposing social groups defined by employment relations.

32   Anthony Musson, 'Sub-Keepers and Constables: the Role of Local Officials in Keeping the Peace in Fourteenth-Century England', *English Historical Review*, 117 (2002), 1–23; Poos, 'Social Context', 35; Whittle, *Development of Agrarian Capitalism*, p. 56.

33   Statute 1351; evidence of enforcement: Poos, 'Social context', 31; Musson, 'Sub-Keepers', pp. 5, 20.

34   Poos, 'Social Context', 30–4; Whittle, *Development of Agrarian Capitalism*, pp. 276–87; Kelsall, *Wage Regulation*, chapter 4.

35   Bennett, 'Compulsory service'; Wales, '"Living at their own hands"'; Paul Griffiths, *Youth and Authority: Formative Experiences in England 1560–1640* (Oxford, 1996), pp. 378–80. Sandy Bardsley discusses women prosecuted for high wages: 'Women's Work Reconsidered: Gender and Wage Differentiation in Late Medieval England', *Past and Present*, 165 (1999). Whittle found that men were likely to be placed in compulsory service in rural Norfolk: *Development of Agrarian Capitalism*, pp. 260–1.

36   Harding, 'Revolt', pp. 183–4.

37   McIntosh, *Controlling Misbehaviour*, pp. 129–34.

The classification of wage workers

The labour laws offer a window into how those in power thought about wage labour and how these ideas crystallised over time. Historians define servants as workers who lived with their employer and were contracted for longer terms, usually a year at a time, and labourers as independent workers who had their own household but relied on wages earned by working for others, typically by the day.[38] Artificers were craftsmen and tradesmen who had a specialist skill acquired via apprenticeship. Vagrants were those with no fixed home or legal source of income. These classifications are so familiar to historians of preindustrial England and elsewhere in Europe that it is easy to overlook their significance. Yet the labour laws played a part in creating these distinctions. They repeatedly classified workers and potential workers into these four main groups, which appeared, in that order, in the Ordinance of 1349. Nonetheless, while these categories were already understood in 1349, some distinctions were blurred in the earliest statutes and became more clearly defined over time.

The common understanding, but also confusion, surrounding the three main types of worker are evident from other fourteenth-century documents, most notably the Poll Tax returns and manorial accounts.[39] The Poll Tax returns of 1380–1 recorded occupations. Rodney Hilton gives the example of the rural parish of Brewood in Staffordshire. Among the 249 taxpayers in 1380–1 were forty-five peasant heads of household (men described as *cultor*), forty artificers or retailers (men or women described by specialist occupations), fifteen taxpaying servants who lived in the households of others (*serviens*, abbreviated as 's') and thirty-five labourers (*labor*), of whom twelve were married and headed their own households.[40] He observes that, as well as living in the households of others, servants were usually unmarried, often female and rarely paid the full tax quota; on the other hand, labourers were more likely to pay the full tax and be married and male. However, Larry Poos notes that 'late medieval England did not possess a completely unambiguous terminology to denote what historians understand by "servant" and "labourer"': some servants lived away from their employer and the term '*famulus*' was used for both types of worker.[41] *Famuli* were manorial employees. They appear in manorial accounts

---

38   E.g. Ann Kussmaul, *Servants in Husbandry in Early Modern England* (Cambridge, 1981), p. 4.
39   Both types of document are in Latin.
40   R. H. Hilton, *The English Peasantry in the Later Middle Ages* (Oxford, 1975), pp. 34–5 and Carolyn Fenwick (ed.), *The Poll Taxes of 1377, 1379 and 1381: Part 2, Lincolnshire to Westmoreland* (Oxford, 2001), pp. 477–8 (the descriptions are in abbreviated Latin); see also Poos, 'Social Context', 24. All people aged over 15 were liable for the tax.
41   L. R. Poos, *A Rural Society after the Black Death: Essex 1350–1525* (New York, 1991), pp. 185–6; see also R. H. Hilton, *Class Conflict and the Crisis of Feudalism* (London, 1985), p. 261.

that survive in their thousands for the period 1250–1450, recording the economy of the large demesne farms owned by manorial lords. Manorial *famuli* were normally paid every quarter or half year and did not necessarily live with their employer. As well as ploughmen, who were typically young unmarried men, they included shepherds and carters, who were more likely to be married with households of their own.[42] Manorial accounts also record payments to casual agricultural workers employed by task or day to thresh, mow and reap, but these workers are rarely named or described. They also frequently record payments to craftsmen such as smiths, carpenters and other building workers, sometimes paid by the task or day and sometimes retained on long-term contracts like *famuli*. Confusion is caused by the fact that both 'servant' and 'labourer' could be used to mean wage workers in general, as well as to refer to more specific types of worker.[43] For instance, the 1349 Ordinance did not use the term 'labourer' and was glossed in the original French as a 'proclamation concerning servants', while the 1351 Statute was entered in the Parliament Roll as 'Statute of Artificers and Servants'.[44] By 1360, however, the 1351 Statute was referred to as 'the Statute of Labourers of old times made'.[45]

The remainder of this section looks in turn at the classification of servants, labourers, artificers and vagrants within the laws. With regards to servants, the labour laws made a transition over time from assuming that servants were manorial *famuli* to using the term 'servant in husbandry'. For instance, the first clause of the 1351 Statute addressed the typical categories of manorial *famuli* when it ordered all 'carters, ploughmen, drivers of the plough, shepherds, swineherds, *deies* (dairywomen), and all other servants' to accept wages at pre-plague levels and 'serve by a whole year, or by other usual terms, and not by the day'.[46] From 1388 Statutes began to set new wage levels,[47] and this involved describing the servants who received different levels of pay, as shown in Table 1.2. Initially, as in 1351, servants were understood as having specialist roles typical of manorial demesne farms, but by the mid-fifteenth century they were divided into groups according to level of skill, gender and age. This transition occurred at the same time that manorial lords largely abandoned direct demesne farming and leased out their demesnes to farmers.[48]

42   M. M. Postan, 'The Famulus: the Estate Labourer in the Twelfth and Thirteenth Centuries', *Economic History Review Supplement* 2 (1954); David Farmer, 'The Famuli in the Later Middle Ages', in R. H. Britnell and J. Hatcher (eds), *Progress and Problems in Medieval England* (Cambridge, 1996); Jordan Claridge and John Langdon, 'The Composition of Famuli Labour on English demesnes, c.1300', *Agricultural History Review*, 63 (2015).

43   On the wider use of 'servant' see Steinfeld, *Invention of Free Labor*, p. 18–22.

44   *SR*, vol. 1, p. 307 and *PR* 1351.

45   *SR*, vol. 1, p. 366.

46   *SR*, vol. 1, p. 311.

47   The earlier statutes had tried to enforce pre-plague wage levels.

48   Bruce M. S. Campbell, *English Seigniorial Agriculture 1250–1450* (Cambridge, 2000), pp. 3, 29.

Table 1.2. Types of servants and their annual wages as described in statutes and wage assessments.

1388 Statute	1431 Wage assessment (Norfolk)	1446 Statute	1495 Statute	1560 Wage assessment (Northants)
Bailiff of husbandry, 28s 4d	Bailiff in husbandry, '20d' [20s] + clothing	Bailiff of husbandry, 28s 4d	Bailiff of husbandry, 31s 8d	Chief servant or bailiff at husbandry [taking] the whole charge of the farm, 45s
Master hine, carter or shepherd, 10s	Plowman, a shepherd, a carter, a maltster, the best, 13s 4d	Chief hind, carter or chief shepherd, 24s	Chief hind, carter or chief shepherd, 25s	Next best servant at husbandry, 36s 8d
Driver of the plough, 7s	The secondary, 10s	Common servant of husbandry, 18s 4d	Common servant of husbandry, 20s 8d	Common servant that can but plough & thresh, 25s
Oxherd or cowherd, 6s 8d				
Swineherd, woman labourer [sic], or deye, 6s	Woman servant of husbandry the best, 10s + clothing	Woman servant, 14s	Woman servant, 14s	Best woman servant [taking] charge of the whole house keeping, 26s 8d
				Best woman servant being a deye, 22s 8d
		Infant aged 14 or less, 9s	Child aged 14 or less, 9s 8d	Common number of meaner sorts, 10s

Sources: *SR* vol. 2, pp. 57 (1388), 338 (1446), 585–6 (1495); E. A. McArthur, 'A Fifteenth Century Assessment of Wages', *English Historical Review*, 13 (1898), 300 (1431); B. H. Putnam, 'Northamptonshire Wage Assessments of 1560 and 1667', *Economic History Review*, 1 (1927), 132. Notes: the value of payments for clothing has been added to the cash wage. The categories of 1446 and 1495 were repeated in 1515–16.

The annual wages listed in Table 1.2 imply annual contracts. However, the statutes remained vague about the length of time servants should be employed for. The Statute of 1351 mentioned working for the 'whole year', but qualified this with 'or other usual terms'.[49] It was not until 1549–50 that a statute specified the requirement that 'all servants of husbandry unmarried' should 'serve by the whole year, and not go by the day wage'.[50] The 1563 Statute of Artificers was again unclear, stipulating that compulsory service for the unemployed should be 'by the year', but not specifying whether normal contracts should always be of that length.[51] Wage accounts from the late sixteenth and early seventeenth centuries show much variation and suggest that a quarter year or six months was the usual understanding of 'a longer term', rather than twelve months.[52] It is also notable that the statutes make no explicit mention of servants living in their employer's household. From 1446 onwards the provision of 'meat and drink' with wages is specified, but this was also the case for day labourers, who received meals when they worked. Nor was the assumption that servants were typically unmarried mentioned until 1549.[53] It seems that neither being married nor having children was seen as a barrier to being placed in service. Instead the key determining factor was whether or not someone had sufficient property to support themselves. The 1446 Statute ruled that 'no man shall be excused to serve by the year' unless they had enough land to provide 'continual occupation' for one man: this suggests that some householders could be placed in service.[54]

Despite the preference for placing people in service, as discussed further in the next section, the laws conceded that casual labourers were also part of the economy. In particular, they were needed to meet peaks in labour demand during the agricultural year. The Ordinance of 1349 did not explicitly address casual labourers as a group. But it did rule that 'any reaper, mower or other workman' should not depart from 'any man's service' before the end of the agreed term. However, the 1351 Statute mentions wage rates by the task and by the day, while the Statute of 1390, which allowed JPs to set local wage rates, attached the description 'labourer' specifically to workers paid by the day. This use of 'labourer' was continued in the fifteenth century. National wage levels set in 1446 acknowledged for the first time labourers who worked outside of agriculture and female harvest labourers, as well as male agricultural labourers. It also set wages for winter and summer, reflecting the different hours of work. By 1495 working hours for labourers and artificers were being described in increasing detail, specifying the number and length of meal breaks and what times of the year it was permissible to have a midday nap. These provisions were repeated in the Statutes of 1515 and 1563. Thus day labourers were an accepted part of England's wage labour force.

50   *SR*, vol. 4, p. 121.
51   *SR*, vol. 4, p. 415.
52   Jane Whittle, 'A Different Pattern of Employment: Servants in Rural England c.1500–1660', in Jane Whittle (ed.), *Servants in Rural Europe c.1400–c.1900* (Woodbridge, 2017).
53   *SR*, vol. 4, p. 121.
54   *SR*, vol. 2, p. 337.

Harvest work was consistently noted as an exception to other guidelines, reflecting a desire to ensure that workers were available at this time of peak demand, even if that transgressed normal boundaries. It was acknowledged as a legitimate cause for the large-scale seasonal movement of workers. The 1351 Statute stated that workers should 'serve the summer ... where he dwelleth in the winter', but made an exception for the people in various upland regions such as 'the counties of Stafford, Lancaster, Derby, Craven [in Yorkshire], of the Marches of Wales and Scotland, and other Places' who may 'come in time of August and labour in other counties, and safely return, as they were wont to do before this Time'.[55] These exceptions continued in the sixteenth century. The 1572 Statute against Vagabondage noted that it did not 'extend to any cockers or harvest folks that travel into any country of this realm for harvest work, either corn harvest or hay harvest, if they do work and labour accordingly'.[56] In 1388 craftsmen were enlisted into the harvest labour force with the order that 'artificers, servants and apprentices, which be of no great reputation, and of which craft or mystery a man hath no great need, in harvest time, shall be compelled to serve in harvest, to cut, gather, and bring in the corn'.[57] This was repeated in 1563 and extended to the hay harvest.

Artificers were seen as a threat to the employing and consuming class via their demands for higher wages or higher prices for the goods they produced. Yet the labour laws went beyond the regulation of prices and wages, usurping the role of craft guilds in regulating entrance into the crafts and work practices. In doing so the government displayed two overriding concerns: one was to protect the primacy of agriculture in the economy, and the other was a fear of craftsmen's independence. The two were connected because structures of landownership allowed the elite to control the agricultural economy via manorial lordship, whereas they had no such control over those employed in crafts and industry. Measures indicate a concern for defining craft workers as separate from the agricultural economy, to which they were nonetheless subjugated, as the requirement for harvest labour indicates. While publicly justified in terms of ensuring the food supply, the primacy of agriculture also served the private interests of the majority of parliamentarians. Nonetheless, craft employment was consistently attractive to workers across the period, providing an escape from servile lord–tenant relations in the fourteenth and fifteenth centuries and a more profitable alternative to agricultural labour for the land-poor in the sixteenth century.

The fear that craft employment was causing a shortage of agricultural labour was first voiced in 1388. That statute specified that no man or women who 'use to labour at the plough and cart, or other labour or service of husbandry' up

---

55 *SR*, vol. 1, p. 312.
56 *SR*, vol. 4, p. 592.
57 *SR*, vol. 2, p. 56.

to the age of twelve was to enter any 'mystery or handicraft'. This plea was sharpened in 1406 when it was stated that 'there is so great scarcity of labourers and other servants of husbandry that the gentlemen and other people of the realm be greatly impoverished'. Property qualifications for entry into crafts were introduced, although in 1429 London gained an exemption from these. The Statute of Artificers of 1563 strengthened parliamentary control further, with wealth and property qualifications set for parents wishing to apprentice children into a comprehensive list of crafts.

The labour laws also increasingly micro-managed the work practices of craftsmen. In 1402 a whole statute was devoted to stopping artificers being paid a full day's pay for holidays or half-days. Hours of work were specified from 1445 onwards, while in 1563 building workers were banned from leaving jobs unfinished. In the sixteenth century journeymen, the most independent and mobile subset of craftsmen, drew particular attention. A statute of 1549 regulating textile workers expressed disapproval of the 'many young folks and servants of sundry occupations' who after completing their apprenticeships were able to work 'at their liberty ... to the intent they will live idly and at their pleasure flee and resort from place to place'. The law banned unmarried journeymen from working for less than three months at a time. In 1563 this was extended to one year, and applied to all unmarried workers and all workers under the age of thirty in all crafts.

The power of the labour laws lay not only in regulating work but in crimi-nalising unemployment. This was recognised in the Ordinance of 1349, which noted in its final clause that 'many valiant beggars as long as they may live of begging do refuse to labour, giving themselves to idleness and vice, and sometime to theft and other abominations', and ordered that none should give alms to anyone able to work so that 'they may be compelled to labour for their necessary living'.[58] Yet there remains confusion about the nature of the people targeted as 'idle' by this and later statutes. This confusion is partly linguistic and partly a matter of interpretation, because the laws applied to a wide range of people. The statutes use the words 'vagrant', 'vagabond' and 'vacabond' interchangeably. Up until the mid-fifteenth century, when the original statutes were written in French, the term vagrant was used. The earliest vagrancy statute in English, that of 1495, used the obsolete term 'vacabond', which derives from the Latin verb *vacere*, meaning 'to be unoccupied or idle', whereas vagabond, like vagrant, derives from the Latin *vagari*, meaning 'to wander'.[59] Throughout the sixteenth century the terms vacabond and vagabond were both used in

58   *SR*, vol. 1, p. 308. 'Valiant' in this context means 'sturdy' or able-bodied.
59   Oxford English Dictionary Online, https://www.oed.com/view/Entry/220882#eid16 067803 [accessed 24 April 2020].

statutes.[60] The interchangeability of the two words highlights the laws' concern both with 'idleness' and unemployment and with 'wandering' and mobility.

Early statutes aimed at the mobile and unemployed also vacillated in their concerns. A 1360 Statute highlighted those who had broken contracts – 'labourers or artificers who absent themselves from their services' – ruling that they should be branded with an 'F' as a 'token of falsity'. In 1383 a statute sought to punish vagrants and 'faitours' who wandered 'from place to place',[61] while in 1388 the focus was on 'every person that goes begging, and is able to serve or labour'. In 1446 it was emphasised that even people with their own house and land could be ordered to serve by the year 'upon the pain to be justified as a vagrant', if their land was insufficient to occupy them fully.[62] A 1495 Statute urged punishment 'of every vagabond, hermit or beggar able to labour'.[63] Concern about vagrancy heightened in the sixteenth century and statutes became increasingly eloquent and detailed in their descriptions of those they sought to punish, but continued to include labourers and unemployed servants in their remit. The 1547 Statute, which notoriously introduced fixed-term slavery as punishment, was aimed at men and women who:

> shall either like a serving man wanting a master or like a beggar … lurking in any house … or loitering or idly wander by the highway's side or in streets in cities, towns or villages, not applying them self to some honest and allowed art, science, service or labour.

A new statute in 1549 noted that 'such common labourers … using loitering and refusing to work for such reasonable wage' would be 'adjudged vacabond'. The statutes of 1572 and 1597–8 set out long lists of different types of people deemed to be 'rogues, vacabonds and sturdy beggars'. Among various categories of fraudsters, travellers and entertainers are 'all common labourers being persons able in body using loitering, and refusing to work for … reasonable wages'.[64]

The vagrancy laws are particularly vivid in their moral judgements of people without property who refused to work under the terms set out in the labour laws, but all the labour laws are imbued with the idea that such people had a duty not just to work but to serve. That is, 'idleness' was not a failure to work per se, but a failure to offer yourself as an obedient employee in return for low wages and thus accept a subservient position in society. The exigencies

---

60   In 1495, 1531, 1536, 1549 and 1576 vacabond was used; 1503–4 and 1572 used both vacabond and vagabond; in 1547 and 1598 the term vagabond was preferred.

61   *SR*, vol. 2, pp. 32–3. 'Faitour' is an obscure medieval term for 'a vagrant who shams illness or pretends to tell fortunes': Oxford English Dictionary Online: https://www.oed.com/view/Entry/67773?redirectedFrom=faitour#eid [accessed 24 February 2020].

62   That is, punished as a vagrant: *SR*, vol. 2, p. 339.

63   *SR*, vol. 2, p. 569.

64   Same wording in both statutes: *SR*, vol. 4, pp. 592, 899.

of agricultural production required the tolerance of some casual seasonal day labour, but the laws indicate that preferred modes of wage labour were longer-term service contracts in which the employer had tighter control over the worker's life as a whole.

Compulsion and subservience as aspects of wage labour

While the creation of the labour laws can be seen as an acknowledgement by those in power that wage labour was more efficient than serfdom at providing a motivated and flexible labour force, they do not indicate an acceptance of 'free' wage labour. Rather than workers choosing when and how to work, and negotiating contracts according to supply and demand, the laws sought to compel people to work for wages and to favour employers in the negotiation of contracts. They were based on principles not of a free labour market but of compulsion and subservience. This section examines how the laws made unemployment illegal and intervened in the nature of labour contracts, considering both the nature of the laws and evidence of enforcement.

The first clause of the 1349 Ordinance ordered men and women aged under sixty who lacked property or a craft to be 'bound to serve him which so shall him require'.[65] Records of the enforcement of compulsory service survive for the late fourteenth century, the mid-sixteenth century and the late sixteenth and seventeenth centuries.[66] It was applied to both women and men, who were placed in year-long service contracts. In some places and periods women seem to have been particularly targeted with this clause.[67] Those who refused to enter compulsory service were prosecuted. A case from Norfolk in 1551 carefully rehearsed the stipulations of the 1349 Ordinance, noting that: 'Robert Gyllam of Hanworth ... who was "strong in body and about the age of 20" and had no craft, property, or living by which to support himself, and was not retained in anyone's service' was ordered into service of husbandry for one year.[68]

Some of those placed in compulsory service were vagrant, in the sense of lacking a permanent home. A short-lived statute of 1572 allowed people to avoid punishment for vagrancy if they entered service, and assize records contain lists of those placed with employers. For instance, in Sussex six people

---

65   SR, vol. 1, p. 307.
66   Bennett, 'Compulsory Service', 17–25; Whittle, *Development of Agrarian Capitalism*, pp. 280–7; Kelsall, *Wage Regulation*, pp. 29–33; Kussmaul, *Servants in Husbandry*, p. 166; K. D. M. Snell, *Annals of the Labouring Poor: Social Change and Agrarian England* (Cambridge, 1985), p. 100; Griffiths, *Youth and Authority*, pp. 350–89; Wales, '"Living at their own hands"'.
67   See footnote 35, above.
68   Whittle, *Development of Agrarian Capitalism*, p. 280.

were indicted for vagrancy on 31 May 1573: three (two men and a woman) were 'bound in service' with named employers, one (a married man) was prosecuted as a vagrant, and two (both women) were discharged.[69] Many of those placed in compulsory service were not vagrants without a home, however. Some lived with their parents; others accused of running 'from place to place like a rogue' nonetheless had a parish of residence.[70] Instead they were defined by being relatively poor, often young, and not actively seeking to enter service.

Evidence from mid-sixteenth-century Norfolk demonstrates that all the mechanisms of enforcement were in use, from petty sessions to detect the 'unemployed' and warrants forcing people into compulsory service to prosecution and imprisonment of those who resisted or absconded.[71] Similar documentation does not exist for other counties. However, a lack of documentation does not necessarily mean a lack of enforcement.[72] We know that quarter sessions continued to be held between the late fourteenth and late sixteenth century, although only fragmentary records survive.[73] Some manorial courts in the period 1450–1550 reported people for 'living suspiciously' and in the sixteenth century occasionally ordered people into service.[74] It is important to note that compulsory service was only likely to appear in the courts if it was resisted. The law allowed employers to force unemployed people into compulsory service with the support of local officials.[75] Further, the threat of compulsory service was sometimes enough to encourage people to enter service by their own arrangement. So the existence of documentation is not necessarily a good measure of the wider effect of the laws.

The range of compulsory work was expanded in 1563 to include not only compulsory service in husbandry by the year in the countryside for men and women aged between twelve and sixty (clause V) but also compulsory service by the year in craft occupations for those with appropriate training who were unmarried or aged under thirty (clause III); more casual forms of compulsory work 'by the year by the week or day' for unmarried women aged twelve to forty in towns (clause XVII); compulsory harvest work by artificers (clause XV); and compulsory apprenticeship in husbandry or crafts for those 'required by any

69   J. S. Cockburn, *Calendar of Assize Records: Sussex Indictments*, Elizabeth I (London, 1975), p. 96.

70   Whittle, *Development of Agrarian Capitalism*, p. 283.

71   Whittle, *Development of Agrarian Capitalism*, p. 285.

72   An argument also made strongly by Bennett, 'Compulsory Service', 15–18.

73   Putnam, *Proceedings*. See pp. cxxi–cxxiv for her comments on geographical and chronological variations in enforcement of the labour laws.

74   McIntosh, *Controlling Misbehaviour*, p. 92.

75   Bennett, 'Compulsory Service', p. 15; Putnam, *Proceedings*, p. cxxiv; John Bellamy, *Criminal Law and Society in late medieval and Tudor England* (Gloucester, 1984), pp. 12–13.

householder' (clauses XVIII, XIX, XXVIII).[76] Unlike compulsory service, which lasted for one year and was paid, compulsory apprenticeship was unpaid and longer term. The 1563 Statute considered compulsory apprenticeship appropriate for those aged eleven to seventeen, lasting until they were twenty-one, or for seven years in crafts.

The idea of compulsory apprenticeship had been developing in law since the Vagrancy Statute of 1536, which ordered that children aged between five and fourteen living by begging or idleness should be placed with masters of husbandry or crafts 'to be taught'.[77] This was developed further by a 1549 statute that specified that, if the parents were beggars, children could be taken from them without their permission and placed as a 'servant without wages, to what labour, occupation or service soever' until they reached the age of eighteen years.[78] These provisions were consolidated in the English poor laws of 1597–1601, which remained in force until 1834 and which allowed those in charge of poor relief 'to bind poor children apprentices' until they were twenty-one (girls) or twenty-four (boys).[79] This applied to 'children of all such whose parents shall not ... be thought able to keep or maintain their children'.[80] Unlike other work-creation schemes for the poor, this provision was commonly and actively pursued until the early nineteenth century.[81] Compulsion was thus an important underlying principle of the labour laws and associated legislation. People who lacked a certain amount of land or level of wealth were assumed to have a duty to serve in wealthier households.

The second strand of the laws set out to undermine workers' power to negotiate labour contracts freely with employers. This was done by setting maximum wage rates and specifying hours of work. Contracts had to be made in public, and workers and employers were sworn to obey these laws twice a year. While breaking labour contracts had been illegal before 1349, the labour laws increased the punishment for workers but not employers,[82] and service was preferred over day labouring. Service, in which the worker became a member of the employer's household, increased the employer's control over the worker.

---

76   SR, vol. 4, pp. 414–22. There were qualifications about the type of householders that could take apprentices; see clauses XVIII and XIX.
77   SR, vol. 3, p. 559 (clause VI).
78   SR, vol. 4, p. 116 (clause X).
79   SR, vol. 4, p. 897 (clause IV).
80   SR, vol. 4, pp. 962–3 (clauses I and III), confirming almost identical statements in 1597.
81   Hindle, On the Parish? pp. 191–223; Katrina Honeyman, Child workers in England 1780–1820: Parish Apprentices and the Making of the Early Industrial Labour Force (Aldershot, 2007); Jocelyn and R. D. Dunlop, English Apprenticeship and Child Labour: A History (London, 1912), chapter 16.
82   Steinfeld, Invention of Free Labor, pp. 3–4, 23–4, 113–14. Servants continued to be imprisoned for leaving service without a master's consent through to the late eighteenth century.

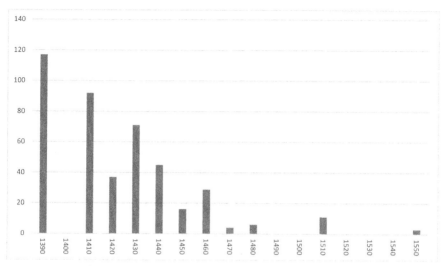

Figure 1.1. Common Pleas cases relating to the labour laws, 1390s–1550s. Source: Indexes to the Court of Common Pleas available from the *Anglo-American Legal Tradition* (AALT) website. Note: one sample year per decade (no data for 1400, 1520, 1540).

During a contract, servants had a duty to obey their master and could be asked to do any work task and work unlimited hours.[83] The employer had a duty to police their servants' behaviour and morals.[84] The laws also controlled mobility, inhibiting people's ability to search for employment freely.

Legal wage rates were set nationally in 1388, 1446, 1495 and 1515 and locally by county from 1390 to 1446 and from 1560 onwards, as shown in Table 1.2.[85] In the late fourteenth century most recorded prosecutions under the labour laws concerned wages, but after 1400 cases concerning broken contracts and compulsory service were more common.[86] Nonetheless, in the late fifteenth century a new wage assessment caused open rebellion in Kent – suggesting that legal wage rates were enforced, at least in certain times and places.[87] Prosecutions for broken contracts were the most persistent type of court case

83 In the early twentieth century servants worked sixteen hours a day, 6.5 days a week: Laura Schwartz, *Feminism and the Servant Problem* (Cambridge, 2019), p. 30.
84 On the legal status of servants see Clark, 'Medieval Labor Law', 346–7; Steinfeld, *Invention of Free Labor*, pp. 27–34. See also Griffiths, *Youth and Authority*, chapter 6.
85 E. A. McArthur, 'A Fifteenth Century Assessment of Wages', *The English Historical Review*, 13 (1898), 299–302; Woodward, 'Background'.
86 Poos, 'Social Context', 30–31; Penn and Dyer, 'Wages and Earnings', 358–9; Bennett, 'Compulsory Service', 16–17.
87 Cavill, 'Problem of Labour'.

citing the labour laws. For instance, these are found in the central court of Common Pleas across the fifteenth century. Figure 1.1 shows the incidence of debt cases where the plaintiff claimed money owing as a consequence of a broken contract and cited the labour laws.[88] The cases come from all parts of the country, from Yorkshire to Kent and from Devon to Norfolk. They were common in the early fifteenth century before tailing off after 1460.[89] Common Pleas cases from fifteenth-century London record the counter-pleas in which defendants explained why they left their employment, as shown in Table 1.3.[90] These demonstrate the difficulties that could emerge during a period of service and the ways employers could use the law to harass former employees.

Table 1.3. Explanations given by London defendants accused of breaking service contracts: Court of Common Pleas, 1399–1500.

Reason	Number
Servant was not retained as claimed	30
Servant left with permission	11
Employer failed to pay wages or to provide adequate food	7
Servant was threatened with unreasonable violence	4
Servant was already employed by someone else	3
Servant did not leave early	1
Contract agreement was conditional	1
Servant accepts charge	1
Legal technicalities or reason not stated	24

Source: Data from Jonathan Mackman and Matthew Stevens, *Court of Common Pleas: the National Archives, Cp40 1399–1500* (London, 2010).

Workers needed to move around freely to seek favourable terms of employment, yet doing so made them liable to prosecution. From 1388 those on the move without documentation could be prosecuted as vagrants. This was confirmed in 1563, when servants were ordered not to leave employment and depart from

88   Relevant cases were identified by using the indexes available from the *Anglo-American Legal Tradition* (AALT) for selected years: http://aalt.law.uh.edu/Indices/CP40Indices/CP40_Indices.html [accessed 18 June 2020].
89   Eastern England (Lincolnshire, Norfolk, Suffolk, Cambridgeshire) and the West Country (Gloucestershire, Wiltshire, Somerset) were particularly over-represented in comparison with their 1377 population estimates.
90   Analysis data from Jonathan Mackman and Matthew Stevens, *Court of Common Pleas: the National Archives, Cp40 1399–1500* (London, 2010), *British History Online* http://www.british-history.ac.uk/no-series/common-pleas/1399-1500 [accessed 18 June 2020].

a parish of residence without a testimonial letter sealed by a constable.[91] As we have seen, the vagrancy laws were explicit in including 'servants out of service', and 'common labourers' within their remit. Punishments for vagrancy set out in the statutes included being imprisoned (1383), set in stocks for three days (1495), whipped (1531), mutilated by having 'the upper part of the gristle of his right ear clean cut off' (1536), branded with a hot iron and placed in slavery for two years (1547, repealed 1549), imprisoned, whipped or compelled to do service (1572) and whipped and detained in a house of correction (1597). Thus servants who left service without permission, or even those who left legally but failed to obtain the necessary documentation, were liable to swift and direct forms of punishment, bolstering the inequality between worker and employer. Employers who failed to pay wages or terminated contracts early could be prosecuted in the courts, but were not subject to such immediate and humiliating punishment. Concern about vagrancy in the sixteenth century thus was not only about groups of beggars and petty thieves moving about the countryside, but about the presence of a large wage-earning class within the population, and the desire to regulate and discipline them in the interests of employers.

To see the labour laws as merely a mechanism to cap wages is to overlook their main intent and impact. The laws were intended to compel people to work for others, and to tip the balance of power between employer and worker heavily towards the employer. They were intended not only to provide a labour force but to enforce subservience and a particular social order. They were enforced not only by bringing cases to court but by immediate action: placing people in compulsory service, putting them in the stocks or whipping them as vagrants. The full power of these laws lay not only in enforcement, which operated more effectively in some counties than others, but in the threat of enforcement, which caused workers to tolerate situations that they might otherwise have rejected.

Conclusions

England's labour laws and associated legislation were subject to continuous development and enforcement from 1349 onwards. The laws specifically concerned with regulating wage labour were tightly related to those punishing vagrancy, which in turn shared aims with the poor laws in seeking to place certain categories of the poor, and those vulnerable to poverty, into employment. The laws demonstrate an increasingly subtle understanding of a variety of types of wage labour, beginning with the perspective of manorial lords in the fourteenth century, but adopting that of more varied types of employer from

---

91   *SR*, vol. 4, p. 416 (clause VII).

the mid-fifteenth century onwards. The young and the poor were particular targets of regulation and the laws aimed to push them into service or pauper apprenticeship in which they could be more effectively disciplined by employers. Compulsion was a central element of the laws and significantly compromised the freedom of people who lacked sufficient property or wealth. While many avoided punishment, the threat of punishment was surely significant in shaping social relations. The laws were hostile to the idea that terms of employment might be determined freely by supply and demand. As a consequence, people were compelled not just to work but to serve others and be subservient. In both their creation and their enforcement, the laws demonstrate a nascent class divide emerging within English society between employers and workers. These relations were not based on a free labour market but were instead shaped by the use of political and legal power to favour those who employed labour against those who provided it.

2

Agricultural Workers and their Contractual Terms of Employment in Marseille, 1349–1400

FRANCINE MICHAUD

Introduction

One of the greatest challenges facing the socio-economic historian of the Middle Ages is to understand the still poorly documented reality of servants attached to household economies. In Marseille, fortunately, from the thirteenth century onwards the evidentiary record becomes less elusive with the commercial expansion of the harbour city. By mid-century the intensity of transactional activities stimulated the production of notarial and judicial records, the oldest series in the French territory. It is also in the middle of that century that the city's prosperity paved the way for the Capetian prince Charles of Anjou, the new count of Provence, to strike a peace treaty with Marseille's rebellious citizens and recognise the community's self-governing institutions and body of laws (c. 1257).[1] Collectively, these sources form a sufficiently solid corpus to draw a picture of the profile and the fate of men and women in the service of the city's propertied classes over several generations. However, the main focus of this essay is on agricultural labourers who worked for urban dwellers in Marseille – the most populous city of Provence – in the decades following the Black Death. Two main arguments are rehearsed here: first, Marseille's economy, despite its overtures to maritime and commercial ventures, relied heavily on its agricultural sector. Chronically dependant on wine and wheat production, and having lost up to half of its pre-plague population by the end of the fourteenth century, the city faced severe labour shortages within a climate of military instability that

1 Georges Lesage, *Marseille angevine. Recherches sur son évolution administrative, économique et urbaine, de la victoire de Charles d'Anjou à l'arrivée de Jeanne 1re* (Paris, 1950), p. 61.

pervaded the county until 1400.[2] Securing the input of agriculturists was vital to its economic recovery. Second, and deriving from the first argument, rural workers represented, with seafarers, the largest and most cohesive group that can be tracked in the extant sources, especially from the mid-century, when Marseille opened its doors widely to migrants, predominantly rural folk. More than half of the 1076 apprenticeship and labour contracts collected between 1248 and 1400 concern seafarers (302), agriculturists (160) and domestics (112).

Given the city's sudden and massive mortality, and the ensuing steady influx of transient and migrant workers it welcomed into its walls, it is of interest to consider the fate of foreign workers in their new surroundings and how they were integrated into the community. Migrants undoubtedly sought to improve their fortune while competing with local hands for decent work conditions. But in a relatively short period of time the labour market went through such a transformation that it was bound to generate some degree of tension in the workplace. When in the fall of 1351 Robert de Rocha sued for breach of contract a certain Jean, a migrant from Brittany, he petitioned the court to have him jailed because, 'as a foreigner, he ought to be suspected of flight.' Himself an English goldsmith, Robert had moved to Marseille, became a citizen, started a family and built there a successful life.[3] Being foreign was thus not an unsurmountable condition in achieving social acceptance, integration and upward mobility, but access to capital and assets was key to such success, which was assuredly denied to most unskilled workers.

The aim of this chapter is to understand how this turbulent period marked by high epidemic mortality and recurring warfare in the larger county of Provence altered the labour conditions and status of rural workers in Marseille.

---

2   Marseille's population hovered around 25,000 before the Black Death: see Édouard Baratier, *La démographie provençale du XIIIe au XVIe siècle. Avec chiffres de comparaison pour le XVIIIe siècle* (Paris, 1961), p. 66 note 1. Throughout the fourteenth century several grain crises (*disettes*) hit Marseille, according to the city council minutes of 1318, 1323, 1340, 1358, 1363 and 1383. The municipal deliberations also contain episodic references to contingency measures regarding wheat supply: see Philippe Mabilly, *Inventaire sommaire des archives communales antérieures à 1790*, vol. 1 (Marseille, 1909). On wheat production, distribution and dependency: Gilbert Buti, 'La traite des blés et la construction de l'espace portuaire de Marseille (XVIIe–XVIIIe siècle)', in Brigitte Marin and Catherine Viroulet (eds), *Nourrir les cités de Méditerranée. Antiquité – Temps modernes* (Paris, 2003), pp. 769–99; Monique Bourin, Sandro Carocci, François Menant and Lluis To Figueras, 'Les campagnes de la Méditerranée occidentale autour de 1300: tensions destructrices, tensions novatrices', *Annales. Histoire, Sciences sociales*, 66 (2011), 670, 673. On Provence's political upheavals and military disturbances in the second half of the century: Martin Aurell, Jean-Paul Boyer and Noël Coulet, *La Provence au Moyen Âge* (Aix-en-Provence, 2005), pp. 275–94.
3   Marseille, Archives départementales des Bouches-du Rhône, Marseille (hereafter ADBRM), 3 B 48, fols 60r–61v (1 October 1351): in the court document, Robert introduced himself as a new resident, *habitator Massilie*; a decade later, in the apprenticeship contract for his eleven-year-old son Antoine, he was 'now citizen of Marseille'. ADBRM, 351 E 25, fol. 73r–v (9 July 1362).

Departing from the formal parameters that regulated household service in the city, the interfacing of administrative, notarial and judicial sources helps capture the profile of servants who sought placement in farming households; the nature, form and conditions of their employment; and their evolving place in the workplace at the turn of the fifteenth century.

Serving in the spirit of the law

With serfdom having all but disappeared in late medieval Provence, wage labour expanded significantly in the course of the fourteenth century, but the central or municipal governments never concerned themselves with comprehensive labour legislation. The earliest known efforts to regulate salaries at the county level were attempted in the midst of the plague epidemic, in August–September 1348, when the Estates General were convened in the royal capital, Aix, at the call of the seneschal of Provence on behalf of Joanna of Anjou, queen of Naples and countess of Provence. The ordinance, though, was never renewed or implemented, as labour regulations were in practice left to local governments, owing in large part to their administrative efficiency and overall political autonomy.[4] Indeed, in the years following the Black Death, Marseille took matters into its own hands. The city council had seemingly deliberated around wages before 1348, for the earliest reference to 'salary' in its deliberation registers dates from December 1325, but this was a misnomer. In reality, what the councillors meant by 'salary' was the 'pricing (called *salarium* in the minutes) of notarial documents and artisans' wares, which are mentioned in the law code'.[5] However, in the wake of the epidemic outbreak in Marseille and in the ensuing decades, wage control – and especially agricultural wages – gained traction. Yet, when the council met on 6 November 1348 to make the labour of ploughmen accessible to other landowners, no specific wages were stated, only the 'usual ones' to be remitted in broad daylight under the penalty of the double, while illicit extra

4 The Ordinance of 5–6 September 1348 recognized that where communities already had their own customs and usages ('juxta ordinationem patrie'), local authorities had jurisdiction over prices and salaries, which compromised its universal enforcement. Furthermore, royal accounts yield no fine collections owing to the violation of the ordinance's provisions: Robert Braid, '"*Et non ultra*": politiques royales du travail en Europe occidentale au XIVe siècle', *Bibliothèque de l'École des Chartes*, 161 (2003), 470 (notes 127–8), 473. If, as Braid suggests, municipal governments in Provence established wage and price lists prior to 1348 (at 444), they have left no documented traces.

5 'Super salariis ipsorum notariorum et omnium aliorum artem mecanicam exercentium, de quibus statuta loquentur': Marseille, Archives Municipales (hereafter AMM), BB 14, fol. 5r (14 December 1325). While the first deliberation register dates from 1319, the series is interrupted between 1340 and 1348, between 1351 and 1357, between 1368 and 1375 and between 1391 and 1400.

earnings would incur a fine of ten *librae*.[6] It is only in late January 1349 that, in order to restrain 'fraudulent manoeuvres by agriculturalists', daily wage figures were provided according to tasks and gender, and capped at four *solidi*.[7] Thereafter the municipal government, time and again, attempted to control agricultural labour.[8] While it decried repeatedly the labourers' *injusta salaria*,[9] a deeper concern was to ensure that Marseille's landowners had unobstructed access to their workforce.[10] But, as with the seneschal of Provence's Ordinance, there is little evidence for the enforcement of the various injunctions, which, at any rate, never made their way into the city's statutory law.

What we do know is that employers continued unabated to enter personal agreements at various salary rates with servants. In the spirit of contractual law, workers engaged freely into labour conventions, in writing or not, for a certain period of time against wages and other forms of income. This explains why the local statutory law, officially codified in the middle of the thirteenth century, remains rather terse on labour relations, for only two statutes draw some boundaries constraining the parties involved. The first statute, applicable to any line of work (*alicuius operis*), forbids employers or employees from violating work conventions without mutual consent or just and reasonable cause.[11] The second statute, though, deals specifically with servant–master relations, underscoring

6   The new provision allowed ploughmen to cultivate their own lands on Fridays and Saturdays, while the remainder of the week (Sunday excepted) had to be served on others' estates: AMM, BB20, fol. 54r.

7   'Super conversatione et augmentatione taxe facte agricolis hominibus cultoribus ve laboratoribus ad evitandum fraudes preconceptas et ad sassiandum [sic] ineffrenatam voluntatem ipsorum': 25 January 1349, AMM, BB 20, fol. 80v. The ubiquitous term *taxa*, meaning also 'tariffs', refers here to wages. If men could cash up to four *solidi* in wages, women were limited by law to two *solidi*, as were male teenagers (*garciones*), unless the latter knew how to prune vines, in which case they could earn an extra six *denarii*.

8   Renewed injunctions added detail or clarification: for instance, 31 March 1349, AMM, BB 20, fol. 107r; 19 June 1349, AMM, BB 20, fol. 155v; 12–14 December 1365, AMM, BB 25, fols 52v–55v; 25 February 1366, AC, BB 25, fols 79r–80r; 7 September 1378, AMM, BB 27, fol. 250r.

9   For instance, during the 1365 harvest season ('hoc presenti tempore messium excoriare') the council allowed men to collect seven *solidi* per diem and women three *solidi* and four *denarii*: 9 June 1365, AMM, BB 24, fol. 205r. The following December, however, in an attempt to limit the workers' 'effrenatas et excessivas solutiones', the government struck a commission to reduce both agricultural workers' and artisans' wages to their just value – 'mercedes eorum reduxisse ad equitatem': 12–14 December 1365, AMM, BB 25, fol. 52v–55v. Years later, another 'moderate' adjustment was also deemed necessary to curb 'unjust salaries' demanded by agricultural male and female labourers: 7 September 1378, AMM, BB 27, fol. 250r.

10   In particular, the landed elite wanted the city ploughmen to make their labour available 'to till the estates about Marseille other than their own farmlands' (*ad cultivandum posses-siones locate in Massilie ... et conducant ad operandum in possessionibus alienis*): 26 November 1348, AMM, BB 20, fols 63v–64r; also, 31 March 1349, AMM, BB 20, fol. 107r; 22 April 1351, AMM, BB 21, fol. 118v; 9 June 1365, AMM, BB 24, fol. 205r–v.

11   In case of violation, a court fine of twenty *solidi* per day would apply, in addition to damages and interest owed to the wronged party: Régine Pernoud (ed.), *Les statuts municipaux de Marseille* (Monaco-Paris, 1949), p. 187 (statute 47, book V).

the subordinate position of the former vis-à-vis the latter: it explicitly forbids servants from defaulting on their masters for higher wages or on account of corporal correction (unless they were victims of brutal beatings – *verbera data atrocia*); otherwise they incurred punishment at the hands of the public authorities and, if they had formally pledged an oath of service (*juratoria cautio*), they would be stripped of all their wages and bonuses and liable to pay any damages sustained by their masters or mistresses.[12] The covenant holding a servant to their commitment was so morally entrenched that not even religious devotion could excuse it, for time and space belonged to the master for the duration of the contract. In a miracle story recorded in Marseille in 1297, an ailing maid was exceptionally remitted the promise to visit Louis of Anjou's shrine in exchange for the cure the saint had granted her, on account that 'she could not fulfil her promise for, as a female servant, she had to stay with her master'.[13]

Within these legal parameters, contractual labourers committed to work for fixed-term employment. Although this time frame could fluctuate according to the parties' preference, the vast majority of agricultural work agreements in Marseille followed a yearly term (75 per cent). While these were concluded in all seasons, the autumn (45 per cent, usually from mid-September to early December) and the early spring months (35 per cent, from mid-February to the end of May) were the busiest hiring periods. Other arrangements – wages, clothing and other extras – depended on the negotiation process between the parties, while the provision of meals, shelter and healthcare (the latter for under-aged workers only) was customarily expected, but not mandatory.[14]

In the municipal code, the term *servientes* broadly defined those who laboured as household dependents, regardless of age, gender, marital status, experience or skills.[15] In both statutory law and city deliberations, agricultural workers were also generically known as manual workers (*operarii*),

12   Pernoud, *Les statuts municipaux*, p. 165 (statute 2, book V). The oath-taking was legally binding but not compulsory: in its absence, servants could terminate their contracts freely without penalty, as a judge explained to a master in a lawsuit (14 March 1390, AMM, FF 564, fol. 34v).
13   'Et quia quod promisit reddere non poterat, quia cum domino stabat ut ancilla, reddita autem promissione sancto, tamen curata extitit et sanata, meritis dicti sancti': Bibliothèque municipale d'Autun, Fonds S 88 (69), *Liber miraculorum sancti Ludovici episcopi*, fol. 24r (the story can be found in the edited codex, in *Analecta Franciscana*, vol. VII [Ad Claras Aquas: Quaracchi-Florence, 1951], 313). The master's control over his servants' time and mobility already evokes the emerging 'new type of unfreedom' characterizing wage labour relations in early modern times: Catharina Lis and Hugo Soly, *Worthy Efforts: Attitudes to Work and Workers in Pre-Industrial Europe* (Leiden, 2012), pp. 494–509, esp. pp. 495–7.
14   Francine Michaud, *Earning Dignity. Labour Conditions and Relations during the Century of the Black Death in Marseille* (Turnhout, 2016), passim.
15   The concept in Marseille shares some, but not all, of the characteristics attributed to northern-European servants in the late Middle Ages and early modern period, as seen in recent scholarship: Jane Whittle, 'Introduction. Servants in the Economy and Society of Rural Europe', in Jane Whittle (ed.), *Servants in Rural Europe 1400–1900* (Woodbridge, 2017), pp. 1–10.

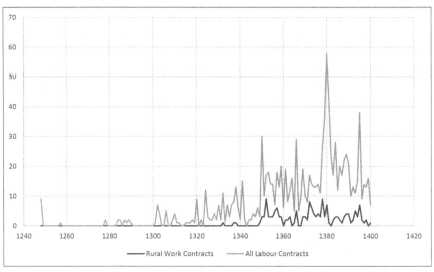

Figure 2.1.   Chronological distribution of labour contracts in Marseille,
1248–1400. Sources: Notarial series E, sub-series 351 (registers 2, 13, 17, 25,
27–32, 35, 37–41, 43–6, 48, 50, 52, 54–5, 57, 62, 69–70, 73, 77, 79–80, 87–9, 92,
647), 352 (register 32), 355 (2–11, 13–31, 33, 35, 37, 73, 75–81), 381 (59–60, 69, 76,
79–82) and 391 (11, 22–7, 31): Archives Départementales des Bouches-du-Rhône
at Marseille; Notarial registers 1321, 1339, 1343–44, 1348 and 1352: Bibliothèque
nationale de France (Paris), Nouvelles Acquisitions Latines, Fonds Mortreuil.

local and foreign (*privati et extranei*),[16] who engaged in 'any rustic output
or labour'.[17] Although these references implied both genders,[18] women were
confined to seasonal work as day labourers, while males also entered long-term
service which,[19] given the salary expenditures involved, prompted many a
master to have labour transactions notarised.[20] This is why female agricultural output is absent from the present study. Another limitation is that only
160 of the thousand and more labour agreements collected between 1248
and 1400 explicitly yield information on agricultural workers, 98 per cent

16   Pernoud, *Les statuts municipaux*, p. 225 (statute. 48, book V).
17   'Agricolis hominibus cultoribus et laboratoribus': 20 January 1349, AMM, BB 20, fol. 8ov.
18   'Tam mares quam femine': 25 January 1349, AMM, BB 20, fol. 81r.
19   Vineyard operations required labour input nearly all year round. See Édouard Baratier,
'Production et exportation du vin du terroir de Marseille, du XIIIe au XVIe siècle', *Bulletin
philologique et historique (jusqu'à 1610)*, I (1959), 242.
20   While an unknowable number of work transactions were agreed orally, without writing,
their traces occasionally surface in litigation or in written contracts drawn up to extend
oral ones. See, for instance, Guillaume Durand, who worked monthly for Pierre de Signes
'verbo et sine scriptura' before extending his contract with a notarial act: 11 October 1355,
ADBRM, 355 E 8, fol. 29r. Although mostly seasonal, informal agreements could be struck
for the longer term: see the case of Guillaume Piché, below note 60.

of which date from the post-plague era (Figure 2.1).[21] As can be expected, a large number found employment with the propertied urban elites, first and foremost knights (*milites*), nobles (*nobiles*) and the gentry (*domini*). Yet the clear majority of masters belonged to the upper-middling groups of society: legal professionals, ploughmen, merchants and artisans who equally depended on a steady workforce to cultivate their lands.[22] In total, labour contracts supported Marseille's landowners – 88 per cent men and 12 per cent women – who employed long-term, dependable manpower to run their property as smoothly as possible in a time of great uncertainty (Table 2.1).

Table 2.1. Landowners' social profile, 1248–1400.

Groups	Total	%	Men	Women
Elite	43	34	37	6
Knights & nobles	(30)		(29)	(1)
Domini	(13)		(8)	(5)
Legal professionals	25	19	21	4
Ploughmen	16	12	15	1
Merchants	15	12	15	
Artisans	29	23	26	3
Subtotal	128	100	114 (89%)	14 (11%)
Unknown	30		26	4
Institutions	2		1	1
Total	160		141 (88%)	19 (12%)

Sources: As for Figure 2.1.

From citizen-ploughmen to foreign fieldworkers

Two distinct categories of agriculturalists were recruited by masters: fieldworkers (*cultores*) and ploughmen (*laboratores*). Both could find employment as either day labourers or resident farm workers, although twice as many ploughmen took up longer-term engagements on farms across the city and its territory.[23] What truly set apart Marseille's ploughmen from fieldworkers,

21 I found only three agricultural work contracts before 1348.
22 Eighty per cent of the collected contracts (128/160) allow for the social identification of masters.
23 Ploughmen were involved in 100 out of 160 contracts collected for this study, but they too took casual work, as evidenced in the judicial records.

though, was their self-identification in the civic body as skilled artisans trained in the *arte laborando*, drawing on both technical mastery and managerial experience; boasting ownership of land, livestock, draft animals and heavy agricultural implements, they enjoyed the full privileges of citizenship.[24] In a display of urban patriotism exhibited on the occasion of a pageant organised for the translation of Saint Louis of Anjou's relics in 1319, the ploughmen's place within the *natio* could hardly be doubted: parading their banner behind the king's and the city's, the *laboratores* ranked ninth among the twenty-six trades in the procession.[25] Wielding a modicum of wealth and professional authority, ploughmen acted as engaged citizens, from performing philanthropic acts – such as the wife who donated a house worth forty florins to the municipal hospital[26] – to offering their expert opinion in policy-making, while their consent was sought by city council to set 'just and reasonable' agricultural wages after the Black Death.[27] Conversely, the landless fieldworkers held no sway in civic life: they were hired to perform menial chores on rural estates and a fair proportion of them, especially by the last quarter of the century, were immigrants (Figure 2.2).[28]

---

24   In Marseille ploughmen were not considered 'less skilled workers' (Christopher Dyer, *Making a Living in the Middle Ages. The People of Britain 850–1520* (New Haven and London, 2002), p. 279), and the *arte laborando*, as routinely stated in labour contracts, was an acknowledged trade that justified the formal training of apprentices (e.g., 3 April 1353, ADBRM, 381 E 79, fol. 7r–v; 24 July 1380, ADBRM, 351 E 50, fol. 148r–v). See also Michaud, *Earning Dignity*, chapter 4; Francine Michaud, 'The Peasants of Marseilles at the Turn of the Fourteenth Century', in Kathryn Reyerson and John V. Drendel (eds), *Urban and Rural Communities in the South of France* (Leiden, 1998), pp. 275–89.

25   May 1319, AMM, BB 11, fol. 53v and fol. 123v. In the context of Provence under the Angevines, Marseille saw itself as forming a distinct political entity from the rest of the county, thanks to the constitutional privileges it had secured through the peace treaty of c.1257 (see note 1 above). Well into the fourteenth century the city council asserted that 'Marseille et la Provence formaient chacune une "nation"' ('Marseille and Provence each formed a "nation"'): Martin Aurell and Jean-Paul Boyer, 'Une journée qui fit Marseille: le 5 décembre 1288', in Thierry Pécout (ed.), *Marseille au Moyen Âge, entre Provence et Méditerranée. Les horizons d'une ville portuaire* (Paris, 2009), p. 209. This concept of *natio* was used and displayed in both official documents and public ceremonials. See also Noël Coulet, 'Entrées royales au XIVe siècle: un rituel du faste et de la cohésion municipale', in Pécout (ed.), *Marseille au Moyen Âge*, p. 223.

26   Mabilly, *Inventaire*, p. 147 (14 January 1378, AMM, BB 27, fol. 260r). As the value of dowries indicates social status, consider Raymond de Cardona, whose wife brought him in marriage 100 *librae*, a three-acre vineyard, and a house near the harbour: 6 August 1322, AMM, 1 II 50, ff. 59v–60r.

27   Their *assensum* was deemed necessary along with that of 'other artisans' ('aliis artistis'): 14 December 1365, AMM, BB 25, fol. 54r–55v; see also Mabilly, *Inventaire*, p. 145 (7 September 1378, AMM, BB 27, fol. 244r).

28   Some 54 per cent of agreements were notarized with foreigners.

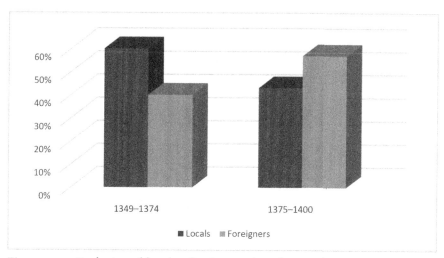

Figure 2.2. Evolution of local vs foreign rural workers under contract in Marseille, 1349–1400. Sources: As for Figure 2.1.

However, as Map 2.1 indicates, more than four in five of all foreign workers (sixty-six of seventy-six contracts) travelled within the familiar parameters of Provence. But this trend became far less pronounced in the last three decades of the century (map inset), when the city's porosity expanded farther, attracting transient workers from further afield, primarily inland and around the western shores of the Mediterranean (larger map), including villages in Catalonia, Piedmont and Calabria (off-map). Indeed, as Table 2.2 shows, over a quarter of them travelled a distance greater than 100km, an impressive range for rural workers. Some were quite young too, such as twelve-year-old Huguet Payen, from the village of Muret in Haute Garonne, who crossed 330km in rugged conditions to find employment in the port city with a farmer and his wife.[29]

Table 2.2. Distance of origin of migrant rural workers, 1349–1400.

Distance in km	1–10	11–20	21–40	41–100	101–200	>200
Proportion of workers	7%	12%	18%	36%	13%	14%

Sources: As for Figure 2.1

29 November 1384, ADBRM, 355 E 30, fols 50v–51v. Most migrants travelled inland through the hilly and rocky terrain leading to Marseille from the backcountry.

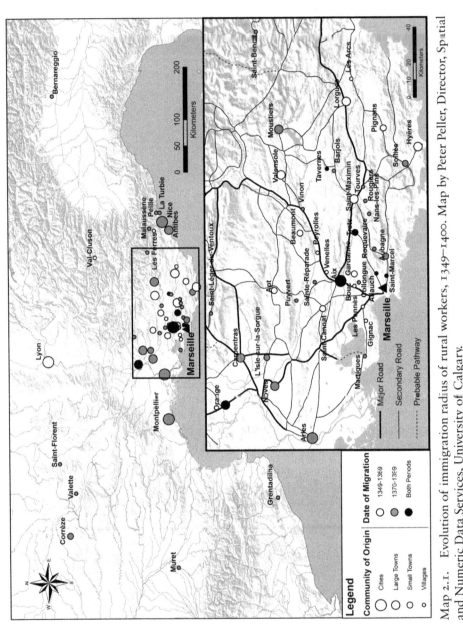

Map 2.1.   Evolution of immigration radius of rural workers, 1349–1400. Map by Peter Peller, Director, Spatial and Numeric Data Services, University of Calgary.

Table 2.3. Communities of origin of agricultural workers in Marseille, 1349–1400.

Cities (*civitas*)	Large towns (*villa*)	Small towns (*villa*)	Villages (*castrum*)
Aix (6)	Antibes (1)	Apt (1)	Allauch (2)
Arles (1)	Carpentras (1)	Aubagne (1)	Aspromonte (1)
Lyon (1)	Hyères (1)	Beaumont (1)	Barjols (1)
Montpellier (2)	Lorgues (1)	Corrèze (1)	*Bernareggio* (1)
Nice (1)	Moustiers (2)	Gardanne (1)	Bouc (1)
	Noves (1)	L'Isle-sur-la-Sorgue (1)	Collongue (1)
	Orange (2)	Pignans (1)	Gignac (1)
	Saint-Maximin (1)	Saint-Cannat (1)	*Grentadilha* (1)
	Valensole (1)	Solliès (2)	Isle (1)
		Trets (2)	La Turbie (1)
			Les Arcs (2)
			Les Ferres (1)
			Les Pennes (1)
			Malaussène (1)
			Martigues (1)
			Muret (1)
			Nans-les-Pins (1)
			Pan de Bona (1)
			Peille (1)
			Peyrolles (1)
			Puyvert (1)
			Roquevaire (3)
			Rougiers (1)
			Saint-Benoît (2)
			Saint-Florent (1)
			Saint-Léger (1)
			Saint-Marcel (3)
			Sainte-Réparade (1)
			Tavernes (2)
			Tourves (1)
			Val-Cluson (1)
			Valette (1)
			Venelles (1)
			Vinon (1)

Sources: As for Figure 2.1

As Table 2.3 indicates, most agricultural workers flocked to Marseille from villages or small towns.[30] But the tangible difference between a rural and an urban community in medieval Provence remains blurred. While population density may have determined the importance and variety of trades that inform the distinction between urban and rural societies, cultural considerations could also bring them closer. Let us consider the number of settlements – a few in existence since Antiquity – spreading north of the Mediterranean, between the Rhône and the Durance valleys, on both sides of the Aurelian way. Sharing a common notarial culture, Provençal valley communities, big or small, routinely interfaced through a tight and intricate network of administrative centres, laced with commercial hubs, markets and trade roads, which, in turn, were stimulated by commodity production and exchange that intensified in the course of the thirteenth and fourteenth centuries.[31] The Black Death, despite its horrendous death toll (some localities losing two-thirds of their populations), did not change these dynamics in fundamental ways.[32] To be sure, contemporaries recognised the binary opposition of 'urban–rural' as a constructed understanding: when a villager from La Bastide des Jourdans, in the Durance valley, was asked by royal officers during a fiscal inquiry to define the word *usage* (custom) that he had just expressed, he responded, tongue in cheek, that he could not, because he was, after all, only a 'grossus homo et ruralis'.[33]

30   Provence did not boast large cities. In fact, before 1348 only seven urban centres had a population of over 10,000 inhabitants: Baratier, *La démographie provençale*, p. 109. Socio-economic historians of the period usually divide Provençal communities into four categories according to the number of fiscal hearths: villages (fewer than 200), small towns (200–400), large towns (400–1000) and cities (over 1,000). They are agreed that the decisive criterion is not the type of habitat but the demography and socio-economic structures. Hence a village had fewer than 1,000 people and, while a small town might have up to 1,800 people and a large one 5,000, the largest city – Marseille – still had fewer than 25,000 inhabitants before the Black Death. Population density, however, by stimulating greater occupational diversification, defined further the urban character of a community, even though artisanal production was not absent from villages: Noël Coulet and Louis Stouff, *Le village de Provence au Bas Moyen Âge* (Aix-en-Provence, 1987), pp. 11, 55.

31   John Drendel, 'Le crédit dans les archives notariales de Basse-Provence (haute vallée de l'Arc) au début du XIVe siècle', in François Menant and Odile Redon (eds), *Notaires et crédit dans l'occident méditerranéen médiéval* (Rome, 2004), pp. 283–4. Scholars now consider notarial culture as a central factor that determined the urban character of the Midi's rural communities: Bourin *et al.*, 'Les campagnes de la Méditerranée', 680.

32   Baratier, *La démographie provençale*, p. 120; Coulet and Stouff, *Le village de Provence*.

33   'An uncouth peasant': cited in Coulet and Stouff, *Le village de Provence*, p. 12, note 49.

After the Black Death: an agriculturalist's golden age?

Threshing, reaping, harvesting, carting, herding and tending mills were common tasks for employees on estates that spread across Marseille's outer territory, including the *bastidae*, the typical fortified agricultural holdings of Provence. Well-to-do citizens, including merchants, jurists and notaries, now owned these thirteenth-century feudal preserves.[34] Prized possessions, they were always entrusted to seasoned ploughmen to run efficiently. For instance, in 1374, notary Pierre Amel had Gaufride Isnard move to his bastide, *Le Sarturan*, a few kilometres north of the city, in order to manage it year round, rain or shine (*per sasones*); Gaufride pledged his word that, 'despite the constant threat of warfare or any other impediments', he would till the land or subcontract 'other competent ploughmen'. In return, he was promised 20 florins of pure gold, 60 shillings' worth of meat, copious quantities of wheat, barley and wine, and a bolt of fabric.[35] This is not an isolated case.

Valued assets in the community, ploughmen, who seemingly had had little incentive to enter into formal labour agreements with urban landowners before the Black Death, now sought long-term employment on others' estates, where they represented 60 per cent of the rural workforce under contract.[36] In general, these specialists commanded higher salaries than fieldworkers, plus substantial extras. Such was the fortune of François Bourgogne, whose earnings included twenty-one florins in hard cash and two florins for his *companagium* – or meat supplement – in addition to 308 litres of wheat, 154 litres of barley and 308 litres of wine.[37] These commodities being worth at least twelve florins at the time, François was poised to earn roughly thirty-five florins, with free lodging.[38] Though a living wage in fourteenth-century Marseille is a notion that resists all available serial sources, it has been said that, by the turn of the fifteenth century, workers' daily wages had risen faster than the cost of the wine they cultivated.[39] Anecdotal evidence also reminds us that a ploughman's income

---

34 Coulet and Stouff, *Le village de Provence*, pp. 26–31.
35 'Sufficiente et idoneos, alios bonos laboratores': 9 April 1374. Paris, Bibliothèque nationale de France, Nouvelles Acquisitions Latines (hereafter BnP, nal), Fonds Mortreuil, 1339, 44. This generous allocation in kind coincides with a period of grain shortage: Félix Reynaud, *Histoire du commerce à Marseille. T. II. De 1291 à 1480* (Paris, 1951), pp. 755–6.
36 Since the commitment involved was never precisely detailed, it remains unclear whether these annual contracts offered a supplement to ploughmen's income or the bulk of it. It is worth noting that by December 1365 the city council complained about the glut of wine on the market (Mabilly, *Inventaire*, pp. 114–15; AMM, BB 25, fols 46r–49r); perhaps small landholders felt the crunch and turned to salaried work to make ends meet.
37 May 1377, ADBRM, 355 E 24, fols 22v–23r.
38 For punctual references to contemporary grain and wine pricing: Reynaud, *Histoire du commerce de Marseille*, pp. 756, 765.
39 Baratier, 'Production et exportation du vin', 244.

could very well approach that of a legal specialist: in 1352, Barthelémie Laurent negotiated twenty-four florins in salary, a florin short of what was earned not long after by Jean André, the city council notary.[40]

As in the rest of Europe, wage inflation followed the 1348 demographic crisis in Marseille, which correlated with monetary devaluations until the mid-1360s.[41] In 1338, city ploughman Jacques Sabrini had received 6.5 *librae* in yearly wages; in 1356, Antoine Catalan, another ploughman, was promised nearly three times that amount – 18 *librae* – to till the land of his very own brother Pierre; one may assume that, given their family relations, 18 *librae* (or 12 florins) was then considered a fair rate for ploughmen.[42] This spike echoes the local government's immediate efforts to maintain or curb rising daily agricultural wages.[43] Although these attempts were repeated on several occasions until the end of the century, all but one of these attempts date before 1365, as if wage inflation abated after this date.[44] The case of Hugues Barral supports that possibility. Hughes had earned fifteen florins in 1352 and when, in 1366, he accepted twenty-two florins from another landlord, the sum included six florins for his wife's domestic work at the master's residence, a rate nearly unchanged for maids from the early 1340s onwards.[45] Yet, even these conditions were hard to find for foreign ploughmen. In 1361, a couple from the village of Gardanne had been offered together only twelve florins; however, seventeen years later a ploughman from the village of Ste-Réparade proved more fortunate and obtained thirteen florins, plus five florins for his wife's domestic service, even though this was still four florins short of Hugues Barral's earnings in 1366.[46] The masters who had initiated these three contracts were all legal professionals and, one must assume, very well acquainted with the various wage practices in the labour market.

---

40 October 1352, AD, 355 E 5, f. 67r–v; 3 March 1358: Mabilly, *Inventaire*, p. 81 (AMM, BB 22, fols 150r–152r).

41 Michaud, *Earning Dignity*, p. 17. Across Provence: Noël Coulet, *Aix-en-Provence. Espace et relations d'une capitale (milieu XIVe s.–milieu XVe siècle)*, vol. 1 (Aix-en-Provence, 1985), pp. 136–7.

42 April 1338, ADBRM, 381 E 60, fol. 11r–v; 14 September 1356, ADBRM, 351 E 647, fols 109v–110v.

43 See above, note 8.

44 Of the half-dozen resolutions passed by the city council specifically on wages before 1400, five date between 6 November 1348 and 14 December 1365 and the last one is from 1378. It can hardly be coincidental that this legislative flurry slowed down with the stabilization of the local currency – the *massiliensis minutum* – when, around 1364, it was established at 32 *solidi* against the Florentine florin of pure gold until 1400.

45 June 1352, ADBRM, 3 B 49, fol. 39r; 28 November 1366, ADBRM, 351 E 28, fol. 241r.

46 September 1361, ADBRM, 355 E 11, fol. 54r–v; 20 February 1378, AD, 355 E 24, fols 131r–132r.

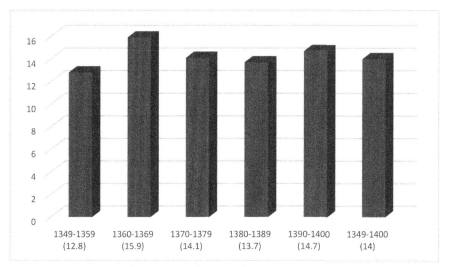

Figure 2.3. Decennial evolution of nominal wages, 1349–1400. Sources: As for Figure 2.1. Wages expressed in florins.

These last examples illustrate that, after the first two decades following the Black Death, salaries had quickly stabilised around fourteen florins (Figure 2.3).[47] Indeed, four out of five rural workers in Marseille earned less than twenty florins throughout the entire period, well below the twenty-four florins and more that ploughmen Barthelémie Laurent and François Bourgogne had been able to negotiate. These professionals belonged to a coterie of established and famed rural workers that only the local elite could afford, and with whom they often repeatedly renewed their association.[48] In a court case of 1397, a miller and two ploughmen were called as expert witnesses to testify on behalf of a prominent landlord about the yearly salary rate for ploughmen in the city: the miller asserted twenty florins, the ploughmen twenty-two florins: the judge accepted the miller's cheaper estimate as the rightful rate.[49] Yet, a quarter of century

47 It is more than possible that in the agricultural labour market, as in other trades in the city (Michaud, *Earning Dignity*, p. 93), a consensus was reached about the 'usual salary' (*consuetum loquerium*) at specific junctures (*hactenus*).

48 Twenty-two landlords disbursed twenty florins or more for agricultural services. A very good example is offered by landowner Pierre Boniface, the wealthy son of a former syndic (Christian Maurel, 'Pouvoir royal et pouvoir municipal (XIVᵉ–XVᵉ siècle)', in Pécout (ed.), *Marseille au Moyen Âge*, p. 225, note 3), who initiated no fewer than six contracts with rural workers (mostly ploughmen) in the 1370s and 1380s, offering them an average of eighteen florins in hard cash (plus extras), well above the average nominal salary at this time (fourteen florins).

49 December 1397, ADBRM, 3 B 580, fol. 51r.

earlier, the city-appointed rectors of the Saint-Esprit hospital had hired a local ploughman to till the fields of the institution for twenty-two florins plus extras: they surely knew the current market price for the best 'artisans of the land'.[50]

While an aristocracy of ploughmen with close ties with the wealthiest and most powerful of the city reaped the greatest gains, relative wage stagnation remained the lot of the majority of agricultural workers with less social capital and fewer personal connections; this was especially so for unskilled and foreign workers.[51] These agriculturalists found employment with small farmers who could not afford experienced ploughmen to the tune of twenty or twenty-four florins. Artisans and especially ploughmen paid less and employed younger staff, often for shorter periods of time.[52]

There were notable exceptions, though, as profit prompted geographical mobility, especially when proximity to the centre allowed propertied peasants to maintain ownership and control over their own land back home. Jean Barnoyn, a specialised gardener and ploughman from Aix-en-Provence, the royal capital, renewed his contracts with noble Pierre Boniface, who gave him preferential salary rates over his other workers, several times. Although for a while Jean resided in Marseille, he never became a citizen, keeping his roots in his hometown; yet, without permanent relocation, he managed to secure handsome earnings while his wife Alice, a professional wetnurse, found lucrative employment in bourgeois households, earning fifteen florins annually, nearly twice the salary of a maid.[53]

Table 2.4. Ploughmen's wages according to their civic status, 1349–1400.

Civic status	Florins (av. *per annum*)
Citizens	16.1
Non-citizens*	12.9
Residents	13
Transients	12.9

Sources: As for Figure 2.1. *Of foreign origins

50   May 1373, ADBRM, 391 E 23, fol. 30v.
51   A parallel could be drawn here with the top-tier *famuli* on English manors at the turn of the fourteenth century, the 'supervisory personnel, ploughmen, carters, shepherds', as opposed to the 'second-tier' *famuli* – the vulnerable workers such as women, youths and elderly: Jordan Claridge and John Langdon, 'The composition of *famuli* labour on English demesnes, c. 1300', *Agricultural History Review*, 63 (2015), 187. In Marseille, however, the term *famuli* referred to low-skilled, younger dependents in both farming and artisanal households.
52   The highest annual salaries ploughmen paid, seventeen and sixteen florins, were to local fellow *laboratores*: 21 December 1390, ADBRM, 351 E 89, fol. 152r; 21 July 1376, ADBRM, 355 E 21, fols 61v–62r.
53   Villagers from Saint-Marcel and Aubagne who were offered citizenship in Marseille also resisted taking permanent residence in the city, as revealed in a council's injunction demanding them to do so: 25 February 1366, AMM, BB 25, fols 79r–80r.

On the whole, though, Marseille proved less attractive to foreign ploughmen, who composed only 35 per cent of all skilled rural workers; and lesser earnings were possibly at play, a fate they shared with unskilled workers – among them a majority of migrants (Table 2.4). Leaving one's homeland to seek salaried work in another community made sense if pushed by necessity, a condition that rarely tipped the negotiation game in favour of the needy. A spirit of adventure interlaced with broken economic opportunities may also have prompted many a ploughman's younger son, such as Hugues Jean in 1357, an orphan from Venelles – a ghost village by 1400 – to flock to Marseille.[54] Borrowing their fathers' professional title by virtue of family training, these youngsters, often plague refugees during the 1350s, fetched only around seven florins – a female wage indeed.[55] This alone explains the weaker nominal salaries earned on average by ploughmen than fieldworkers in that decade alone, an anomaly noted in Figure 2.4.

However, in the last quarter of the century, the wage gap between locals and outsiders, ploughmen and fieldworkers, started to close as the migratory flux intensified in the city (Figure 2.5). To explain this evolution, we have to turn to yet another factor that initially advantaged Marseille's ploughmen above all other agriculturalists: work transacted through credit.[56] Local custom dictated that employees be paid in three instalments: at the beginning, at the mid-point and at the contract's end. From the master's perspective, the first instalment represented a form of loan extended to the worker, who was bound to repay it through his labour at the fourth month mark. Statutory law explicitly made masters first creditors of their employees above all others, a disposition that only surges in contracts after 1348.[57] In court, employers frequently cited the second statute of the fifth book of the municipal code to gain cause against their defaulting servants,[58] provided they had not fled town. Such was the case of Antoine Étienne, a city ploughman who absconded on his promise to work for noble Pierre Amel after the latter had allegedly paid at great expense Antoine's release from prison for debt.[59] Another aristocrat, Guillaume Martin, had been more fortunate with a fieldworker from the Alpine village of Saint-Benoît, Guillaume Piché. In the summer of 1384, Piché had walked away at the peak of harvest time (probably to gain higher daily wages on some other landlord's estates). But by Michaelmas his master had had him arrested and incarcerated until a local ploughman stepped forward to serve as surety, so Guillaume could resume his work for an extra year, the

54   Baratier, *La démographie provençale*, pp. 90, 136.

55   Such as Durand Vénitien, a sixteen-year-old, who self-identified as 'ploughman': 5 June 1352, ADBRM, 355 E 6, fol. 7r–v.

56   Drendel, 'Le crédit dans les archives notariales'. For northern Europe in general: Phillipp Schofield and Thijs Lambrecht (eds), *Credit and the Rural Economy in North-western Europe, c. 1200–1850* (Turnhout, 2009).

57   Pernoud, *Les statuts municipaux*, pp. 198–9 (statute 18, book VI).

58   Pernoud, *Les statuts municipaux*, p. 165.

59   June–22 December 1397, AMM, FF 580, fols 46v–51v.

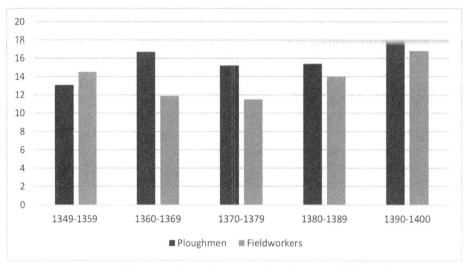

Figure 2.4.   Decennial wage evolution between ploughmen and fieldworkers, 1349–1400. Sources: As for Figure 2.1. Wages expressed in florins.

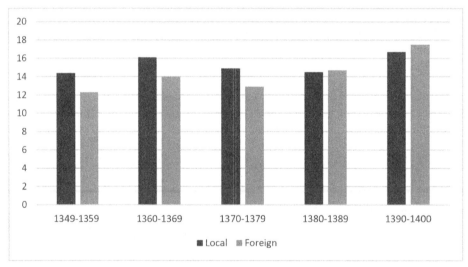

Figure 2.5.   Decennial wage evolution between local and foreign rural workers, 1349–1400. Sources: As for Figure 2.1. Wages expressed in florins.

term of his earlier engagement; he also promised the court to give Pierre the twenty-one florins he had been offered in salary – although he had pocketed only seven florins – in addition to sixteen florins for damages and interest: that is, eight florins for each of the two unworked harvest months.[60] This last and hefty penalty, nearly five times Guillaume's monthly salary, matches the daily wages paid to rural workers over two months of service during harvest in this time period.[61] Perfectly in line with the spirit of the municipal code, these punitive measures were meant to enforce servants' loyalty towards and dependence on their masters.

Since defection was a major concern among employers, many demanded sureties.[62] This presupposed a system of warranties resting on personal assets, reputation and social networks.[63] This is why masters offered better work conditions to city ploughmen, who, they knew, enjoyed the necessary collateral values through personal relations and, especially, real estate, which foreigners lacked, as goldsmith Robert de Rocha had pointed out in his lawsuit against his migrant employee.[64] Hence, when a jurist hired a city ploughman to work at his bastide in the spring of 1366, the latter accepted the transfer of all his chattels to his master's urban residence as surety and let him place a lien on his own vineyard.[65] Women's access to real estate property among this professional class through matrimonial endowment also reinforced the position of ploughmen, who relied on their wives, mothers and even mothers-in-law as personal sureties to secure good wages.[66] In order to seal his work contract with the noble Guillaume Martin in 1362 Laurent Prosii turned to his wife Baudine, who pledged her city-centre house. The precaution proved wise, as six months later, after Laurent had failed to show up for work, Baudine remitted ten florins to Guillaume as a penalty for her husband's defection.[67]

60   1–19 October 1384, ADBRM, 3 B 103, fols 139r–142v.
61   Eight florins coincides roughly with the 6.8 *solidi* paid to day labourers in addition to their meals, an attractive sum compared to the 1.8 *solidi* Guillaume received daily according to his yearly contract. Information on the daily wages is provided from contemporary court cases: 15 June 1390, AMM, FF 565, fol. 96r; 6 June 1392, AMM, FF 570, fol. 67r.
62   While nine in twelve lawsuits initiated by landholders concerned a breach of contract, more than 25 per cent of all 160 agreements made with agricultural workers explicitly contained a *fidejussor* (guarantor) clause.
63   Bourin *et al.*, 'Les campagnes', 691.
64   See above, note 3.
65   May 1366, ADBRM, 351 E 28, fol. 70r–v.
66   Twenty-three out of forty *fidejussores* were wives or female relatives.
67   July 1362, ADBRM, 351 E 28, fol. 83r–v.

'A place where one could safely harvest': the levelling trend

The velocity of money in the post-plague years accelerated credit flow, but also dependency on labour relations. For instance, in 1359 Bernissio Belloni promised before the tribunal to till the land of the noble Guillaume Vivaud for twelve florins, ten of which were immediately handed over to his creditor Raymond de Montillis, while his wife Hugua served as security for his debt.[68] The corpus is replete with similar stories of ploughmen owing money to their masters – current or prospective – or third parties, sometimes even contracting in judicial or prison courtyards labour engagements by means of protracted repayment.[69] In time, spiralling debt considerably mitigated one's bargaining power: when Guillaume Maximin sold his services to the noble Jacques Létourneau in 1374 he was promised only thirteen florins, minus half the sum his master had paid on his behalf to clear a debt, while the remainder would be paid, as a precaution, only at exit time.[70] Nine years later, Jean Venelle pledged to till the land of François Galli, a local aristocrat, in return for sixteen florins immediately after contracting a debt of fifteen florins with merchant Louis Benedict. The transaction was sealed at the royal court and secured by Jean's father, also a ploughman, as his legal guarantor.[71] It is precisely in this context that the wage gap narrowed between ploughmen and lesser skilled workers, foreign or local.

This trend also coincides with landlords already experiencing cash shortages, even insolvency. By the late 1360s the vast majority of labour litigations revolved around servants suing their masters for back pay. Disputes brought by rural workers primarily concerned lesser landowners, but even the wealthiest employers, better equipped to face adversity, had to rely on saleable commodities to obtain cash.[72] When Antoine Bruni accepted work with Antoine de Roques Neuves, he warned the aristocrat that if he failed to receive his second instalment he would walk away – a pre-emptive move copied by others.[73] For his part, the noble Guillaume Martin had no choice but to sell quantities of his wine when his servant demanded to be paid.[74]

68   For instance: 5 October 1359, ADBRM, 355 E 10, fols 65v–66r; 5 November 1350, ADBRM, 355 E 3, fol. 129r.
69   Fourteen direct indebtedness cases were found in the contracts, in addition to numerous references to the courthouse where labour arrangements were concluded.
70   June 1374, ADBRM, 391 E 24, fols 33v–34r.
71   October 1383, ADBRM, 355 E 29, fols 52v–53r.
72   Out of 176 lawsuits, 36 cases were initiated by rural workers.
73   November 1373, ADBRM, 351 E 32, fol. 185v.
74   October, ADBRM, 3 B 103, fol. 141r. Among other examples: 11 October 1393, AMM, FF 571, fol. 15r; 30 October 1394, AMM, FF 574, fol. 179v.

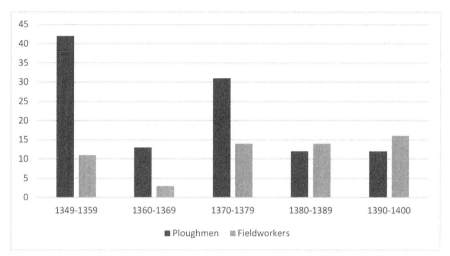

Figure 2.6.   Evolution of ploughmen and fieldworkers under contract,
1349–1400. Sources: As for Figure 2.1.

As migrants now flowed into the city at a much higher rate and from
farther afield, limited liquidity may further explain wage stabilisation, but
also renewed competitive opportunities for outsiders (Figure 2.6).[75] According
to a well-known contemporary eyewitness in 1392, Francesco Datini's agent
in Provence, 'Marseille was one of the few places where one could safely
harvest and trade' – and, one might add, make a fair living, even for foreign
rural workers.[76] That peasants from Roquevaire, Noves, La Turbie, Vinon
or Aubagne could then earn twenty florins and more in pure gold a year, in
addition to their board and lodging plus benefits, all conditions no foreigners
had secured in the quarter of century following the Black Death, illustrates
the shift.[77] Guillaume Piché, the Alpine villager mentioned earlier, is a telling
example of migrants' improved prospects: his ability to gain twenty-one florins
in 1384, the support he had found in the community to release him from prison

75   On money supply reduction in the Midi at the end of the fourteenth century: Bourin
et al., 'Les campagnes', 687 and note 84.
76   R. Brun, 'Annales avignonnaises de 1382 à 1410, extraites des Archives Datini', *Mémoires
de l'Institut historique de Provence*, 12–14 (1935–38), cited in Aurell, Boyer and Coulet, *La
Provence au Moyen Âge*, p. 292. At the time, robber baron Raymond de Turenne spread the
practice of *pâtis* (or ransoms) against villages that were threatened with having their crops
burnt: Aurell, Boyer and Coulet, *La Provence au Moyen Âge*, p. 291.
77   July 1380, ADBRM, 355 E 37, fol. 10r; 29 October 1380, ADBRM, 351 E 50, fol. 225r–v;
7 June 1379, ADBRM, 391 E 27, fol. 54v; 27 December 1396, Fonds Mortreuil, BnF, n.a.l.,
1344, fols 199v–200r; 6 August 1390, ADBRM, 351 E 62, fol. 24r; 23 July 1393, ADBRM
351 E 92, fol. 41r.

for debt and his renewed contracts within the Martin family, a leading aristo-
cratic household, all speak volumes about his integration in the community
since migrating there as a simple farmworker (*brasserius*) four years earlier,
when he could only gain two-thirds of his current wages.[78] For his part, Antoine
Bermond, an agriculturist of foreign origins, had also found in the middle of
the 1390s a stable position with the Saint-Jacques family, a noble lineage in
the city. In the process, Antoine had steadily increased not only his wages but
also his place in society by gaining citizenship, having in all likelihood acquired
landed property in order to earn it.[79]

Conclusion

Marseille's wider opening to foreign rural workers toward the end of the
century puts into perspective the traditional advantage enjoyed by the *laboratores*' families of old stock, who had long identified with the civic body. After
the Black Death, the municipal government did not envision harsh labour
laws in its attempts to reduce rampant inflation, in part because citizen
ploughmen were both landowners and wage earners, and sought instead a
rough consensus around labour policies.[80] Despite the economic stress created
by the demographic crisis, Marseille's political elite did not overtly rule along
class-divided lines or opt for anti-immigration measures, unlike some other
governments across Christendom.[81]

However, the city ploughmen's relatively secure position within the
community started to dwindle under the gradual, but unstoppable, competition
in the work market from foreign rural workers. This trend, occurring in the last
quarter of the century, proved a protracted effect of the second outbreak of the
1361 epidemic in Provence which, compounded by years of military insecurity

---

78   January 1380, ADBRM, 351 E 48, fol. 116v; 17 April 1381, ADBRM, 351 E 52, fol. 19r;
1 October 1384, ADBRM, 3 B 103, fol. 139r.
79   Antoine contracted his labour with the Saint-Jacques family at least three times during
this period: 6 April 1394, ADBRM, 355 E 79, fol. 5r; 2 July 1395, ADBRM, 355 E 80, fol.
53v; 25 October 1397, ADBRM, 355 E 81, fol. 75r. However, in 1398 he toiled for a wealthy
landowner, apothecary Antoine Simon: ADBRM, 351 E 79, fol. 94r–v.
80   In so far as legislation 'revealed how the elites felt about wage labour and wage workers',
Marseille's ruling class were compelled to take into consideration the ubiquitous economic
situation of the ploughmen, not just the needs of 'merchant entrepreneurs and wealthy
master artisans' to secure cheap labour, as in other regions at this time: Lis and Soly, *Worthy
Efforts*, pp. 438–9.
81   Such as England, where parliament favoured the landed classes, or Florence, where the
government vied to protect its citizens' interests against those of rural workers and migrants:
Samuel Cohn, 'After the Black Death: Labour Legislation and Attitudes Towards Labour in
Late-Medieval Western Europe', *Economic History Review*, 60 (2007), 457–85.

across the county, saw the deepening of local communities' dislocation. These very circumstances stimulated, in turn, an unprecedented migration flux toward Marseille, the safest urban centre in the region. By then, the velocity of money had slowed down and indebtedness accrued, further precipitating a process of socio-economic displacement within Marseille's own agricultural class.

We will remember the disdain for landless foreign workers that the goldsmith Robert de Rocha, an English immigrant himself, had expressed in his 1351 lawsuit; years later, he pronounced in his own son's apprenticeship contract that 'a trade is what keeps a man honest with God's help'.[82] The sudden and growing presence of foreign fieldworkers in post-plague Marseille partly challenged this view: it arguably enhanced labour competition, helping to suppress 'unbridled' wages and reduce not only the traditional advantage held by ploughmen but also, in broad strokes, the social hierarchies among the agricultural class.[83] No doubt this change provoked an identity crisis among Marseille's *labora-tores*, who had customarily positioned themselves in the social arena as citizen artisans and not as mere low-skilled interlopers.[84] Only a thorough proposo-graphical study on Marseille's ploughmen in the second half of the fourteenth century would add depth and texture to a process that saw them lose a firm grip on the labour market.[85] This process, all the same, also saw rural migrants set down new roots in a time of both insecurity and opportunity, and carve for themselves a place in the recovering community that was Marseille, a city 'hungry for men' that had little choice but to opt for sustainable coexistence.

---

82   See above, note 3.

83   On this point: Pere Orti Gost and Lluís To Figueras, 'Serfdom and Standards of Living of the Catalan Peasantry before and after the Black Death of 1348', in Simonetta Cavaciocchi (ed.), *Schiavitù e servaggio nell'economica europea secc. XI-XVIII. Serfdom and Slavery in the European Economy, 11th–18th Centuries* (Florence, 2014), p. 163.

84   As a result, they were poised to experience an 'increasingly narrowly based "hierarchy of belonging"': Lis and Soly, *Worthy Efforts*, p. 460. This was a period of social contraction, when the trades – a traditional leverage for social mobility – had become far less accessible to the lower and middling classes: Michaud, *Earning Dignity*.

85   This may also help explain what can be gleaned from the labour litigation records: a culture of distrust that surreptitiously permeated work relations, prompting the perception of alterity to take new forms towards landless newcomers, many unskilled. On the increased degree of animosity between masters (especially ploughmen and small artisans) and their servants, the majority foreign to the city, see Michaud, *Earning Dignity*, chapter 5.

3

The Ties that Bind: *Mezzadria* and Labour Regulations after the Black Death in Florence and Siena, 1348–c.1500

DAVIDE CRISTOFERI[1]

During the so-called 'crisis of the late Middle Ages' labour regulations played a major role in shaping rural economy and society in central Tuscany via the development of an extractive sharecropping system known as *mezzadria*.[2] This trend – closely connected to the political and economic dominance of the urban elites in the region – was unique in late medieval Europe.[3] *Mezzadria* worked as an inequality-regulating institution by dividing half (*mezzo* in Italian) of the input, such as the purchase of sowing seed, oxen, tools and manure, and half of the output between the lessor and the lessee. Lessees were typically smallholders or landless peasants who often lived in the lessor's farmhouse, while lessors were usually absentee urban landlords. Townsmen, who had other sources of revenue, were able to increase their wealth by sharing just part of

---

1 This research is part of the GINI project 'Economic Growth and Inequality. Explaining Divergent Regional Growth Paths in Pre-Industrial Europe from late Middle Ages to Nineteenth Century' supported by Ghent University and conducted jointly by the Economics and History Departments.

2 See P. Jones, 'From Manor to Mezzadria: a Tuscan Case-Study in the Medieval Origins of Modern Agrarian Society', in N. Rubinstein (ed.), *Florentine Studies: Politics and Society in Renaissance Florence* (London, 1966), pp. 193–241; D. Herlihy and Ch. Klapisch-Zuber, *Tuscans and their Families: a Study on the Florentine Catasto of 1427* (New Haven, 1985). Regarding sharecropping in general see T. J. Byres, *Sharecropping and Sharecroppers*, Library of Peasant Studies, 6 (London, 1983).

3 See for a discussion R. J. Emigh, *The Undevelopment of Capitalism: Sectors and Markets in Fifteenth-Century Tuscany* (Philadelphia, 2009). For instance, in most areas of the Low Countries sharecropping disappeared over the course of the Middle Ages and was only temporarily implemented in period of deep crisis: E. Thoen and T. Soens, 'The Low Countries, 1000–1750', in E. Thoen and T. Soens (eds), *Rural Economy and Society in North-western Europe. Struggling with the Environment: Land Use and Productivity* (Turnhout, 2015), pp. 221–58, at p. 227.

their income from land – avoiding time-consuming day-to-day management – while peasants were kept at a subsistence level.[4] This was assured by the size of the landholding, designed for the subsistence of both the lessor and the lessee and to fully exploit the labour input of the latter. Furthermore, the share of the input, the repayment of debts and a series of extractive clauses hindered any form of capital accumulation on the part of the lessee. In this way, *mezzadria* perpetuated wealth inequality and land concentration during the late Middle Ages and the early modern period.[5]

The development of this sharecropping system was already taking place in the late thirteenth-century Tuscany through the growing land investment of urban market elites: craftsmen, merchants, bankers, notaries, urban patricians and nobles.[6] For instance, in the early fourteenth-century Sienese countryside almost 46 per cent of real estate was owned by city dwellers and 81 per cent of their land was leased out in *mezzadria*. According to the area, the rural population was mainly composed of smallholders who worked as seasonal wage labourers or tenants, as well as of sharecroppers and leaseholders.[7] The trend was similar in the Florentine countryside.[8] After the Black Death, however, the economic and demographic factors that had favoured this land consolidation process were at stake. The labour force dropped dramatically, wealth and land were redistributed among the survivors, rural wages rose and some agricultural land was abandoned.[9] In this context, city governments such as those of Florence and Siena reacted to support urban land investment

---

4   Concerning the rationale of sharecropping, see D. A. Ackerberg and M. S. Botticini, 'The Choice of Agrarian Contracts in Early Renaissance Tuscany: Risk Sharing, Moral Hazard, or Capital Market Imperfections?' *Explorations in Economic History*, 37 (2000), 241–57.

5   See D. Cristoferi, 'Socio-Economic Inequalities in Fifteenth-Century Tuscany: the Role of Mezzadria System', in G. Alfani and E. Thoen (eds), *Inequality in Rural Europe: Late Middle Ages–18th century* (Turnhout, 2020), pp. 81–101.

6   Jones, 'From Manor', pp. 193–241.

7   Peasants owned 31 per cent of the land surface and preferred direct farming (74 per cent) to sharecropping (18 per cent) and tenancy (6 per cent), while religious institutions controlled 17 per cent of land surface, mostly run via sharecropping (52 per cent) and other leases (41 per cent). Elaboration of the author from a sample of twenty Sienese villages recorded in the Sienese cadaster (*Tavola delle Possessioni*) of 1316–20 and published in G. Cherubini, 'Proprietari. contadini e campagne senesi all'inizio del Trecento', in G. Cherubini, *Signori contadini borghesi* (Florence, 1974), pp. 231–312, at p. 280 (table 11) and p. 297 (table 15).

8   See D. Herlihy, 'Santa Maria Impruneta: a Rural Commune in the Late Middle Ages', in Rubinstein (ed.), *Florentine Studies*, pp. 242–76; O. Muzzi and M.D. Nenci, *Il contratto di mezzadria nella Toscana medievale*, vol. 2, *Contado di Firenze, secolo XIII* (Florence, 1988), pp. 92–9.

9   See G. Piccinni, 'L'evoluzione della rendita fondiaria alla fine del Medioevo', in A. Cortonesi and G. Piccinni (eds), *Medioevo delle campagne. Rapporti di lavoro, politica agraria, protesta contadina* (Rome, 2006), pp. 57–95. For an European perspective, see J. Drendel (ed.), *Crisis in the Later Middle Ages. Beyond the Postan–Duby Paradigm* (Turnhout, 2015).

and share-contracts through labour regulations and specific agrarian policies between 1348 and the third decade of the fifteenth century.[10] Notably, the aim was to bind peasants to land, curbing the rise of wages. The convergence of interests between ruling urban elites and city dwellers as *mezzadria* landowners made such coercion of labour possible.[11]

Previous research has addressed this topic by focusing on specific case studies or trends such as changes in share-contracts and policies.[12] A comparative study encompassing labour regulations and their impact on labour market, share-contract clauses and peasants' conditions across Tuscany is yet to be written. This essay provides a first step in this direction by comparing the post-Black Death labour regulations of Florence and Siena, the major city states in fourteenth- and fifteenth-century Tuscany. It integrates the findings of the existing studies on labour policies and share-contracts' evolution with a new study of twenty-four Florentine laws between 1348 and 1431.[13] Previously,

---

10   For European comparisons, see Whittle and Michaud in this volume. Regarding the mechanisms behind the negotiation and production of statutory law in Mediterranean city-communes see D. Lett (ed.), *La confection des statuts dans les sociétés méditerranéennes de l'Occident (XIIe–XVe s.). Statuts, écritures et pratiques sociales* (Paris, 2017); D. Lett (ed.), *Statuts communaux et circulations documentaires dans les sociétés méditerranéennes de l'Occident, XIIe–XVe siècle* (Paris, 2018).

11   For instance, the motivations of a law in 1446: 'in this way the rural properties of the city-dwellers will be saved for the benefit of the city as well as of that of agriculture [...] for the good and utility of the city, of its inhabitants, of the countryside as well as for the development of agriculture [...] to which as the most needed thing we should always care, especially for the preservation of the properties of the city-dwellers'. See G. Piccinni, *Il contratto di mezzadria nella Toscana medievale*, vol. 3, *Contado di Siena 1348–1528. Appendice: la normativa 1256–1510* (Florence, 1992), pp. 431–3 (document XLIV). For a theoretical framework: B. J. P. van Bavel, *The Invisible Hand? How Market Economies have Emerged and Declined since AD 500* (Oxford, 2016), pp. 251–88; D. Acemoglu, S. Johnson and J. A. Robinson, *Institutions as a Fundamental Cause of Long-Run Growth*, in P. Aghion and S. N. Durlauf (eds), *Handbook of Economic Growth*, volume 1a (London, 2005), pp. 386–464.

12   See Piccinni, *Il contratto di mezzadria*; Piccinni, 'La politica agraria del comune di Siena', in Cortonesi and Piccinni (eds), *Medioevo delle campagne*, pp. 207–92; S. K. Cohn, *Creating the Florentine state. Peasants and Rebellion, 1348–1434* (Cambridge, 1999); S. K. Cohn, 'After the Black Death: Labour Legislation and Attitudes Towards Labour in Late-Medieval Western Europe', *Economic History Review*, 60 (2007), 465–75.

13   The *Registri delle Provvisioni* of Florence is a series of laws discussed and approved by the assemblies of the commune of Florence and recorded as public laws in specific registers: Archive of Florence (hereafter ASFi), Provvisioni, 36, fol. 154v (25 August 1349); 40, fols 27r–27v (3 December 1352); 42, fols 114v–115r (21 August 1355); 42, fols 161r–161v (9 December 1355); 43, fol. 146v (12 September 1356); 46, fol. 101r (22 February 1358); fols 71v–72r (2 December 1363); 52, fols 34r–34v (3 October 1364); 65, fols 44v–46v (4 June 1377); 68, fols 113v–115v (17 August 1379); 72, fols 171r–172r (20 October 1383); 74, fols 204v–205r (8 December 1385); 80, fols 197r–198v (2 December 1391); 88, fols 182r–183v (14 October

these laws have mostly been analysed to address rural immigration and the state-building process in the Florentine countryside.[14]

Such comparison allows (i) an exploration of differences and similarities in labour regulations between Florence and Siena; (ii) an evaluation of their effectiveness in the short and long terms; and (iii) an explanation of how and why they achieved the binding of peasants to land as sharecroppers by the end of the fifteenth century. The analysis is organised in three sections. The first focuses on the labour regulations that attempted to curb the profit shares and claims of sharecroppers between the two plagues of 1348 and 1363. The second covers the immigration and fiscal policies developed between 1364 and 1435 in order to cope with the further drop in population and the labour force. This includes a consideration of supplementary Sienese laws up to 1470.[15] The third analyses the reasons behind the policies discussed and their short- and long-term impacts.

I

One of the most important consequences of the Great Plague was the steady rise of wages and prices across Europe following the fall in population.[16] Tuscany was also affected by these dynamics.[17] During the months of August

---

1399); 88, fols 226r–227r (7 November 1399); 88, fols 328v–329v (23 February 1399 (1400)); 91, fols 146v–147r (20 September 1402); 93, fols 193r–193v (3 February 1404/(1405); 101, fols 333r–334r (24 January 1412/1413); 101, fols 334r–334v (24 January 1412/1413); 105, fols 215v–216v (22 November 1415); 107, fols 215r–215v (5 May 1417); 112, fols 143r–144r (18 October 1422); 113, fol. 217r (7 February 1423 (1424)); 114, fols 63v–64v (5 December 1424); 117, fols 122v–123r (26 June 1427); 117, fol. 123r (26 June 1427); 118, fols 116v–117v (20 November 1427); 120, fols 461v–462r (8 February 1429/1430); 120, fols 491r–491v (13 February 1429/1430); 121, fols 72r–72v (26 October 1430); 122, fols 2r–2v; 2v–3r; 4r–5r (16 April 1431).

14 See Cohn, *Creating*; Cohn, 'After the Black Death', 465–75.

15 See Piccinni, 'La politica agraria', p. 238.

16 See J. H. Munro, 'Wage-Stickiness, Monetary Changes, and Real Incomes in Late-Medieval England and the Low Countries 1300–1500: Did Money Matter?' *Research in Economic History*, 21 (2003), 185–297; B. J. P. van Bavel and J. L. van Zanden, 'The Jump-start of the Holland Economy During the Late-Medieval Crisis, *c*.1350–*c*.1500', *Economic History Review*, 57 (2004), 503–32; J. Fynn-Paul, *The Rise and Decline of an Iberian Bourgeoisie. Manresa in the Later Middle Ages, 1250–1500* (Cambridge, 2015), pp. 211–53; S. Broadberry, B. M. S. Campbell, A. Klein, M. Overton and B. van Leeuwen, *British Economic Growth 1270–1870* (Cambridge, 2015), pp. 247–60.

17 See A. B. Falsini, 'Firenze dopo il 1348. Le conseguenze della peste nera', *Archivio Storico Italiano*, 121 (1971), 425–503; G. Piccinni, 'Siena e la peste del 1348', in R. Barzanti, G. Catoni and M. De Gregorio (eds), *Storia di Siena*, vol. 1, *Dalle origini alla fine della Repubblica* (Siena 1995), pp. 225–38; S. Tognetti, 'Prezzi e salari a Firenze nel tardo Medioevo: un profilo', *Archivio storico italiano*, 153 (1995), 263–333. See for a critical approach S. K. Cohn, *Paradoxes of Inequality in Renaissance Italy* (Cambridge, 2021), pp. 11–20.

and September 1348, when the epidemic was ending and agrarian contracts were normally renewed, rural workers started demanding better conditions. Most of their requests concerned the clauses regulating the division of the capital input and output in the *mezzadria* contract, which effectively determined the wage of sharecroppers. The chronicles of Marchionne di Coppo Stefani and Matteo Villani noted:

> The rural labourers from the *contado* wanted such lease-contracts so that, we can say, almost all the harvest to be collected was taken by them. Furthermore, they have learnt to take in lease the oxen at the lessor's risk, then to work for a wage for others during the periods requiring their work in the field [of their lessors], then to deny debts and payments. As a consequence, severe laws were approved against these troubles; but the cost of rural labourers rises, so that it seemed that they themselves owned the landholding because of all the benefits they wanted such as the oxen, the sowing seed, the loans and other advantages.[18]

> The rural labourers wanted to be paid for the oxen and the sowing seed as well as to work the best land and to abandon the others: our government thought to impose order in these matters through a good deliberation as well as to stop these abuses through certain laws; however, whatever [measure] they took, they did not reach to make up, so it seemed convenient to leave the development and the remedy of these abuses to God. However, they were still ongoing in 1362, without any remedy or failure.[19]

First, the lease of the oxen: before 1348, the lessee was often responsible for providing or purchasing the draught animals.[20] After 1348, sharecroppers asked to pay only half of this cost or, alternatively, required the lessor to buy the oxen 'at his own risk', without sharing with the lessee the cost of purchasing the animals.[21] Likewise, sharecroppers frequently asked the lessors to pay for seed.[22] Another type of demand involved loans to run the *mezzadria* landholding: after 1348, lessees refused to pay old debts and requested further loans. By doing so

---

18 Translation by the author from N. Rodolico (ed.), *Marchionne di Coppo Stefani, Cronica fiorentina* (Bologna, 1903–13), pp. 232–3.

19 Translation by the author from G. Porta (ed.), *Matteo Villani, Cronica* (Parma, 1995), p. 112.

20 G. Pinto and P. Pirillo, *Il contratto di mezzadria nella Toscana medievale*, vol. 1, *Contado di Siena XIII–1348* (Florence, 1987), pp. 43–56, at p. 55; Muzzi and Nenci, *Il contratto di mezzadria*, pp. 92–9.

21 Piccinni, *Il contratto di mezzadria*, pp. 131–56, at p. 151. A pair of oxen was generally replaced every four to five years in late medieval Tuscany. See Herlihy and Klapisch-Zuber, *Tuscans*, pp. 118–20.

22 See Pinto and Pirillo, *Il contratto di mezzadria*, pp. 43–56, at p. 55; Muzzi and Nenci, *Il contratto di mezzadria*, pp. 92–9; Piccinni, *Il contratto di mezzadria*, pp. 131–56, at p. 151.

they probably aimed to increase their buying power on the commodity market while simultaneously reducing their liability for capital inputs such as oxen and sowing seed.[23] In addition, sharecroppers sold their labour as seasonal wage workers to profit from high wages. Finally, the scarcity of labour supply led sharecroppers to concentrate on the best land available, while poorer land was abandoned.[24] To sum up, as many lessors complained, 'almost all the harvest was taken' by the lessees, reducing landowners' profit.

In order to counteract these threats, 'severe laws' and 'good deliberation' were immediately approved by the city councils of Florence and Siena. In September 1348 the major Sienese assembly enacted a series of laws 'against tenants, share-croppers and labourers'.[25] The measures adopted were not reported, but they all aimed to fight the 'ferocious, inhuman and ungrateful purpose' shown by rural workers and to remove their ability 'to plan or to put in practice anything damaging [to] city-dwellers and rural landowners'.[26] The motivation behind these measures was the desire to protect and advance landownership among Sienese city dwellers.[27]

In Florence, only one year after the epidemics, in August 1349, a committee was ordered to write new laws to control sharecroppers and rural wage labourers.[28] Previously, the commune had briefly attempted to control the wages of the lower and marginal strata of the city's labourers. Furthermore, it never tried to limit the hyper-inflated prices for food and basic commodities as French and English governments did.[29] The measures against rural workers, according to the deliberations of the commune, were aimed specifically at dealing with the abandonment of landholdings by sharecroppers.[30] Florentine landlords feared this trend would raise rural wages further, increase costly competition among lessors and thus reduce their rate of profit from the land. As a consequence, Florentine city councils explicitly forbade rural workers

---

23   See Piccinni, 'L'evoluzione della rendita', pp. 57–95.

24   Such concentration probably led to a rise in land productivity in the long run: *ibid.*

25   Piccinni, *Il contratto di mezzadria*, document XIV (1348).

26   *Ibid.* The greed for money of Florentine servants and labourers after the Black Death is noted also by Giovanni Boccaccio: see V. Branca (ed.), *Giovanni Boccaccio. Decameron* (Turin, 1956), p. 9.

27   This process never stopped in the Sienese territory, even in time of crisis: for instance, in 1348, the volume of property transactions reached 55,000 florins and was mainly land purchases by city-dwellers. See A. Bacciu, *Per una analisi prosopografica della società senese: lo spoglio della Gabella dei contratti del 1348* (Siena, 2013), pp. 18–20.

28   ASFi, Provvisioni, 36, fol. 154v (25 August 1349).

29   In this regard, Cohn argues for the severity of Florentine laws in comparison with these countries. See Cohn, 'After the Black Death', 463–7.

30   ASFi, Provvisioni, 36, f. 154v (25 August 1349). The motivation of a law of 1355 states that 'because the land that remains inhabited and uncultivated is a serious damage to the [city-dwellers'] possession and against the good and the peace in the city'. See ASFi, Provvisioni, 42, fols 114v–115r (21 August 1355).

from either withdrawing from any share-contract or from cultivating any land they had taken in lease without the approval of their lessors for the next three years.[31] The fine levied was a hundred *lire*, a sum 'well beyond the wherewithal of the wealthiest peasants in second half of the fourteenth century'.[32]

This law was regularly re-enacted until 1363.[33] In 1352, however, new measures were introduced.[34] First, landlords were entitled to sue their lessees if they were not working or if they damaged land taken in lease or left it unculti-vated. Moreover, any such lawsuit should be reported to the Florentine officials in charge of grain provisioning. In this way, the daily conflicts between lessors and lessee were removed from court officials in rural communities. This measure can also be considered a major step in the development of the *mezzadria* system: it claimed for the city the economic, political and judicial management of share-cropping. For the same reason Sienese city councils moved to bring into the city all legal disputes between rural communities and city dwellers concerning the limits of commons and private properties in 1446.[35]

In addition, new regulations were made concerning the micro-economy of this system, the detailed clauses of the *mezzadria* contract.[36] The target was a series of payment in kind, such as a certain amount of pork, capons and eggs, that the lessee had to provide by contract to compensate the landlords for the use of the stables, garden and services of the *mezzadria* farm.[37] The sharecroppers' refusal to pay for these services may have indirectly challenged the property rights of the landlords. Moreover, pig breeding and poultry were probably profitable for sharecroppers in times of high price inflation.[38] The law of 1352 compelled the lessee to deliver to the landlord half of the pork, capons and eggs produced up to a certain quantity.

Few years later, in 1355, a series of new laws blamed ill-defined 'peasants' for damaging Florentine real estates and for threatening tenants.[39] Those respon-sible were defined as rebels and outlaws and were apparently mainly targeting properties of Florentine craftsmen, widows and orphans. Similar attacks had been reported before the Black Death as a consequence of the tensions raised by

---

31   ASFi, Provvisioni, 36, fol. 154v (25 August 1349).

32   Cohn, 'After the Black Death', 468.

33   See ASFi, Provvisioni, 40, fols 27r–27v (3 December 1352); 43, fol. 146v (12 September 1356); 46, fol. 101r (22 February 1358); fols 71v–72r (2 December 1363).

34   ASFi, Provvisioni, 40, fols 27r–27v (3 December 1352).

35   Piccinni, *Il contratto di mezzadria*, document XLIV (1446).

36   ASFi, Provvisioni, 40, fols 27r–27v (3 December 1352).

37   See Pinto and Pirillo, *Il contratto di mezzadria*, pp. 43–56; Muzzi and Nenci, *Il contratto di mezzadria*, pp. 92–9; Piccinni, *Il contratto di mezzadria*, pp. 131–56.

38   See G. Piccinni, 'Le donne nella mezzadria toscana delle origini', in Cortonesi and Piccinni, *Medioevo delle campagne*, pp. 153–203; Tognetti, 'Prezzi e salari', 275–300.

39   See ASFi, Provvisioni, 42, fols 114v–115r (21 August 1355); 42, fols 161r–161v (9 December 1355).

city dwellers' land purchases, which led to the impoverishment of rural inhabitants and communities in the Florentine territory.[40] Behind the rhetoric, these
new accusations show the failure of the measures adopted up to that point.[41]

The new laws approved in that year, once again, attempted to ensure the
cultivation of city dwellers' landholdings. The laws ordered rural communities
to take abandoned properties in lease in order to protect and cultivate them.
Specific attention, moreover, was given to costly perennial crops such as fruit
trees and vines, in which city dwellers concentrated most of their investment.[42]
All the members of these communities as well as their heirs and the local
officials were required to guarantee the rental fee demanded by the landlords.
A committee composed of both city dwellers and rural inhabitants was created
to establish the amount to be paid in cases of disagreement.[43]

Despite the Florentine measures approved between 1348 and 1363 being
described as 'the most repressive labour laws enacted anywhere in post-plague
Europe', their effectiveness when it came to the tug-of-war between lessors and
lessee was probably low, as suggested by the increasing severity of the constant
re-enactments.[44] The same may be suggested for the law approved by Siena in
1348.[45] Both policies seemingly focused on curbing the claims of sharecroppers
and tenants rather than those of wage labourers. This was because *mezzadria*
and tenancy were channelling most land investment from the city, while the
direct management of farms using rural wage labour played a lesser role in
Tuscan agriculture.

II

The second outbreak of the plague in 1363 served a death blow to population
recovery and pushed the Florentine and Sienese rulers to change their strategy in
order to cope with the consequences of a further fall in the labour force.[46] Both

40   One can consider them as a reaction to the progressive levelling down of rural social
layers. See ASFi, Provvisioni, 35, fols 94v–95r (22 January 1347).

41   See the quote from Matteo Villani above.

42   Regarding landlords' investment in cash crops and new plantation see C. M. De La
Roncière, *Un changeur florentin du Trecento: Lippo di Fede del Sega, 1285 env.–1363 env.*
(Paris, 1973), pp. 120–36.

43   This interpretation of the deliberation differs from that proposed by Cohn, 'After the
Black Death', 468.

44   See *ibid.*, 468–9, where it is suggested that 'such severity may well reflect an unreality
about these laws'.

45   See Piccinni, 'La politica agraria', pp. 240–1.

46   The plague of 1363 was even worse in some areas of Tuscany, killing most of the
youngsters born after 1348: S. K. Cohn, 'Epidemiology of the Black Death and Successive
Waves of Plague', *Medical History Supplement*, 27 (2008), 74–100. The records of the Sienese

the governments of Florence and Siena now switched to the indirect regulation of the labour market through, first, new tax policies and, second, new immigration policies. In this respect, the term *agrarian policies* is a better description than labour regulations of the series of measures approved.[47] The aims were still the same, however: curbing the rise of wages and sharecroppers' output shares, binding sharecroppers to land and preserving the rate of profits from landownership. These methods had been previously applied by Siena and Florence, favouring fiscal categories closest to the economic interests of city dwellers and attracting new immigrants with better conditions.[48] The main difference now was in the target: Florence heavily taxed the population of the mountains rather than that of the plains and hills near the city, while Siena exempted sharecroppers but not rural communities and wage labourers from taxation.

Between 1364 and 1371 Florentines approved a new immigration law and developed an unequal fiscal system across rural society. In October 1364 they attempted to attract labourers from outside the Florentine state to work as sharecroppers or tenants (but not as independent farmers) by granting them an exemption of six years from all the taxes and services normally due from rural inhabitants.[49] Between 1364 and 1431 Florentine city councils passed at least twenty-six laws and decrees favouring both immigration and the return of the Florentine peasants who had left the area 'because of war, famine, debts, and especially excessive taxes', 'no matter what tenurial relations they contracted'.[50] The change was radical, as shown by comparing the title of the decree in 1352,

---

city-councils reported that the countryside had been emptied of its labour force in 1364, and had suffered a great loss in population and grain yields in southern Tuscany in 1370 and 1373 and another plague in 1374: G. Piccinni, *Nascita e morte di un quartiere medievale. Siena e il borgo nuovo di Santa Maria a cavallo della peste del 1348* (Pisa, 2019), p. 154; G. Piccinni, 'Siena, il grano di Maremma e quello dell'Ospedale. I provvedimenti economici del 1382', *Bollettino Senese di Storia Patria*, 120 (2013), 174–89, at 179–80.

47   Piccinni, 'La politica agraria', p. 212.

48   Siena favoured sharecroppers against rural communities via distributing the tax burden in 1288, 1298, 1306, 1329, 1331 and 1337. See *ibid.*, pp. 223–4. Immigration policies had also been enacted by Florence and Siena before the Black Death. See Cohn, 'After the Black Death', 473–5.

49   ASFi, Provvisioni, 52, fols 34r–34v (3 ottobre 1364).

50   Cohn, *Creating*, p. 230. See also Cohn, 'After the Black Death', 472–3. Regarding the laws, see ASFi, Provvisioni, 65, fols 44v–46v (4 June 1377); 68, fols 113v–115v (17 August 1379); 72, fols 171r–172r (20 October 1383); 74, fols 204v–205r (8 December 1385); 80, fols 197r–198v (2 December 1391); 88, fols 182r–183v (14 October 1399); 88, fols 226r–227r (7 November 1399); 88, fols 328v–329v (23 February 1399 (1400)); 91, fols 146v–147r (20 September 1402); 93, fols 193r–193v (3 February 1404 (1405)); 101, fols 333r–334r (24 January 1412 (1413)); 101, fols 334r–334v (24 January 1412/1413); 105, fols 215v–216v (22 November 1415); 107, fols 215r–215v (5 May 1417); 112, fols 143r–144r (18 October 1422); 113, fol. 217r (7 February 1423/1424); 114, fols 63v–64v (5 December 1424); 117, fols 122v–123r (26 June 1427); 117, fol. 123r (26 June 1427); 118, fols 116v–117v (20 November 1427); 120, fols

which was 'against rural workers', while that forty years later was 'to favour rural workers returning at work'.[51]

After 1371 and especially between 1383 and 1402, fiscal reform led to an unequal redistribution of the tax burden across the Florentine territory[52] created by the type of tax levied in the countryside (*estimo del contado*) in the fourteenth century. It was based on a mixed system of analytical and arbitrary assessment. First, the city governments or tax officials established and distributed the overall amount to be collected among the various communities. At this stage, Florentine patrons could influence the redistribution of the total share in order to favour some communities over others. Second, the share was split among the households of each community by local officials and councils on the basis of an evaluation of the tax capacity of each household according to wealth (measured in land and animals) and the number of adult male workers.

The implicit goal of such an unequal redistribution of taxes was to support land investment by the city dwellers in the plains and the hills near Florence.[53] On the one hand, Florentine elites protected the villages where they had previously or recently established their patronage as *mezzadria* landlords by lessening the tax levied there.[54] On the other, they burdened the mountainous areas on the borders of the state, which was unsuitable for Florentine land investment because it was too distant and infertile (see Figure 3.1).[55] In this way, they channelled the internal and external immigration towards the plains and the hills near Florence, resulting in a stable or increasing population between 1365 and 1427.[56]

However, the unequal fiscal pressure exerted by Florence on the periphery emptied the mountain villages on the borders of people. Indebted villagers from the Apennines chose to escape into the territories of Bologna, Romagna and Pistoia, rather than hand over almost half of the value of their land in

---

461v–462r (8 February 1429/1430); 120, fols 491r–491v (13 February 1429/1430); 121, fols 72r–72v (26 October 1430); 122, fols 2r–2v; 2v–3r; 4r–5r (16 April 1431).

51   See ASFi, Provvisioni, 40, fols 27r–27v (3 December 1352); 80, fols 197r–198v (2 December 1391).

52   It should be also noticed that taxes could be levied more than once per year and according to the needs of the city-commune. See Cohn, *Creating*, pp. 55–61.

53   A survey of land purchases in the plains near Florence shows that the 'majority of sales (forty-one sales or 37 per cent) took places between villagers' in 1364–71, while in 1370–1401 the trend was reversed. Exchanges of rural properties between Florentines increased, exchanges between peasants fell and 'urban buyers doubled the number of rural buyers in the acquisition of rural lands in the plains near Florence'. See *ibid.*, pp. 102–3.

54   *Ibid.*, pp. 107–8: 'heavy tax burdens on those from lowland and hill villages near the city, where citizens possessed their farms and profited from their sharecroppers' production and well-being, would have threatened the economic resources of these same urban rulers and proprietors; in effect they would have become a tax on themselves'.

55   *Ibid.*, pp. 104–5.

56   *Ibid.*, pp. 80–9, at pp. 86–8.

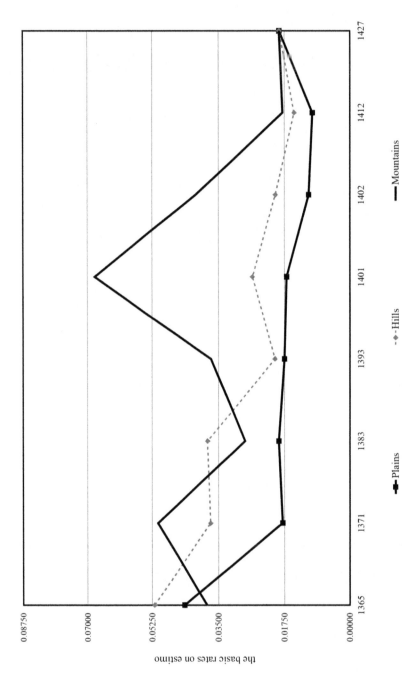

Figure 3.1. Tax rates in the *contado* of Florence: mountains, hills and plains, 1365–1427. Source: Elaboration of the author from Cohn, *Creating*, p. 89 (figure 3.4). Each year in the x-axis represents a new *estimo* made. The figure is based on data from the *estimi* of 25 villages of the *contado* of Florence.

taxes.[57] Indebtedness also influenced sharecroppers' mobility, but they tended to move within the Florentine state, usually to work for another landowner who was willing to pay off their debts.[58] In 1427 a new fiscal system called the *Catasto* introduced a standardised analytical assessment of the wealth of all Florentine households. This removed the inequality in tax distribution among the Florentine settlements, but inequalities between sharecroppers and other rural workers remained. Sharecroppers were assessed as propertyless and were taxed only on the able-bodied men of the household, while their landlord paid for half of the property leased out in *mezzadria*. In contrast, smallholders and farmers were taxed for all the land they held. Thus, the *Catasto* continued to make *mezzadria* more attractive than wage labour or farming during the whole fifteenth century.[59]

In December 1364 the Sienese city council approved two new laws in the same day. The first defended *mezzadria* workers against over-taxation from rural communities.[60] The deliberation claimed that local representatives were over-burdening sharecroppers to discourage them from working for the city dwellers. This was a form of resistance against the land purchase process and dated back to the end of the thirteenth century in the Sienese territory.[61] The Sienese council used the upsurge of this type of conflict to strengthen the bond between the city dwellers and their sharecroppers and to support sharecroppers in contrast with the rest of the peasantry. This was done via exemptions from taxes and services due from the rural community. The taxes due from share-croppers to Siena were reduced and the only services required were guarding the settlement where they lived in case of war and payment of damage done by their livestock. All other taxes and services due as members of the rural community were suspended if they were working for city dwellers.[62]

The second law, like that of 1348, addressed the increasing number of wage labourers as opposed to sharecroppers and the rising cost of labour. Both trends were causing land leased out by the city dwellers to be left uncultivated. The measure proposed was subtle: all the able-bodied men who were not directly

57   *Ibid.*, p. 75.
58   The mobility of labourers beyond the borders (12 per cent from the plains, 15 per cent from the hills, all because of the debts), across the *contado* (49 per cent from the plains, 33 per cent from the hills of the total population) or within each *pieve* (28 per cent in the plains, 44 per cent in the hills) between 1383 and 1412. Data assessed for fourteen villages in *ibid.*, p. 37). For Siena see Piccinni, 'La politica agraria', pp. 217–18.
59   See Herlihy and Klapisch-Zuber, *Tuscans*, pp. 1–27.
60   Piccinni, *Il contratto di mezzadria*, document XV (1364).
61   See Piccinni, 'La politica agraria', pp. 223–4. For Florence, see footnote 40.
62   If sharecroppers were landless they had to pay to their community only three *lire* or thirty *soldi*, depending on whether they were provided with a pair of oxen or not. Local officials not respecting the measure must be fined fifty *lire*. See Piccinni, *Il contratto di mezzadria*, document XV (1364).

cultivating a certain amount of land, no matter if owned or leased, had to pay a tax of twenty *soldi* per month (around 0.66 *soldi* per day in a thirty-day month).[63] In this way, wage labour became immediately less profitable compared with sharecropping. The highest daily wage recorded in 1364 was one *soldo* per day: accordingly, wage labourers risked losing over 60 per cent of their salary in taxes.[64]

Despite these laws, however, social control over rural workers in the Sienese territory was still difficult: in 1368 a law was approved to punish the flight of indebted sharecroppers with detention.[65] This crime was perceived as even more serious than in other parts of central Tuscany because of the severity of the demographic crisis in the Sienese territory.[66] As the population did not recover, between 1398 and 1431 Sienese rulers were forced to change strategy by approving new Florentine-like immigration policies in favour of foreigners and fugitive labourers: in 1398, a ten-year fiscal exemption was granted to foreigners (usually Florentines) migrating to Siena and its countryside. In 1413, 1425 and 1427 five years' relief from the payment of previous debts was granted to all the sharecroppers who had escaped from the territory.[67] In addition, Sienese councils further reduced the taxes paid by sharecroppers to the community of residence in 1427.[68] Only in 1460 was the series of tax exemptions granted to foreigners abolished, probably because of increasing fiscal demands from the city and the slightly decreasing need for labourers from abroad by this time.[69]

63   The amount of land to cultivated ranged between twelve *staiora* (1.5ha.) and six *staiora* (0.75ha.) according to the proximity to the city. See *ibid*.

64   The deliberation reports that the highest salary requested by wage labourers was twelve *denari* per day: that is, eighteen *soldi* for working thirty days. See *ibid*.

65   See *ibid*., document XVI (1368). Further measures against sharecroppers escaping abroad were adopted in 1435 (against those helping fugitive sharecroppers) and in 1460 (sharecroppers escaping with the harvest and draught animals were to be hanged). See *ibid*., documents XLV (1435) and XLVI (1460).

66   In 1440, for instance, a 'shortage of labourers' near Siena was reported. See Piccinni, 'La politica agraria', p. 218 n. 87. In the fifteenth century many Sienese communities were recorded as unable to pay taxes because they were abandoned, underpopulated or inhabited by unpropertied peasants: see M. Ginatempo, *Crisi di un territorio. Il popolamento della Toscana senese alla fine del Medioevo* (Firenze, 1989).

67   See Piccinni, *Il contratto di mezzadria*, documents XXV (1413), XXIX (1425) and XXXII (1427).

68   Propertied and unpropertied sharecroppers must pay their community only three *lire* per pair of oxen owned or leased. All the other payments due to communities were abolished. See *ibid*., document XXXIII (1427).

69   See *ibid*., document XLVI (1460).

III

The impact of the policies developed by Florentine and Sienese rulers after 1348 was twofold. In the short term, the labour regulations enacted between 1348 and 1363 mostly failed in their primary aim, to curb the rise in profits among sharecroppers. Rising rural wages were complained about, but not directly addressed. Instead, urban elites attempted to preserve sharecropping-friendly labour-market conditions through heavy fines across a vast territory troubled by epidemics and warfare. The tax and immigration policies developed after 1363 also failed to sustain the recovery of the rural population, apart from in the areas near Florence. The loss of population was, once again, too heavy and continuously worsened by outbreaks of the plague (in 1374, 1383, 1400) and warfare to be rapidly compensated for by immigration and new births.[70] In Central Tuscany a positive demographic trend was well established only after 1450, while pre-1348 population levels were reached one century later.[71]

In the long term, the policies enacted after 1363 contributed significantly to the development of the *mezzadria* system, further increasing the profits from land for city dwellers and reducing the share of profit for the peasants. The change of strategy, target and method explains the success of these agrarian policies, together with the slow demographic recovery. However, such success was not immediate. Landlords (implicitly) preferred to intensify their capital input and to pay higher salaries to sharecroppers rather than hiring free wage labourers. They stuck to the *mezzadria* system or to tenancy.[72]

This choice was supported by the profitability of land investment even in times of labour scarcity. Indeed, the concentration of labour on the most fertile land increased the land productivity there through the cultivation of cash crops such as vines and orchard and olive trees.[73] The fall in the labour force together with immigration across the territory and towards the cities, moreover, may have lowered or kept stable the price of land.[74] Both these factors could explain, together with specific agrarian policies, the increase of land purchase by Florentine city dwellers after the 1370s, when the number of urban buyers was double that of rural buyers.[75] In Siena, land consolidation probably never stopped: after 1348 urban landlords kept purchasing land from rural inhabitants, while in 1446 a deliberation reported that Sienese landowners had the

---

70   See Cohn, *Creating*, p. 226; Cohn, 'Epidemiology of the Black Death', 74–100.
71   See Herlihy and Klapisch-Zuber, *Tuscans*, pp. 60–73.
72   See Ackerberg and Botticini, 'The Choice of Agrarian Contracts', 241–57.
73   See Piccinni, 'L'evoluzione della rendita fondiaria', pp. 57–95.
74   Cohn, *Creating*, pp. 101–3.
75   See footnote 53.

'most fertile and good by nature' land in the Sienese territory and peasants only 'infertile and meagre' properties.[76]

As a consequence, binding peasants to the land as sharecroppers was crucial in order to maintain the profitability of land investment.[77] Not surprisingly, there was a decrease in short-term share-contracts (one to six years) in the Sienese territory after 1363 and through the fifteenth century (see Figure 3.2). Such trend represented a win–win situation for both parties. In longer tenancies (seven to nine years, or even perpetual) the lessor benefited from the higher and more constant availability of labour input provided by the contract, while the lessee, for his part, could profit from a stability of income and benefits such as loans and capital input. Furthermore, a longer stay allowed him to benefit from longer-term investment such as the planting of new crops. A shorter contract (on average three years), on the contrary, increased the uncertainty of the lessee, which was high when he risked being deprived of the landholding and farmhouse.

Finally, post-1363 agrarian policies, implicitly or explicitly, targeted free wage labourers, who were more vulnerable to daily or seasonal wage fluctuations than sharecroppers or tenants. The aim, however, was not to curb their salaries, which kept growing until the 1470s, but to discourage sharecroppers or new immigrants from becoming (seasonal or daily) wage earners. In this respect, Florentine and Sienese rulers shifted from directly regulating the labour market (up until 1363) towards influencing it via taxation (after 1363). Furthermore, at the micro-level, urban landlords may have used loans and capital flows, and improvements of labour conditions, to create socio-economic ties. This is suggested, first, by the growing competition among Sienese landowners to 'buy with great loans the few sharecroppers available', as noted in 1427;[78] and, second, by the negative correlation between numbers of short-term contracts and those of leases providing livestock and loans for the lessee observed between 1364 and 1469 (see Figure 3.2). In both cases, sharecroppers were kept in the employ of a lessor. Such a sharp use of tax policies and loans has similarities to some nineteenth- and twentieth-century fiscal policies in African colonies.[79]

76   See footnote 27 and Piccinni, *Il contratto di mezzadria*, document XLIV (1446).

77   'In some cases, [among the contracts of land purchase between peasants and city-dwellers analysed between 1370 and 1401] a second transaction followed on the same day and place: a short-term lease or *mezzadria* contract converted the former village proprietor into the urban landlord's tenant on the very property which moments before he had owned.' See Cohn, *Creating*, p. 103.

78   See Piccinni, *Il contratto di mezzadria*, document XXXII (1427).

79   Between the late nineteenth and the early twentieth centuries there was a 'prevalence of domination mechanisms in the South African migrant labour system, with the state playing a prominent role to ensure that black workers were "cajoled into selling their labour power by expropriation of land, imposition of taxation, and similar non-market inducements", and then ensuring their submission by treating the migrant "as an alien without rights

Despite these similarities, the policies adopted by Florence and Siena differed somewhat in target and timing between 1364 and 1434. On one hand, the Sienese city councils focused on dividing sharecroppers from wage labourers and rural communities. They also adopted immigration policies thirty years later than Florence, despite an even harsher demographic crisis. Finally, their laws show a more explicit awareness of their purpose than do the Florentine ones.[80] On the other hand, Florentine rulers reacted earlier to labour scarcity by developing new immigration policies. However, they may not have succeeded without the 'informal' tax exemptions they granted as patrons to the areas near Florence to protect the renewal of capital flows towards the countryside. In this regard, Florentine rulers apparently showed less awareness of the relevance of the sharecroppers in their government policies than they did as individual investors.

In order to fully explain such differences between Florence and Siena in facing similar issues, further research is needed. However, the discrepancy between the agrarian policies of the two cities might be explained by the (i) the divergent socio-economic features of the two cities and (ii) the diversity of their countrysides. For instance, land purchase was often considered as one type of investment among many (such as textile production, money changing, banking, merchandising and public bonds) by late medieval Florentine city dwellers. Furthermore, it was not the most important (in term of money) among the higher classes in the first half of the fifteenth century.[81] In contrast, land accumulation was fundamental for Sienese nobles and members of the ruling class, especially after the crisis in Sienese banking at the end of the thirteenth century.[82] In addition, the Florentine *contado* differed from the Sienese one because of the larger rural population living in the fertile area around the city and because a larger area was intensively cultivated. The territory around Siena, in contrast, despite its lesser population and productivity, was more fundamental to the Sienese economy and society.[83]

The final achievement of both sets of policies, however, was the same. The *mezzadria* system was well established in Central Tuscany by the end of the fifteenth century. For instance, the number of householders working as sharecroppers increased from 25 to 29 per cent in the whole territory under the rule of Florence between 1427 and 1469. This growth was even stronger in the most

---

of citizenship"'. See R. Hamann and R. Bertels, 'The Institutional Work of Exploitation: Employers' Work to Create and Perpetuate Inequality', *Journal of Management Studies*, 55 (2017), 394–423.

80   See, for instance, footnote 11.

81   See Herlihy and Klapisch-Zuber, *Tuscans*, pp. 28–59, 93–130.

82   See G. Piccinni, *Fedeltà ghibellina affari guelfi. Saggi e riletture intorno alla storia di Siena fra Due e Trecento* (Siena, 2008). See also the land purchase attested in 1348, footnote 27.

83   See Herlihy and Klapisch-Zuber, *Tuscans*, pp. 28–36, 93–130; Piccinni, 'La politica agraria', pp. 207–92.

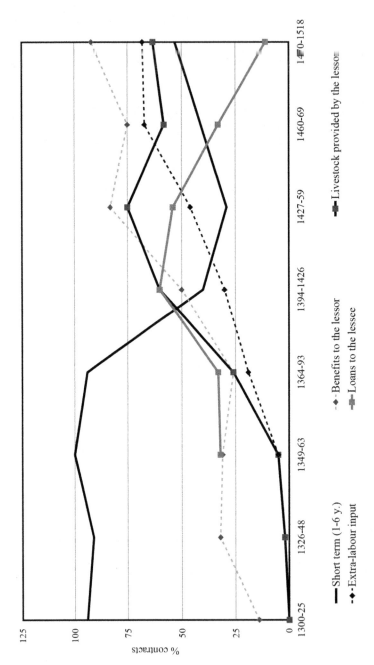

Figure 3.2. Clauses distribution in Sienese share-contracts, 1300–1518. Source: Elaboration of the author from Pinto and Pirillo, *Il contratto di mezzadria*, pp. 44, 52–3 (1300–25 = 88 contracts); (1326–48 = 143 contracts); Piccinni, *Il contratto di mezzadria*, pp. 149–54 (1349–63 = 19 contracts) (1364–93 = 78 contracts) (1394–1426 = 10 contracts) (1427–59 = 24 contracts) (1460–69 = 12 contracts) (1470–1518 = 92 contracts). The breakpoints are those proposed in the literature used and follow the changes in labour regulations and agrarian policies identified by Piccinni in the Sienese laws. See *ibid.*, pp. 11–88.

fertile areas where city dwellers concentrated their investment: in these regions, sharecroppers represented 39 per cent, 50 per cent or even the majority of the inhabitants by the end of the fifteenth century.[84] The trend was similar in the Sienese territory: in 1460, the tax levied by Siena on rural inhabitants was called the 'tax on the sharecroppers' in some communities.[85] Moreover, while in 1351 there was only one Sienese village where all the inhabitants were sharecroppers, by the end of the fifteenth century the number of settlements entirely composed of sharecroppers had increased to thirty-eight, covering half of the territory of the province of Siena.[86]

Such developments can explain why rural labour regulations disappeared during the fifteenth century – after 1431 in Florence, and after 1470 in Siena. The spread of *mezzadria* provided the labour market control previously pursued by landlords through agrarian policies. This is evident in Sienese documentation: between 1427 and 1459 share-contracts started to explicitly refer to labour regulations in order to enforce specific clauses. After 1500, great landowners began to introduce standardised contracts to run all their estates in *mezzadria* and to apply the same conditions to all their sharecroppers.[87] In this regard, the replacement of individual negotiation with fixed clauses for large group of sharecroppers represents the final step of the establishment of the *mezzadria* system.

An important role was also played by the peasants: after 1348, some of them – but how many and to what extent is still a matter of debate – were recovering part of their 'landed losses' from other villagers and city dwellers using profits from higher wages. These purchases, however, were mainly scattered strips and plots of land rather than *mezzadria* farms and landhold-ings.[88] Others, in contrast, turned to seasonal or daily wage labour, which was more remunerative in times of lower grain prices and rising salaries (see Figure 3.3). This group, however, was highly varied, including smallholders

---

84   South-west of Florence sharecroppers reached 39 per cent of the population between 1427 and 1469, while north-west of the city they increased 10 percentage points, to 32 per cent. See Herlihy and Klapisch-Zuber, *Tuscans*, pp. 116–19. In the territory of S. Giovanni in Petroio in Mugello (30km northwards from Florence), sharecroppers were 56 per cent of the residents in 1504. See D. Cristoferi, '"I nostri contadini solevano istare molto meglio per lo addrieto che ora": mezzadria, proprietà cittadina e disuguaglianza economica in Toscana, sec. XV–XVI', in G. Nigro (ed.), *Economic Inequality in Pre-Industrial Societies: Causes and Effects* (Florence, 2020), pp. 275–300.

85   Piccinni, *Il contratto di mezzadria*, document XXXIII n. 1.

86   The chronological increase of villages inhabited only by sharecroppers: 1350 = 1; 1400 = 4; 1430 = 14; 1450 = 26; 1500 = 38. See *ibid.*, pp. 97–101 (tables 3 and 4).

87   Standardized contracts applied the same clauses (length, extra-works, benefits to the landlords, etc.) to all the sharecroppers working properties of the same lessor, usually a big landlord such as a religious institution: *ibid.*, pp. 140–5.

88   See Cohn, *Creating*, pp. 98, 101–3.

or leaseholders who turned to occasional wage labour, as well as servants and daily wage earners, and was mostly complementary to the management of properties owned by city dwellers, religious and welfare institutions that were leased rather than sharecropped.[89]

More importantly, many peasants, instead of purchasing land or working as wage labourers, preferred to use their temporary bargaining power to pay lower rents or to increase their buying power on the commodity market and to diminish their participation in capital input into the *mezzadria* system: that is, they preferred to risk less. Loans, tax exemptions, lessors' capital input and the access to food, credit and shelter provided by the *mezzadria* system were more attractive to landless peasants than daily wage labour or independent farming, especially in period of crisis.[90] The peasants' preference for sharecropping is further explained by the century-long process of land expropriation led by the city dwellers. By then, many peasants were already bound to land through the *mezzadria* system, while their capacity for entrepreneurship was limited by their dependency on their lessors.[91] In this regard, it is not surprising that only a minority of peasants purchased land in the Florentine plains after the Black Death.[92]

Once population levels recovered in the fifteenth century, however, the share-cropping system framed by Sienese and Florentine labour regulations and city dwellers' land purchases contributed to reversing the situation in favour of the landowners. Peasants started to lose the bargaining power acquired between 1348 and 1363, while the city dwellers' profits from land grew again. Between 1471 and 1500, for instance, we observe a decrease in the value of rural daily wages in the Florentine territory.[93] In the Sienese countryside, sharecropping contracts with longer terms and loans started to decrease in number since 1459. In contrast, clauses requiring sharecroppers to provide extra works for free and special benefits to the lessor multiplied (see Figure 3.2).

Extra works consisted of tasks such as planting new vineyards and olive and fruit trees, grafting fruit trees, cartage services and clearing and tillage activities, in addition to the usual maintenance of the landholding. Benefits were (small) payments in cash, an unequal division of valuable products such as wine or industrial crops and the delivery of a certain amount of commodities produced

---

89 See F. Panero, 'Il lavoro salariato nelle campagne dell'Italia centro-settentrionale dal secolo XII all'inizio del Quattrocento', in A. Cortonesi, M. Montanari and A. Nellie (eds), *Contratti agrari e rapporti di lavoro nell'Europa medievale* (Bologna, 2006), pp. 179–202, at pp. 194–201.
90 Regarding the risk-avoiding factors explaining the persistence of *mezzadria* see Ackerberg and Botticini, 'The Choice of Agrarian Contracts', 241–57.
91 See Emigh, *The Undevelopment of Capitalism*, pp. 131–67.
92 See footnote 53.
93 Wage labour further shrank to seasonal works: Tognetti, 'Prezzi e salari', 305–8.

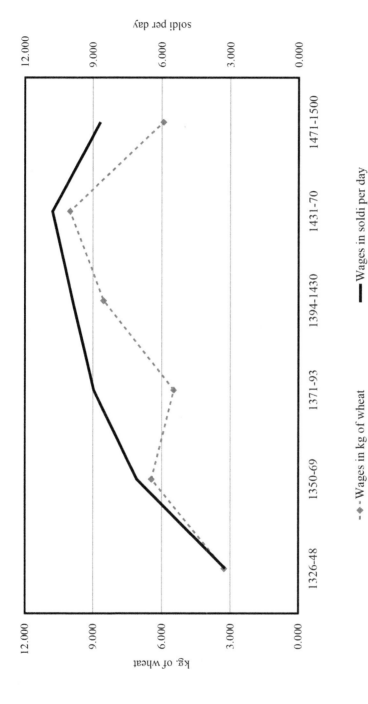

Figure 3.3. Nominal and real rural wages in the Florentine countryside, 1326–1500. Source: Elaboration of the author from Tognetti, 'Prezzi e salari', 309 (table 14). Each point represents the average of all the data on daily wages collected within that ten-year interval, expressed in kg of wheat and in *soldi* per day.

by the sharecropper, such as wax, timber, honey and capons. If the terms were not fulfilled, the lessee could be deprived of the landholding. Labour regulations, moreover, supported the landowners who demanded extra works in order to increase the profits from land.[94] Despite such clauses being found in pre-Black Death contracts, their growth in number and details during the fifteenth century reflects the increasing negotiating power of the lessors.[95] Essentially, lessors asked sharecroppers to pay back the higher share of land investment lessors were providing through loans, oxen and building services. These operations, furthermore, particularly benefited the landlord, since they took a long time to increase land productivity.[96]

Such a trend was also evident in the Florentine territory. During the second half of the fifteenth century a priest claimed: 'our peasants used to be better off in the past than now [...] in many villages, they also pay for oxen and sowing seeds and [...] they must do it in this way because they have increased a lot in numbers'.[97] Furthermore, capital flows together with the concentration of labour input provided by the sharecroppers increased the value of the land owned by the city dwellers. For instance, landed wealth increased by up to 40 per cent in the Florentine territory, while Sienese landowners claimed to own the best land available and to make great investments through the fifteenth century.[98] Sharecroppers were caught up in a spiral: in order to profit from their own efforts they were induced to renew the share-contract at almost any cost, no matter the length, the labour input required or the loans provided.

To conclude, post-Black Death labour regulations, fiscal laws and immigration policies enacted by Florentine and Sienese elites successfully interacted, in the long term, with demographic changes and peasants' agency in establishing the *mezzadria* system at the core of Tuscany. In the short term, these measures failed to curb the rise of agricultural wages and the claims of the peasants, but they laid the foundation of a share-tenancy mostly beneficial

---

94   In 1427 Sienese city-councils established fines of twenty *soldi* per olive tree and ten *soldi* per fruit tree for every sharecropper, tenant and farmer who would not plant two fruit trees and two olive trees or four fruit trees per each landholding. The lessor should pay back his lessee with one silver *grosso* per olive tree and one *soldo* per fruit tree: Piccinni, *Il contratto di mezzadria*, document XXXI (1427).

95   See Pinto and Pirillo, *Il contratto di mezzadria*, pp. 44–52.

96   Recently planted vines or olive trees require some years (seven for the vines, nine to ten for the olive tree) to reach full productivity.

97   See G. Folena (ed.), *Motti e facezie del pievano Arlotto* (Milan–Naples, 1953), p. 218 motto CLV.

98   In the Florentine territory of Petroio in Mugello, the number of landed estates worth over 250 golden florins increased from 58 per cent to 73 per cent between 1427 and 1512. In the same period, the revaluation of the landed property of the city-dwellers was up to 40 per cent. See Cristoferi, '"I nostri contadini"', p. 280. Regarding the claims of the Sienese landowners, see Piccinni, *Il contratto di mezzadria*, pp. 17–8 and document XLIV (1446).

for the landowners as soon as the labour supply recovered. Peasants, for their part, mainly chose to remain within a less risky system in a period of high uncertainty, profiting from its short-term benefits. When these benefits were reduced by population recovery, peasants were already bound to land within the *mezzadria* system. Through its ties, however, the *mezzadria* contract was able to keep the tenant and his family at subsistence level, providing land, food, shelter, oxen and credit. In this way, Florentine and Sienese labour regulations ensured the profitability of land investment and made Tuscan rural society stable in the long term, despite its growing economic inequality.

PART II

THE REGULATION AND CLASSIFICATION OF
LABOUR IN EARLY MODERN EUROPE

4

Slaves, Servants and other Dependent People: Early Modern Classifications and Western Europe's Self-Representation

RAFFAELLA SARTI[1]

Introduction

This essay discusses how servants, slaves and other dependant people were classified by early modern Europeans through the analysis of the writings of ancient Greek, Italian, French and English authors, including philosophers, jurists, authors of directions on household management and travellers. After analysing common descriptions of servants and slaves, the issue of slavery in relation to the self-representation of Western Europe is briefly discussed. Finally, the chapter addresses various forms of dependence in different European countries from the late Middle Ages to the early nineteenth century as they were described by contemporaries.

Long traditions of historical studies have addressed serfdom;[2] rural and

---

1 Submitted Nov. 2020. English revision by Clelia Boscolo. I thank Patrizia Delpiano for her comments.
2 Marc Bloch, 'Le servage dans la société européenne', in Marc Bloch, *Mélanges historiques*, vol. 1 (Paris, 1963), pp. 261–528, partially translated by William R. Beer as *Slavery and Serfdom in the Middle Ages: Selected Essays* (Berkeley, 1975). More recent works: Michael L. Bush (ed.), *Serfdom and Slavery: Studies in Legal Bondage* (Abington, 1996); Karl Kaser, 'Serfdom in Eastern Europe', in David I. Kertzer and Marzio Barbagli (eds), *History of the European Family*, vol. 1 (New Haven, 2001), pp. 4–62; Tracy Dennison, *The Institutional Framework of Russian Serfdom* (Cambridge, 2011); Simonetta Cavaciocchi (ed.), *Schiavitù e servaggio nell'economia europea secc. XI–XVIII – Serfdom and Slavery in the European Economy 11th–18th centuries* (Florence, 2014).

domestic service in Europe;[3] and Atlantic[4] and Mediterranean slavery.[5] Yet these traditions have developed rather independently from each other. Relationships and commonalities were thus partly overlooked, or described as if, in Europe, there was a linear transition from ancient slavery to medieval serfdom and then to free modern service.[6] Only recently have historians focused on themes such as the presence and status of Mediterranean slaves in areas far from the Mediterranean; the hinterland's involvement in the Atlantic slave trade's interest networks; the presence and status, in the Old Continent, of slaves

3   Raffaella Sarti, 'Historians, Social Scientists, Servants, and Domestic Workers: Fifty Years of Research on Domestic and Care Work', *International Review of Social History*, 592 (2014), 279–314, also published in Dirk Hoerder, Elise van Nederveen Meerkerk and Silke Neunsinger (eds), *Towards a Global History of Domestic and Caregiving Workers* (Leiden, 2015), pp. 25–60; Jane Whittle (ed.), *Servants in Rural Europe 1400–1900* (Woodbridge, 2017); Fabrice Boudjaaba and Francisco García González (eds), *El trabajo doméstico y sirviente en la Europa rural (ss. XVI–XIX). Diversidad de modelos regionales y formas de dependencia*, special issue of *Mundo Agrario*, 18 (2017); Isidro Dubert and Vincent Gourdon (eds), *Inmigración, trabajo y servicio doméstico. En la Europa urbana, siglos XVIII–XX* (Madrid, 2017).

4   For example, Olivier Pétré-Grenouilleau, *Les traites négrières. Essai d'histoire globale* (Paris, 2004); David Brion Davis, *Inhuman Bondage. The Rise and Fall of Slavery in the New World* (Oxford–New York, 2006); Lisa A. Lindsay, *Captives as Commodities. The Transatlantic Slave Trade* (Prentice Hall, 2008); Michael Zeuske, *Sklavenhändler, Negreros und Atlantikkreolen: eine Weltgeschichte des Sklavenhandels im atlantischen Raum* (Berlin–Boston, 2015). On emancipation see Gabriele Turi, *Schiavi in un mondo libero. Storia dell'emancipazione dall'età moderna a oggi* (Rome–Bari, 2012). For a good overview see Patrizia Delpiano, *La schiavitù in età moderna* (Rome–Bari, 2009).

5   Salvatore Bono, *Schiavi musulmani nell'Italia moderna: galeotti, vu' cumprà, domestici* (Napels, 1999); Salvatore Bono, 'La schiavitù nel Mediterraneo moderno: storia di una storia', *Cahiers de la Méditerranée*, 65 (2002), 1–16; Giovanna Fiume, *Schiavitù mediterranee. Corsari, rinnegati e santi di età moderna* (Milano, 2009); Giuliana Boccadamo, *Napoli e l'Islam. Storie di musulmani, schiavi e rinnegati in età moderna* (Naples, 2010); Roger Botte and Alessandro Stella (eds), *Couleurs de l'esclavage sur les deux rives de la Méditerranée (Moyen-Âge – XXè siècle)* (Paris, 2012); Fabienne Guillen and Salah Trabelsi (eds), *Les esclavages en Méditerranée. Espaces et dynamiques économiques* (Madrid, 2012); Sara Cabibbo and Maria Lupi (eds), *Relazioni religiose nel Mediterraneo. Schiavi, redentori, mediatori (secc. XVI–XIX)* (Rome, 2012); Andrea Pelizza, *Riammessi a respirare l'aria tranquilla: Venezia e il riscatto degli schiavi in età moderna* (Venice, 2013); Serena di Nepi (ed.), *Schiavi nelle terre del Papa. Norme rappresentazioni, problemi a Roma e nello Stato della Chiesa in età moderna*, special issue of *Dimensioni e Problemi della Ricerca Storica*, 26 (2013); Simonetta Cavaciocchi (ed.), *Schiavitù e servaggio*; Salvatore Bono, *Schiavi: una storia mediterranea (XVI–XIX secolo)* (Bologna, 2016); Giulia Bonazza, *Abolitionism and the Persistence of Slavery in Italian States, 1750–1850* (London, 2019).

6   For instance, Henri Jean-Baptiste Grégoire, *De la domesticité chez les peuples anciens et modernes* (Paris, 1814), pp. 1–40.

brought from the colonies; and the long-term survival of different forms of personal dependence in Europe.[7]

Furthermore, some historians have now recognised that 'unfree labor and forms of coercion were perfectly compatible with market development': 'economic growth between the seventh and the mid-nineteenth century in Russia, Europe, and the Indian Ocean region was achieved through the wide use of bondage and legal constraints on labor'.[8] When bonded labour eventually collapsed (only 'with the second Revolution and the rise of the welfare state', according to Alessandro Stanziani[9]), there was widespread expectation that secure employment would expand to an increasingly larger share of the worldwide population – as working people who enjoyed new rights were initially only a small minority, mainly located in the West. On the contrary, in many countries nowadays workers experience a loss of rights and rising insecurity, and this is particularly apparent in Europe, where for a long time labour was associated with growing rights. Additionally, there is a revival of paid domestic work and even of slavery.[10]

Besides the present socio-economic situation, the critique of Western civilisation and colonialism by post-colonial studies has also prompted new sociological, anthropological, economic and historical scrutiny of slavery, bondage and any other form of unfree labour, both now and in the past. Research covers the entire world, including areas that for a long time were only marginally considered, such as North-Western and Central Europe.

This chapter contributes to this strand of studies focusing, as mentioned, on the description and classification of slaves, servants and other dependent

---

7 For instance, Robert J. Steinfeld, *The Invention of Free Labor: the Employment Relation in English and American Law and Culture, 1350–1870* (Chapel Hill, 1991); Sue Peabody, *There Are no Slaves in France: the Political Culture of Race and Slavery in the Ancien Régime* (Oxford, 1996); Suzy Pasleau and Isabelle Schopp (eds), with Raffaella Sarti, *Proceedings of the Servant Project*, vol. 2, *Domestic Service and the Emergence of a New Conception of Labour in Europe* (Liège, 2005); vol. 3, *Domestic Service and the Evolution of the Law* (Liège, 2005); Andrea Weindl, 'Slave Trade of Northern Germany from the Seventeenth to the Nineteenth Centuries', in David Eltis and David Richardson (eds), *Extending the Frontiers. Essays on the New Transatlantic Slave Database* (New Haven, 2008), pp. 250–71; Raffaella Sarti, 'Tramonto di schiavitù. Sulle tracce degli ultimi schiavi presenti in Italia (sec. XIX)', in Felice Gambin (ed.), *Alle radici dell'Europa: Mori, giudei e zingari nei paesi del Mediterraneo occidentale, secoli XVIII e XIX* (Florence, 2009), pp. 281–97; Alessandro Stanziani, *Bondage. Labor and Rights in Eurasia from the Sixteenth to the Early Twentieth Centuries* (New York, 2014); Bono, *Schiavi*; Felix Brahm and Eve Rosenhaft (eds), *Slavery Hinterland: Transatlantic Slavery and Continental Europe, 1680–1850* (Woodbridge, 2016).
8 Stanziani, *Bondage*, p. 1.
9 *Ibid.*, p. 2.
10 Raffaella Sarti, *Servo e padrone, o della (in)dipendenza. Un percorso da Aristotele ai nostri giorni* (Bologna, 2015 [*Quaderni di Scienza & Politica*, no. 2]), pp. 11–22; Sarti, 'Historians'.

people by early modern authors. Understanding how Europeans perceived and described them is important to reach a more precise knowledge of the past, to assess Westerners' self-representation and to pinpoint the differences between past and present. The results of this analysis may well surprise some readers.

Living tools

Commenting 'with morals and reflexions' on the *Fables of Aesop and Other Eminent Mythologists*, English author, pamphleteer and defender of royalist views Sir Roger L'Estrange (1616–1704) explained that a servant beating his master's dog to the point of making it run away was 'the Master's Instrument' 'as the Cudgel [was] the Servant's'.[11] Such a representation of a servant goes back to Aristotle, who argued that the *doulos* (servant/slave) is a living tool of his master, even though he is not excluded from mankind. He does not belong to himself but to his master; he has no will and no individual identity.[12] Only the master is the active subject; the slave acts as his tool.[13]

Such a representation of the slave as a master's tool was highly ideological: social history has shown that slaves (in Ancient Greece and elsewhere) had some agency.[14] Nonetheless, it was reproduced for over 2,000 years in dozens of texts very different in content, aim and audience.[15] For instance, early modern directions on household management, which inevitably dealt with servants' government, often described servants as living tools. 'Servants are living rational tools owned mainly for the service and utility of their own masters',[16] states, for instance, a short book that took this sentence almost literally from the Senese author Alessandro Piccolomini (1508–1578).[17] Piccolomini associated servants and tools to the point of maintaining that servants would rust if they spent

---

11   Roger L'Estrange, *Fables of Aesop and Other Eminent Mythologists: With Morals and Reflexions*, 2nd ed. (London, 1694), p. 205.
12   Aristotle, *Politics*, Book 1 (A), 1255b. On this issue there is a huge literature that cannot be addressed here.
13   Aristotle also wrote that 'How slaves should be employed, and why it is advantageous that all slaves should have their freedom set before them as a reward, we will say later', but he never explained it. Aristotle, *Politics*, Book 7, 1330a.
14   See Moses Finley, *Ancient Slavery and Modern Ideology* (London, 1980) and a reappraisal by Kostas Vlassopoulos, 'Slavery, Freedom and Citizenship in Classical Athens: Beyond a Legalistic Approach', *European Review of History*, 16 (2009), 347–63.
15   Sarti, *Servo e padrone*, pp. 37–40.
16   Pompeo Vizani, *Breve trattato del governo famigliare* (Bologna, 1609), pp. 36–7.
17   Alessandro Piccolomini, *Della institution morale* (Venice, 1575), p. 524, revised edition of the book *De la institutione di tutta la vita de l'homo nato nobile e in città libera* (Venice, 1542).

time without working.[18] The poet and writer Torquato Tasso (1544–1595) also argued that servants were tools,[19] as did the French Jesuit Jean Cordier (1599–1673): he explained that Aristotle defined servants as *instruments animez* [sic], clarifying that, if they were as they should be, they would act only according to their master's will.[20]

Aristotle's position was also mentioned, to quote another genre, in the eighteenth-century edition of the well-known *Iconologia* by Cesare Ripa (1555/1560–1622), expanded by Cesare Orlandi. Servitude (*Servitù*) is represented as a poor, dishevelled young woman with a yoke or a big stone on her shoulders. She is dishevelled – the author explained – because servants, who are 'an active living tool provided with reason', are prevented from caring for themselves by having to care for their masters.[21] Eighteenth-century books on trade, to mention another example, normally considered colonial slaves 'in the manner of Aristotle, as *living tools or instruments*': 'their humanity is invisible: they are not subjects but objects, tools or instruments of production', Catherine Larrère explained.[22]

These examples show the long-term persistence of the representation of servants as living tools, still attested in the nineteenth century,[23] its presence in texts different in content and purpose, and its use in different cultures and countries. Such definitions were used not only to refer to chattel slaves but also while speaking of servants' management in Western Europe, when most servants were no longer slaves, as recognised by some writers. The first-mentioned booklet spoke of servants who served out of personal choice, unlike oxen and horses, which were irrational living tools.[24] The recourse to the tool metaphor and the simultaneous recognition of the servants' freedom appears confusing to us, as in the case of Cordier, who, after approvingly mentioning Aristotle's definition of servants as living instruments, argued that servants should not obey masters who give them orders contrary to Christian ethics.[25]

18   Piccolomini, *De la institutione*, p. 231; Piccolomini, *Della institution morale*, p. 547. See also Silvano Razzi, *Economica christiana, e civile* (Florence, 1568), p. 244.
19   Torquato Tasso, *Il padre di famiglia*, in Ettore Mazzali (ed.), *Torquato Tasso. Opere*, vol. 2 (Naples, 1969), pp. 503–66, at p. 537.
20   Jean Cordier, *La famille saincte* (Lyon, 1662), p. 847.
21   Cesare Ripa, *Iconologia (…) notabilmente accresciuta (…) dall'abate Cesare Orlandi*, vol. 5 (Perugia, 1767), pp. 102–3.
22   Catherine Larrère, 'Économie politique et esclavage au XVIIIe siècle, une rencontre tardive et ambiguë', in Olivier Pétré-Grenouilleau (ed.), *Abolir l'esclavage. Un réformisme à l'épreuve (France, Portugal, Suisse, XVIIIe–XIXe siècles)* (Rennes, 2008), pp. 209–23 (215, emphasis in the original); see also pp. 211, 214, 216.
23   Antonio Rosmini-Serbati, *Filosofia del diritto*, vol. 2 (Milan, 1843), p. 296, note 1.
24   Vizani, *Breve trattato*, p. 36.
25   Cordier, *La famille saincte*, pp. [8]49–50.

Some writers who used the tool metaphor admitted that it was no longer possible to follow Aristotle in every detail. Piccolomini, for instance, wrote that in Ancient Greece, according to the law, a master had total power over those who were bought or captured through a fair war, whereas in his own times such a custom was forbidden in Italy and masters were left with only limited power over servants – that is, as much power as servants freely accepted by agreeing to serve in exchange for wages, day by day.[26] Similarly, Tasso argued that in ancient times servants were slaves captured in war, whereas in his times they were mainly free people, for whom rewards were necessary.[27] Nonetheless, they described servants as their masters' tools: clearly, they did not consider being a tool and being free as contradictory conditions.

Types of servant, degrees of dependency

The comparison between past and present was only one aspect of the efforts made by early modern writers to classify different kinds of servant. With regard to these classifications, which I have also analysed elsewhere,[28] I focus here on two issues: the inclusion of slaves among servants, and the characterisation of the differences between free and unfree servants. The opposition between free and unfree servants implies a clear-cut dualism, and some authors classify servants accordingly. 'You can have two different kinds of servant at your service', explained the Jesuit Fulvio Fontana, at the beginning of the eighteenth century. 'You can have servants whose condition is that of slaves, or you can have free servants who serve in exchange for a salary.'[29] Yet such a dualism is absent in many other early modern texts: several authors suggest complex classifications that include different degrees of dependency, classifying a large variety of situations under 'umbrella terms' such as servitude (*servitù*) and servant (*servo*), as can be illustrated with examples showing the spread of such classifications in a large variety of texts written over a long period.

The Tuscan physician and writer Francesco Tommasi, the author of a manual on household management (1580), distinguished 'natural servitude' – that is, the servitude 'by which ignorant people serve the learned, and the weak the strong'; 'legal and positive servitude', according to which those who are made 'weak, and defeated by force serve the winners, and the more powerful'; and 'mercenary' servitude, which was more complex than the others because

26   Piccolomini, *Della institution morale*, p. 522.
27   Tasso, *Il padre di famiglia*, p. 532.
28   Raffaella Sarti, 'Who are Servants? Defining Domestic Service in Western Europe (16th–21st Centuries)', in Pasleau, Schopp and Sarti (eds), *Proceedings of the Servant Project*, vol. 2, pp. 3–59.
29   Fulvio Fontana, *Il padrone instruito* (Milan–Bologna, 1710), p. 31.

'some servants serve for wages, but not out of good will'; others 'out of good will, and not for reward' and others 'neither out of good will nor for reward' and therefore resemble 'donkeys who are not handled except with a stick'.[30]

Similarly, the Croatian philosopher and politician Nicolò Vito di Gozze (1540–1610), also the author of a book on the management of the family (1589), argued that servants were of 'varying and different kinds': 'servants by nature', 'servants by law', 'servants by remuneration' and servants 'by virtue or pleasure'. The servants by nature were the 'barbarous and uncouth people' living in the countryside. The servants by law were the slaves. The servants by remuneration were free people who placed themselves in the service of a master: among them, some served in exchange for board and clothing only; others received an additional salary; others worked 'for remuneration only', seeing to all their needs by themselves. Finally, there were those who served not 'for money or out of compulsion, but for mere and sincere pleasure, feeling great affection towards their master's virtue'. The ones in this position were called servants, but they were 'not truly so', as they were, rather, 'courtiers'.[31]

Such classifications imply a complex understanding of the servants' conditions: some servants were people naturally unable to be free and thus destined to serve; others – those whom we would define as slaves – were forced to serve; others served (more or less) voluntarily in exchange for a reward, others out of good will or virtue, or for pleasure. The aforementioned authors strived to distinguish different cases, creating ordered taxonomies. They did not suggest binary classifications opposing free and unfree servants; rather, they described different degrees of dependence and freedom and different reasons why people might serve.

This might sound surprising if we consider that in classical Roman law there was a clear-cut distinction between free and unfree people (*liberi et servi*), and Roman law was a reference for medieval and early modern jurists in a large part of Europe, although within the juridical pluralism common at the time.[32] In fact, even though the distinction free/unfree was important for some authors, such as Ippolito Bonacossa,[33] from the Middle Ages jurists, too, were complicating the free/unfree people opposition, and their classifications could be even

30   Francesco Tommasi, *Reggimento del padre di famiglia* (Florence, 1580), pp. 198–201.
31   Nicolò Vito di Gozze [Nikola Vitov Gučetić], *Governo della famiglia* (Venice, 1589), pp. 100–16.
32   Beatrice Pasciuta, '"Homines aut liberi sunt aut servi". Riflessione giuridica e interventi normativi sulla condizione servile fra medioevo ed età moderna', in Giovanna Fiume (ed.), *Schiavitù religione e libertà nel Mediterraneo tra medioevo ed età moderna*, special issue of *Incontri mediterranei*, 17 (2008), pp. 48–60; Alice Rio, *Slavery After Rome, 500–1100* (Oxford, 2017), p. 1.
33   Ippolito Bonacossa (*De servis vel famulis tractatus* (Venice, 1575)) makes clear that his treatise is about the 'homo liber' who, because of his poverty, is forced to work as a servant.

more complex than those described above.[34] Jurist and cardinal Giambattista De Luca (1614–1683), the author of an influential legal text (1673), acknowledged a difference between free and unfree people. Yet this was embedded in a complex and far from dualistic classification. He distinguished between personal, real and mixed servitude. Personal servitude could be active or passive: active servitude was servitude seen from the vantage point of the individual who enjoyed service; 'passive personal servitude' was the servitude of an individual forced to serve someone else. According to De Luca, there were several types of the latter: a first kind implied a radical change in the legal status of the person who served because such a person lost his/her freedom and became a 'servant in perpetuity'. De Luca (who, unlike many other jurists, wrote his treatise in Italian, not in Latin) made it clear that, in Italian, the name for this kind of serving person was *schiavo*, slave (in legal books written in Latin, the language might create some confusion: the Latin term *servus* meant slave, whereas the Italian word *servo* was increasingly used in relation to 'free' servants; in relation to unfree servants, the term *schiavo* was used, a term that originally was an adjective referring to people from the Slavic regions).[35]

According to De Luca, another kind of personal passive servitude was that of a free person who was forced to perform some service for a master. He or she could be forced to work because of a contract (*locatio operarum*, in Italian 'contratto di locazione delle sue opere') and, in this case, according to De Luca, his or her condition was legally called, in Italian, *famulato* (in Latin *famulus* meant servant). Terms such as *famulo*, *famiglio* and *familiare* were certainly used in Italian, yet servants who served on a contractual basis were defined in many other ways, too. De Luca added that an individual could be forced to render some services to a master also because of the 'quality' (i.e. the 'status') of the master himself. Such was the case of the servitude of children towards their fathers, or that of vassals towards their lords.[36] De Luca's definition was extremely wide and ambiguous: servants, slaves, children and vassals were all involved in some kind of servitude. Furthermore, he considered the members of the regular clergy (monks, friars, nuns) similar to servants because, if they acquired something, it belonged not to them but to their monasteries.[37]

---

34   Pasciuta, '"Homines aut liberi sunt aut servi"'.
35   Grégoire, *De la domesticité*, p. 26 and Luigi Cibrario, *Della schiavitù e del servaggio e specialmente dei servi agricoltori* (Milan, 1868), vol. 1, p. 2; Charles Verlinden, 'L'origine de *sclavus* = esclave', *Archivium Latinitatis Medii Aevi*, 17 (1942), 97–128; Charles Verlinden, *L'esclavage dans l'Europe médiévale*, vol. 2 (Bruges, 1977), pp. 797–8 and 999–1010 (annexe I: Encore sur les origines de *sclavus* = esclave); Didier Bondue, *De «Servus» à «Sclavus». La fin de l'esclavage antique (371–918)* (Paris, 2011).
36   Giovanni Battista De Luca, *Il Dottor Volgare*, vol. 4 (Rome, 1673), pp. 7–25.
37   *Ibid.*, p. 16.

Other authors, too, distinguished different types of servant and, while trying to elaborate comprehensive classifications, included under the heading of *servo* (or similar ones) people ranging from slaves to the pope, *Servus servorum dei* (the servant of God's servants). As recalled by several authors, according to the Gospel, Christ came 'not to be served, but to serve' (Matthew 20:28; Mark 10:45). 'Although in ancient times the title of "servant" was disgraceful, once it had been assumed by Christ himself it became very honoured', don Pio Rossi (1581–1667) claimed, and this was the reason why it was used by the pope, too.[38] Rossi argued that even the king should be a servant, providing a representation that is often seen as an eighteenth-century elaboration, but was actually already present in ancient times: 'The good Prince', who was 'entrusted with the wellbeing of his people, must serve all of his subjects'.[39]

Such an extended and blurred notion of servant might appear confusing to our eyes. It created problems and conflicts in early modern times, too.[40] Yet, it was consistent with the *Weltanschauung* prevalent in early modern European societies, which generally represented themselves as networks of people involved in dependency and service relationships. Almost everybody might be considered a servant. However, this did not imply that all those who might be defined as servants were equal – rather the opposite, as inequality was at the very core of most early modern societies.[41]

No longer slaves? Slavery and European identity

Slaves were often presented as a case of extreme dependency within a wide range of 'species of servitude'. At the same time, many authors argued that slavery, widespread in the past, was extinct or uncommon in their times: 'And even if such a species of servitude [i.e. slavery] is dealt with very frequently in Roman civil laws, nonetheless in our times it is in practice very rare', De Luca wrote in the seventeenth century.[42] Several authors, however, admitted that slaves continued to exist. Piccolomini argued that it was not convenient for a Christian to serve another Christian beyond what he voluntarily undertook to

38 Pio Rossi, *Convito morale*, vol. 1 (Venice, 1639), p. 433.
39 *Ibid.* Rossi wrote that Agamemnon thought that he was a servant and slave of his vassals. According to Seneca, *De clementia*, I, 8, 1: *ista* [= the role of the emperor] *servitus est, non imperium*.
40 Sarti, 'Who are Servants?'
41 Sarti, *Servo e padrone*, vol. 1, *passim*; Sarti, 'Who are Servants?' A similar point is made by George Boulukos, 'Social Liberty and Social Death: Conceiving of Slavery beyond the Black Atlantic', in Srividhya Swaminathan and Adam R. Beach (ed.), *Invoking Slavery in the Eighteenth-Century British Imagination* (Farnham–Burlington, 2013), pp. 175–90.
42 De Luca, *Il Dottor Volgare*, vol. 4, p. 12.

do, but he acknowledged that a custom similar to the ancient one was followed 'among us with barbarous people of a religion other than ours', such as Tartars, Moors and Turks, 'whom we sometimes buy for our service'.[43]

Interestingly, according to the 1454 version of the Statutes of the city of Bologna, in force until 1796, having and keeping male and female slaves from the Slavic lands, the land of the Tartars and other overseas places was allowed.[44] As early as 1256 Bologna had abolished slavery and freed serfs.[45] Yet explicit exceptions to the prohibition of slavery and of personal dependency had been foreseen by the Statutes in the fourteenth century,[46] as also happened in other cities, such as Florence.[47] However, the places of origin of slaves changed, if compared with those mentioned in the Bologna Statutes. The year before the publication of the 1454 version, the Turks had conquered Constantinople and soon after took possession of the Genoese and Venetian colonies on the Black Sea. This reduced the slave trade from the East, which was compensated by increasing imports of slaves from Africa to Italy (this lasted until the mid–late sixteenth century, when the Atlantic slave trade absorbed most of the African flow), and by 'Turks' captured by pirates and corsairs, and during wars.[48]

In 1673, De Luca argued that in his times a Christian was not allowed to keep a fellow Christian as a slave; thus, in Europe, soldiers captured in wars no longer became the slaves of the winners; rather, they were prisoners of war. It was different for Turks captured in wars or by corsairs: they became slaves, and were then mainly employed as rowers on galleys or (less frequently) as

43   Piccolomini, *Della institution morale*, p. 523.

44   Filippo Carlo Sacco, *Statuta Civilia et Criminalia Civitatis Bononiae*, vol. 1 (Bologna, 1735), p. 508. Giuliana Vitale, 'Servi e padroni nella Napoli del XV secolo', *Prospettive Settanta*, n.s., 10 (1988), 306–32, here 326, mentioned a similar case.

45   Armando Antonelli (ed.), *Il "Liber Paradisus" con un'antologia di fonti bolognesi in materia di servitù medievale (942–1304)* (Venice, 2007); Armando Antonelli and Massimo Giansante (eds), *Il "Liber Paradisus" e le liberazioni collettive nel XIII secolo: cento anni di studi (1906–2008)* (Venice, 2008).

46   The possibility of having Slavic slaves and slaves from oversea countries was probably introduced in the Bologna statutes in 1376, the reference to Tartars in 1454. Besides the 1454 Statutes, I checked the following: Archivio di Stato di Bologna, *Governo del Comune, Statuti*, vol. 10 (1335); vol. 11 (1352); vol. 12 (1357); vol. 13 (1376, c. 245v); vol. 14 (1389, c. 318).

47   In Florence a decree of 6 August 1289 forbade serfdom, whereas a decree dated 2 March 1363 permitted the importation of foreign slaves, provided they were not Christians: see Agostino Zanelli, *Le serve orientali a Firenze nei secoli XIV e XV* (Florence, 1885), pp. 24, 64; Iris Origo, 'The Domestic Enemy: The Eastern Slaves in Tuscany in the Fourteenth and Fifteenth Centuries', *Speculum*, 30 (1955), 321–66, here 324, 335; Samuela Marconcini, 'Una presenza nascosta: battesimi di "turchi" a Firenze in età moderna', *Annali di Storia di Firenze*, 7 (2012), 97–121, here 109.

48   Bono, *Schiavi*; Raffaella Sarti, 'Bolognesi schiavi dei "Turchi" e schiavi "turchi" a Bologna tra Cinque e Settecento tra Cinque e Settecento: alterità etnico-religiosa e riduzione in schiavitù', *Quaderni storici*, 36 (2001), 437–73, with further references.

household servants.[49] The role of Christian religion in making slavery rare was stressed by many authors. Piccolomini had argued that Italians ruled over their slaves at their will only until the latter became Christians.[50] Similarly, Tommasi had stressed the difference between the ancient Greeks, Romans and Muslims, on the one hand, and Christians on the other. According to the first, only the master could decide to free a slave, whereas, thanks to the Christian religion, all human beings were acknowledged to be free and made confident in the freedom granted by Christ our saviour. More pious than other religions, Christianity tolerated the slavery of infidels captured by Christians, yet only until these infidels converted to Christianity or were able to buy their freedom, thus becoming free again.[51]

Interestingly, already some sixteenth-century European authors described the presence of slaves in their societies as uncommon and considered the absence or scarcity of slaves as a feature that distinguished their civilisation from the ancient and from contemporary people whom they considered as barbarous and/or infidel. Furthermore, they presented slavery with Christian owners as less severe than other forms, thanks to the possibility for slaves to be freed as a consequence of conversion or self-liberation. However, not every author considered slavery in Europe as a rare phenomenon or an 'easy' condition. For instance, Paolo Caggio – perhaps because he lived earlier (he died in 1562) and was a Sicilian – spoke of slaves as a usual possession and a useful presence in a household.[52] While many studies have shown that slaves were numerous in sixteenth-century Sicily,[53] the descriptions of slavery as a marginal condition elsewhere in Italy are not confirmed by historical research: slaves have turned out to be present more or less everywhere, although they were generally not

49   De Luca, *Il Dottor Volgare*, vol. 4, pp. 13–14.
50   Piccolomini, *Della institution morale*, p. 523.
51   Tommasi, *Reggimento*, p.194.
52   Paolo Caggio, *Iconomica* (Venice, 1562), pp. 41–7.
53   Antonio Franchina, 'Un censimento di schiavi nel 1565', *Archivio Storico Siciliano*, n.s., 32 (1907), 374–420; Matteo Gaudioso, *La schiavitù in Sicilia dopo i Normanni* (Catania, 1926); Giovanni Marrone, *La schiavitù nella società siciliana dell'età moderna* (Caltanisetta–Rome, 1972); Rossella Cancila, 'Corsa e pirateria nella Sicilia della prima età moderna', *Quaderni storici*, 36 (2001), 363–78; Giovanna Fiume, *Il santo moro: i processi di canonizzazione di Benedetto da Palermo (1594–1807)* (Milan, 2002); Giuseppe Bonaffini, 'Corsari schiavi siciliani nel Mediterraneo (secoli XVIII–XIX)', *Cahiers de la Méditerranée*, 65 (2002), 301–10; Maria Sofia Messana, 'La "resistenza" musulmana e i "martiri" dell'islam: moriscos, schiavi e cristiani rinnegati di fronte all'inquisizione spagnola di Sicilia', *Quaderni storici*, 42 (2007), 743–72; Antonino Giuffrida, 'La legislazione siciliana sulla schiavitù (1310–1812). Da Arnaldo Villanova al consultore Troysi', in Alessandro Musco (ed.), *I Francescani e la politica. Atti del Convegno internazionale di studio, Palermo 3–7 Dicembre 2002* (Palermo, 2007), pp. 543–59.

numerous.[54] The difference between Caggio's comments and those by other authors cannot be explained only by regional differences.

The importance attributed to Christianity in making slavery rare supports the idea that many narratives were ideological and did not mirror social practices. Conversions, in particular, did not play the role suggested by Piccolomini and Tommasi. Rather, things were more or less as De Luca outlined in the late seventeenth century: slavery was forbidden among Christians. This meant that capturing Christians was forbidden. Capturing infidels was allowed. Infidel slaves who converted to the Christian religion would remain slaves.[55] Furthermore, in some circumstances (not mentioned by De Luca) native Christians, too, might be enslaved.[56] Orthodox Christians subject to Ottoman rule could be captured and kept as slaves; in 1674, the year after the publication of De Luca's work, the city authorities of Rome allowed people to buy Orthodox Christian slaves.[57] East-European Christians, even Catholics from Poland, captured and trafficked by Tatars and Turks, might arrive in Italy as slaves: in 1628, after requests by the king of Poland to the king of Spain, in the Kingdom of Naples, then under Spanish rule, the trading of Polish slaves was forbidden.[58] Christians enslaved as rowers by the Ottomans might be kept in slave-like conditions when Western Europeans captured the ships where they served; in theory, this was illegal, but galley slaves might not be able to claim their freedom before a tribunal and/or demonstrate their religion.[59]

54   Bono, *Schiavi*; Bono, *Schiavi musulmani*.
55   De Luca, *Il Dottor Volgare*, vol. 4, pp. 18–19. In my article 'Bolognesi schiavi' (see footnote 48), written when research on conversion was scarce, I tentatively suggested that conversions that took place in the so-called Case dei Catecumeni (institutions encouraging conversion), especially in the Papal State, might imply liberation. Later studies have not confirmed my hypothesis, even though some slaves believed that they would be freed after converting: see Marina Caffiero, 'Battesimi, libertà e frontiere. Conversioni di musulmani e ebrei a Roma in età moderna', in Giovanna Fiume (ed.), *Schiavitù e conversioni nel Mediterraneo*, special issue of *Quaderni storici*, 42 (2007), 821–41; Pietro Ioly Zorattini, *I nomi degli altri. Conversioni a Venezia e nel Friuli Veneto in età moderna* (Florence, 2008), p. 33; Peter A. Mazur, 'Combating "Mohammedan Indecency": The Baptism of Muslim Slaves in Spanish Naples, 1563–1667', *Journal of Early Modern History*, 13 (2009), 25–48; Marconcini, 'Una presenza nascosta', 110; Peter A. Mazur, *Conversion to Catholicism in Early Modern Italy* (New York–London 2016), p. 35; Marina Caffiero, 'Non solo schiavi. La presenza dei musulmani a Roma in età moderna: il lavoro di un gruppo di ricerca', in Sara Cabibbo and Alessandro Serra (eds), *Venire a Roma, restare a Roma. Forestieri e stranieri fra quattro e settecento* (Rome 2017), pp. 291–314.
56   Sarti, 'Bolognesi schiavi'; Bono, *Schiavi*, pp. 53–4.
57   Wipertus Rudt de Collenberg, 'Le baptême des musulmans esclaves à Rome aux XVIIᵉ et XVIIIᵉ siècles', *Mélanges de l'École française de Rome*, 101 (1989), 9–181, 519–670, here 537.
58   Ginesio Grimaldi, *Istoria delle leggi e magistrati del Regno di Napoli*, vol. 10 (Naples, 1772), p. 470.
59   Sarti, 'Bolognesi schiavi'; Bono, *Schiavi*, p. 53.

Inconsistencies between representations of Europeans as the protectors of personal liberty and the acknowledgement of the presence of slaves in Europe can be found later and elsewhere, too. In the eighteenth century the heading *domestiques* in the French *Encyclopédie* stated that in France there were no slaves, and that all servants were free.[60] On the contrary, the heading *esclave*, after claiming that 'at the present time all individuals are free', described legislation that, from 1716 onwards, allowed slaves from the colonies to be brought to France and kept as slaves.[61] Furthermore, under the heading *galérien* (convicts condemned to work as rowers on galleys), slaves popped up as an obvious presence: when 'the convicts are brought to the harbours, they are divided into crews with the slaves',[62] the author M. Durival junior explained. Only at the very end of the entry did he explain that the *galérien* were criminals condemned according to the law, whereas the slaves were 'men captured during the wars against the infidels'. Durival claimed that, 'according to the rights of war, they should be considered prisoners, but we reduce them into a kind of slavery because of our right to retaliation'.[63]

Similarly, in Britain, the jurist William Blackstone (1723–1780), in his *Commentaries on the Laws of England* (1765–1770), observed that 'pure and proper slavery does not, nay cannot, subsist in England', such that 'an absolute and unlimited power is given to the master over the life and fortune of the slave'. He made it clear that 'now it is laid down, that a slave or negro, the instant he lands in England, becomes a freeman; that is, the law will protect him in the enjoyment of his person, his liberty, and his property'.[64] However, in England there were slaves brought from the colonies without becoming free as soon as they breathed the English air. A first important step against slavery in Britain would be made only in 1772, with the well-known sentence by Lord

60   [Antoine-Gaspard Boucher d'Argis], 'Domestiques', in *Encyclopédie, ou Dictionnaire raisonné des sciences, des arts et des métiers*, vol. 5 (Paris, 1755), p. 29.

61   [Antoine-Gaspard Boucher d'Argis], 'Esclave', in *Encyclopédie*, vol. 5, pp. 939–43. France's most important court, the Paris *Parlement*, did not register the measures of 1716 and 1738; thus, the only valid rule within its jurisdiction was the old free-soil principle. From the 1750s, people of African origin who petitioned for their freedom before the court of Paris's Admiralty were freed: see Peabody, *There Are no Slaves*.

62   M. Durival, 'Galérien', in *Enciclopédie*, vol. 7 (Paris, 1757), p. 445.

63   *Ibid.* See also André Zysberg, *Les galériens: Vies et destins de 60 000 forçats sur les galères de France (1680–1748)* (Paris, 1991); Gillian Weiss, 'Infidels at the Oar: A Mediterranean Exception to France's Free Soil Principle', *Slavery & Abolition*, 32 (2011), 397–412.

64   William Blackstone, *Commentaries on the Laws of England*, vol. I (Oxford, 1765), chapter 14, p. 411. See also p. 123: 'And this spirit of liberty is so deeply implanted in our constitution, and rooted even in our very soil, that a slave or a Negro, the moment he lands in England, falls under the protection of the laws, and with regard to all natural rights becomes *eo instanti* a freeman.'

Mansfield.[65] Blackstone, besides arguing that proper slavery could not exist in Britain, rejected slavery, stating 'And indeed it is repugnant to reason, and the principles of natural law, that such a state should subsist anywhere.'[66] Yet, interestingly, he admitted the existence of something that we cannot define as other than slavery in an ambiguous passage where he spoke of people bound to perpetual service 'by contract or the like'. Blackstone reconciled the rejection of slavery with the legitimation of uninterrupted perpetual service by presuming that a valid contract or something similar to a contract existed between a (former?) slave and his master, stressing the similarities between such contract and that of an apprentice:

> And now it is laid down, that a slave or negro, the instant he lands in England, becomes a freeman; that is, the law will protect him in the enjoyment of his person, his liberty, and his property. Yet, with regard to any right which the master may have acquired, by contract or the like, to the perpetual service of John or Thomas, this will remain exactly in the same state as before: for this is no more than the same state of subjection for life, which every apprentice submits to for the space of seven years, or sometimes for a longer term.[67]

Again, on the one hand there was a general discourse rejecting slavery, while on the other the rejection was not really effective: discourses on slavery show the gap between early modern Europeans' representation of their civilisation and their practices, even though their notions of freedom might be rather different from ours[68] and the distinction between free and unfree people far from clear-cut.

Slaves, apprentices, villains, servants, labourers

Like other scholars, Blackstone viewed slavery as both radically distinguished from and ambiguously associated with other types of service/servitude. Apprentices, with whom Blackstone associated the 'perpetual service' of

---

65   William M. Wiecek, 'Somerset: Lord Mansfield and the Legitimacy of Slavery in the Anglo-American World', *The University of Chicago Law Review*, 42 (1974), 86–146; Carolyn Steedman, 'Lord Mansfield's Women', *Past and Present*, 176 (2002), 105–43; Andrew Lyall, *Granville Sharp's Cases on Slavery* (Oxford–London, 2017).

66   Blackstone, *Commentaries*, p. 411.

67   *Ibid*. Blackstone made his initial statements even more ambiguous in later editions: see Folarin O. Shyllon, *Black Slaves in Britain* (Oxford, 1974), pp. 59, 65–6, 76; Edlie L. Wong, *Neither Fugitive nor Free: Atlantic Slavery, Freedom Suits, and the Legal Culture of Travel* (New York–London, 2009), pp. 40–1; Lyall, *Granville Sharp's Cases*, pp. 38–42.

68   Steinfeld, *The Invention*, p. 4; Douglas Hay and Paul Craven, *Masters, Servants, and Magistrates in Britain and the Empire, 1562–1955* (Chapel Hill, 2004), p. 5.

(former?) slaves, were one of the four 'sorts of servants' which he distinguished after stressing that 'pure and proper slavery' could not exist in England.
According to his classification, 'the first sort of servants (...) acknowledged by
the laws of England' were 'menial servants; so called from being *intra moenia*,
or domestics', generally hired for a year. 'Another species of servants' – he
wrote – 'are called apprentices (from *apprendre*, to learn) and are usually bound
for a term of years, by deed indented or indentures, to serve their masters, and
be maintained and instructed by them.' 'This is usually done', he continued,
'to persons of trade, in order to learn their art and mystery; and sometimes
very large sums are given with them, as a premium for such their instruction.'
'A third species of servants are labourers, who are only hired by the day or the
week, and do not live *intra moenia*, as part of the family.' Finally, he mentioned
'a fourth species of servants, if they may be so called being rather in a superior,
a ministerial, capacity; such as stewards, factors, and bailiffs: whom however
the law considers as servants *pro tempore*, with regard to such of their acts, as
affect their master's or employer's property'.[69]

That there were no longer slaves in England and that foreign slaves became
free as soon as they landed on its shores had also been written, a century before
Blackstone, by Edward Chamberlayne (1616–1703) in his *Angliae Notitia, or
The Present State of England* (first published anonymously in 1669 and then
republished several times). 'Foreign Slaves in *England* are none, since Christianity
prevailed. A Forreign Slave brought into *England*, is, upon Landing, *ipso facto*
free from Slavery, but not from ordinary Service', Chamberlayne wrote, without
giving more details about what he meant by ordinary service (perhaps perpetual
service, as in Blackstone's view).[70] When Chamberlayne wrote his work, slaves
who entered England were probably less numerous than in Blackstone's times,
since England's involvement in the slave trade grew significantly from the late
seventeenth century.[71] Like Blackstone, Chamberlayne dealt with slavery while
speaking of different kinds of servant: after noting that servants' conditions had
improved since the time when England was considered to be 'the Purgatory of
Servants', he explained that 'ordinary Servants are hired commonly for one year,
at the end whereof they may be free (giving warning three months before)'. It
was considered 'indiscreet to take a Servant without Certificate of his diligence
and of his faithfulness' by his former master. Servants were to be corrected by
their masters and mistresses and resistance was 'punished with severe penalty';
killing one's master was 'accounted as a Crime next to High Treason'.[72]

69 Blackstone, *Commentaries*, pp. 413–15.
70 Edward Chamberlayne, *Angliae Notitia, or The Present State of England* (London,
1676), p. 299.
71 See http://www.slavevoyages.org/assessment/estimates; William A. Pettigrew, *Freedom's
Debt: The Royal African Company and the Politics of the Atlantic Slave Trade, 1672–1752*
(Chapel Hill, 2013), pp. 11–12.
72 Chamberlayne, *Angliae Notitia*, p. 299.

In the same chapter, entitled 'On Servants', he also discussed villeinage: 'some lands in *England* are holden in *Villanage*, to do some particulars Services, to the Lord of the Mannor, and such Tenants may be called the Lords Servants'. He then explained that

> there is a two-fold Tenure called *Villanage*, one where the Tenure onely is Servile, as to plough the Lords Ground, sow, reap, and bring home his Corn, dung his Land, &tc. The other, whereby both the Person and Tenure is servile, and bound in all respects, at the disposition of the Lord; such persons are called in Law, *Pure Villains*, and are to do all Villanous Services.

He concluded that 'of such there are now but few left in England',[73] and then described what he presented as the 'the nearest to this condition', which were apprentices. These were 'a sort of pure Villains or Bond-slaves', but differed in that 'Apprentices are Slaves, onely for a time, and by Covenant; the other are so, at the will of their Master.'[74] While Blackstone no longer mentioned villains among servants, listing labourers instead, both he and Chamberlayne associated apprentices and slaves, which might appear surprising to a contemporary sensibility. The harsh conditions of apprentices, in fact, surprised some travellers even in early modern times. Europeans from different countries had peculiar perceptions of the differences in the freedom enjoyed by (different kinds of) servants in different European nations.

The perception of internal differences in Europe

The Italian historian and satirist Gregorio Leti (1630–1701), in his work *Del Teatro Brittanico* (1683), among many other aspects of English life, commented on the condition of servants. Leti's main source was precisely Chamberlayne's *Angliae Notitia*: he translated some parts almost literally, adapted others and added his own views, explanations of words and concepts that might have been obscure to Italians, and comparisons with Italy and France. He claimed that female and male servants' condition in England, in the past described as their purgatory, had improved and was as elsewhere. Servants were normally hired for a year and could leave their masters (or be dismissed) only after serving the entire agreed period and giving notice three months in advance. Before being hired, they should present a certificate from their previous masters. Thanks to this custom, English masters trusted their servants more than the French and Italians. Servants were thus better protected by their masters. Furthermore, their wages were higher than in Italy and France. Yet they were forced to work

73   *Ibid.*, pp. 299–300.
74   *Ibid.*, p. 300.

very hard, and were punished harshly if they were insolent or disobedient; killing one's master or mistress was punished as if it were treason against the state. While in the past the use of slaves had been widespread, it had disappeared a long time before; and, according to Christian customs, foreign slaves became free as soon as they landed on English shores, despite remaining bound to ordinary service. In his view, the condition of some peasants called villeins (*villani*) was truly servile, to the extent that they should be called servants (*servidori*) rather than tenants (*affituali*). Such a condition was truly unhappy, as it was impossible to consider the condition of perpetual servitude as happy. A similar condition was that of apprentices, which Leti considered a truly servile one. Yet, while villains experienced long-life bondage, apprentices were normally bound for seven years or even less, depending on their contracts.[75]

While Leti was surprised at the servile conditions of English villeins, the English Dr Moore, in his *View of Society and Manners in Italy* (1781), published about a century after Leti's *Teatro Brittanico*, maintained that

> Though the inhabitants of the Italian Cities were the first who shook off the feudal yoke, and though in Naples they have long enjoyed the privilege of municipal jurisdiction, yet the external splendour of the nobles, and the authority they still exercise over the peasants, impose upon the minds of the *lazzaroni*; and however bold and resentful they may be of injuries offered by others, they bear the insolence of the nobility as passively as peasants fixed to the soil. A coxcomb of a *volanti* [the volante was a kind of servant] tricked out in his fantastical dress, or any of the liveried slaves of the great, make no ceremony of treating these poor fellows with all the insolence and insensibility natural to their masters; and for no visible reason, but because he is dressed in lace, and the others in rags. Instead of calling to them to make way, when the noise in the streets prevents the common people from hearing the approach of the carriage, a stroke across the shoulders with the cane of the running footman, is the usual warning they receive. Nothing animates this people to insurrection, but some very pressing and very universal cause; such as a scarcity of bread.[76]

In his view, the Neapolitan poor were similar to serfs (peasants tied to the soil) even though Italian cities had abolished serfdom early. Furthermore, he mentioned the presence of slaves, both in the previous passage and while speaking of the construction of the royal palace in Caserta:

---

75 Gregorio Leti, *Del Teatro Brittanico*, vol. 1 (London, 1683), pp. 454–6; Raffaella Sarti, '"The Purgatory of Servants": (In)subordination, Wages, Gender and Marital Status of Servants in England and Italy in the Seventeenth and Eighteenth centuries', *Journal of Early Modern Studies*, 4 (2015), 349–51.
76 John Moore, *A View of Society and Manners in Italy*, vol. 2 (London, 1781), pp. 164–5.

Among the workmen employed in finishing this palace and the gardens, there are one hundred and fifty Africans; for as the King of Naples is constantly at war with the Barbary States, he always has a number of their sailors prisoners, all of whom are immediately employed as slaves in the gallies, or at some public work.[77]

Interestingly, he used the term slave also in relation to people condemned to forced labour:

There are at present at Casserta, about the same number of Christian slaves; all of these have been condemned to this servitude for some crime, some of them for the greatest of all crimes; they are, however, better clothed and fed than the Africans. This is done, no doubt, in honour of the Christian religion, and to demonstrate that Christians, even after they have been found guilty of the blackest crimes, are worthier men, and more deserving of lenity, than Mahometan prisoners, however innocent they may be in all other respects.[78]

In summary, Moore dealt with serfdom, abolished without leading to a substantial improvement of the condition of the poor, as well as with domestic servants, including slaves; with African slaves employed in services other than domestic, and even with 'Christian slaves', a definition that might seem inconsistent with many triumphant speeches on the role of Christianity in the abolition of slavery.

That slavery and serfdom were two components of the same category had been argued in 1755 by the heading *Esclavage* of the *Encyclopédie*, too: 'there are two types of slavery or servitude, the real and the personal one'. The real one, according to the heading, tied the slave (*esclave*) to the soil, the personal one referred to household management and to the person of the master. The more abusive slavery was that which was both real and personal.[79] Slavery (*esclavage*) had been abolished in most of Europe in the fifteenth century, yet too many survivals of slavery still existed in Poland, Hungary, Bohemia and several places in low Germany, and in some small way even in French customs.[80] What we would probably define as serfdom was included in the heading about slavery.[81]

While opinion on the differences between types of servant and slave existing in different European countries changed over time, the persistence of feudal forms of dependence was still stressed, for instance, by Mittre in 1837: in his

---

77   *Ibid.*, p. 305.
78   *Ibid.*
79   Louis de Jaucourt, 'Esclavage', *Encyclopédie*, vol. 5, pp. 934–9, here p. 934.
80   *Ibid.*, p. 936. See also [Boucher D'Argis], 'Esclave', p. 940.
81   Rebekka von Mallinckrodt, 'There are no Slaves in Prussia?' in Brahm and Rosenhaft (eds), *Slavery Hinterland*, pp. 109–32, p. 115 argued that in the Holy Roman Empire 'the debate about the abolition of slavery and the dispute over the elimination of serfdom were interconnected'.

view, French masters and servants were freer than English ones to part company (*de se quitter réciproquement*), even though English norms were not always respected. The opposite happened in 'the Northern countries', Austria and Prussia, where feudal distinctions remained strong.[82]

Some decades earlier, it was exactly the freedom to leave one's master that had been presented by the *Encyclopédie* as the distinctive feature of free servants in comparison with slaves: 'In France, where there are no slaves, all servants (*domestiques*) are free'; they could leave their masters when they wanted. When they broke their contracts, masters could only claim compensation for damages, although some exceptions to this rule existed.[83] Conversely, English servants could be imprisoned for breach of contract, because it was a criminal offence. Yet, according to the English, this did not affect personal freedom as long as people entered service voluntarily. While the French *Encyclopédie* stressed the freedom to leave one's master as the distinguishing feature of free servants, in England the freedom to enter service, rather than to leave, was seen as crucial.[84]

In England, to the surprise of some French commentators, there were also people forced to serve. Domestic service implies 'a contract between two free people', Abbot Grégoire wrote in 1814. 'Nevertheless, in England, there are cases where the law seems to curb freedom, since some people can be forced to enter service; but this is a barrier that the policy maker thought he had to erect against laziness.'[85] As Blackstone explained, rehearsing the measures of the Statute of Artificers (1563), which repeated those of Statute of Labourers (1351), and which are known to have been enforced well into the eighteenth century: 'All single men between twelve years old and sixty, and married ones under thirty years of age, and all single women between twelve and forty, not having any visible livelihood, are compellable by two justices to go out to service, for the promotion of honest industry.'[86] In fact, norms forcing people to serve in order to reduce vagrancy and and/or to guarantee (unpaid or low cost) manpower to feudal lords, farmers and others existed in several European countries,[87] thus contributing to blurring boundaries among different types of serving people.[88]

82 Marius-Henri-Casimir Mittre, *Des domestiques en France* (Paris–Versailles, 1837), 203–4.
83 [Boucher D'Argis], 'Domestiques', p. 29. In France, there were some laws, only partly enforced, limiting the servants' freedom to leave: see Sarti, 'Freedom', pp. 8–9.
84 Steinfeld, *The Invention*, pp. 96–7.
85 Grégoire, *De la domesticité*, p. 178.
86 Blackstone, *Commentaries*, p. 413.
87 See the chapters on England, the Low Countries, Denmark, Norway, Sweden and Iceland in this volume.
88 See also Sarti, 'Freedom'.

Conclusion

This essay has outlined how early modern writers perceived, described and classified what we today define slaves, serfs and servants, or free and unfree servants both in their own countries and in other European ones. It has offered examples from different places, periods and cultures showing that slaves were generally described as part of larger categories of different serving people: in some cases, such categories were so large that almost anybody could be included in them. This did not imply that all those who were included were considered equal, or that differences among them were overlooked: rather the opposite.

The essay has mainly concentrated on the classification of slaves and servants and on the features associated with them. In most texts there is no simple dualistic opposition between free and unfree servants: rather, slaves are considered one kind of servant within a wide range of cases. It would be interesting to analyse how such categories were used, for instance in court cases,[89] and how people in their everyday life suffered, used, manipulated and challenged the labels of slave, servant or serf.[90] Yet such endeavours lie beyond the scope of this essay, which focuses on categories found in books.

As for the absence of slaves, it was seen as a distinctive feature of more civilised people. This implied ignoring or minimising the slaves' actual presence, or resorting to inconsistent arguments to reconcile the rejection of slavery in principle with its acceptance and/or justification in practice. In the *Encyclopédie*, the heading *esclavage* denounced that 'almost in the space of the century following the abolition of slavery in Europe, the Christian powers, having conquered different countries, allowed the buying and selling of humans in those countries where they thought it was advantageous to them to have slaves, ... forgetting the principles of Nature and Christianity, which make all men equal'.[91] In many cases, such 'forgetfullness' led to inconsistent statements. According to Leti, for instance, 'peoples of Holland enjoy a liberty, which any republic in the world has never had a greater'.

'Holland', he wrote,

> does not bear slaves nor bought servants, and when a gentleman who has a slave enters the lands of Holland [the slave] is immediately understood to be frank, and free, and the right of the master above him is void, being [the

---

89   For instance, Rebekka von Mallinckrodt, 'Verhandelte (Un-)Freiheit. Sklaverei, Leibeigenschaft und innereuropäischer Wissenstransfer am Ausgang des 18. Jahrhunderts', *Geschichte und Gesellschaft*, 43 (2017), 347–80.

90   Raffaella Sarti, 'The True Servant. Self-definition of Male Domestics in an Italian City (Bologna, 17th–19th Centuries)', *The History of the Family*, 10 (2005), 407–33; Sarti, *Servo e padrone*, pp. 89–154; Raffaella Sarti, 'Le "nom de domestique" est un "mot vague". Débats parlementaires sur la domesticité pendant la Révolution française', *Mélanges de l'École française de Rome. Italie et Méditerranée modernes et contemporaines*, no. 131/1 (2019), 39–52.

91   De Jaucourt, 'Esclavage', p. 936.

slave] able to go at his pleasure or remain free in Holland without fear of any violence, and the master will lose the servant, and the money with which he has bought it.

At the same time, he described the Dutch slave trade in detail, complaining that – because of inhuman treatment – at least half the Africans transported on Dutch ships normally died during the passage, which reduced the trade's profitability. He defined the Africans as unhappy but seemed to consider it natural that they were enslaved; nor did he apparently perceive any inconsistency between the Dutch love for freedom and their engagement in the slave trade.[92]

In fact, things were even more complex than denounced by the French *Encyclopédie*. Christians allowed slavery not only in their colonies. In some European contexts, from the Middle Ages to the nineteenth century, slavery was never abolished;[93] in others, as shown above, there were laws allowing the import of slaves, be it medieval Bologna or eighteenth-century France; in others still, the import of slaves, though forbidden, was tolerated, thus creating ambiguous situations, as in England and Holland. Most authors were rather reticent to recognise that there were slaves in early modern Europe. Yet they spoke of slaves and did not simply contrast their condition with that of free people. Rather, they suggested that there might be several ranks of dependence and freedom, as was actually the case in most contexts.

92 Gregori Leti, *Teatro Belgico. Parte Seconda* (Amsterdam, 1690), pp. 29–30, 310–11. The situation of slaves arriving in Holland was less fortunate than argued by Leti; see Dienke Hondius, 'Access to the Netherlands of Enslaved and Free Black Africans: Exploring Legal and Social Historical Practices in the Sixteenth–Nineteenth centuries', *Slavery & Abolition*, 32 (2011), 377–95.
93 Sarti, 'Tramonto'; Giuffrida, 'La legislazione'.

5

The Servant, the Law and the State: Servant Law in Denmark–Norway, c.1600–1800

HANNE ØSTHUS[1]

On 11 March 1777 the servant Sibilla Christensdatter Hæg was interviewed by the chief of police in Oslo. Sibilla had complained to the police that her master, the merchant Hans Frederich Holmboe, had dismissed her illegally. According to the law, a servant in Oslo in the late eighteenth century could leave service on only two specific dates during the year,[2] but Sibilla had been turned out on a different day. She therefore wanted compensation and asked to be paid maintenance for the time she had been without work as well as being awarded her full wages.[3] The police court, which ruled in the case four months later, disagreed. The dismissal was legal, according to the court, because Sibilla had violated paragraph 5 of the law, which gave masters the right to fire servants for 'stealing, drunkenness, insubordination or similar things'.[4] Specifically, the court claimed Sibilla had acted, in the words of the court, 'defiantly' towards her mistress and master. She was also faulted for being 'reckless' when minding her employer's two children, resulting in one child falling and hitting his head and the other being found with marks on his arm from Sibilla having grabbed him.[5] Sibilla partly disputed these claims, alleging that the first child had fallen and hit his head against a chair when she was forced to put him down on the

1   I would like to thank the participants of the workshop 'Labour Laws in Preindustrial Europe: The Coercion and Regulation of Wage Labour, c.1300–1850' (22 May 2020), particularly Charmian Mansell, Thijs Lambrecht, Hilde Sandvik, Vilhelm Vilhelmsson and Jane Whittle, for their valuable feedback.
2   Act of 3 December 1755, § 1 and 5.
3   Regional State Archive Oslo (hereafter SAO), Oslo police, minutes of the interrogations nr. I, 11 March 1777, pp. 124–6.
4   Act of 3 December 1755, § 5.
5   SAO, Oslo police court, minutes nr. 3, 12 June 1777, pp. 703–4.

floor in order to make up his cradle.[6] Yet, despite declaring the dismissal legal, the ruling was ambiguous: as she had requested, Sibilla was awarded her full wages. Furthermore, her master was fined for hiring Sibilla without checking her references, which the law stated that employers were obliged to do.[7]

As Sibilla's case reveals, servants and masters in Oslo in the 1770s were subject to legislation that stipulated when and how servants could enter and exit service. The law also required that employers issued references upon termination of the contract and demanded references upon hiring. In addition, the law provided rules for how servants and masters should solve potential conflicts. The decree that regulated all these issues in Oslo in 1777 was part of a larger body of laws, acts and ordinances that regulated service within the Danish–Norwegian state in the pre-industrial period. This chapter examines this legislation.

Previous research has mostly examined servant law from a local perspective or with present nation-states as a starting point.[8] Here, I investigate this body of law from the perspective of the seventeenth- and eighteenth-century Danish state. This state will be referred to as Denmark–Norway in this chapter. By taking Denmark–Norway as a starting point, I argue that we can both find connections and commonalities that go beyond today's national borders and identify local and regional idiosyncrasies. As demonstrated in other research, local demands were often addressed in discussions on how to regulate work through servant law.[9] By combining the perspective of the state with the perspective of a specific region or area we can see how different labour regimes and demands on labour interacted with both local and central servant

6   SAO, Oslo police, minutes nr. 1, 11 March 1777, pp. 124–6.
7   SAO, Oslo police, minutes nr. 3, 12 June 1777, pp. 703–4.
8   A. Faye Jacobsen, *Husbondret. Rettighetskulturer i Danmark 1750–1920* (Copenhagen, 2008); S. Sogner, 'The Legal Status of Servants in Norway from the Seventeenth to the Twentieth Century', in A. Fauve-Chamoux (ed.), *Domestic Service and the Formation of European Identity. Understanding the Globalization of Domestic Work, 16th to 21st Centuries* (Bern, 2004), pp. 175–87; H. Østhus, 'Contested Authority. Master and Servant in Copenhagen and Christiania, 1750–1850', unpublished PhD dissertation (European University Insititute Florence, 2013) looks at both Denmark and Norway, but there is very little on other geographical areas of the Danish state. This also applies to much research that looks at servant legislation primarily through the study of other topics, such as poverty, or on labour laws more generally.
9   Such arguments are less explicit in research on servant legislation, but more so in research on poverty, which often also deals with servant legislation. S. Dyrvik, 'Avgjerdsprosessen og aktørane bak det offentlege fattigstellet i Norge 1720–1760', in K.-G. Andersson (ed.), *Oppdaginga av fattigdomen. Sosial lovgivning i Norden på 1700-talet* (Oslo, 1983), pp. 109–84; G. Á. Gunnlaugsson, 'Fattigvården på Island under 1700-talet', in Andersson (ed.), *Oppdaginga av fattigdomen*, pp. 185–215; H. Róbertsdóttir, *Wool and Society. Manufacturing Policy, Economic Thought and Local Production in 18th-century Iceland* (Gothenburg, 2008).

legislation. The aim of this study is therefore to give a survey of the servant laws in the Danish kingdom during the seventeenth and the eighteenth centuries by examining common themes in the servant legislation as well as pointing out some differences between areas and over time.

Servant law affected many people: at least 10 per cent of the population in the European parts of Denmark–Norway worked as servants in the eighteenth century, and there were probably as many in the seventeenth century. Additionally, since service was primarily a position occupied by the young and unmarried, an even larger segment of the population had worked as a servant at one point in their life. This chapter is a study of legislation that affected servants, and not a survey of the implementation of that legislation. The time period, c.1600–1800, has been chosen because of the substantial number of servant laws that were issued during this period, particularly after the implementation of absolutism in 1660.

Servant law in Denmark–Norway

When Sibilla Christiansdatter Hæg went to court in Oslo in 1777, Denmark–Norway was a kingdom with changing borders and minor colonial claims. At the turn of the eighteenth century it included, in addition to Denmark and Norway,[10] Iceland and the Faeroe Islands in the Atlantic and the Duchies of Schleswig and Holstein in the Holy Roman Empire, the Caribbean island of St Thomas, the small port of Tranquebar on the Coromandel coast in south-east India and the fort Fredriksborg on the West African coast, controlled through a treaty with the kingdom of Fetu. At the end of the eighteenth century, the borders had changed somewhat: in the Caribbean, the islands of St Jan and St Croix were added to form the island group of the Danish West Indies. In Africa, five new forts were built, but some were also lost. In Asia, a trade station was set up in Serampore in Bengal under the name Fredriksnagore and the Nicobar Islands were claimed for the Danish king. In Europe, there was an attempt to recolonise Greenland, and the king sought to consolidate his power in Schleswig and Holstein, although the areas retained their particular status as duchies.

One way to seek control over this varied and changing area was through legislation, including legislation over labour. After the introduction of absolutism in 1660, the impetus for common legislation increased and came to fruition in 1683, when a law code for Denmark was issued. Poul Erik Olsen has contended that, in addition to the king, the Law Code was one of very few common

---

10   The borders of Denmark and Norway also changed, particularly in the seventeenth century.

features connecting an otherwise disparate state.[11] Five years later, in 1687, the Danish code was followed by the Norwegian Law Code. Despite being initially prepared by a separate law commission that was meant to revise earlier national Norwegian law codes, the Norwegian Law Code copied the Danish Law of 1683 in most respects.[12] Importantly in the context of this chapter, the sections and paragraphs dealing with servants in the Danish Law of 1683 and the Norwegian Law of 1687 are almost identical: the later Norwegian law largely copied the language of the earlier Danish version.[13]

In principle all inhabitants of Danish lands should have been subject to the king's law, although who an inhabitant was and what Danish lands were were both questioned and changing during the seventeenth and eighteenth centuries. The Norwegian Law Code of 1687 was valid in Norway and the Faroe Islands. The Danish Law Code of 1683 applied everywhere else, with exceptions for Greenlanders in Greenland and Tamils in Tranquebar.[14] In Holstein, under the Holy Roman Empire, Carolingian law applied. In Schleswig, the situation was different still. There, the medieval law of Jutland remained the valid law in general, but the Danish Law Code of 1683 was used in some areas. During the eighteenth century, however, the Danish Law Code and the law of Jutland were both increasingly replaced by Carolingian law.[15]

In Iceland the legal situation was also somewhat different. The medieval law book *Jónsbok*, which was in part modelled on a Norwegian Law Code from 1274, was never formally abandoned, but the Norwegian and Danish Law Codes partly came to replace it.[16] When it came to servant legislation it was less necessary to implement those law codes because an Icelandic ordinance issued in 1685 regulated service.[17] Its concurrence in time with the Danish and Norwegian Law Codes of the 1680s is interesting and, although there were differences, the Icelandic ordinance of 1685 laid out many of the same rules as the Danish and Norwegian Law Codes, most notably on hiring and firing and on the obligation to serve.[18] According to historian Hrefna Róbertsdóttir the act

---

11   P. E. Olsen, 'Kolonirigets organisering', in M. Bregnsbo (ed.), *Danmark. En kolonimagt* (Copenhagen, 2017), p. 201.

12   S. Dyrvik, *Truede tvillingriker, 1648–1720* (Oslo, 1998), pp. 295–303.

13   The Danish Law of 1683, hereafter DL, 3-19. The Norwegian Law of 1687, hereafter NL, 3–21. One telling difference is between the hiring days: DL 3-19-9 and NL 3-21-9. Hiring days continued to change from place to place and over time.

14   Olsen, 'Kolonirigets organisering', p. 201.

15   F. Thygesen, 'Danske Lovs indflydelse i hertugdømmet Slesvig', in D. Tamm (ed.), *Danske og Norske lov i 300 år* (Copenhagen, 1983), pp. 255–87. A servant law for both Holstein and Schleswig was issued by the Danish king in 1844.

16   P. Sigurðsson, 'Danske og Norske Lov i Island og de islandske kodifikationsplaner', in Tamm (ed.), *Danske og Norske lov i 300 år*, pp. 347–66.

17   Act of 2 April 1685.

18   Particular thanks to Vilhelm Vilhelmsson for pointing this out.

of 1685 was 'a response to a request ... from Copenhagen',[19] but formulated by officials in Iceland. As such it shows the interaction between the central power in Copenhagen and local elites and officials in Iceland.

Another example of the contact between local and central authorities on the development of labour and servant law can be found in Norway in the 1730s. At that time, the state actively elicited feedback from local civil servants on how to deal with poverty and what was framed as a shortage of servants.[20] Some of those civil servants sought advice from the peasantry and reported back to central authorities that the peasantry wanted stricter rules on service. The district judge in an area in south-east Norway, for example, reported that the public 'urgently asked' that the law be changed, that regulations on service should be tightened, and that vagrants should not be permitted to live in the countryside at all.[21]

In Iceland the 1685 decree was followed by a number of other decrees and acts in the late seventeenth and particularly in the eighteenth centuries, for example on obedience and order in the household, on compulsory service and on passports and mobility control.[22] Similarly, in other areas of Denmark–Norway a considerable number of decrees were issued to supplement or revise the rules given in the Law Codes of the 1680s. We can get an impression of the number by investigating two compilations of legal acts that were published in the late eighteenth and early nineteenth centuries. In both compilations, servants were grouped together with vagrants, a point I will return to later in this chapter when addressing laws on compulsory service. One of the compilations listed twenty-nine legal acts and decrees within the category 'servants and vagrants' just in the years between 1670 and 1795. That number excluded tax codes, as well as a number of acts issued for certain towns or regions and national law codes.[23] The other compilation, listing more minor acts and ordinances from 1660 to 1800, referred to 112 decrees grouped as being legislation on 'servants and vagrants', but here too the list is far from complete and numerous servant laws were omitted.[24] Moreover, there were few overlaps between the two compilations.

---

19   Róbertsdóttir, *Wool and Society*, p. 153.

20   Dyrvik, 'Avgjerdsprosessen og aktørane', pp. 109–84.

21   The National Archive of Norway (RA), 'Om tjenestefolk og løsgjengere' 1733–4, pakksaker, stattholderembetet, letter to H. Eseman.

22   Gunnlaugson, 'Fattigvården på Island', pp. 198–9; Róbertsdóttir, *Wool and Society*, pp. 157–69.

23   J. H. Schou, *Alphabetisk Register over de Kongelige Forordninger og aabne Breve samt andre trykte Anordninger som fra Aar 1670 af ere udkomne* (Copenhagen, 1795).

24   L. Fogtman, *Alphabetisk Register over de Kongelige Rescripter, Resolutioner og Collegialbreve, Aar 1660–1800. Anden Part, L–Æ* (Copenhagen, 1806).

The number of laws, acts, decrees and ordinances dealing with servants, then, was considerable.[25] Most of them applied to a certain town or region. The particular act used and referenced in Sibilla Christensdatter Hæg's case in Oslo in 1777, for instance, was originally issued in 1755 to apply in the city of Copenhagen but was extended to all chartered towns, Oslo among them, in the Norwegian region *Aggershuus* in January 1776. In August the same year, most of this Copenhagen act also became law in Bergen.[26] Just extending a law wholesale was not common practice, but having a particular piece of servant legislation that applied to one or several towns or regions was not unusual. Another example relates to Tranquebar, a small port on the south-east coast of India. Here we find a decree regulating service dated 17 February 1785.[27] Before this, no specific Danish servant law for this area seems to have existed, although the Danish Law Code should have been in effect, except for Tamils. The act of 1785 dealt with hiring days and gave rules on when servants had to give notice in order to change employers lawfully. Such rules were needed, according to the local Danish colonial government in Tranquebar, because servants left work without prior notice, leaving their masters without help.[28] Similar sentiments were expressed repeatedly in legislation from the European part of the kingdom, but, as in this act from Tranquebar, the motivation usually referenced the local or regional context.

In addition, there existed in Denmark–Norway laws that did not take geography as their starting point but sought to regulate servant keeping among Jews.[29] Despite the number of geographically or, as in the case of Jews, religiously limited decrees, we can also identify three themes that appeared repeatedly in servant legislation in the period 1600 to 1800; the extraction of taxes, regulating the relationship between master and servant, and compulsory service. We now turn to these three subjects.

25   The chapter will therefore not include all servant legislation issued within the kingdom. For overviews of servant laws see also for Denmark Faye Jacobsen, *Husbondret*, pp. 439ff; for Denmark and Norway Østhus, 'Contested Authority', pp. 359–65; for Iceland Vilhelm Vilhelmsson's chapter in this volume.

26   Act of 7 Aug. 1776.

27   S. Rastén, 'Beyond Work. The Social Lives and Relationships of Domestic Servants under Danish Rule in Early Colonial Bengal', in N. Sinha, N. Varma and P. Jha (eds), *Servants' Pasts: Sixteenth to Eighteenth Century South Asia* (Hydrabad, 2019), pp. 268–9; J. S. Izquierdo Díaz, 'The Trade in Domestic Servants (Morianer) from Tranquebar for Upper Class Danish Homes in the First Half of the Seventeenth Century', *Itinerario*, 43 (2019), 197–9.

28   Rastén, 'Beyond Work', pp. 268–9.

29   Act of 12 March 1725; Act of 6 August 1734; Act of 4 July 1747; Act of 13 December 1748.

Extracting taxes

The historian Sølvi Sogner, who has written extensively on servants in Norway,
observed how, through the sixteenth century, 'all tax levies have special
provisions for servants'.[30] The taxes were mostly imposed to extract money
for poor relief and war, but, in that century, taxes on servants were also issued
to help fund various government spending schemes, such as the wedding of a
princess or a king's coronation.[31] During the seventeenth century, taxation
increased substantially in Denmark–Norway. Moreover, the tax system was
reformed and many taxes transformed from provisional to permanent, trends
that continued into the eighteenth century. In fact, taxes became one of the
main sources of income for the crown during this period, particularly after
the introduction of absolutism in 1660. Historians have even regarded these
developments significant enough to warrant the use of the term 'the fiscal state'
as shorthand to describe the period.[32]

At the offset, servants, both as taxable objects and as tax-paying subjects,
were on the periphery of this system. A number of different taxes existed, but
as a general rule the most important were calculated based on the value of the
land in the countryside. The urban population usually paid tax on their real
estate, wealth and/or trade.[33] This meant, therefore, that many people who
had no land or property, servants among them, would not be taxed, at least not
directly. To remedy this, a number of provisions were enacted to collect taxes
from some of those who fell outside this system, and several drew servants into
the tax system. The number of tax levies that in some way included servants is
too copious to list here, but generally they can be categorised into three main
types: the 'consumption tax' that included the so-called 'family tax' and the
'people's tax'; various poll taxes; and tax to extract poor relief.[34]

---

30   Sogner, 'The Legal Status of Servants', p. 180.

31   17/18 (1539), 27/13 (1541), 38 (1544), 46 (1545), 147 (1560), 236/6 (1567), 266 (1569),
279 (1571), 323 (1574), 327 (1574), 335 (1574), 344 (1576), 476 (1582), 550 (1588), 656 (1595),
676 (1596), 729 (1600). Found in H. Winge, *Lover og forordninger 1537–1605. Norsk lovstoff
i sammendrag* (Oslo, 1988).

32   The levels and subsequent burdens of taxation have, however, been intensely debated.
A particularly lively debate was that among Norwegian historians in the 1980s and 1990s,
wherein it was argued that Norwegian peasants paid less tax than their Danish counterparts,
particularly in the eighteenth century. Important contributors to this debate were Kåre
Lunden, Stein Tveite, Knut Mykland and Øystein Rian. For a take by a Danish historian,
see O. Feldbæk, *Nærhed og adskillelse 1720–1814* (Oslo, 1998), p. 95. For a more recent
contribution to the debate, see T. Bjerkås, 'Et nytt blikk på befolkningen? Om 1723-matrik-
kelens konsekvenser og årsakene til dens fall', *Heimen*, 51 (2014), 126–45.

33   Dyrvik, *Truede tvillingriker*, pp. 243–4.

34   We also find a number of taxes levied on servants, particularly urban servants, to help
finance the poor: Act of 27 April 1758 (Copenhagen); Act of 9 May 1760 (towns in the region
of *Skiælland*); Act of 28 April 1787 (the region of *Skiælland*).

Poor relief tax was to some extent a continuation of earlier tax revenue, but by the eighteenth century it was primarily levied on some urban servants, particularly in Copenhagen.[35] Poll tax was usually collected when the need for state finances were particularly desperate, often in connection with warfare. In the belligerent period 1678–1713, for example, servants and children over the age of ten or fifteen (depending on the specific tax levy) in the Danish countryside were taxed fifteen times.[36] In 1762, a poll tax was imposed on everyone over the age of twelve, servants among them. This tax law was collected in every part of the state: from 1762 in Denmark, Norway, Schleswig and Holstein and from 1765 also in Iceland, the Faroe Islands and *Finnmarken*, the northernmost region of Norway.[37] Other poll taxes were more concentrated in scope, time frame and geography: in 1711, for example, all waged servants in Norway were ordered to pay one-sixth of their salary in tax.[38]

The 'family tax' and 'people tax' were included in the tax category 'consumption' (*Consumtionen*), an early modern VAT. 'Consumption' mostly meant urban consumption, but in the countryside a 'family tax' (*Familieskat*) was imposed on members of a household, servants included. It was to be paid by public servants and certain other (usually) non-peasant groups in rural society, with varying measures of inclusion and exclusion depending on which income category they were deemed to belong to.[39] The so-called 'people's tax' (*Folkeskat*) was a tax on servants, urban and rural, with specific regulations and tax rates for town and country.[40] In the Danish countryside, the 'people's tax' also included farmers' servants, whereas in Norway it did not. Whether this constituted the actual taxation of Danish rural servants in contrast to servants in Norway's countryside remains unclear.

An important question in this respect concerns who actually paid the 'people's tax': the servant or the master? According to the legislation, it was the duty of the master to ensure the payment of the tax. Indeed, this was standard practice in all tax levies directed at servants, as it was with taxes that fell on other members of the household, such as wives, relatives and children. This, of

---

35   *Ibid*.

36   C. Rafner, 'Fæstegårdmændenes skattebyrder 1660–1802', *Fortid og nutid*, 33 (1986), 90, table 1.

37   Feldbæk, *Danmark-Norge. Nærhed og adskillelse*, p. 96.

38   H. M. Kvalvåg, 'Tjenerne som samfunnsgruppe 1711: En undersøkelse om tjenerhold og tjenernes lønnsnivå hos oppsitterne i det sønnenfjeldske Norge', unpublished MA dissertation (University of Bergen, 1974), p. 1.

39   Dyrvik, *Truede tvillingriker*, pp. 243–5. For example: Act of 1 February 1672 (Denmark); Act of 8 November 1680 (Norway), Act of 24 January 1682 (Norway); Act of 31 December 1700 (Denmark); Act of 24 December 1760 (countryside Denmark); Act of 22 December 1761 (countryside Norway); Instruction 23 August 1777 (towns Norway); Instruction 9 November 1782 (Denmark).

40   *Ibid*. Abolished in 1813.

course, was in line with the general ideology that saw the master as the representative of the household and all its members. In rural Denmark, in addition, manorial lords were responsible for collecting taxes from the household heads.[41] However, although revealing when it comes to power structures and ideology, this manner of tax collecting obscures any potential tax contribution from servants. A number of the tax levies on the 'people's tax', poll taxes and poor relief tax did explicitly allow the master to deduct the tax from the servant's wage.[42] Thus there was a possibility that servants in some cases did pay tax. On the other hand, a number of the tax levies also decreed that the tax was to be paid whether the servant received a wage or not.[43]

If we compare the tax levies of the sixteenth century with those of the seventeenth and eighteenth centuries, we find some suggestive differences. Whereas the wording in the laws for the sixteenth century suggested that servants paid taxes on what they earned *aside* from their wages,[44] in the seventeenth century servants were no longer taxed on what additional income they might earn. This change was already evident in the late sixteenth-century tax codes, and mirrored changes in the servant legislation that sought to restrict the servant's access to additional income beyond his or her wage. The state no longer wanted servants to be able to earn extra money from keeping sheep, trading, or growing flax or cereals and so on.[45] This also meant that they could no longer tax what became illegal activities. To a certain extent, taxation also became less gendered: while the earlier tax ordinances mostly concerned themselves with male servants, female servants were increasingly taxed in the late seventeenth and eighteenth centuries.

Regulating the relationship between master and servant

The second topic that repeatedly appeared in legislation on servants in pre-industrial Denmark–Norway concerned the relationship between master and servant. This included regulations on the servant contract, such as rules

41   The collection of the 'consumption tax' was also leased out for some time. Rafner, 'Fæstegårdmændenes skattebyrder', 88; S. Imsen and H. Winge (eds), *Norsk historisk leksikon* (Oslo, 2004), 'Konsumpsjon'; Act of 31 December 1700, chapter III, § 1.

42   Rafner, 'Fæstegårdmændenes skattebyrder', 88; Kvalvåg, 'Tjenerne som samfunnsgruppe', p. 31; Act of 9 May 1760 (towns in the region of *Skiælland*).

43   Act of 31 December 1700, chapter III, § 1 (countryside Denmark); Decree of 23 August 1777, §1 (towns in Norway, servants over the age of 15); Decree 9 November 1782 (Denmark); Decree of 28 April 1787 (towns in the region of *Skiælland*).

44   Sogner, 'The Legal Status of Servants', p. 180.

45   For more on this, see H. Østhus, 'Servants in Rural Norway c. 1600–1900', in J. Whittle (ed.), *Servants in Rural Europe 1400–1900* (Woodbridge, 2017), pp. 122–3.

on hiring and firing.[46] The latter was, as we saw, the crux in the case between servant Sibilla Christensdatter Hæg and her master Hans Frederich Holmboe. She argued she had been fired without cause, while he claimed she had been fired because she had acted in a manner that broke the law. Legislation that dealt with the master—servant relationship also included rules on the master's right to chastise his servant.[47] Below we will see how this became a disputed factor in the late seventeenth-century slave-holding society of St Thomas in the Caribbean. Furthermore, legislation compelled the master to facilitate the religious education of his servants, to care for them in the event they fell ill and to pay their wages on time.[48] The servants, on the other hand, were obliged to respect and obey their masters and mistresses.[49]

As such, and as we will also see regarding laws on compulsory service, the legislation portrayed the master—servant relationship as much more than a purely contractual relationship. The master's responsibility for their servants' religious education was a palpable expression of this and was sometimes elaborated in the legislation. In an act issued in 1691, the king saw the need – through a particular decree devoted to the issue – to remind masters and parents in the Danish countryside that they had a legal obligation to allow their servants and children to partake in the annual 'visitation', in which their knowledge of Christianity would be tested by the church.[50] In 1746 an act on 'house discipline' (*Huustugt*) was issued in Iceland with the express purpose of furthering knowledge of God as well as advancing peace between parents and children and masters and servants.[51]

Although the length and level of detail of the 1746 act were unusual, similar demands about servants' and masters' duties towards each other were often part

---

46 DL 3-19-9, 3-19-14, 3-19-15; Act of 2 April 1685, § 7, 8, 9 and 11 (Iceland); NL, 3-21-9, 3-21-14, 3-21-15; Act of 3 June 1746, § 125 and 26 (Iceland); Act of 9 August 1754, §9, 12 and 13 (Norwegian countryside); Act of 3 December 1755, § 1–9 (Copenhagen and chartered towns in *Aggershus* region, also applied to Bergen from 1776); Act of 23 March 1770; § 1–6 (countryside Denmark); Act of 21 May 1777, § 2,3 and 5 (the Faroe Islands); 17 February 1785 (Tranquebar); Act 25 March 1791, § 6–11 (countryside Denmark).

47 DL 6-5-5 and 6-5-6; Act of 2 April 1685, § 10 (Iceland); NL 6-5-5 and 6-5-6; Act 3 June 1746, § 8 and 16 (Iceland); Act of 25 March 1791, § 14 (countryside Denmark).

48 DL 1683 2-6-2 and 6-3-2; Act of 2 April 1685, § 16 (Iceland); NL 1687 2-6-2 and 6-3-2; Act of 3 December 1739 (Denmark); Act of 3 June 1746, § 5, 6, 7, 23 and 24 (Iceland); Act of December 1755, § 20 (Copenhagen and chartered towns in *Aggershus* region); Act of 21 May 1777, § 3 and 7 (Faroe Islands); Act of 25 March 1791, § 15, 16, 18 and 19 (countryside Denmark).

49 DL 1683 6-2-4, Act of 2 April 1685, § 10 (Iceland); NL 6-2-4; 3 Act of 3 June 1746, § 16, 17 and 19 (Iceland); Dec. 1755, § 15 (Copenhagen and chartered towns in *Aggershus* region); 25 March 1791, §14 (countryside Denmark).

50 Act of 28 February 1691.

51 Act of 3 June 1746.

of the master–servant laws. We find another example in a decree on policing in the Danish countryside in 1791. The need for such a law, according to the introduction of the ordinance, was to ensure that order was kept in the household so that 'both masters' authority over their servants can be enforced and servants can be protected from unjust treatment from the masters'. The act therefore sought to list the 'the limits on the paternal power and impress on the servants the obedience they owe their masters'.[52]

Insubordination was considered to be a valid legal reason to dismiss your servant and was explicitly mentioned in many decrees. It could even lead to the defiant servant being imprisoned.[53] In the case of Sibilla Christensdatter Hæg we saw how insubordination as a dismissible offence existed in practice and could lead to an actual dismissal in a court of law. However, this case also illustrates how courts interpreted law, here by categorising certain behaviour as insubordination. In my previous research on court cases between masters and servants in Oslo and Copenhagen in the late eighteenth century I found that a large number of different types of behaviour could be subsumed under the heading of disobedience and be judged illegal.[54]

This and other research on legal practice has revealed that breaches of master–servant law did come up in court. Although there is still need for further study, particularly of the seventeenth century and of rural areas, it seems that court cases between masters and servants were most common in urban areas of Denmark–Norway and from the second half of the eighteenth century. Predominantly such cases were concerned with issues related to contract and pay, particularly with illegal dismissal, absconding and unpaid wages. Some also addressed the use of corporal punishment, but only a few dealt with what has been termed the paternalistic side of the master–servant relationship, namely care of sick servants and the facilitation of religious education and church attendance.[55] Master–servant law, then, was enforced, but with substantial geographical variations and differences when it came to types of offence. Strict laws were tempered by pragmatism, where the authorities often tried to

---

52   Act of 25 March 1791, introduction.
53   Act of 1755, § 5 (Copenhagen, chartered towns in *Aggershus* region, Bergen); Act of 21 May 1777, § 2 (the Faroe Islands); Act of 25 March 1791, § 14 (countryside Denmark).
54   Østhus, 'Contested Authority'.
55   B. Gjerdåker, 'Om tenarar i Lofoten 1754–1818', *Heimen*, 17 (1977), 469–83; K. Ojala, 'At tjene for kost og løn hos godtfolk i 1700-talets Odense', *Fynske årbøger* (2005), 28–38; K. Ojala, 'Opportunity or Compulsion? Domestic Servants in Urban Communities in the Eighteenth Century', in P. Karonen (ed.), *Hopes and Fears for the Future in Early Modern Sweden, 1500–1800* (Helsinki, 2009), pp. 206–22; Faye Jacobsen, *Husbondret*; Østhus, 'Contested Authority'.

reconcile the feuding parties, which again was in line with the general practice in Nordic courts at the time.[56]

If we leave legal practice and return to what is the main focus of this chapter, servant legislation, we find substantial changes over time when it came to laws on the relationship between master and servant. While the sixteenth century had few legal regulations on this,[57] in the seventeenth and eighteenth centuries the number of legal clauses and decrees on one or more of these issues grew.[58] This reflected a general trend in which an increasingly ambitious state sought to control more and more aspects of society. With regard to the master–servant relationship this meant not only a growing number of more detailed decrees and acts but also that the legislation laid out how the state, through various officials and the police, should solve conflicts between masters and servants.[59] This, of course, also meant that they could interfere in the relationship between masters and servants.

Compulsory service

In 1777 the court in Oslo fined Sibilla's master for not asking for references from her former master. Demands for written testimonials appeared over and over in the servant laws from at least the seventeenth century,[60] and were usually coupled in the law with demands that some sort of local civil servant or priest should issue 'passports' to servants on the move.[61] The purpose was to control

56 S. Sogner, 'Conclusion: The Nordic Model', in E. Österberg and S. Sogner (eds), *People Meet the Law. Control and Conflict-Handling in the Courts* (Oslo, 2000), pp. 271–3.

57   148/6 (1560, on the Hanseatic community in Bergen); 167/30–31 (1562, concerned with crown land, aristocracy and towns); 343/32 (1575, areas of Marstrand and Viken). Found in Winge, *Lover og forordninger*.

58 For example, DL 3-19, NL 3-21, Act of 3 June 1746 (Iceland); Act of 9 August 1754 (Norway), Act of 3 December 1755 (Copenhagen, from 1776 extended to all towns in *Aggershus* county and Bergen); Act of 21 May 1777, § 2 (Faroe Islands).

59   Act of 22 October 1701, chapter III, § 6 (Copenhagen); Act of 24 March 1741, §1 and 2 (Copenhagen); Act of 9 August 1754, § 14; Act of Act of 3 December 1755, § 22 and 23 (Copenhagen etc.); Act of 7 August 1776, § 25 (Bergen); Act of 21 May 1777, § 6 (the Faroe Islands); Act of 8 December 1769 (Trondheim); Act of 25 March 1791, § 20–32 (Danish countryside).

60 Law of 1562, section 31, 156/30 and 31 (men and in towns, on crown lands and noble lands), in Winge, *Lover og forordninger*. Also referenced in Faye Jacobsen, *Husbondret*, pp. 439–40. For legislation that applied to men and women, see DL 3-19-12; Act April 1685, § 8 (Iceland); NL 3-21-12; Act 3 June 1746, §26 (Iceland); Act of 19 August 1754, § 12 (countryside Norway); Act of 3 December 1755, §11; Act of 21 May 1777, § 5 (the Faroe Islands).

61 For example: DL 3-19-8 and 10; NL 3-21-8 and 10; Act of 3 June 1746, § 26 (Iceland); Memo on 9 October 1762 (women in Aalborg region); Memo 21 November 1789 (Lolland

mobility and hinder vagrancy. In one act issued in 1701 an explicit connection between references, passports and what was thought of as dangerous mobility and criminality was expressed outright: in a statement outlining the reasoning behind the ordinance, it was explained that, because numerous people in the countryside did not bother to obtain the necessary passports or references, altered the ones they did receive or faked such documents the country was in danger of 'filling up' with vagrants and other criminals.[62]

Legislative attempts to limit and control mobility can be traced back to the Middle Ages, a time when Denmark and Norway were separate kingdoms. In regional laws from the twelfth century, we find early developments towards control over the mobility of segments of the population. In these laws, historians have also identified the transition from the slavery of the Viking Ages to 'free labour'.[63] Restrictions on mobility developed in later law codes, in which traces of the unfree labour of earlier periods largely disappeared from the legislation. In a decree from 1260 for Norway it was declared that farmers had trouble getting people to work for them because people wanted to go on trade trips instead of working the land. Similar reasoning was found in legislation up until the eighteenth century: people had to be induced with threats of legal consequences to work for farmers. In 1260 the solution was a ban on trading: persons who did not possess a specific amount of wealth were prohibited from travelling on trade trips between Easter and Michaelmas (29 September).[64] These restrictions on mobility were repeated in the first nationwide Norwegian Law Code, issued in 1274.[65] The Icelandic lawbook *Jónsbok* was largely based on this law,[66] and in Sweden a law code of the 1350s largely repeated these restrictions.[67]

Despite differences between and within regions and between town and country, from the seventeenth century Denmark–Norway legislation almost everywhere mandated that those without a farm, a cottage or a profession were

---

region, on type of paper used); Act of 25 March 1791, § 13 (Danish countryside); Memo 16 March 1793 (Zealand region, male servants and soldiers); 22 March 1793 (male servants enrolled in the military).

62 Act of 19 February 1701.

63 T. Iversen, *Trelldommen. Norsk slaveri i middelalderen* (Bergen, 1997), pp. 255–70. There are older written laws for Norway than for Denmark. For Denmark, see B. Poulsen, 'A Classical Manor in Viking Age and Early Medieval Denmark', *Revue belge de philologie et d'histoire*, 90 (2012), pp. 451–65.

64 'Haakon Haakonsens rettarbot', 1260.

65 'Magnus Lagabøtes Landslov', 1274.

66 Sigurðsson, 'Danske og Norske Lov i Island', p. 348.

67 P. Borenberg, *Tjänstefolk. Vardagsliv i underordning. Stockholm 1600–1635* (Gothenburg, 2020), p. 142. The king behind this law, Magnus Eriksson, was the great grandson of the king behind the Norwegian law code of 1274, Magnus Lagabøte.

obligated to take work as servants.[68] By then the medieval seasonal restrictions on travel had been replaced by year-round limitations on mobility. Movement was also structured around fixed moving days and half-year or year-long contracts for servants. In addition, issues of mobility and obligatory service became increasingly associated with vagrancy, which was criminal. By the late seventeenth century, people who were obligated to work as servants but refused were classified as vagrants.

By the eighteenth century, compulsory service as it was presented in a number of acts and decrees was aimed at forcing specific groups of the population into service and away from other types of work, particularly self-employment and day labour. An ordinance applicable to the countryside in Norway issued in 1754, for example, prescribed in quite typical language that everyone from 'the peasant's estate' without a farm or a profession was obliged to enter annual service. The reason, according to that ordinance, was '[t]o check the scarcity of servants among the public, which apparently has arisen from the fact, that a considerable amount of people of both sexes would rather live on their own than work for the farmer'.[69]

Here we find ideas similar to those expressed in the medieval legislation cited above: people did not want to work as servants and laws were necessary to ensure that they did. Typically, however, the 1754 act referred to the scarcity of available labour in the Norwegian countryside at that particular time. Similar mentions of a particular situation in a particular region or area can be found in a number of other decrees as well. In an ordinance valid on the Faroe Islands from 1777 we are told that tramps and people going around begging for wool were to be blamed for a shortage of servants in the countryside and for harvest failure.[70] The solution was the same as in the 1754 law for Norway and other legislation from the seventeenth and eighteenth centuries: forcing people into service and punishing those who refused as vagrants. In an act from Iceland that removed the possibility of some people labouring by the week, issued in 1783, reference was again to a lack of people willing to work as servants. Instead the act claimed that people in Iceland hired themselves out on much shorter contracts for high wages or went tramping around the countryside selling 'useless goods' and renting out livestock illegally.[71]

---

68 For example: DL 3-19-4; NL 3-21-4; 9 February 1684 (Norway, men); 2 April 1685 (Iceland); 28 July 1728 (women, Copenhagen); 2 December 1741, chapter 3, § 2 (Eastern region Norway); 3 June 1746 (Iceland); 29 April 1754 (countryside Norway); 3 December 1755, § 17 (Copenhagen and chartered towns in *Aggershus* region); 2 April 1762 (women, Denmark); 21 May 1777: § 9, 11 and 12 (Faroe Islands); 19 February 1783 (Iceland), 25 March 1791 (countryside Denmark).

69 Act of 9 August 1754, § 3.

70 Act of 21 May 1777, introduction.

71 Act of 19 February 1783, introduction and §1.

Some of the specificities of unwanted labour thus varied somewhat from place to place and over time: in the Faroe Islands in 1777 it was begging for wool, in Iceland in 1783 it was selling goods and renting livestock. In the act regulating service in Copenhagen from 1755 we find an urban example of unwanted economic behaviour: unmarried women were not allowed to 'run around selling fruits and similar items'. Instead they were ordered to work as servants.[72]

Demands on and for labour

Compulsory service demonstrates how the state preferred young, unmarried people without a farm or a trade to work as servants. But how, then, did compulsory service connect with the policies of taxation touched on above, which taxed some servants and servant keeping, and therefore seemingly undermined the policy of encouraging as many as possible to enter service? First, taxes fell primarily on servant keeping and on servants in some and not all households. Second, those who did not enter service were taxed more heavily than those who did. In the 'people's tax' of 1700 in Denmark, healthy people without a farm, cottage or position as a servant were taxed at six times the rate of a farmer's servant.[73] In the Norwegian countryside in 1762, such people would pay eight times as much as servants if they were men, and six times as much if they were women.[74] Taxation was consequently used to make living outside service costly, while the laws on compulsory service sought to make it illegal.

The laws demonstrate that the authorities assumed that if potential servants could decide for themselves they would choose not to be servants, thus making it necessary to force them into service. Without obligatory service there would be a scarcity of servants, it was claimed. A shortage of servants hurt agricultural production, and day wage labourers were not seen as a solution to the labour supply shortage. On the contrary, day wage labour and self-employment were highly restricted for several reasons: first, it was assumed to be a life on the margins that could easily lead to vagrancy and criminality. Second, it was argued that day wage labour inflated wages. These two claims were not seen as contradictory, as it was assumed that a day labourer would rather go idle than work for low pay, thus pressuring the desperate farmer in need of extra hands to pay higher wages or leading the demanding day wage labourer to live in poverty rather than accept low wages. Third, for the young and unmarried the state considered service, in which you usually lived with your employer,

---

72   Act of 3 December 1755, § 17.
73   Act of 31 December 1700, chapter III, § 1.
74   Act of 22 December 1761, chapter II, § 3.

as something desirable. It reflected the idea that people without a place in a household were masterless, and masterless people were unruly elements that threatened the stability and order of the state.

Besides these general concerns, there were differences within Denmark–Norway regarding who was allowed to work as a day wage labourer and would therefore be exempt from the obligation to serve. These differences reveal certain variations in how the authorities sought to structure the wage labour market. In the overarching law codes of 1683 and 1687, married people with a farm or a cottage would be allowed to perform day wage labour, as well as fishermen during wintertime and threshers, as the law put it, when they were needed.[75] This, then, was the general rule for Denmark–Norway. The requirements were also similar in an act for the Danish countryside in 1791, although certain soldiers were also allowed to do day labour according to this decree. In addition, and in contrast to the earlier general law codes and the Norwegian act of 1754, married people who had 'always supported themselves with day labour' were allowed to continue to do so. Furthermore, the 1791 act stated that neither aliens nor the country's own subjects should be 'hindered' from finding employment as day labourers in agriculture as long as they were equipped with the correct passports.[76]

The obligatory service laid out in the 1791 act for the countryside in Denmark was more lenient than the 1754 act for the Norwegian countryside,[77] the act of 1777 for the Faroe Islands or the act of 1783 for Iceland. The Icelandic act was particularly harsh and repealed a previous decree allowing people with a specific quantity of wealth to work on their own.[78] The Norwegian, Icelandic and Faroe Island acts all also required that cottars and farmers had to send the sons and daughters they could not employ themselves to work as servants. Similar requirements do not seem to have existed in legislation for Denmark.[79] Comparable obligations were, however, found in Swedish servant acts.[80]

These differences between the Faroe Islands, Iceland, Norway and Denmark, while not substantial, might be explained by the different demands on labour. Agriculture in the Danish part of Denmark–Norway was geared towards production for sale to a greater extent and thus the need for casual wage labour

75   DL 3-19-5 and 6 and NL 3-21-5 and 6.
76   Act of 25 March 1791, §1.
77   Act of 9 September 1754, §2 and 4.
78   Act of 3 June 1746, §15; Act of 19 February 1783, § 1. § 8 allowed fishermen to work as day wage labourers.
79   Act of 2 December 1741, part V (*Aggershus* region); Act 9 August 1754, § 3; Act 21 May 1777, § 11; 19 February 1783, § 7. There were some differences: Norway and Faroe Islands: sons and daughters; Iceland: only sons.
80   C. Uppenberg, *I husbondens bröd och arbete. Kön, makt och kontrakt i det svenska tjänstefolkssystemet 1730–1860* (Gothenburg, 2018).

was greater than in the other European parts of Denmark–Norway. In addition, before 1800 men in rural Denmark were subject to additional mobility restrictions through the existence of adscription, which legally prohibited them from leaving the manor.

A whole alternative set of legislation restricting men's mobility thus already existed in Denmark, making rules on compulsory service less necessary. In the late 1780s and early 1790s new liberal ideas inspired legislative changes such as the lifting of adscription. Its abolition was part of what was at the time seen as a trio of laws that promoted 'freedom', which also including a temporary easing of censorship and the abolition of the slave trade in 1792. The 1791 act relating to service, however, was less of a direct expression of such ideas, although some observers of life in the Danish countryside found it far too indulgent: one argued that no man or women should be able to leave the parish in which they were born before they turned twenty-eight or thirty.[81]

It is unclear to what degree the laws on compulsory service were followed, and it falls outside the scope of this chapter to investigate this. Most research on the practice of compulsory service has been limited to a specific county or town, but such studies have shown how the eagerness and possibility of enforcement varied over time and from place to place. At some places at certain times the laws on compulsory service were enforced, but more often enforcement was less rigorous.[82] Several of those prosecuted were merely instructed to find employment as servants, but a number of young men and women were also confined to correction houses, particularly in cases where such a workhouse could be found in the vicinity. It is, however, important to remember that for most people in Denmark–Norway service was not a permanent position, but something one did before marriage. The master–servant relationship was a contractual relationship you were allowed to exit and, despite the laws, young people worked in a variety of different situations and positions. For instance, in the northernmost part of Norway, which we will return to shortly, there was a group of young unmarried men called 'selvfosterkarer' who lived independently or with their parents and supported themselves by fishing and day wage labour.[83]

We now turn to two examples of the connection between local labour demand and servant law; *Finnmarken* in the northernmost part of Norway and the Danish West Indies in the Caribbean. Despite finding different solutions, both sought to recruit labour. In *Finnmarken* immigration was encouraged, in

---

81   P. A. Wedel, *Hvorfor er det saa vanskeligt at holde Tienestefolk?, og hvorledes kan dette daglig voxende Onde bedst afhielpes? En Undersøgelse gieldende for alle danske Huusfædre, og især for Landmanden* (Odense, 1799), p. 7.

82   Østhus, 'Servants in Rural Norway', pp. 117–18.

83   Particular thanks to Hilde Sandvik for pointing this out.

part by exempting settlers from taxation.[84] In addition, several legal measures were implemented specifically to encourage and to some extent to force servant immigration to the area. For one thing, the obligation to work as a servant was included in several decrees valid in the area, reinforcing the general laws of compulsory service.[85] Additionally, and in contrast to the general servant legislation for rural Norway, a number of these laws applied only to men, thus revealing how it was first and foremost young male manpower that was sought after in this area. Another measure was to force people convicted of crimes to work as servants in this region. A decree from 1762, for example, directed that people from *Finnmarken* sentenced to the correction house should instead work as servants for two to four years in the area.[86] Their labour was seen as too valuable to confine it to a correction house.

In the Danish West Indies, African slaves came to be the favoured worker after efforts to recruit voluntary migrants, indentured servants and convict labour failed.[87] In addition, we find some workers who were labelled 'servants', meaning people who had entered into a contractual relationship. They were subject to the servant legislation in the Danish Law Code of 1683, which was affirmed as valid on the islands in 1734 and 1755. Slaves were also partly subject to that law, but they were defined as 'property' and were not covered under the sections of the law dealing with service. The Danish Law Code's paragraphs 6-5-5 and 6-5-6, which gave mistress and masters the right to punish their servants and children, could be employed in the punishment of slaves. However, Gunvor Simonsen notes an interpretation of authority that was different to the practice of European Denmark–Norway. In the early period of colonisation, 1670–1700, Simonsen found that the state actually assumed the power to punish, thereby taking it away from the slave owner. Around 1700 there was a shift in this policy, which ended in 1733 with the issuing of an ordinance that delegated very wide powers to punish slaves to slave owners, and to all white inhabitants on the islands over slaves.[88] At the same time, in the European part of Denmark–Norway, the opposite trend was in motion: there the state slowly infringed on masters' authority over their servants, for example in easing servants' access to courts to address their grievances.[89]

84   Act of 25 April 1778, § 37. Mostly reiterated in an act of 20 August 1778 § 34, with some changes.
85   Act of 25 April 1702; Act of 20 August 1778 § 34, 40 and 42.
86   Act of 8 June 1762.
87   J. Heinsen, *Mutiny in the Danish Atlantic World. Convicts, Sailors and a Dissonant Empire* (London, 2017).
88   G. Simonsen, 'Sovereignty, Mastery, and Law in the Danish West Indies, 1672–1733', *Itinerario*, 43 (2019), 283–304.
89   Østhus, 'Contested authority'.

Conclusion

This study of servant law has emphasised four points: first, in Denmark–Norway between 1600 and 1800 a large number of different law codes, acts, decrees and ordinances on service and servants were issued. The quantity can partly be attributed to a general increase in law making in the Danish kingdom in this period, but it also reveals the interest the state took in this particular subject.

Secondly, it was argued that when we examine this substantial body of servant law three themes emerge: i) the extraction of taxes, ii) the relationship between master and servant, and iii) compulsory service. The state primarily sought tax revenue through the taxation of land, and the landless servant was of little interest here. Despite this, the servant was drawn into the tax system through specific tax levies that included poll taxes, the tax category of 'consumption tax' and poor relief. As such, the tax policy can also be connected with other aspects of the servant legislation: it assigned the task of tax collection to the master, thus emphasising that the servant was a member of a household where the master was the head. Conversely, the punishment meted out in the law for young, unmarried people of 'the peasant estate' who were not in service reveals how the state viewed this as an undesirable position, partly because such masterless people were assumed to live unruly lives. The master–servant relation was a contractual relationship with legal regulations on when and how to enter and exit service, but the law also compelled the servant to obey his master and mistress and obliged the master and mistress to care for their servants.

Thirdly, laws that regulated service dealt not only with servants but also with other types of worker and social group, particularly vagrants, beggars and itinerant people, but also soldiers, foster children and grown children, apprentices and, at times, even tenant farmers. These different groups were seen as connected by the lawmakers. A consistent concern was to compel young people to take steady employment as servants by criminalising those who did not and labelling them as vagrants and beggars. Another category, soldiers, were often drawn from among actual and potential servants, and the law sought to keep male servants in the countryside where they would be available for the military. Their importance is also evident from some of the tax levies, where soldier–servants were exempt from taxation.

The fourth observation of this study of servant law concerns the geography of the servant legislation. Servant law consisted of national legislation; the law codes of 1683 for Denmark and 1687 for Norway contained almost identical rules for servants and applied to most of Denmark–Norway, but servant law was also made up of regional and local decrees. In absolutist Denmark–Norway the king was the only lawmaker on paper; studies have shown how local elites sought to influence servant law, sometimes arguing for stricter policies than those preferred by the central administration in Copenhagen. In the decrees and ordinances themselves, we have seen how a specific local situation was often cited: the particular situation in the 1780s in Tranquebar warranted a specific ordinance there in 1785; in *Finnmarken* in northern Norway the laws compelled certain criminals to work as servants to ensure a supply of workers, and in Iceland in 1746 lawmakers saw the need for a whole ordinance devoted to the subject of 'house discipline'. Despite these differences, however, a recurrent complaint was that there was a local, regional or national shortage of servants. The persistent solution to this persistent complaint was to seek to force a substantial segment of the population into service.

6

Labour Legislation and Rural Servants in the southern Low Countries, c.1600–1800

THIJS LAMBRECHT

The topic of this chapter – labour regulation of the rural workforce – is largely absent from the rich historiography on social, economic and political developments in the Low Countries during the pre-industrial period. In sharp contrast to urban labour markets, which were heavily regulated by the guilds, rural labour markets in the Low Countries are often represented as arenas where employers and workers bargained without much legal constraint and where wage formation and bargaining was relatively free compared with other European regions.[1] This representation of rural labour markets and the emphasis on the absence of labour laws in the Low Countries is perhaps most explicit in the research of Bas van Bavel. In his sweeping survey of the medieval economic history of the Low Countries, van Bavel juxtaposes different regions within the Low Countries with respect to labour market institutions. In none of the regions analysed by van Bavel are legal interventions in the operation of the labour market cited as a significant influence. Although regions clearly differed in master–servant/employer–worker relationships, these differences were not the result of legal interventions in the labour market.[2] While such claims certainly apply to some parts of the Low Countries during the late medieval period, research for the later periods has been nonexistent. The potential to examine the impact of labour laws on social and economic rural relations during the early modern period, however, certainly exists. In the early 1930s the Dutch legal historian Jan Willem Bosch published an extensive survey of urban

---

1 See, for example, B. J. P. van Bavel, J. Dijkman, E. Kuijpers and J. Zuijderduijn, 'The organisation of markets as a key factor in the rise of Holland from the fourteenth to the sixteenth century: a test case for an institutional approach', *Continuity and Change*, 27 (2012), 355–7.

2 B. J. P. van Bavel, *Manors and Markets: Economy and Society in the Low Countries, 500–1600* (Oxford, 2010), pp. 205–10.

and rural regulations on service and servants. His work contains references to dozens of specific clauses, bylaws and regulations on servants and service from the late medieval period to the late eighteenth century.[3] Although his research focuses heavily on urban settlements and urban domestic service, there are multiple references to legal provisions relating to rural servants. In this chapter I want to take a closer look at labour regulations concerning service in the Low Countries during the seventeenth and eighteenth centuries. As most of the legal provisions concern servants in husbandry, I direct attention to this category of rural workers. As such, this chapter can be viewed as a chronological extension of previous research on labour legislation during the sixteenth century.[4] The first part of the chapter looks at labour laws relating to rural service from a comparative perspective. In particular, it examines the similarities and differences between regions within the county of Flanders with respect to the legal position of rural servants and their employers. Whereas this first section relies almost exclusively on published normative sources, the second part of the chapter is largely based on unexplored archival material and explores the policing and enforcement of compulsory service.

Labour legislation in the southern Low Countries constitutes an interesting and peculiar case study because, in contrast to a number of other European countries, political centralisation did not result in growing state interference in the operation of labour markets during the early modern period. As an extensive survey of government intervention in economic matters has shown, labour market policies were largely absent from the actions of central government in the southern Low Countries.[5] Until the end of the eighteenth century, this domain of economic intervention was left to the local and regional urban and rural bodies of governance.[6] In the cities, labour market policies and regulations were developed in tandem with the politically powerful guilds of Flemish

3   J. W. Bosch, 'Rechtshistorische aanteekeningen betreffende de overeenkomst tot het huren van dienstpersoneel', *Themis*, 92 (1931), 355–418 and 93 (1932), 23–92, 215–77. The survey of legislation relating to servants in the Southern Low Countries in P. Godding, *Le droit privé dans les Pays-Bas méridionaux du 12e au 18e siècle* (Brussels, 1987), pp. 471–2 is instructive but incomplete.

4   T. Lambrecht, 'The Institution of Service in Rural Flanders in the Sixteenth Century: A Regional Perspective', in Jane Whittle (ed.), *Servants in Rural Europe, 1400–1900* (Woodbridge, 2017), pp. 37–55.

5   E. Aerts, 'Economische interventie van de centrale staat in de Spaanse en Oostenrijkse Nederlanden (1555–1795)', in C. de Moreau de Gerbehaye, S. Dubois and J.-M. Yante (eds), *Gouvernance et administration dans les provinces belgiques, XVIe–XVIIIe siècles*, vol. 2 (Brussels, 2013), pp. 399–452.

6   H. Soly and C. Lis, 'Labour Laws in Western Europe, 13th–16th Centuries: Patterns of Political and Socio-Economic Rationality' in M. van der Linden (ed.), *Working on Labor: Essays in Honor of Jan Lucassen* (Leiden, 2012), p. 319.

and Brabantine cities.[7] In the countryside, the labour market policies were elaborated and shaped by either local village officials or aldermen in charge of a larger rural district. The result of this institutional and political fragmentation is that information about labour legislation is scattered over dozens of (mostly unpublished) bylaws of local and regional institutions. This is one of the main reasons why labour market regulation in the countryside has been largely neglected by rural historians.

The origins of these decentralised labour policies can be traced back to the Middle Ages and reflect the political fragmentation of the Low Countries. Both urban and rural political elites possessed substantial autonomy in economic policy.[8] Central powers could propose economic measures, but the approval and implementation of these central policies ultimately depended on the explicit endorsement and cooperation of local and regional political institutions. During the sixteenth century, the central institutions of the Habsburg Low Countries took a number of initiatives concerning the operation of rural labour markets, but always in concert with local and regional political elites. For example, on 5 November 1530 large parts of the coastal provinces of the Low Countries were inundated following a massive flood. These exceptional circumstances resulted in swift government action, including the proclamation of labour legislation. The aim of these laws was to allocate all available labour to the reconstruction of the dikes and draining of the flooded land. The labour laws issued by the government prohibited emigration from the region and instituted strict wage control in the coastal regions. These measures were not imposed top-down by the central government, but were negotiated and elaborated in consultation with the regions.[9] A similar pattern emerges when the central government tried to introduce uniform wage legislation in 1561. A draft of this bill was circulated among the local and regional political authorities. This wage bill, however, never passed because some local and regional authorities firmly opposed the provisions in this piece of labour legislation, albeit for different reasons. Some regions stated outright that maximum wage rates would be detrimental to their economic interests. Others added that they saw no

7   J. A. van Houtte and R. van Uytven, 'Wirtschaftspolitik und Arbeitsmarkt in den Niederlanden vom Spätmittelalter bis zur Schwelle des Industriezeitalters', in H. Kellenbenz (ed.), *Wirschaftspolitik und Arbeitsmarkt* (Vienna, 1974), pp. 47–68.
8   J. Dumolyn, 'Privileges and Novelties: The Political Discourse of the Flemish Cities and Rural Districts in Their Negotiations with the Dukes of Burgundy (1384–1506)', *Urban History*, 35 (2008), 5–23.
9   J. Lameere, *Recueil des ordonnances des Pays-Bas. Deuxième série: 1506–1700*, vol. 3 (Brussels, 1902), pp. 78–9; C. Dekker and R. Baetens, *Geld in het water. Antwerps en Mechels kapitaal in Zuid-Beveland na de stormvloed in de 16e eeuw* (Hilversum, 2010), pp. 53, 91–2. On the reconstruction of dikes in Flanders following the flood of 1530 see also A. de Kraker, 'Een kwestie van geld en organisatie. Dijkaanleg en dijkherstel in noordoost-Vlaanderen tijdens de zestiende eeuw', *Tijdschrift voor Waterstaatsgeschiedenis*, 2 (1993), 26–37.

reason to regulate wages as there were no labour shortages or problems with labourers demanding high wages. Significantly, some also opposed the wage bill because they felt that labour policies and regulations were the exclusive responsibility of regional authorities. A wage bill introduced by the central government was viewed as a potential infringement on their political privileges. Ultimately, divergent economic and political interests resulted in the failure of the bill.[10] When wage levels soared in the 1580s as a result of depopulation and warfare, the central government adopted another policy. This new approach to the problem of labour shortages and wage inflation was clearly inspired by the legislative failure of 1561. In 1588, local and regional authorities were solicited to introduce maximum wages and labour legislation in their jurisdictions to deal with rising wages, but, in contrast to 1561, they now enjoyed considerable agency and freedom in designing labour legislation. As research has shown, local and regional responses to the request of government varied substantially. Some regions responded with new labour laws and maximum wages, whereas others did not intervene in the labour market in any way.[11] The central government could stimulate local and regional authorities to develop labour legislation and endorsed such initiatives, but, ultimately, the scope and content of labour laws was left to the discretion of regional authorities.

At the regional level, labour legislation for rural settlements was developed by colleges of aldermen that governed rural districts (so-called 'châtellenies' or 'kasselrijen') and enjoyed extensive legal and political power. At this regional level, labour legislation was developed through specific bylaws, which could have a temporary or permanent character. In the latter case, the specific provisions were included in written customs. Labour laws included in these customs had a permanent character and applied to all labour contracts concluded in that region. In the early decades of the seventeenth century, dozens of local and regional customs and separate bylaws were codified and ratified by the central government.[12] These written customs constitute a most important source for reconstructing labour legislation in the countryside during the early modern period. First, because they contain only legislation that had a permanent character, they can inform us about the long-term and structural features of

10   C. Verlinden and J. Craeybeckx, *Prijzen- en lonenpolitiek in de Nederlanden in 1561 en 1588–1589. Onuitgegeven adviezen, ontwerpen en ordonnanties* (Brussels, 1962) and C. Verlinden, 'Economic Fluctuations and Government Policy in the Netherlands in the late XVIth century', *Journal of European Economic History*, 10 (1981), 201–6.

11   C. Verlinden, 'Twee documenten over prijzen en lonen voor Vlaanderen en Gent (1588)', *Standen en Landen*, 4 (1952), 103–34; H. De Schepper, 'Une législation de circonstance aux Pays-Bas sous le gouvernement personnel d'Alexandre Farnèse, 1579–1589', in E. Bousmar, P. Desmette and N. Simon (eds), *Légiférer, gouverner et juger. Mélanges d'histoire du droit et des institutions (IXe–XXIe siècles) offerts à Jean-Marie Cauchies à l'occasion de ses 65 ans* (Brussels, 2016), pp. 289–90.

12   See the list in G. Martyn, *Het Eeuwig Edict van 12 juli 1611* (Brussels, 2000), pp. 146–52.

labour legislation in a region. Second, because they were codified during the same period, they offer ample opportunities for comparative analysis.

Table 6.1. Scope and content of labour legislation in the county of Flanders, c.1610–1650.

Rural district	Entry into service	Premature departure/ dismissal	Compulsory service
Assenede (1619)	X		
Belle (1632)	X	X	
Bergues (1617)	X	X	X
Boekhoute (1630)	X		
Bruges (1619)	X	X	X
Furnes (1615)	X	X	X
Kaprijke (1641)	X		
Cassel (1613)	X	X	
Waas (1645)	X		

Sources: Assenede: *Costumen ende usantien, der stede ende ambachte van Assenede* (Gent, 1775), p. 15; Belle: *Costumen der stede ende casselrie van Belle* (Gent, 1633), pp. 320–3; Bergues: *Costumen der stede, casselrye, ende vassalryen van Berghen Ste Winocx* (Gent, 1617), pp. 48–52; Boekhoute: *Costumen van den ambachte van Bouchaute* (Gent, 1775), p. 25; Bruges: L. Gilliodts-Van Severen, *Coutume du Franc de Bruges*, vol. 1 (Bruges, 1879), pp. 244–8; Dendermonde: *Costumen der stede ende lande van Dendermonde* (Gent, 1775), p. 23; Furnes: L. Gilliodts-Van Severen, *Coutumes de la ville et chatellenie de Furnes*, vol. 2 (Brussels, 1896), pp. 172–5; Kaprijke: F. de Potter and J. Broeckaert, *Geschiedenis van de gemeenten der provincie Oost-Vlaanderen. Tweede reeks – arrondissement Eekloo*, vol. 2 (Gent, 1872), p. 74; Cassel: *Costumen ende usantien vanden steden ende casselrie van Cassele* (Gent, 1613), p. 253; Waas: State Archives Ghent (hereafter SAG), Hoofdcollege Land van Waas, nr. 2693.

For a number of regions in the county of Flanders, the customs and bylaws of the first half of the seventeenth century are compared in Table 6.1. There were considerable differences between regions in the scope of their labour laws. In some regions, laws were developed in some detail and their scope was relatively wide. In others, labour legislation was only marginally developed in the customs. Importantly, in some regions no labour legislation at all was included in the customs at this stage.[13] In the absence of labour legislation,

13   The customs of these regions have not been included in Table 6.1.

relations between employers and labourers were governed only by contract law. This meant that, in the case of contract breach, for example, employers and labourers could claim damages in court, but no additional punishment or legal consequences would follow from contract breach. Labour laws could contain provisions on contract law, but also frequently imposed additional punishment for those who breached labour contracts and agreements. In that sense, labour law could both replace and supplement existing laws.

Although the provisions concerning labour contracts and agreements in the customs had a permanent character, they were not inflexible. For example, the customs of the district of Assenede were officially ratified by the government in 1619. As can be seen from Table 6.1, the scope of labour legislation was restricted. In later periods, however, labour legislation in this district became more elaborate. The bylaws of the district from 1629 added specific provisions concerning the punishment of premature departure by servants, while a revision of the bylaws from 1730 dealt with the fines imposed on both servants and employers for breach of contract.[14] In the district of Courtray, there is no reference to labour legislation in the seventeenth-century customs. However, from 1703 onwards specific provisions about hiring servants appear in the bylaws.[15] These two examples show that bylaws were a flexible instrument that allowed local and regional institutions to introduce new labour laws and adjust existing legislation. This flexibility, importantly, also offered the local and regional legislators the possibility to construct tailor-made legislation.

Before turning to the specific content of labour legislation regarding rural servants, it must be noted that, in theory, servants (like other mobile groups) were subject to specific identification procedures when they moved between villages. As part of a wider Counter-Reformation programme in the Southern Low Countries, internal migrants were required to produce a so-called 'testimonium vitae' from the 1570s. This was a written statement produced by the priest and aldermen of their former residence and contained information on their religious and moral qualities.[16] Some communities translated these government instructions into a condition for servants to work in their community. Immigrant servants in Kaprijke, for example, were expected to produce such a certificate of 'good' religious and moral conduct within a fortnight of their entry into the community.[17] Research, however, shows that

---

14 SAG, Ambacht Assenede, nr. 22 (1629) and nr. 23 (1730).

15 *Reglement op den styl van proceduren ende sallarissen voor de wetten ende jurisdictien ghelegen binnen de casselrye van Cortryck* (Brussels, 1704), p. 19.

16 M. Cloet, 'De personalisering van de zielzorg na Trente. Ambities en realisaties in de Mechelse kerkprovincie', *Trajecta: tijdschrift voor de geschiedenis van het katholiek leven in de Nederlanden* (2000), 19–23.

17 F. De Potter and J. Broeckaert, *Geschiedenis van de gemeenten der provincie Oost-Vlaanderen. Tweede reeks – arrondissement Eeklo*, vol. 2 (Gent, 1872), pp. 71–2.

in most cases servants changed employment and crossed parish borders without producing and submitting such a certificate. Due to the intense mobility of servants, village officials struggled to apply and enforce these instructions.[18] In practice, therefore, servants could move from village to village without much administrative supervision and control.

Entry into service

The most common element of rural labour regulation in this part of the Southern Low Countries related to entry into service (see Table 6.1).[19] In most regions, legal provisions ensured the execution of a labour contract by both parties. In particular, these sections of the labour laws were designed to ensure that servants presented themselves to their employer at the agreed date. In Flanders, servants were mostly hired several weeks or even months before they started work and moved to the household of their employer.[20] This time gap between the verbal agreement and the physical entry of the servant in the employer's household was potentially risky as one party could choose not to honour their contractual obligations. The motives could be diverse. For servants, higher wages or better overall working conditions with another employer could be reasons to fail to fulfil their promised labour contract.[21] Employers, on their part, might have found cheaper or more highly skilled servants. Measures concerning entry into service, therefore, were important elements of labour law as it provided some security that the contract would be honoured. In all regions, customary law dealt with these specific challenges and stipulated the consequences for both servants and employer for this aspect of contract breach. In all customs breach of promise by both servant and farmer was punished, but the fines and additional sanctions were far from uniform.

The verbal or written agreement between a farmer and a servant was usually sealed with a so-called God's penny or hiring penny.[22] This hiring penny was a

18   K. Bergé, *Kerkelijk leven in de landelijke dekenij Deinze, 1661–1762* (Louvain, 1981), p. 86; H. Vervaeke, 'Het kerkelijk leven in de dekenij Deinze onder deken Michiel Zachmoorter (1612–1660) en bisschop Antoon Triest (1622–1657)', *Het Land van Nevele*, 13 (1982), 241.
19   A few customs also contain provisions on the exit from service with an individual employer. These clauses specified when the servant and/or farmer had to give notice. See, for example, *Costumen der stede, casselrye, ende vassalryen van Berghen*, pp. 49–50. These clauses have not been included in this analysis of labour laws.
20   T. Lambrecht, *Een grote hoeve in een klein dorp. Relaties van arbeid en pacht op het Vlaamse platteland tijdens de 18de eeuw* (Gent, 2002), pp. 148–9.
21   As suggested by some contemporary legal texts. See n. 24.
22   Ann Kussmaul, *Servants in Husbandry in Early Modern England* (Cambridge, 1981), p. 32.

small denomination coin given by the farmer to the servant. The acceptance of this hiring penny was not merely symbolic, but also entailed legal implications and obligations. By handing over and accepting the God's penny, servants and employers committed themselves to execute the conditions of the labour contract. In some regions, servants enjoyed a small window of opportunity to return the God's penny to the farmer. In the district of Waas, the restitution of the hiring penny within three days liberated the servant from any obligation vis-à-vis an employer.[23] Many contemporary texts suggest that servants in particular abused this system. In some cases, labour legislation was developed with an explicit reference to the servant's abuse of the God's penny. According to these legal texts, servants successively negotiated with multiple employers and entered service with the employer that offered the best terms. As a result, some farmers found themselves without servants.[24] In all regions, servants who failed to show up for work as agreed faced a fine. Also, if they hired themselves to multiple employers, they were meant to enter service with the employer from which they received the hiring penny first. In addition to a fine, there were also other consequences for servants who failed to show up for service. In this respect, significant differences between the regions can be observed. In the district of Kaprijke such behaviour was sanctioned with a temporary ban from the village.[25] In some other regions, the physical removal from the village was preceded by public exposure at the pillory.[26] Frequently, as was the case in Assenede, a servant or labourer fined for failure to show up or execute work was also barred from seeking employment in the village.[27] Most of the regional

23   The bylaws of Zandhoven from 1665 state that the hiring penny had to be returned within twenty-four hours to render the labour agreement null and void. See *Kort begryp van verscheyde placaerten ende ordonnantien soo gheestelijcke als werelijcke* (Brussels, 1734), p. 202. Some communities allowed servants up to eight days to return the hiring penny. See G. De Longé, *Coutumes du Kiel, de Deurne et de Lierre* (Brussels, 1875), p. 22.

24   See, for example, the preamble of the bylaws on servants in the district of Waas from 18 January 1645 in SAG, Hoofdcollege Land van Waas, nr. 2693. The clause dealing with the hiring penny in the bylaws of the rural district of Nevele from 1704 refers to 'great inconveniences' for the employers resulting from this malicious practice. See D. Berten, *Coutumes des seigneuries enclavées dans le Vieuxbourg de Gand* (Brussels, 1904), pp. 513–14. In the district of Courtray the bylaws from 1703 adopted the term 'disorder' to describe the effects of servants not honouring their labour contracts. See *Reglement op den styl van proceduren ende sallarissen*, p. 19.

25   De Potter and Broeckaert, *Geschiedenis*, p. 74.

26   The bylaws for the district of Lummen from 1613 were particularly harsh on servants who did not enter service. Interestingly, servants were not fined but were banned from the village for two years and either had to suffer exposure at the village pillory for three consecutive days or undertake a penal pilgrimage to Milan. See L. Crahay, *Coutumes du Comté de Looz, de la seigneurie de Saint-Trond et du Comté impérial de Reckheim*, vol. 2 (Brussels, 1872), p. 558.

27   *Costumen ende usantien, der stede ende ambachte van Assenede* (Gent, 1775), p. 15.

customs stated that servants were expected to compensate employers finan-
cially for the economic damage they had caused by not showing up for service.
Farmers could hire another servant to take their place and claim reimbursement
of these costs from the servants that reneged on their contractual obligations.

Labour laws protected the interests not only of the employer but also of
the servant. In this respect, one could argue that labour legislation was quite
balanced. Farmers who refused to employ servants they had hired were indeed
also fined and had to compensate servants for their financial loss. Normally
employers had to pay the full wages owed to the servant. However, in some
regions the fines for such infractions were different between employer and
servants. In the district of Furnes refusal to enter service was sanctioned with
a fine of 12 £ parisis, but refusal to hire a servant by the employers was only
sanctioned by 6 £ parisis.[28] To the extent that the different fines for a similar
infraction reflect the priorities and concerns of the lawmakers, the political
elites in the district of Furnes clearly viewed breach of contract by the servants
as a more pressing problem than refusal to hire on the part of the employers.

Premature departure and dismissal

The second most common topic dealt with in labour legislation was the
early departure or dismissal of servants. From the viewpoint of the employer,
premature departure of a servant could have a significant impact. There was only
a short window of opportunity to hire servants throughout the year. Servants
were hired on yearly or half-yearly contracts starting in May or October.[29]
After these dates, it could be difficult to find servants, as most of them would
be employed. Early departure of a servant, therefore, could result in short-term
labour shortages on a farm. For the servant, too, early dismissal could spell
bad news and result in temporary unemployment. Specific provisions were
included in labour legislation to protect both employer and servant against such
situations. Importantly, not all departures of servants before the end of their
term were treated as punishable offences. Marriage in particular was considered
a valid reason to end service prematurely. In other words, labour laws not only
explicitly recognised the life-cycle character of service but also prioritised the
formation of new households over the labour needs of rural employers. Also,
in case of sickness a servant could leave employment without incurring any fine
or financial punishment. Finally, some regions also stated that unreasonable of

28   Gilliodts-Van Severen, *Coutumes de la ville*.
29   See L. Vervaet, 'The Employment of Servants in Fifteenth- and Sixteenth-Century
Coastal Flanders: A Case Study of Scueringhe Farm near Bruges', in Whittle (ed.), *Servants
in Rural Europe*, pp. 23–4.

unlawful behaviour on the part of the employers constituted a valid reason to put an early end to a service term. In the absence of these conditions, breach of service had important financial implications. In all regions, servants were fined and forfeited their wages when they left employment prematurely. In other words, the employer owed the servant nothing in this case. The fines that servants incurred varied regionally. The district of Bergues offered the servant the option to resume his/her service if they were not able to pay the fine.[30] In most districts, however, early departure by the servant resulted in the permanent severance of the master–servant relationship.

The customs of most regions treated servants and employers on an equal legal footing. Servants and employers incurred the same fine for breach of contract. Also, in most cases employers were expected to pay the servant full wages if they dismissed them during their term. Servants, therefore, certainly enjoyed protection under the labour laws against early dismissal from their employers. The district of Bruges was a region where some important inequalities can be observed in this respect. Servants who left their employment before the end of their term and without the consent of the master forfeited their wages and incurred a fine of 6 £ parisis. Farmers, on the other hand, could send away their servants before the end of their term without incurring substantial additional costs. First, farmers were not fined for such actions. Second, they were also not expected to pay servants their full yearly wages. Servants could be dismissed prematurely through payment of the wages owed to them up to that date in addition to the equivalent of a week's earnings. Importantly, this clause specified that employers only owed wages in proportion to the working time ('naer rate van tyde') that had elapsed.[31] The customs, therefore, assumed that labour efforts of servants were equally distributed over time. This, off course, was not the case during the early modern period. Some months were characterised by higher work intensity and longer working days. In theory, farmers in this region could hire servants shortly before the peak season and dismiss them shortly afterwards without incurring a fine or substantial costs. To what extent farmers in the district of Bruges made active use of this flexible and cheap severance option is not known. Most probably, this option offered by regional labour laws was not exploited to its full potential by farmers as this would ultimately reflect badly on individual employers and prevent them from attracting servants. Farmers with a reputation of dismissing servants prematurely would undoubtedly have encountered difficulties in hiring workers. More research is required to determine to what extent premature dismissal was actively prosecuted in rural courts. Farm accounts indicate that the potential of the labour laws was not fully exploited by employers. For example, a farmer

---

30 *Costumen der stede, casselrye, ende vassalryen, ibid.*
31 Gilliodts-Van Severen, *Coutume, ibid.*

named Jacob Haeghebaert recorded in his notebook that one of his manser-vants left his farm without notice before the end of his term. He wrote that he was offended by this behaviour, but apparently did not pursue this breach of contract in court.[32]

Compulsory service

As can be seen from Table 6.1, compulsory service was not widespread. Most regions in the southern Low Countries did not resort to compulsory service as part of their local and regional labour market policies, making such coercive forms of labour control quite unusual. All references to compulsory service in labour laws originated in the county of Flanders. In particular, compulsory service was only encountered in the Flemish regions bordering the North Sea, such as the districts of Bergues, Bruges and Furnes. In these regions compulsory service clauses targeted young unmarried adolescents who were living on their own. In the district of Bergues, the young could not live independently from their parents unless they had the explicit permission of the village aldermen. In addition, they could not take up temporary residence in inns. Instead, they were expected to hire themselves to farmers of the district in exchange for a 'reasonable wage' ('redelicken loon').[33] Infractions were sanctioned with a fine of 10 £ parisis, but magistrates could also impose higher fines or other forms of punishment as they saw fit. In the district of Bruges the customs specifically targeted unmarried youths of the poorer sections of the population. Those who did not hire themselves were liable to be fined 6 £ parisis. Those who rented rooms to or housed such individuals also faced a fine of 6 £ parisis. As in Bergues, young people were expected to enter service with the farmers of the district. Thus the labour laws not only targeted the young unmarried labouring population but also those who enabled such people to live outside of service. Interestingly, the fines that were imposed on both recalcitrant youths and those who housed them accrued partly to individuals who denounced such behaviour and activity. The labour laws specifically stated that informers were entitled to half of the monetary fine.[34] Clearly, the aldermen of the district speculated that a financial stimulus would result in widespread social control and reporting.

The clauses relating to compulsory service in this region were not a novelty of the early seventeenth century. Compulsory service first appeared in Flemish labour laws in the 1550s and 1560s. Mortality crises and rising nominal wages spurred the aldermen of the coastal districts to introduce more strict and

---

32   Anonymous, 'Uit een familieboek', *Biekorf*, 11 (1900), 73.
33   *Costumen Berghen Ste Winocx*, p. 51.
34   Gilliodts-Van Severen, *Coutume du Franc, ibid.*

coercive labour laws to deal with the alleged labour shortages and subsequent 'unruly' attitudes of the rural workforce.[35] Significantly, these measures were not restricted to the specific challenges that characterised the rural labour market during the 1550s and 1560s. When new customs were compiled in the early seventeenth century, compulsory service was again included in the regulations. This indicates that the aldermen did not view compulsory service as a temporary measure to deal with short-term challenges, but considered it a useful instrument to get a permanent and strong grip on some parts of the labouring classes. Such coercive labour strategies were related to the specific social, demographic and agrarian characteristics of these coastal regions. First, the coastal regions in Flanders were characterised by large holdings. In comparison to more inland regions, a larger share of the soil was occupied by farms employing wage labour provided by day labourers, migrants workers and servants.[36] Second, wage labourers in this region were relatively scarce. The slow transition to agrarian capitalism was accompanied by long-term demographic decline. Large tenant farmers were able to extend their holdings at the expense of small and middle-sized family farms. These farms were dismantled and integrated into larger holdings. This resulted in emigration from the region and comparatively low population densities.[37] Moreover, permanent immigration by labourers was restricted to avoid pressures on local poor relief resources. Thirdly, the nature of agrarian production should also be taken into account. The large farms in the coastal regions increasingly specialised in pastoral agriculture during the early modern period. Dairy production and the fattening of cattle became the most important form of agriculture in this region.[38] This resulted in specific patterns of labour demand. Whereas in arable agriculture the demand for labour was highly seasonal, pastoral husbandry was characterised by a need for permanent year-round employees. Living-in servants provided an answer to these specific labour requirements. Therefore, the unique

35   Lambrecht, 'The Institution', pp. 52–3.
36   T. Lambrecht, 'Agrarian Change, Labour Organization and Welfare Entitlements in the North-Sea Area, c.1650–1800', in S. King and A. Winter (eds), *Migration, Settlement and Belonging in Europe 1500–1930s: Comparative Perspectives* (New York–Oxford, 2013), pp. 205–9 and A. Vervaeke, 'Met recht en rede(n). Toegang en gebruik van burgerlijke rechtbanken in het Brugse Vrije, 1670–1795', unpublished PhD dissertation (Vrije Universiteit Brussel, 2018), pp. 210–14.
37   D. Dalle, *De bevolking van Veurne-Ambacht in de 17de en de 18de eeuw* (Brussels, 1963), pp. 74–83; K. Dombrecht, 'Plattelandsgemeenschappen, lokale elites en ongelijkheid in het Vlaamse kustgebied', unpublished PhD dissertation (Ghent University, 2014), pp. 60–74.
38   P. Vandewalle, *De geschiedenis van de landbouw in de kasselrij Veurne, 1550–1645* (Brussels, 1986), chapter 4 and E. Thoen and T. Soens, 'Elevage, prés et pâturage dans le comté de Flandre au moyen âge et au début des temps modernes. Les liens avec l'économie régionale', in F. Brumont (ed.), *Prés et pâtures en Europe occidentale* (Toulouse, 2008), pp. 79–99.

combination of large commercial farms, low population densities and pastoral specialisation probably explains why coastal regions in particular resorted to compulsory service in their labour laws. Compulsory service gave employers a powerful means of attracting labour to their farms not only in sufficient quantity but also in the specific form they desired as a permanent workforce of productive adolescents employed for longer periods. As the next section illustrates, the clauses concerning compulsory service did not constitute dead letters in these regions but were actively enforced to police particular segments of the rural labour force.

Policing unmarried men and women in Furnes

Regulations concerning compulsory service were most elaborate and detailed in the rural district of Furnes, on the North Sea coast. They were first introduced in 1559, elaborated at different stages in the second half of the sixteenth century and ratified and codified at the start of the seventeenth century.[39] In the customs ratified in 1615, the section on compulsory service comprised more than half of all the labour regulations.[40] As in other coastal regions, compulsory service targeted young unmarried men and women who were living independently. Unlike in other regions, officials in this region adopted a specific terminology to designate this group. In the sources, individuals who qualified for compulsory service were described as *eenclipte lieden*.[41] They were defined not by their age but through a combination of marital status, wealth, occupation and living conditions. Although there is no explicit reference to their marital status, compulsory service in this region targeted those individuals who were not married. Compulsory service specifically targeted the poorer sections of the rural population, as the clauses did not apply to those who were wealthy enough to live from the proceeds of their economic and financial assets. Only those who lacked financial security, such as day labourers, were targeted by the compulsory service clauses. In addition to wealth and income, occupation mattered too. Craftsmen were exempted if they could show that they enjoyed steady employment through their professional activities. Finally, compulsory service applied to those who were either living on their own as tenants of

39   See Gilliodts-Van Severen, *Coutumes Furnes*, vol. 2, p. 526 (1559 and 1565); A. Viaene, 'De loonregeling van 1588 voor Veurne en Veurnambacht', *Annales de la Société d'Emulation de Bruges*, 72 (1929), 189–90 (1588) and State Archives Bruges (hereafter SAB), *Découvertes*, nr. 152 (1594).

40   Gilliodts-Van Severen, *Coutumes Furnes*, vol. 2, pp. 172–3. The section about servants contains ten articles, of which six deal with compulsory service.

41   In Middle Dutch and the dialect of the western part of Flanders the term *eenclipt* (and its variations) means unmarried or single and applied to both men and women.

cottages, had taken up residence as a lodger, or who were still living with their with their parents. Individuals that fitted this description were expected to hire themselves as living-in servants with the farmers of the district.[42] In general, these *eenclipte lieden* were expected to secure employment as regular servants did. Farmers, however, did not have to offer them a customary term of six or twelve months' employment, but could hire them for shorter periods. As such, they were a very flexible category of workers that could be hired and dismissed as employers saw fit.

Forcing people into service was achieved by way of fines and taxation. Those who did not seek employment in service were liable to a hefty fine of 30 £ parisis. Interestingly, anybody who signalled or denounced such people to the authorities could claim half of the fine. In addition to fines, the district of Furnes also resorted to fiscal means to direct unmarried adolescents to service. In contrast to other regions in Flanders, unmarried adolescents could be taxed individually in the district of Furnes. There was a clear strategy behind these high fines and taxes. Both were aimed at decreasing the net earnings of *eenclipte lieden*, so that making a living on one's own became either challenging or impossible. This deliberate sabotage was designed to make the prospect of service more attractive and rewarding compared to casual day labouring. Finally, and in contrast to other regions, the customary law of Furnes introduced permanent monitoring of this group. Local officials were instructed to draft two lists each year (in May and November) and report the individuals that did not comply with these regulations. In theory, therefore, the aldermen of the district recorded detailed information about the number of *eenclipte lieden* in each village. Within the Low Countries the region of Furnes stands out as a consequence of this combination of fiscal, legal and monitoring mechanisms, constructed to identify and force young people into service.

Although the specific provisions regarding compulsory service remained in force until the 1790s, this does not mean that they were being applied with equal vigour throughout the seventeenth and eighteenth centuries. Unfortunately, there are no direct sources that record the number of *eenclipte lieden* that were fined each year nor are there large numbers of successive lists of people that were deemed fit for service. As a consequence it is difficult to assess how these legal provisions on compulsory service translated into actual policies over the long-term. However, there is some indirect information that sheds some light on these matters. Throughout the late seventeenth and eighteenth centuries rules about compulsory service were repeatedly brought to the attention of the rural population. Separate ordinances dealing with *eenclipte lieden* were published in 1696, 1702, 1721, 1722, 1732, 1737, 1752, 1761, 1779 and 1790.[43] As can be

42   Gilliodts-Van Severen, *ibid.*
43   City Archives Furnes, Old Archives, nrs. 342–6.

seen from the timing of the ordinances, the first half of the eighteenth century was characterised by high activity. Between 1696 and 1790 ten ordinances were issued, but most of these date from the first half of the 1700s. In light of the social and economic evolution of this region this is no surprise. As a border region situated between France and the Spanish Low Countries, the district of Furnes was at the forefront of a number of military campaigns. Warfare resulted in population decline through increased mortality and emigration. Population dropped by some 25 per cent between 1688 and 1697 and recovered only slowly, reaching its pre-war level around the middle of the eighteenth century.[44] The numerous ordinances on compulsory service during the first half of the eighteenth century are clearly connected to the slow population recovery and the subsequent labour shortages. During this period, the aldermen of the districts made extensive use of the possibilities offered to them in the customs to force people into service.

In most cases, no new measures were instituted by the separate ordinances, which simply restated the customary rules about compulsory service as codified in 1615. There are, however, some minor but significant changes that appear in the ordinances during the eighteenth century. One significant difference compared with the early seventeenth century concerns the timing of the production of lists of *eenclipte lieden*. Traditionally, these had to be produced in May and November of each year. The timing was informed by the dates governing the hiring season. In the coastal regions contracts of servants started or ended on either Mayday or 1 October. The *eenclipte lieden* that would have figured on lists produced in May and November were those who were not hired to start work on Mayday or 1 October. Therefore, these lists were probably primarily used to prosecute and fine adolescents who had not hired themselves in the last hiring period. From 1732 onwards, lists had to be produced in March and September: that is, before the hiring seasons started. The function of these lists clearly changed from a tool to punish and fine adolescents to an instrument to identify potential servants and pressure them into service. The earlier dates at which these lists had to be produced possibly signals that *eenclipte lieden* were policed more actively during the first half of the eighteenth century. This new form of active policing was undoubtedly inspired by complaints from village elites in the coastal regions about the lack of labourers and servants. In 1728 complaints reached the aldermen about labour shortages in the region. In their eyes, part of the problem was caused by depopulation. This resulted in labour shortages, especially during the harvest period.[45] Also, farmers complained about the refusal of young people to serve. In 1732, for example, the villagers of Oostduinkerke testified that labour shortages were also the result of the refusal

44   Dalle, *De bevolking.*
45   City Archives Furnes, Old Archives, nr. 343 (1728).

and reluctance of the poorer sections of the population to enter service. Young people were accused of idleness, as they spent part of the working week lying on their backs in the sun near the sea; they refused to enter service, even at the promise of high wages.[46] Such complaints – real or fictive – probably inspired the aldermen to strengthen their grip on these adolescents. A second transformation that occurred during the eighteenth century concerns the language adopted in some of the ordinances. In 1721, for example, the refusal to enter service was described as detrimental to the 'common good' of the region and living on one's own was portrayed as a life in idleness. Clearly, in the course of the eighteenth century a more hostile discourse emerged regarding unmarried adolescents. Although the measures adopted during the eighteenth century did not differ substantially from the early seventeenth-century customs, the language in which such concerns were voiced had shifted.

As noted above, the aldermen of the district placed great emphasis on the production of lists that would allow them to police this part of the population. Unfortunately, few of these lists have survived. Only the results of the enquiry ordered by the district from 1779 have been preserved.[47] These lists, and the information they contain, are instructive on a number of points. First, they allow us to gauge the extent of the 'problem' of unmarried adolescents living on their own. In sharp contrast to some of the complaints, it was only a marginal problem. Most villages recorded no adolescents living on their own. In most cases only a handful of individuals were identified that met the requirements for compulsory service. Possibly, this could hint at the overall success of these policies on compulsory service. The village official of Stavele, for example, noted that as a result of the 1779 ordinance some *eenclipte lieden* had left the village. Some lists also indicate that the provisions on compulsory were no dead letter. In the village of Oostduinkerke one young man was identified as working for wages and living with his brother. Although he had been ordered by the district aldermen to enter service a year earlier, he continued working for daily wages. Mary Blieck, a young woman living with her mother, was reported to have been offered work by multiple farmers in the village, but she repeatedly refused to hire herself as a servant. The lists contain many names of both young males and females that had served in the past (with the names and locations of their past employers), but were now living on their own. These examples hint at the active supervision of young people deemed fit for service, but equally indicate that some were reluctant to serve.

Whereas most of the lists record only the names and place of residence of these *eenclipte lieden*, some village officials provide more details on the nature of the work and living conditions. Men seem to have been employed on a daily

---

46   City Archives Furnes, Old Archives, nr. 343 (1728).
47   City Archives Furnes, Old Archives, nr. 1122.

basis in a number of economic sectors. Many worked in agriculture, but some also combined agrarian work with textile weaving, construction work and other forms of day labouring. Women who refused to enter service were mostly active in the textile sector as spinsters or sold their services as washerwomen. Overall, young men made up the majority. In sixteen villages, the officials recorded sixty-six males against eight females who were fit for service but refused to comply with the clauses on compulsory service. The age of the majority of these people was not recorded. While most were probably in their twenties or early thirties, some older unmarried individuals were listed. Some men were listed aged forty and over, which suggests that age was certainly not the main criterion to identify these people as eligible for compulsory service.

One final element that we can reconstruct from the lists concerns the living conditions of the *eenclipte lieden* (see Table 6.2). For seventy-five out of eighty-four individuals we have more information about their household situation. As can be seen from the table, most of them opted for a non-family solution for their living conditions. Males and females resided most frequently with non-family members. In practice this meant that they took up residence in rooms or parts of cottages in exchange for rent. In many cases, multiple *eenclipte lieden* shared a room or part of a cottage. *Eenclipte lieden* also resided frequently with family members. These could be the parents or one of their siblings. As expected, only a minority of these people literally lived on their own. Only seven men were listed as the occupants of a cottage. For women, apparently, renting a cottage was not a realistic option. Importantly, although they were described as 'living on their own', this was not reflected in their household situation, as most of the *eenclipte lieden* resided with their families or secured a place as a lodger.

Table 6.2. Living conditions of *eenclipte lieden* in the district of Furnes, 1779.

	Males	Females	Total
With parent(s)	8	4	12
With sibling(s)	11	2	13
With others	32	11	43
Cottage	7	0	7
Unknown	8	1	9

Source: State Archives Furnes, *Old Archives*, nr. 1122.

As stated above, the region of Furnes was unique in its efforts to police and identify adolescents that could be coerced into service. Unsurprisingly, these policies were not exclusively achieved through the labour laws. In the case of Furnes, village elites utilised a supplementary mechanism to force young people into service. The parochial poor relief institutions in this region – called *armendissen* – were also transformed into labour market instruments. In the course of the eighteenth century, parish support became conditional upon compliance with the labour laws. In particular, households or individuals could be coerced to send their children into service through the withdrawal of parish support. This became a standard practice in this region during the eighteenth century. In 1753, for example, the poor law officials of Leisele decided to suspend all parish support to households that had children old or fit enough to serve. Only after these children had entered service was parish support granted again.[48] Similar practices also prevailed in other villages in this district. In 1776, the parish officials of Reninge distributed grain to needy households conditional upon the entry of their children into service.[49] As expenditure on poor relief increased in the course of the eighteenth century, village elites sought new ways to control and guide the working lives of the labouring poor.[50] In these cases, the enforcement of the labour laws and the clauses on compulsory service in particular were achieved through the poor laws. As in England, labour legislation operated in tandem with the poor laws to control and supervise young servants and their parents.[51]

Conclusions

This chapter has explored some of the characteristic features of labour legislation in one region of the Low Countries. The analysis of rural labour legislation in Flanders during the seventeenth and eighteenth centuries has revealed a number of new insights. Although only a selection of local and regional bylaws was scrutinised, some distinct patterns and characteristics emerge. First, in all regions where labour legislation was incorporated into customary law, the material and financial interests of both servants and employers were addressed. Both servant and employer could be held accountable for breaking a contractual agreement. However, this protection did not result in equal treatment in the law. With respect to entry into service, the fines for servants were sometimes

---

48   SAB, OA Leisele, nr. 40.
49   SAB, OGA Reninge, nr. 172.
50   T. Lambrecht and A. Winter, 'An Old Poor Law on the Continent? Agrarian Capitalism, Poor Taxes, and Village Conflict in Eighteenth-Century Coastal Flanders', *Economic History Review*, 71 (2018), 1182–3; T. Lambrecht and A. Winter, 'De vele gezichten van zorg. Armoede en armenzorg op het platteland in het graafschap Vlaanderen tijdens de achttiende eeuw', *Tijd-Schrift*, 7 (2017), 53–5.
51   See, for example, T. Wales, '"Living at Their Own Hands": Policing Poor Households and the Young in Early Modern Rural England', *Agricultural History Review*, 61 (2013), 19–39.

higher than those for employers. In addition, further punishment was a likely prospect for servants in some regions. Whereas servants could be temporarily expelled or even barred from employment in the village when they failed to honour their contracts, such additional and profound corrective measures did not apply to employers refusing to hire a servant as promised. A similar picture emerges with reference to early departure or premature dismissal. In no region could a master dismiss servants before the end of their term without some compensation. However, as the example of the district of Bruges indicates, the specific rules concerning premature dismissal were designed with the interests of employers in mind. Looking at the fines and regulations for such infractions, we find that early departure by the servants was frequently sanctioned more heavily than premature dismissal by the employer. The clearest expression of deliberate inequalities in legal labour regimes is to be found in the regulations about compulsory service. In this legal regime, the interests and freedom of servants were unequivocally subordinate to the economic interest of rural elites. Within the Low Countries, the most unequal labour laws were those concerning compulsory service.

In the case of Flanders, the differential treatment and position of servants and farmers in labour laws conforms to a specific spatial pattern. The scope and nature of labour laws in Flanders changes with the economic and social geography of the region. Close to the coast, where commercial farms dominated the landscape and waged workers supplied most of the labour, labour laws were elaborate and gravitated towards the interests of the farmer. It is here that we most frequently encounter additional punishment for servants, unequal fines and compulsory service. In inland regions, characterised by a majority of small peasant holdings and fewer waged labourers, masters and servants were treated more equally and labour legislation was less elaborate.[52] In addition to the nature and scope of labour legislation, there were also differences in the timing of the introduction of labour laws. In coastal Flanders the first labour legislation was already introduced during the early fifteenth century and by the 1560s the regions of Bergues, Bruges and Furnes possessed elaborate and detailed labour laws.[53] There is a marked contrast with the more inland regions, where labour legislation did not emerge until the 1640s or later. The timing, scope and content of labour legislation, therefore, was clearly linked to the underlying rural economic structures. Importantly, this differentiated geography of labour laws probably also hints at differences in political leverage and access to power. It seems that large farmers in the coastal regions experienced few barriers in convincing the aldermen of the district to tailor the labour

52   For a succinct but complete overview of the differences between coastal and inland Flanders during the late medieval and early modern period see E. Thoen, 'Rural Economy and Landscape Organization in Pre-Industrial Flanders', *Sartoniana*, 32 (2019), 247–76.
53   Lambrecht, 'The Institution', 50–4.

laws to their needs. In inland Flanders, labour laws were not deliberately skewed towards the interests of large commercial farmers although they could also have benefited from a strong bargaining and legal position on the labour market. Although commercial farmers in both coastal and inland Flanders had similar interests with respect to waged labour, the inland commercial farmers could not translate their specific interests into labour legislation. This suggests that farmers in coastal Flanders had more political leverage than their counterparts in the more inland regions.

Admittedly, the evidence of regulation of the rural labour market in Flanders by way of legislative measures relies heavily on normative sources and stipulations. If, how and when labour legislation was used by both servants and masters is a topic that requires more research. In the case of compulsory service, the evidence from the 1770s indicates that those targeted by such measures were reluctant to comply with their forced employment and subordinate position. Also, the survival of lists of recalcitrant independent adolescents proves that clauses on compulsory service were no dead letter. At the same time, the inclusion of compulsory service into the legal toolkit of rural elites did not mean that those targeted by the law were constantly harassed into service. As the case of Furnes illustrates, the efforts of rural elites with respect to enforcing compulsory service were heavily influenced by demographic developments. Importantly, compulsory service could also be enforced through alternative ways. In periods of growing poverty and dependence on public welfare, it was probably much easier and more effective to use the threat of withholding relief to ensure that young adolescents entered service. The example of coastal Flanders illustrates, once again, that labour laws and poor laws often strategically operated in tandem to discipline and control rural labourers in regions where capitalist agriculture dominated.[54]

---

54   C. Lis and H. Soly, *Poverty and Capitalism in Pre-Industrial Europe* (New York, 1979) and C. Lis and H. Soly, *Worthy Efforts: Attitudes to Work and Workers in Pre-Industrial Europe* (Leiden–Boston, 2012), chapter 7.

Dimensions of Free and Unfree Labour in the Swedish Servant Acts, 1664–1858

CAROLINA UPPENBERG

The Servant Acts regulated labour relations for a large part of the population through compulsory service and other coercive measures, while at the same time creating a labour market where servants and masters could meet and decide whether to enter labour relations or not. In this chapter, the Servant Acts issued by the Swedish Crown, from the first one issued in 1664 to the sixth and last one in 1833, are analysed from the theoretical perspective of free/unfree labour.

Service in rural, pre-industrial Sweden was ubiquitous. Although exact numbers are not easily discerned, studies suggest servants made up 10 to 20 per cent of the population during the whole period under study here. The demographic structure followed the European marriage pattern already in the seventeenth century, so most servants were lifecycle servants, meaning that they served during adolescence and early adulthood and left service when they married.[1] This should not be exaggerated, however; older servants existed as well, but generally the position was associated with youth and unmarried status.[2]

Servants in early modern Sweden were neither as unfree as slaves nor as free as modern wage labourers, but rather part of an intrinsic system of free and unfree dimensions that structured the labour market. Admittedly, to use the term 'free labour' is risky, both since it could be questioned whether a modern-day wage labourer is free and since any freedom for most people in a pre-industrial setting was severely curtailed. Free labour should not be conflated with any

---

[1] Beatrice Moring, 'Nordic Family Patterns and the North-West European Household System', *Continuity and Change*, 18 (2003), 77–109; Christer Lundh, *The World of Hajnal Revisited: Marriage Patterns in Sweden 1650–1990* (Lund, 1997); Christer Lundh, 'The Social Mobility of Servants in Rural Sweden, 1740–1894', *Continuity and Change*, 14 (1999), 57–89.
[2] Cristina Prytz, 'Life-Cycle Servant and Servant for Life: Work and Prospects in Rural Sweden c.1670–1730', in Jane Whittle (ed.), *Servants in Rural Europe 1400–1900* (Woodbridge, 2017), pp. 95–111.

inherently positive meaning of the word 'free', but should rather be understood in the Marxist sense of a free worker as someone legally free to choose between work and hunger. As such, although work is almost always surrounded by constraints, there is both a theoretically and practically different logic between labour extracted through legal and physical compulsion and labour extracted through economic compulsion. As will be shown, these can be combined in a labour contract, and this is the reason for a thorough study of different dimensions of certain labour relations. In the article 'Labor – free or coerced?' Robert J. Steinfeld and Stanley L. Engerman argue for a better understanding of the history of labour by scrutinising how laws constructed the coercive practices of work relations; what measures different laws admitted the state, employers and workers; and how free and unfree dimensions formed each part of the labour contract.[3] Following Steinfeld and Engerman, I take it as my theoretical starting point that legal and physical compulsion in labour relations is of a different kind than economic compulsion, and that the different nature of compulsion needs to be analysed for each step of the labour extraction process.[4] A detailed extension of this model is suggested by Marcel van der Linden.[5]

In practice, the option that the Servant Acts posed service against was day labouring: that is, working on short contracts for different employers. Day labouring by people without a clear household affiliation – 'masterless' people – was what the regulations of the Servant Acts aimed to counteract. This means that a servant was distinguished from a day labourer not by the work tasks performed but by the specific position and connection to the employer. A servant became part of the household in which he or she served, but was at the same time a contracted labourer who could resign once the contract ended. Therefore, the specificities of the servant contract can also be used as a tool to understand the development of labour relations at large. In this chapter, this is done by unpacking the free and unfree dimensions of the Swedish Servant Acts. I use the theoretical perspective of free/unfree labour as an analytical tool to dissect the dimensions of the servant institution that were stated in law, in order to empirically analyse the Swedish Servant Acts and to theoretically expand the free/unfree labour debate with this example.[6]

3   Robert J. Steinfeld and Stanley L. Engerman, 'Labor – Free or Coerced? A Historical Reassessment of Differences and Similarities', in Tom Brass and Marcel van der Linden (eds), *Free and Unfree Labour. The Debate Continues* (Bern, 1997), pp. 108–9.
4   Steinfeld and Engerman, 'Labor – Free or Coerced?' pp. 109–15.
5   Marcel van der Linden, 'Dissecting Coerced Labor', in Marcel van der Linden and Magaly Rodríguez García (eds), *On Coerced Labor: Work and Compulsion after Chattel Slavery* (Leiden, 2016), pp. 293–322. See also Christian G. De Vito, Juliane Schiel and Matthias van Rossum, 'From Bondage to Precariousness? New Perspectives on Labor and Social History', *Journal of Social History*, 54 (2020), 644–62.
6   A similar analysis concerning the Danish/Norwegian servant legislation is made by Hanne Østhus, 'Tvunget til tjeneste? Tjenesteplikten i Danmark-Norge på 1700-tallet og

There are two debates in previous research that I would like to refer to as reasons for adopting this model in an analysis of the Servant Acts. The first is related to the importance that used to be attributed to the existence of a free peasantry in western Europe.[7] Landed Swedish peasants belonged to an estate with both political power and economic opportunities to act in the land market as well as the labour market.[8] However, the peasantry was not without internal antagonism. In fact, the Servant Acts serve as an illustration of this, since they were decided upon in parliament, in which the landed farmers, but not the landless or semi-landless part of the peasantry, were represented.[9] Although the group of landed farmers were free – indisputably, in comparison with peasants under serfdom – there are reasons to add more nuance to the free-peasants perspective. If the term 'peasantry' is taken to include all people working the land, including servants who were children of both landed farmers and of landless people, unfree dimensions were prevalent. Therefore, this study adds a detailed analysis of free/unfree dimensions of the labour laws affecting a large part of the rural, pre-industrial population, which in turn nuances the labelling of western Europe as characterised by free peasants and eastern Europe by unfree peasants.[10]

The second reason for using the perspective of free/unfree labour is related to previous research on Servant Acts. The focus in previous studies has been on economic and demographic aspects, with the Acts being understood as an effect, rather than a driving force in themselves. Furthermore, in previous research the development towards a free market has been taken for granted, and the story of the development of the Servant Acts has been told against this background. This means that the seventeenth-century Acts have been understood as a way to ensure the availability of soldiers during the many wars of the time. Mercantilist ideas about the advantages of a large, hard-working and poorly paid population have been used as the explanation of the increasingly detailed and restrictive Acts of the eighteenth century. In contrast, the

begynnelsen av 1800-tallet', *Arbetarhistoria*, 163–4 (2017), 26–31.

7   Trevor H. Aston and Charles H. E. Philpin (eds), *The Brenner Debate: Agrarian Class Structure and Economic Development in Pre-Industrial Europe* (Cambridge, 1995).

8   Carl-Johan Gadd, 'The Agricultural Revolution in Sweden 1700–1870', in Janken Myrdal and Mats Morell (eds), *The Agrarian History of Sweden. From 4000 BC to AD 2000* (Lund, 2011), pp. 118–64.

9   The double role of peasant farmers as originators of the servant legislation and employers of servants is addressed in Carolina Uppenberg, 'Masters Writing the Rules: How Peasant Farmer MPs in the Swedish Estate Diet Understood Servants' Labour and the Labour Laws, 1823–1863', *Agricultural History Review*, 68 (2020), 238–56.

10   For a call for the nuancing of the labelling of free and unfree labour, but in the context of slavery, indentured service and free wage labour, see Douglas Hay and Paul Craven, 'Introduction', in Douglas Hay and Paul Craven (eds), *Masters, Servants, and Magistrates in Britain and the Empire, 1562–1955* (Chapel Hill, 2004), p. 28.

Acts of the nineteenth century have been understood as the first steps towards a liberalised labour market. The quantity of restrictive measures in the Acts have also been attributed to variations in harvest results and regional labour market features. Although there are merits to these perspectives, I argue that they veil two important aspects. Firstly, the servant legislation was not only a feature of the labour market but also shaped the relationship between the state, masters and servants. Secondly, the Servant Acts show a remarkable continuity over the centuries that is not explained with this perspective.[11]

Another reason for adding to these previous studies is that they have mostly assumed that the strict legislation could not have been followed.[12] I have previously studied how and when the Swedish Servant Acts were followed through an analysis of court cases and found that the legislation was actively used by masters and servants and often enforced rather strictly.[13] I make some references to show how legislation was used in practice, and I argue that the legislation was part of the lived experience of both masters and servants. However, the main focus of this article is not about compliance, but is on the careful segregation of the free and unfree dimensions of the regulations of servants and masters. Although legal clauses cannot reveal how people lived their lives, it is not possible to reveal how people lived without knowledge of the laws surrounding them. The structure of the article follows van der Linden's suggestion to analyse three steps of labour relations: entry, labour extraction and exit.[14]

---

11   Arthur Montgomery, 'Tjänstehjonsstadgan och äldre svensk arbetarpolitik', *Historisk tidskrift*, 53 (1933), 245–76; Gustaf Utterström, *Jordbrukets arbetare: levnadsvillkor och arbetsliv på landsbygden från frihetstiden till mitten av 1800-talet. Del 1* (Stockholm, 1957), pp. 234–319; Börje Harnesk, *Legofolk: drängar, pigor och bönder i 1700- och 1800-talens Sverige* (Umeå, 1990). This is, of course, not only true in studies of Swedish servant law: see a discussion about the lack of studies taking the statutes seriously in Hay and Craven, 'Introduction', pp. 11–27; Samuel Cohn, 'After the Black Death: Labour Legislation and Attitudes towards Labour in Late-Medieval Western Europe', *Economic History Review*, 60 (2007), 457–85. A Swedish exception is Monica Edgren, *Från rike till nation: arbetskraftspolitik, befolkningspolitik och nationell gemenskapsformering i den politiska ekonomin i Sverige under 1700-talet* (Lund, 2001). The focus of her study is how the Servant Acts defined and structured citizenship and the role of a citizen that was made available to men and women through the Servant Acts.
12   Utterström, *Jordbrukets arbetare*, pp. 250–1; Harnesk, *Legofolk*, p. 38.
13   Carolina Uppenberg, *I husbondens bröd och arbete: kön, makt och kontrakt i det svenska tjänstefolkssystemet 1730–1860 [Servants and Masters. Gender, Contract, and Power Relations in the Servant Institution in Sweden, 1730–1860]* (Gothenburg, 2018); Carolina Uppenberg, 'The Servant Institution during the Swedish Agrarian Revolution: The Political Economy of Subservience', in Jane Whittle (ed.), *Servants in Rural Europe 1400–1900* (Woodbridge, 2017), pp. 167–82.
14   Van der Linden, 'Dissecting Coerced Labor', p. 298.

Entry

Entry into the servant institution or the servant contract was freely chosen to the extent that people could not be sold or born into the position, nor legally be hindered from leaving their employer after the contracted work year. Servants and masters were also free to find each other. In principle, a servant could not be forced to start working for a certain master, nor could a master be forced to employ a certain servant. But under the heading of *laga försvar* (literally legal/orderly protection, hereafter translated as legal protection), the Servant Acts shaped the servant position through compulsion. The Servant Acts implicitly assumed that the servant position would be open to anyone willing to work. The scarcity of labouring people, rather than unemployment, was deemed a problem. Thus, the Acts created the servant position as a position of last resort, and it made legal compulsion part of the forming of the contract.

In medieval times service was imposed on people lacking the means to support themselves, defined as a certain sum of money.[15] When the first proper Servant Act was issued in 1664, its first paragraph stated that every man of the peasantry not being a peasant farmer or having access to land should go into service or otherwise be forced into military service. The fundamental change was that money could no longer save a man from the obligation to go into service. This means that legal compulsion was strengthened with the introduction of the Servant Act. However, women were treated differently in this first Servant Act. For them, it was enough that they could show an honest way of supporting themselves.[16] The same wordings for both men and women were kept in the second Servant Act, issued in 1686, but with one important addition. The Swedish Crown now saw the need to interfere not only with the freedom of its young and landless subjects but also with masters and their employment decisions in order to ensure a fair allocation of servants. This was done through the introduction of a limit to the number of male servants each master could employ. The allowed number of servants was based on the size of the farm.[17]

---

15   Martin Andersson, 'Husbönderna, statsmakten och klasskampen: varför "gemene man" i Bispberg ville ha lägre löner', *Arbetarhistoria*, 173–4 (2020), 50–9.

16   Servant Act 1664 §1. Title and date for Swedish laws (hereafter referred to as 'Servant Act [year]'): *Kongl. Maj:ts stadga och påbudh, om tienstefolck och legohjon. 30 Aug. 1664; Kongl. Maj:ts stadga och förordning, angående tienstefolck och legohjon [...]. 23 Nov. 1686; Kongl. Maj:ts förnyade stadga och förordning angående tienstefolck och legohjon. 6 Aug. 1723; Kongl. Maj:ts förnyade stadga och förordning angående tienstefolck och legohjon. 21 Aug. 1739; Kongl. Maj:ts nådiga legostadga för husbönder och tjenstehjon. 15 Maj 1805; Kongl. Maj:ts förnyade nådiga lego-stadga för husbönder och tjenstehjon. 23 Nov. 1833.*

17   Servant Act 1686 §1–2. For details about the distribution, see Uppenberg, *I husbondens bröd och arbete*, p. 269.

With the two Servant Acts issued in the eighteenth century, in 1723 and 1739, obligatory service was strengthened and further details were added. In principle, the same ideas guided the Acts. It was not enough to support oneself, and the motivation expressed in the first paragraph of the Acts was that the Crown wanted to discourage people from vagrancy, indolence and being prowlers or lodgers.[18] The acceptance of an honest occupation for women was abandoned with the 1723 Act and replaced with another alternative: that women who had caring responsibilities for old parents or small children were exempt from obligatory service.[19] This may have been of greater practical effect, as caring responsibilities must have been more prevalent than decent work opportunities. Nevertheless, it meant that legal restrictions on female labour converged towards those placed on men, as it forced women lacking the necessary position (as landed or as carer) into compulsory service.

In the 1723 Act, the restriction on the allowed number of servants in each household was extended to women, and the interference in the affairs of masters was dramatically sharpened, as the master's own children were now to be counted as part of the labour force of the household.[20] There was a total threshold per household that employers could not exceed. If the total number of working people in the household exceeded this limit, the master could be accused of holding too many servants, even if some of them were his own children. Thus, these excess children did not enjoy proper legal protection and needed to find employment. This meant that the wording of the Act forced children of a certain age out of their parental home and into the household of someone else. In the following Act, issued in 1739, this was mitigated with the paragraph that one son and one daughter could be exempt from the allowed number.[21] The inclusion of the master's own children in the allowed labour force was repealed in 1747, although the general restriction on the number of servants remained in place until 1789.[22]

It might not be very surprising that clauses regulating masters' behaviour were more contested and repealed earlier than those regulating servants; in general the Servant Acts ensured masters' access to labour. But in my previous studies, in which I examined court cases, I found that masters' behaviour was more closely monitored and more often punished by the court than the behaviour of servants. Even though a master with an especially pressing situation could

18   Sw: 'Inge Landstrykare, Lösdrifware, Lättingar eller Inhyseshion böra uti Wårt Land och Rike tålas', Servant Act 1739 art. 1 §1.
19   Servant Act 1723 §1.
20   Servant Act 1723 §2.
21   Servant Act 1739 art. 3 §1–3.
22   *Kongl. Maj:ts nådige förordning angående hemmans klyfning. Gifwen Stockholm i råd-cammaren then 30 junii 1747*; *Kongl. Maj:ts öpna nådiga försäkran och stadfästelse å swenska och finska allmogens fri- och rättigheter. Gifwen Stockholms slott then 4 April 1789.*

be allowed to employ an extra servant, this could not be decided freely by the master but needed permission from the court. And the punishment of masters for employing servants without using them all year round was much more common in the court than cases of servants running away.[23] However, masters were punished economically, while servants were also punished physically (for example with whipping or incarceration). This means that it is important not only to take employment relations into account but to acknowledge the legislative context and different ways that compulsion was administered.

During the nineteenth century compulsory service was becoming more contested, but it was not abandoned until the last Servant Act was issued in 1833. In the 1805 Servant Act, service was not compulsory for married people 'who were registered and living in a certain place, pledged to honest and continuous work'.[24] However, in 1811 and 1819 new decrees were issued in order to stress that this did not mean that young, landless people should get married and just live for the day, working irregularly.[25] By 1833, the specific demand for landless people to choose service rather than any other way of supporting themselves was replaced by the demand to support oneself. But if that demand was not met, landless people could still be forced into the servant position.[26] The servant position was no longer the position of last resort for landless people, although it continued to be a common position in which labour extraction was surrounded by unfree dimensions, as is developed below.

Marcel van der Linden describes two forms of coercive acts related to labour unfreedom: constrained choice and physical compulsion.[27] But since constrained choice includes everything from free wage labour to self-sale into slavery in this model, it is not clear that the 'constrained choice' category is enough to capture the specificities of the servant position, or changes over time. To be subject to the Servant Acts in the first place meant to be landless, and to be a landless person in a pre-industrial setting was to be a person with constrained choices. What made the choice of the servant position special was thus not that it was constrained but that it worked as the last resort of free choice of employer. The choice not to take up the servant position led to physical compulsion.

---

23   Uppenberg, *I husbondens bröd och arbete*, pp. 117–22, 134–7, 150–4; Uppenberg, 'The Servant Institution', pp. 176–9.
24   Sw: 'å Landet äro gifte samt å wisst ställe mantalsskrifne och boende, der de till arbete sig förbundit och ärligen försörja', Servant Act 1805 art. 1 §1.
25   *Kongl. Maj:ts nådiga påbud om en noga efterlednad af Kongl. Maj:ts d. 15 maji 1805 utfärdade nådiga stadga för husbönder och tjenstehjon; gifwit Drottningholms slott den 30 augusti 1811; Kongl. Maj:ts nådiga kungörelse angående flyttningstiden för tjenstehjon. Gifwen Stockholms slott den 22 april 1819.*
26   Servant Act 1833 art. 1 §1.
27   Van der Linden, 'Dissecting Coerced Labor', p. 296.

The clauses on legal protection targeted a specific group and gave them the following options: take up service in a household of your choice that is eligible to offer legal protection; go into military service (for men); take care of elderly parents (for women); or find yourself a landed position (a constrained choice indeed). If the person did not adhere to this, he or she would be put in another group, no longer one with constrained choices but rather under compulsion (mediated without money): a group that could be physically forced, either into a household as a servant or into convict labour. The service position was defined by its lack of definition: if one did not belong to any other defined group, one had to be a servant. In this way, the servant position was the last resort of legal and acceptable occupations. On the other side were illegal and immoral ways to support oneself – vagrancy, theft, prostitution. Although obligatory service was less strict after the Act of 1805 and especially after 1833, the need to find legal protection still shaped the lives of the landless.

Extraction of work

Once a master and servant had found each other and the contract had been sealed with a small sum of money changing hands, the relations between them were heavily regulated. While the Crown restricted both masters and servants concerning entry into the relationship, the Acts distributed the power differently once the work year started, with far-reaching rights for masters and far-reaching duties for servants. Marcel van der Linden defines labour extraction as based on three components: compensation, conditional force and commitment.[28] All three were covered in the Servant Acts.

Compensation for servants was of two kinds: payment in kind and a cash wage. In kind wages were made up of lodging, food and clothes, so that a servant, if correctly treated, should have everything for his or her daily needs. Although this was of great importance and probably a major incentive for any willingness to take up the position, it cannot be said to characterise a free labour relation, on two points. Firstly, it deprived servants of the freedom of using their wages as best suited them and made it much harder to accumulate resources in order to one day find themselves another position. Secondly, although in kind wages made up a safety net, it did not set servants' work apart from various kinds of unfree labour. Even in slavery or convict labour, workers were generally provided with food, lodging and clothes. Furthermore, not until the Servant Act of 1805 did insufficient food or lodging become a legitimate reason for servants to leave in advance, if the situation had not become better after repeated requests.[29] Before

28   Van der Linden, 'Dissecting Coerced Labor', pp. 306–10.
29   Servant Act 1805 art. 2 §4.

that, it was rather the other way around. In the 1723 Act it was said that servants should be satisfied with the food and lodging that the master could provide, and anyone unfairly rejecting this who thereby discouraged others from taking up service in that household should be fined and forced to apologise in public.[30] This meaure was retained in the Act issued in 1739.[31]

Money wages, on the other hand, did set servants apart from unfree labour. In previous Swedish research Börje Harnesk argued that a money wage was a sign of subservience, and therefore servants preferred other kinds of compensation, such as the possibility to keep sheep. I have found a similar pattern regarding the desire to get compensation in the form of increased independence, but, in contrast to Harnesk's finding regarding money wages, I argued that cash wages were part of striving for independence.[32] However, the Servant Acts created restrictions on wage payments in several ways. Masters were not allowed to pay their servants with part of the household's produce. Already in the first Servant Act, of 1664, the clause regulating wages stated that no servant may request, and no master offer, the use of land or the profits of making and selling of beer or liquor. This was repeated and made more detailed in the following Acts. By the Act of 1805, the details were reduced while the essence was kept – wages should only be paid in cash and with clothes. In the last Servant Act, issued in 1833, wage rates were made a free agreement between the parties.[33]

The other check on servants' independence was maximum wage rates, in force from 1686 until 1805. Both masters offering and servants accepting wages higher than stipulated risked being fined.[34] The regulations of wages and maximum wage rates deprived servants of the possibility to negotiate, but also deprived masters of the possibility to increase work extraction, and meant that the economic pressure to increase labour intensity was weak. Although it is plausible that masters and servants found many ways to negotiate in the daily running of things, the main mechanism allowed by the Acts for masters to increase labour intensity was the right to chastisement – that is, physical means rather than economic, and a feature well known from unfree labour relations.

Coercion, the second part of the scheme by van der Linden in defining unfreedom in labour extraction, was an intrinsic part of the servant contract. Chastisement – that is, corporal punishment – was addressed in the Servant Acts as an important way to make servants work and behave – and both were the responsibility of the master.[35] In accordance with the definition of the servant position above as more of a status than defined by its work tasks, the

---

30   Servant Act 1723 §10.
31   Servant Act 1739 art. 7 §8.
32   Harnesk, *Legofolk*, pp. 141–8; Uppenberg, *I husbondens bröd och arbete*, pp. 171–93.
33   Servant Act 1664 §7; 1686 §7; 1723 §10; 1739 art. 5 §4; 1805 art. 5 §1; 1833 art. 5 §31.
34   Servant Act 1686 §7; 1723 §10; 1739 art. 5 §3.
35   Servant Act 1664 §5; 1686 §5; 1723 §6; 1739 art. 7 §1; 1805 art. 2 §3; 1833 art. 2 §5.

Servant Acts showed more interest in the behaviour of the servant than in how much or how efficiently he or she worked. This made chastisement a workable measure since, quoting van der Linden, 'coercion can be applied to enforce discipline, but hardly as a punishment for a lack of creativity'.[36] Creativity was not an important part of the servant institution as formulated by the Servant Acts. Servants should be 'pious, loyal, diligent, obedient and not evade any of the duties that the master reasonably ordered'.[37] This list refers both to the actual working practices and to the behaviour of the servant in relation to the master, thus capturing the intertwined roles of master–servant relations. Chastisement was to be administered at the judgement of the master, and did not include any reciprocity. The servant could go to court if he or she thought that the chastisement received had overstepped the 'legitimate', 'due' and 'moderate' use defined in the Acts, since outright battery resulting in bleeding wounds or serious injury was not allowed; but as long as it was deemed rightful chastisement, the servant needed to receive it with submissiveness.[38]

The Servant Acts also contained a number of coercive measures at a more detailed level. A servant could not demand to get his or her wages before the end of the work year, thus creating a lock-in effect. Moreover, servants' behaviours were addressed: they were not allowed to use their money at the alehouse, nor could they refuse to work during certain holidays.[39] Neither were servants, as defined by the live-in arrangement, allowed to store their belongings at any other place than in their master's household. The master was even ordered to arrange for the servant's chest to be transported when contracting a new servant.[40] Such features had the effect of putting the servant's whole life in the hands of the master. The year-long contract with food and lodging provided had the obvious benefit of being a safety net, but the detailed coercive features meant it was not a free labour contract.

While chastisement was a coercive measure for making servants work and behave, the main coercive feature for keeping servants in their position was the one-year contract. This was already established in the 1664 Servant Act, although at that time half a year could be accepted, a possibility that was abandoned with the generally stricter and more comprehensive Acts from 1723

---

36 Van der Linden, 'Dissecting Coerced Labor', p. 309.
37 Sw: 'Gudfruchtige, trogne, flitige och hörsamme, och icke undandraga sig alt thet arbete och sysslor, som husbonden thy skiäligen befaller och föresätter'. Quote from the Servant Act 1739 art. 7 §1, but the same wordings were part of all Acts.
38 Sw: 'skälig', 'tillbörlig', 'måttlig', Servant Act 1664 §5; 1686 §5; 1723 §6; 1739 art. 7 §1; 1805 art. 3 §6; 1833 art. 3 §10.
39 Servant Act 1723 §12; 1739 art. 7 §9–10; 1805 art. 3 §13; 1833 art. 3 §16.
40 Servant Act 1664 §6; 1686 §8; 1723 §4; 1739 art. 6 §2; 1805 art. 3 §14, art. 8 §1; 1833 art. 3 §17, art. 8 §43.

onwards.[41] What differentiated this labour contract from others was not that the length was regulated, but rather two other features: that it was not possible for the servant to leave the contract in advance, and that the alternative to staying in the position was to be violently brought back. Masters could demand help from local authorities to bring servants back, which was done by force if necessary. If the master did not want the servant back, the servant who had left in advance lacked legal protection. It is crucial to note that, although obligatory service was no longer in place after 1833, the one-year contract was still reinforced by the threat of being violently brought back.[42]

Generally, the message of the Servant Acts, especially during the eighteenth century, was that masters and servants needed to get along during the contracted year. Even if both parties were unhappy with the arrangement, they could not just leave each other. This means that force in the servant institution cannot be understood only as part of the relationship between master and servant. The state had goals other than labour extraction in imposing conditions that curtailed the freedoms of masters and servants; it sought to control landless subjects by delegating this responsibility to masters. When the chastisement of adult servants (males older than eighteen years and females older than sixteen years) was prohibited in 1858, this came with another change in the servant contract which is also the reason this year is the end of the period of study in this chapter. Since chastisement rather than giving notice was prescribed in cases when the master was unhappy with the servant, the abandonment of this force after 1858 was compensated with an increased right for masters to give notice.[43] This points to the argument made in the introduction: that economic and physical compulsion are different ways of organising and extracting labour, speaking to different kind of logics, and that this was visible also to the actors of the time.[44] However, not all parts of the labour contract became subject to economic compulsion at the same time, which is why it is important to categorise the different parts of the labour relationship and follow its development over time.

Commitment, the third way to extract labour in van der Linden's definition, was covered in the Servant Acts as well, as in the demand for diligent labour discussed above. But did servants take pride in working as servants, and therefore do their best? It is of course likely that many servants did appreciate the household members with which they lived, that they thought the food was acceptable and the work load reasonable, and therefore wanted to contribute to a well-managed production, partly for 'the joy of working together', as van

---

41   Servant Act 1664 §3; 1686 §3; 1723 §4; 1739 art. 6 §1; 1805 art. 7 §1; 1833 art. 8 §44.
42   Servant Act 1664 §5; 1686 §5; 1723 §6; 1739 art. 6 §4; 1805 art. 9 §8; 1833 art. 9 §52.
43   *Kongl. Maj:ts nådiga kungörelse, angående [...] ändring af 5, 9 och 10 §§ i legostadgan 1833.* 1 Oct. 1858.
44   Steinfeld and Engerman, 'Labor – Free or Coerced?' p. 115.

der Linden puts it.[45] Likewise, it is plausible that many others strongly disliked their subordinate position, thought they were unjust treated with unreasonably hard work and inferior provision, and only waited for a chance to get out of the servant position. There are signs of servants taking pride in doing a good job – and of masters being somewhat ambivalent about this. In the didactic literature from the time, the importance for masters and mistresses showing superior knowledge of the work process and never signalling the fragility of their position by asking servants for advice were strongly underlined. One recurring theme in this literature was servants taking pride in feeding the livestock of their employing household better than the livestock of neighbouring households.[46]

The master–servant relation was not only a work relation, not only supposed to bring more arms and hands into agricultural production, but also a hierarchical household relation. Masters became masters when they employed servants, and as such their position as household heads and important figures in the local community was consolidated. Therefore, highly competent, motivated servants, who identified themselves with the household in which they were employed and took personal pride in its success, could be a threat to the master's position.

Exit

There were three ways to leave the servant contract, with alternatives ranging from free to unfree. As with entry, there was a fundamental difference between leaving one employer for another and leaving the servant position altogether. The way to end a servant contract that could be freely chosen was to leave one employer after a full work year in order to start working for another employer. Although servants did use this opportunity extensively, as shown by servants' frequent moves every year or every second year, it was surrounded by detailed regulations creating insecurity, as detailed below.[47] The second way to end the servant contract was to leave the servant position altogether. This was legal if the servant had an alternative that offered legal protection, but, as shown in the entry section above, these were not numerous. The third way was, of course, to run away, an alternative that brought the threat of being fined as well as physically brought back if found, and otherwise being accused of vagrancy.

45   Van der Linden, 'Dissecting Coerced Labor', p. 309.
46   Uppenberg, *I husbondens bröd och arbete*, pp. 218–23; Reinerus Broocman, *En fulständig swensk hus-hålds-bok om swenska land-hushåldningen* (Norrköping, 1736).
47   Lundh, 'The Social Mobility of Servants', 81–2; Carl-Johan Gadd and Hans Christian Johansen, 'Scandinavia, 1750–2000', in Eric Vanhaute, Isabelle Devos and Thijs Lambrecht (eds), *Making a Living: Family, Income and Labour* (Turnhout, 2011), p. 303.

Van der Linden distinguishes between exit through physical compulsion, constrained choice and death. Physical compulsion could take the form either of being forced to leave or of being forced to stay, and being forced to leave could be through the decision of the employer or other forces,[48] To start with 'other forces', the servant institution was a relationship between servant, master and the Crown. For most of the decisions, the Crown delegated its power over people to masters, so that masters had the right to decide about work organisation and treatment. The master's right to the servant's labour for the full year was also emphasised in the Acts, so that even a servant with a legitimate reason to leave had to wait until it was time to give notice. But there were occasions when the master was deprived of his mastery, as with the decision of how many servants each master could employ. Another such instance was military service.

Military service – another kind of unfree labour – stood in a complex relationship to the servant institution, as for men it was both an alternative to service and a punishment for not having taken up the position as servant. In time of peace, the Crown did not have the right to take servants out of their master's house, but in time of war this right was extended. However, for periods of drill, the Crown forced male servants out of their masters' households and, if this period exceeded one month, the servant did not have the right to come back to his former servant position. For the master, this meant that he could employ another servant, but for the servant it meant lacking legal protection and thus being at risk for vagrancy accusations.[49] While this is neither the first nor the last time a state used force to acquire military labour, the relationship between peasant farmers, servants and military need for labour created a particular set of relationships. It has been argued that it was through placing the burden of conscription onto servants and other landless people that the Crown managed to create a comparatively strong group of peasant freeholders with political influence and the ability to pay taxes.[50]

The Servant Acts strived to uphold the one-year contract, but did allow masters to give notice in advance if no measures, including chastisement, had brought relations with a servant to satisfaction. This satisfaction rested on the ability and knowledge of the servant to do the tasks required, and the behaviour of the servant. However, giving notice could not be done without reason, as in that case the servant was entitled to compensation. This meant that, even though servants could be forced to leave by their employer, it was a constrained right for masters. To be given notice is of course part of any labour relation, but the reasons for classifying this as physical compulsion are twofold. The first reason is that a servant who had been forced to leave his or her position in

48   Van der Linden, 'Dissecting Coerced Labor', pp. 310–13.
49   Servant Act 1739 art. 1 §1, art. 6 §5; 1805 art. 1 §1, art. 8 §7; 1833 art. 1 §1, art. 8 §50.
50   Mats Hallenberg, 'Bönder och alla dom andra: om statsbildning och social skiktning under svensk stormaktstid', *Arbetarhistoria* 173–4 (2020), 60–9.

advance risked accusations of vagrancy and, by extension, incarceration. The second reason is the lack of reciprocity between master and servant in ending the contract. Not until the Act of 1805 was the servant's right to exit addressed; before that, only punishment for leaving in advance was specified.[51]

While being forced to leave, by employer or by another power, could be part of the servant position, it was being forced to stay that set the servant contract apart and constituted a major unfreedom. If a servant left his or her position in advance, the master could demand help from the local authorities to physically bring back the servant. If the master did not want the servant back, the servant could not just try to find another position; quite the contrary, as any master shielding a servant who had run away could be fined. It was only if the servant had been wrongfully sent away that he or she was free to find another household to work in. The Servant Act 1739 explicitly stated that a servant who had run away and whom the master did not want to take back should be considered a vagrant. The servant also had to pay back any wages received. These fines could be issued even if the servant had only planned to run away.[52] Another obstacle to running away was that anyone 'not known' at a certain place needed to show a passport issued by the authorities explaining his or her reason for travelling.[53] This was in force from 1812, but servants were also subject to specific regulations concerning their movements before that date. 'Less approved' servants could not move between regions, and servants in certain sparsely populated counties could not move unless there was a food crisis or they had found an opportunity to get married or inherit a farm in another county.[54]

Robert Steinfeld points out the importance of distinguishing between freely entered contracts and unfreedom once under a contract, and describes it as a major turning point when people no longer handed over the power over their lives for the contracted period to someone else by signing a contract, but rather kept the right to withdraw his or her labour at any point without punishment other than the economic: 'The great political virtue of economic persuasion was that it left the ultimate decision formally to the laborer.'[55] Although changes during the nineteenth century made the servant contract somewhat easier to dissolve for both master and servant, the servant could not withdraw his or her labour at any point of his or her choice. This long-lasting feature of the Servant Acts made even mid-nineteenth-century servants subject to physical compulsion.

---

51   Servant Act 1664 §5; 1686 §5; 1723 §6; 1739 art. 4 §11, art. 7 §1; 1805 art. 2 §3–5, art. 3 §6; 1833 art. 2 §5–6, art. 3 §10.

52   Servant Act 1664 §5; 1686 §5; 1723 §6; 1739 art. 6 §4; 1805 art. 8 §8; 1833 art. 8 §52.

53   Theresa Johnsson, *Vårt fredliga samhälle: 'Lösdriveri' och försvarslöshet i Sverige under 1830-talet* (Uppsala, 2016), pp. 100–3.

54   Servant Act 1739 art. 8 §6–7; 1805 art. 3 §1–2.

55   Robert J. Steinfeld, *The Invention of Free Labor: The Employment Relation in English and American Law and Culture, 1350–1870* (Chapel Hill, 1991), p. 148.

The unfreedom of the contract had its end after a full work year, but this rule was not without exceptions. The most important was the detailed regulation regarding children as servants. In the Act of 1723 the paragraph stated that if a master took an orphan into the household, that person should stay as a servant in the household until the master had been compensated for the cost, according to a judge. Even after that, the servant should preferably not take up service at someone else's household but stay with his or her benefactor. This was further developed in the Act of 1739, in which 'boys and girls' should stay for three years and, if they had also been taught certain skills, they should stay until the master thought he had been compensated. It was also added that a servant having been saved from begging or military service could be forced to teach another servant to the same skill level before he or she was allowed to leave, and that any 'poor man's child' taken in as a servant under the age of twelve years should stay until he or she turned eighteen.[56] Although one could say that children are always unfree since they are under parental jurisdiction, in the Servant Acts even adult servants who had started working as children could be hindered in ending their contract if their masters thought they had not yet been compensated for the cost of upbringing.

Van der Linden distinguishes between forced to stay and exit with constrained choice, and both were prevalent in the servant position. During the contracted work year, servants were forced to stay by the use of violent treatment from authorities if necessary. However, during the short period in which a change of employer was allowed, the degree of freedom increased significantly. At that time, servants could set employers against each other, accept a position with one master and, if receiving a better offer elsewhere, change his or her mind and take up employment at that place instead. However, once the contract was sealed, a year of subservience began, with very little opportunity to leave.

There were practical hindrances to making use of this short-lived freedom of choice, and the wordings of the Servant Acts also indicate that masters trying to hinder their servants from leaving by putting up practical obstacles was not unheard of. The basic rule was that if none of the parties gave notice the servant contract continued over the next year, making it a de facto permanent position. There was a certain period of time of a few weeks up to two months open for giving notice and negotiating with a new employer, but these two processes were separated in time. This meant that a decision first had to be made to terminate the contract and only when this decision was made were masters and servants allowed to find a new servant or a new situation. The time period changed with the different Servant Acts issued, so that under the 1664 and 1686 Acts servants and masters could give notice two months before the day a new contract started (at Michaelmas, 29 September), and thereafter start finding new employment

56   Servant Act 1723 §9; 1739 art. 6 §3.

or a new servant six weeks before at the earliest. In 1723 the period for giving notice started on 10 August, and allowed only two weeks, 14–29 September, for making new agreements. New time periods were also specified in all the later issued Acts.[57] This created a potentially powerful check on leaving the contract, since a person was not only uninformed regarding the treatment of servants at a new place but not even allowed to make agreement with another household prior to the decision to quit the present employment.

Although gathering information about other possibilities was still allowed, there was a fine line not to be passed, because a potential employer could be accused of enticing the servant away from his or her master.[58] That 'stealing' servants was morally wrong was an ideological underpinning of the servant institution, which also points to labour relations that were a relationship not only between the master and the servant but also between masters. Masters were understood as having a common master-interest in reducing the mobility of servants. Steinfeld analyses this moral understanding as a consensus needed to uphold the strict rules of unfree labour, and sees the eroding of this understanding as the necessary ground for new labour contracts to take form.[59]

The servant needed a document, the so-called *orlovssedel*, showing that he or she was free from the former employer, before making an agreement with a new one. This document was issued by the former employer after the servant or the master had given notice, but the wordings of the Acts showed a concern that masters could withhold this document or simply leave the household for those weeks in order to prevent the servant from finding a new position. The Acts covered for such events by allowing servants to give notice in the presence of trusted men if the master was absent.[60] This meant a balancing of interests. In order to legitimate compulsory service and other unfree dimensions of the servant position, servants' right to change employer was one legitimate interest. However, masters' right not to engage in a competition on market terms in order to receive servants was another interest of importance.

The last alternative in van der Linden's scheme for leaving is death, which characterised the most unfree labour relations such as chattel slavery. Servants were not bound to their position for life, but the Acts did prescribe what to do with the contract if a master died. In the Acts of 1805 and 1833, although the possibilities for ending the contract in advance had been somewhat increased, not even the death of a master meant the end of the servant contract. If the master's heirs wanted to keep the servant, he or she had to stay. The same was

---

57   Servant Act 1664 §4, 6; 1686 §4, 6; 1723 §4–5; 1739 art. 4 §1–2, art. 5 §1–2; 1805 art. 7 §1; 1833 art. 7 §39.
58   Servant Act 1664 §5; 1686 §5; 1723 §6; 1739 art. 4 §10; 1805 art. 7 §4; 1833 art. 7 §42.
59   Steinfeld, *The Invention of Free Labor*, p. 169.
60   Servant Act 1664 §6; 1686 §6; 1723 §5, 1739 art. 4 §3–4; 1805 art. 4 §6–7, art. 7 §3; 1833 art. 4 §27–28, art. 7 §41.

true if the master sold the farm – the new owner could demand to keep the servant. And if the master moved to another farm, the servant was required to follow.[61] This shows how free and unfree dimensions were combined in unexpected ways, and that the story of the development of a free wage labour market cannot be told as a steady progression.

Conclusions

Although demographic and economic explanations provide important perspectives on labour legislation, laws create differing interests between the parties with their own internal logic. It has been shown here that coercive measures and compulsory service were surprisingly stable features of the servant position over a long time period, although the economic structure and work opportunities outside the servant institution changed profoundly. In the nineteenth-century Acts compulsory service became less strict and some features associated with a capitalistic labour market were introduced: freer wage setting, enhanced possibilities to end the contract and more alternatives to service. But a servant could still be violently brought back, chastised if misbehaving and unable to leave his or her position even if the master died or moved away. Only when the, sometimes contradictory, regulations are carefully unpacked, is this made clear.

Studying the labour laws from the perspective of different logics and tracing free and unfree dimensions emphasises the remarkable continuity of the Servant Acts that has not been possible to explain with demographic or economic features. Van der Linden's model was developed for labour relations that are usually understood as unfree, if not outright slavery, indentured labour or coercive colonial practices. The model thus focuses more on the individual's possibilities in unfree systems than on structural unfreedom. There were no visible chains in the Swedish servant institution and unfreedom was more structural than individual. Servants did not necessarily feel particularly unfree themselves, since they did what other people did and they could change employer after one year if they wished. Legal compulsion and violent measures were more of a threat than actual, day-to-day practice for most servants. But what an analysis based on this model makes clear is that the servant position was a position of last resort – any step outside the institution was a step towards being chased as a vagrant or physically forced back. The servant could not, as Steinfeld puts it, withdraw his or her labour at any point.

Although the choice of which specific master to work for was mostly free for servants, the position was surrounded by unfree – violent – dimensions. If a landless person did not go into service, he or she was subject to violence. If

---

61   Servant Act 1805 art. 8 §4–6; 1833 art. 8 §47–49.

a servant did not work faithfully, the same was true. And, finally, if a servant left his or her position in advance, violent capture and return was a risk. A pre-industrial landless person might not have had many choices, but still this inherent lack of choices was not enough for the state, which formed the servant institution through its demand that people had legal protection – that is, a legally recognised place in a household. The principle of legal protection created the servant position as a position of last resort, and all measures for labour extraction were reinforced by the threat of being punished as a vagrant if the servant did not meet them. The one-year contract, chastisement and payment in kind kept the servant in his or her place. While the servant position should not be thought of as a prison for the young, landless population, neither should it be thought of as a labour market in which people could switch freely between different types of labour contracts. It is rewarding here to distinguish between the individual servant's contract and the servant position or institution. While the laws distinguished between masters and servants and made them two separate entities, in practice individuals could go between the groups during their life course. The possibility of leaving the position means that coercive measures might have been easier to endure. Nevertheless, the institution of service was unfree in many respects. Without keeping both of these features in mind at the same time, it is not possible to explain the historical development of labour.

This study has raised questions about the story of contrasts between the free peasants in north-western Europe and unfree peasants in eastern Europe. A large part of the peasantry of Sweden was not free, and not only were they unfree once in the master–servant relationship, but they were also subject to compulsory service and physical compulsion. The political and economic effects of this unfreedom have yet to be studied more thoroughly and placed in their comparative perspective.

PART III

THE EXPERIENCES OF REGULATION

8

Objecting to Youth: Popular Attitudes to Service as a Form of Social and Economic Control in England, 1564–1641

CHARMIAN MANSELL

In 1563 the Statute of Artificers explicitly laid out an agenda for regulating labour for large swathes of England's population. The statute ruled that those between the ages of twelve and sixty who had not secured an apprenticeship or position in service and were not contracted to work for at least half a year should be compulsorily placed in annual service. Only those who owned (or whose parents owned) goods to the value of £10 or land worth 40s annually were exempt. Maximum wage rates were set locally by Justices of the Peace and labour mobility was controlled: to seek work elsewhere, servants were to produce testimonials, complete with seal, from two honest householders and a constable of their city, town or village.[1] In theory, the Statute applied to anyone of working age, but in practice it targeted unmarried labouring men and women below the age of thirty. We might assume that their freedoms were suddenly and severely curtailed by this legislation. However, the Statute was not an innovation in policy. Ordinances and acts aiming to control labour were introduced from as early as the Black Death. In 1349 the Ordinance of Labourers was enacted to regulate employment and wages at a time when labour supply was diminished and surviving workers could demand higher wages.[2] By the mid-sixteenth century there were new perceived threats to stable employment structures. Maximum wage rates, last set in 1515, were now untenable for workers due to price inflation and, consequently, higher wages

---

1 R. H. Tawney and Eileen Power (eds), *Tudor Economic Documents: Being Select Documents Illustrating the Economic and Social History of Tudor England* (London, 1951), pp. 338–50.
2 For a detailed discussion of the 1349 Ordinance of Labourers, see Jane Whittle, 'Attitudes to Wage Labour in English Legislation, 1349–1601' in this volume.

were demanded. Although it had a less pronounced demographic effect than the Great Pestilence of 1347–9, a wave of influenza epidemics in the late 1550s augmented the crisis.[3] The Statute of Artificers was therefore an elaboration and consolidation of earlier legislation that addressed these challenges to the national labour market.[4]

Early scholarship on the Statute focused on the economic concerns and political agendas that explain its introduction.[5] The extent of its enforcement has since been analysed as a barometer of socio-economic attitudes; records of the petty and Quarter Sessions expose those who did not comply with the legislation, while advice to constables printed in legal handbooks indicates growing concern amongst authorities.[6] However, records of the enforcement of the law offer only a picture of those who were reported to the authorities for various infringements (which included leaving service before the end of covenant, living at one's own hands, and paying or accepting higher wages than the established maximum rates). Many people did not meet the Statute's wealth threshold but lived by their own means without a stable annual wage, and yet they were not reported by local constables.[7] It is difficult to quantify how many people successfully lived out of the institution of service, but it is clear that alternative employments were available to labouring young men and women.

Through the study of prosecutions, an additional concern of contemporary lawmakers has been exposed. Magistrates' notebooks resonated with the same perceived vices of young, unmarried people – sex outside marriage, disorder and disobedience – that were proclaimed in moralists' tracts. It is argued that these vices held significant explanatory power for the stringent enforcement of

3   See F. J. Fisher, 'Influenza and Inflation in Tudor England', *Economic History Review*, 18 (1965), 128; Donald Woodward, 'The Background to the Statute of Artificers: The Genesis of Labour Policy, 1558–63', *Economic History Review*, 33 (1980), 33–4.

4   Woodward, 'The Background', 33.

5   For example, see S. T. Bindoff, 'The Making of the Statute of Artificers', in S. T. Bindoff, J. Hurstfield and C. H. Williams (eds), *Elizabethan Government and Society* (London, 1961), pp. 56–94; Woodward, 'The Background', 32–44; Fisher, 'Influenza and Inflation in Tudor England', 120–9.

6   See Tim Wales, '"Living at their own Hands": Policing Poor Households and the Young in Early Modern Rural England', *Agricultural History Review*, 61 (2013), 19–39; D. Hay 'England 1562–1875: The Law and Its Uses', in D. Hay and P. Craven (eds), *Masters, Servants and Magistrates in Britain and the Empire, 1562–1955* (Chapel Hill, 2004) pp. 59–116; F. G. Emmison, *Elizabethan Life: Home, Work and Land, from Essex wills and sessions and manorial records* (Chelmsford, 1976), pp. 146–74; J. A. Sharpe, *Crime in Seventeenth-Century England: A County Study* (Cambridge, 1984), pp. 183–4, 197–8.

7   Charmian Mansell, 'Female Service and the Village Community in South-West England 1550–1650: The Labour Laws Reconsidered', in Jane Whittle (ed.), *Servants in Rural Europe 1400–1900* (Woodbridge, 2017), pp. 77–94.

the labour legislation, particularly against women.[8] The 1563 policy-makers made no explicit reference to this concern; only the aim to 'banish idleness' is set out in the Statute's preamble. While the Statute came to be used to control vice, this was not necessarily the original intention of the legislators.[9] What is clear is that authorities came to see the Statute as a solution for tackling economic problems as well as concerns over the socialisation and morality of young people. Service became a remedy for both.[10]

In studying the Statute, popular attitudes towards young people and labour have been overlooked in favour of studying the effectiveness of the machinery of the state. Enforcement of the Statute was dependent on the cooperation of parish officials, who were often forced to mediate between central government mandates and their neighbours' interests.[11] Socio-economic control of young people probably accelerated in the seventeenth century as Puritan ideologies of the middling sort (who often held prominent local offices) formed the basis of regulating sinful behaviour.[12] However, Marjorie McIntosh and Margaret Spufford contend that regulating activity predates the Puritan movement.[13] Martin Ingram notes in his study of church courts that some villages sought to control misbehaviour around 1600, even when Puritanism was not evidently at work.[14] Although her focus is not specifically on young people, McIntosh instead highlights the combined actions of local society and governing elites. Her work on the reporting of offences to local courts indicates that, while parliamentary proclamations and statutes were issued to address these perceived social problems, action was effected by local leaders. They were usually men (though occasionally women) from well-established, respectable households who knew how to engage with the legal system to tackle these problems.[15]

---

8   Wales, '"Living at their own Hands"', 32–3, 35; Paul Griffiths, *Youth and Authority: Formative Experiences in England, 1560–1640* (Oxford, 1996), p. 60.
9   Tawney and Power, *Tudor Economic Documents*, p. 339.
10 Griffiths, *Youth and Authority*, p. 60.
11 For a fuller discussion of the role of constables in appeasing neighbours and the state, see Joan Kent, *The English Village Constable 1580–1642: A Social and Administrative Study* (Oxford, 1986); Keith Wrightson, 'Two Concepts of Order: Justices, Constables and Jurymen in Seventeenth Century England', in John Brewer and John Styles (eds), *An Ungovernable People: The English and their Law in the Seventeenth and Eighteenth Centuries* (London, 1980), pp. 21–46.
12 Keith Wrightson and David Levine, *Poverty and Piety in an English Village: Terling, 1525–1700* (Oxford, 1979), pp. 198–220.
13 Marjorie K. McIntosh, *Controlling Misbehavior in England, 1370–1600* (Cambridge, 1998), p. 4; Margaret Spufford, 'Puritanism and Social Control?' in Anthony Fletcher and John Stevenson (eds), *Order and Disorder in Early Modern England* (Cambridge, 1985), pp. 41–57.
14 Martin Ingram, *Church Courts, Sex and Marriage in England, 1570–1640* (Cambridge, 1988), pp. 166–7, 233–7.
15 McIntosh, *Controlling Misbehavior*, esp. pp. 2, 24–33.

But a key question remains unanswered: if society was so keen to regulate behaviour, *how* was it possible for young men and women to live outside service? Christopher Hill marks the 1563 Statute of Artificers as an important milestone in determining how labour was conceptualised in the late sixteenth and early seventeenth centuries. He notes that the poor were exploited and compulsorily forced into wage labour (i.e. service), thus rendering them 'unfree'.[16] Robert Steinfeld points out that, even when the labouring poor 'freely' entered into a contract of service, the contract was legally binding and their freedom was therefore curtailed. They could not depart from service and were forced to serve.[17] While Keith Wrightson, McIntosh and others debated the importance of Puritanism in driving social regulation, Hill reminds us of the broad spectrum of opinions that was held in early modern England in relation to those without means. He points out that at the very same time that Puritans and other reformers were 'evolving a doctrine of the dignity of labour' others – primarily those of working status such as members of the Digger movement – were displaying a hatred of wage labour.[18] Enforcement of the labour laws was surely, then, a mixed bag. It is small wonder that many individuals living outside service fell through the cracks of the legislation.

Church courts offer a glimpse of the working lives of young people and their labour patterns.[19] These records may not seem an obvious choice for studying labour legislation; explicit references to the Statute and its enforcement are rare in church court depositions, as it did not fall within the remit of these courts. However, they reveal much about attitudes towards young people and labour. Alexandra Shepard's work on the language of poverty and labour used in church court depositions has been pivotal in unpicking how ideas of credibility were fused with economic worth. She demonstrates that appraisal of one another's worth incorporated both material wealth and ideas of morality and work ethic.[20]

This chapter deploys Shepard's approach of using church court depositions as evidence of popular attitudes to social rank and position, while also building

16   Christopher Hill, 'Pottage for Freeborn Englishmen: Attitudes to Wage Labour in the Sixteenth and Seventeenth Centuries', in C. H. Feinstein (ed.), *Socialism, Capitalism and Economic Growth: Essays Presented to Maurice Dobb* (Cambridge, 1967), p. 340.
17   Robert Steinfeld, *The Invention of Free Labour: the Employment Relation in English and American Law and Culture, 1350–1870* (Chapel Hill, 1991), chapter 2 but esp. p. 24.
18   *Ibid.*, p. 347.
19   See, for example, Alexandra Shepard, 'Poverty, Labour and the Language of Social Description in Early Modern England', *Past and Present*, 201 (2008), 51–95; Mansell, 'Female Service and the Village Community', pp. 77–94; Charmian Mansell, 'The variety of women's experiences as servants in England (1548–1649): evidence from church court depositions', *Continuity and Change*, 33 (2018), 315–38.
20   Alexandra Shepard, *Accounting for Oneself: Worth, Status, and the Social Order in Early Modern England* (Oxford, 2015); Shepard, 'Poverty, Labour', 51–95.

upon my own previous work on the Statute of Artificers.[21] It explores the extent to which the economic and social concerns expressed in the Statute mirrored the concerns of society. And it does so through a close examination of the grounds upon which opposing parties in the church courts discredited the testimonies of unmarried witnesses aged thirty and under. Depositional evidence is drawn from the church courts of the dioceses of Bath and Wells, Exeter, Gloucester and Hereford. This is a region of England for which we know little about the extent to which the Statute of Artificers was enforced. The chapter focuses on objections (known as exceptions) to the testimonies of witnesses recorded in sixty-three sample cases heard in these courts between 1564 (the year after the Statute was introduced) and 1641. These objections rarely explicitly expressed living outside service as a key marker of vice among young people. Rather, objections more commonly centred on the lack of a fixed place of residence, whether that was in service or the family home. Lacking a position in service was also largely absent in articulations of other perceived vices of young people: principally, sex outside marriage and theft. The legislative power of the Statute encourages us to focus on service as the solution to problems of youth. But, in reality, the relationship between the two was less straightforward. Early modern society's conceptual framework for the regulation of young people's labour and sociability was much broader than the Statute mandated.

Sources and methodology

Church courts heard a range of non-criminal disputes between parishioners. Organised along diocesan lines, they were responsible for prosecuting sin and maintaining morality within parishes. Aggrieved parties pursued suits against their neighbours over defamation, payment of tithes, breaches of marital contracts and bequests made in wills. The court also made its own enquiries into parishioners' behaviour through periodic visitations. The bishop and his deputies made circuits around the diocese to root out and prosecute miscreants, thereby generating what was known as *ex officio* complaints in the church courts, in which adultery, non-attendance at church and clerical misdemeanours loomed large.

When witnesses were required to provide evidence in a case, they were asked to respond to a set of questions (articles) drawn up by the plaintiff(s) in relation to the alleged offence committed by the defendant(s). Their responses were recorded along with a short biography of the witness, which detailed their age, marital status or occupation and place of residence. A form of cross-examination of the witness by the defendant (known as an interrogatory)

---

21   Mansell, 'Female Service and the Village Community', pp. 77–94.

was permitted, and questions were designed to discredit their testimonies. In this process, defendants summoned their own witnesses who testified their objections (exceptions) to the plaintiff's witnesses. This process could be reciprocated by the original plaintiff until a resolution was reached (usually out of court, as few verdicts survive).

Pastoral works from as early as the twelfth century set out who was considered an appropriate witness in the church courts. In 1216, Tancred in his *Ordo Judicionis* labelled the testimonies of 'the unfree, children, and the poor' as unacceptable. Women were not entirely excluded from the church courts; in the courts studied here they represented up to around 20 per cent of all witnesses. But serious reservations were expressed about female testimony.[22] Age was also an important determinant in assessing the quality of a witness.[23] The result was that across the late medieval and early modern periods, female witnesses were produced in fewer numbers than their male counterparts and younger deponents appeared less frequently than older witnesses.[24]

Exceptions raised against witnesses fed into these ideas of who was deemed suitable. By the sixteenth century, serfdom had virtually vanished in England. In this context, being 'unfree' to testify might therefore be better understood not as bondage to a lord but in relation to economic or familial ties to the litigant party. Doubt was cast on those hired by the party as a servant or apprentice, those indebted to them, or members of their biological family. This, however, did not prevent servants, apprentices or family members from testifying. Exceptions made to witnesses are sometimes hyperbolic, often representing extreme views designed to discredit the opposing party's witnesses. Contradictory assessments of character were often given in the courts, depending on whose side the witness was on. However, the accuracy of these assessments of a witness' character is of lesser importance here. The types of accusation levelled at witnesses were typically commentaries on their economic activities (including wealth and labour) and their social behaviours (including intellect, sobriety, morality and neighbourliness). For the words of an opposing witness to serve as an effective and plausible exception (thereby rendering the target witness' deposition

---

22   Bronach Kane, *Popular Memory and Gender in Medieval England: Men, Women and Testimony in the Church Courts, c.1200–1500* (Woodbridge, 2019), p. 49.

23   Laura Gowing, for example, notes that in London church court depositions the young were frequently undermined by defendants who suggested that their youth made them less credible witnesses. See Laura Gowing, *Domestic Dangers: Women, Words and Sex in Early Modern London* (Oxford, 1996), p. 50.

24   Mansell, 'The variety of women's experiences', 322; Charmian Mansell, 'Female Servants in the Early Modern Community: a Study of Church Court Depositions from the Dioceses of Exeter and Gloucester, c.1550–1650', unpublished PhD dissertation (University of Exeter, 2016).

unsuitable or untrustworthy), they had to play to established mentalities and vocabularies of misbehaviour and disorder.

Characterising objections

The sample of cases is drawn from sixty-three church court suits, predominantly from Somerset and Gloucestershire (outlined in Table 8.1).[25] A large proportion (52 per cent) were generated by defamation disputes, representing the largest single type of case in the sample. The cases produced a total of 323 'objection-raising witnesses' (witnesses brought to court to pass judgment and raise exception to a witness who had already given testimony) and 212 'objectionable witnesses' (witnesses whose testimonies were objected to). For example, Sibill Woodward of Fownhope in Herefordshire testified in 1600 in a defamation suit that the plaintiff, Elizabeth Williams, had been called a 'foule hoore' by the defendant Johan Smith. Elinor Smith, however, was produced by the defendant to claim that Sibill 'did live incontinentlie with one Thomas Noven', thereby attempting to discredit her as a trustworthy witness. In this case, Elinor Smith is an 'objection-raising witness' and Sibill Woodward is an 'objectionable witness'.[26] Only 20 per cent of objection-raising witnesses were women, fitting with wider gender patterns of witness populations in the church courts. The gender composition of the 212 objectionable witnesses is strikingly different: 40 per cent were women. When accounting for gender disparity in witness production across the church courts, women were proportionally more likely to be targeted than their male counterparts.

In the short biographies outlined at the beginning of their depositions, female witnesses were identified by their marital status and male witnesses by their occupation. Married and single women comprised roughly equal proportions of objection-raising witnesses (45 and 39 per cent respectively). But married women represented a slightly lower proportion of objectionable witnesses than single women (35 per cent compared with 45 per cent). Widows made up just 20 per cent of objection-raising witnesses and 16 per cent of objectionable witnesses. Single women were therefore more frequently the target of church court exceptions than their married or widowed counterparts. This statistical analysis therefore echoes the findings of previous scholarship suggesting that young unmarried women's behaviour was more frequently criticised than that of other social groups.

---

25   The sixty-three suits form part of a transcribed collection of church court depositions for a wider study of church courts I am currently working on.
26   See Herefordshire Archive and Records Centre (hereafter HARC), HD4/2/11, Elizabeth Williams vs Joan Griffithes (1600). These are not terms employed in the church courts but are descriptions I have devised to distinguish between these different types of witness.

Table 8.1. Distribution of cases and witnesses across the church courts of the dioceses of Bath and Wells, Exeter, Gloucester and Hereford, c.1564–1641.

Church court	Cases	Objection-raising witnesses			Objectionable witnesses		
		F	M	All	F	M	All
Diocese of Bath and Wells (Somerset)	27	31	112	143	36	57	93
Diocese of Exeter (Devon and Cornwall)	9	10	46	56	17	26	43
Diocese of Gloucester (Gloucestershire)	21	18	77	95	26	36	62
Diocese of Hereford (Herefordshire)	6	5	24	29	7	7	14
Total	63	64	259	323	86	126	212

Sources: Somerset Heritage Centre: DDCd Vols 15, 18, 20, 25, 27, 28, 30, 32, 34, 36, 38, 44, 45, 50, 51, 55, 64, 65, 71, 80, 131; Devon Heritage Centre: Chanter Vols 855a, 860, 861, 864, 866, 877; Gloucestershire Archives: GDR Vols 25, 32, 65, 79, 100, 114, 121, 148; Herefordshire Archive and Records Centre: HD4/2/13, HD4/2/11.

Both objection-raising and objectionable male witnesses held a broad range of occupations, although two notable differences are apparent. Servants were more frequently among those targeted, while gentlemen were more prominent among those raising objections. However, objection-raising witnesses were not exclusively drawn from the upper circles of society. Husbandmen were the most numerous occupational category in both groups.[27] Yeomen, tailors and weavers were also prominent, demonstrating that the power of raising exception to a witness did not simply lie in the hands of the wealthiest. Interestingly, a small number of objection-raising witnesses were also recorded as *objectionable* witnesses; tables could easily be turned and those objecting to witnesses could suddenly find themselves on the receiving end, sometimes revealing their own hypocrisy.

The median age of objection-raising witnesses was forty, while those they criticised had a median age of thirty-two.[28] Objections were clearly more

27   This pattern largely mirrors the occupational structure of early modern rural society. A high proportion of husbandmen is found in the diocese of Bath and Wells court (43 per cent of all stated occupations), where a large amount of the data studied was collected. The other three courts recorded proportions of between 26 and 32 per cent.

28   Keith Thomas suggests that age was given more precisely for those under the age of twenty. My findings suggest that those in their twenties also gave their ages with precision. See Keith Thomas, 'Numeracy in Early Modern England', *Transactions of the Royal Historical Society*, 37 (1987), 128.

frequently made against testimonies of the young. But inverse age patterns are found when drilling down to look at the gender of the 155 objectionable witnesses whose ages are stated: sixty-four were women, and around 60 per cent of them were under thirty. By contrast, around 60 per cent of the ninety-one male witnesses were over thirty. Age itself could be raised as an objection to a witness. The vitriolic objections that witnesses levied were littered with words associated with youth, such as 'boy', 'girl', 'wench' or simply 'young'. Paul Griffiths identifies these words as linguistically reflecting transitional states from youth to adulthood.[29] The oldest objectionable witnesses described as 'young' were two women and a man all aged thirty. No married person was labelled as 'young', reinforcing the importance of marital status in gaining social standing and credibility.

Sometimes objection-raising witnesses hazarded a guess at the age of a witness in order to prove their youth and discredit their testimony. Husbandman John Nayle of Iron Acton in Gloucestershire described Elizabeth Bampton in 1612 as 'aboute the age of fifteene or sixteene yeares & knoweth not what belongeth to an oath being a simple person'.[30] The median age of those identified as 'young' was twenty, indicating that these accusations of youth were accurate: indeed, Joanna Tintinye of Moorlinch in Somerset noted in 1606 that James Allyn was 'scarce xxty [20] yeeres old'. In the brief biography at the beginning of his own testimony, he confirmed that he was twenty years old.[31] Women were much more frequently the target of age-related character slurs: nineteen of the thirty-one witnesses (61 per cent) for whom youth-related language was used were women. In only one case was old age suggested as a reason to discount someone's testimony. In 1605, twenty-one-year-old John Arney of Westbury in Somerset described yeoman Richard Hardweech as 'a hastye forward ould man'. From his own testimony, we know that Richard was sixty years old.[32] There was clearly, then, an age dynamic to taking exception with witnesses in court. Objectionable witnesses were on average younger than those objecting to them and age-related slurs were frequently used to cast doubt on their testimonies.

The key objections against the testimonies of young people that touch on the themes of labour regulation and social control can be broadly grouped into four main categories: 1) criminal or antisocial behaviour; 2) poverty; 3) vagrancy; 4) work. The first category of objection primarily reflects witnesses' observations of social misbehaviour, whereas the final three relate to economic concerns,

---

29   Griffiths, *Youth and Authority*, p. 21.
30   Gloucestershire Archives (hereafter GA), GDR/114, Cressett Cox vs Silvester Nayle (1612).
31   Somerset Heritage Centre (hereafter SHC), DDCd30 and DDCd38, Margaret Huckbridge vs Agnes Salter (1606).
32   SHC, DDCd28, John Hardweech vs William Bowlting (1604).

although these distinctions are of course not absolute. An accusation of theft against a witness could hint at their economic position (and many of those who were labelled as thieves by counter witnesses were described as poor). But the accusation of theft was also an accusation of immorality and dishonesty, indicating the overlap between these categories. Nonetheless, the categories provide a useful framework to help think about the dual concerns of the Statute of Artificers: labour regulation and social control. They also help us to think about the intersection of the Statute with other legislation, including vagrancy laws and poor laws. Table 8.2 sets out the number of witnesses who were described using terms that fell within these broader categories: 145 witnesses were accused of antisocial behaviour, while 165 were objected to on grounds that we might label 'economic' (poverty, vagrancy and work). The following sections explore in detail the objections that fell within these two groupings and what they can tell us about popular attitudes towards the young.

Table 8.2. Categories of objections raised against witnesses in the church courts of the dioceses of Bath and Wells, Exeter, Gloucester and Hereford, c.1564–1641.

Age	Criminal or antisocial behaviour			Poverty			Vagrancy			Work		
	F	M	All	F	M	All	F	M	All	F	M	All
30 and under	35	34	69	30	24	54	7	10	17	16	18	34
Over 30	21	55	76	16	30	46	1	3	4	3	7	10
Total	56	89	145	46	54	100	8	13	21	19	25	44

Sources: As in Table 8.1.

Working lives of young people

In early modern society people were frequently assessed and categorised according to their economic standing. A person's place in society could be framed around their material or monetary worth or descriptions of their labour, as Shepard's work has shown.[33] This section considers how objection-raising witnesses levied 'economic' objections to young men and women's working and living arrangements. It assesses the extent to which these objections intersected with the ideas of service embodied in the Statute of Artificers. The restrictions on labour presented by the Statute affected women more acutely than men.

33   Shepard, *Accounting for Oneself*; Shepard, 'Poverty, Labour', 51–95.

Men could seek alternative work to service, learning a trade as an apprentice (although the poorest strata in society could not afford this). Labouring women's options in the Statute were fewer, yet they nonetheless sought alternatives to service. For example, Craig Muldrew has shown that spinning opportunities for women could be lucrative and allow them to enjoy freedoms outside service.[34] Assessing the wages and productivity of spinners from the late sixteenth to the early nineteenth century, however, Jane Humphries and Ben Schneider have argued that there was no high-wage economy in spinning in pre-industrial England.[35] But women of the south-west certainly engaged in this form of labour: Anne Combe of Chudleigh in Devon lived with her mother and father in 1598, getting her living by carding and spinning.[36] They also sought other alternative employments: Grace Kinge, a nineteen-year-old from Yeovil in Somerset, was described in her 1629 deposition as a bonelace maker.[37] Labouring men also sought alternative work, sometimes on a seasonal basis. In 1633, twenty-five-year-old fuller John Catford of Dulverton in Devon told the court that he had been hired in the harvest season to rake.[38] This seasonal work was not uncommon for young women either.

Requiring unmarried people to work in service meant there was an expectation they would live away from their parents in the homes of their masters and mistresses. Some alternative forms of labour likewise took place in the homes of others, but young people also continued to live and work in the familial home. Numerous young witnesses in the church courts described living at home with parents. In 1573 Edward Jackette of Meysey Hampton in Gloucestershire told the court that he 'dwelleth together with his father & soe as yet hath little of his owne'.[39] Shepard notes that dependence on parents was sometimes framed explicitly as a form of 'training at home, acquiring experience, and serving a family enterprise in advance of their inheritance'.[40] Even servants expressed reliance on parents. In the statement of her worth made in interrogatory questioning, servant Alice Gullock of Farmborough in Somerset deposed in 1610 that 'she is a mayden and hath but little more then her apparrell, but she dependeth chieflie uppon her parents'.[41]

---

34   See C. Muldrew, 'The "Ancient Distaff" and "Whirling Spindle": Measuring the Contribution of Spinning to Household Earnings and the National Economy in England, 1550–1770', *Economic History Review*, 65 (2012), 498–526.

35   J. Humphries and B. Schneider, 'Spinning the Industrial Revolution', *Economic History Review*, 72 (2019), 126–55.

36   Devon Heritage Centre (hereafter DHC), Chanter 864, Jane Iverye vs Pentecost Ball and Andrew Fole (1598).

37   SHC, DDCd65, Marie Bashiler vs Joanna Hilson (1629). Grace is one of the very few female witnesses (other than servants) for whom an occupational description is recorded.

38   SHC, DDCd75, Aldred Cruse vs Spurwaie (1633).

39   GA, GDR/25, Edyth Snell vs Martyn Bradford (1572).

40   Shepard, *Accounting for Oneself*, p. 208.

41   SHC, DDCd44, Sara Kelston vs Richard Kelston (1610).

Tim Wales notes the mid-seventeenth-century preoccupation of authorities with poor young people living at home with their parents.[42] But parishioners in the south-west used their discretion when actively policing young people who lived at home, often using wealth as a key determinant in deciding when to take legal action. Mary Smith of Brampford Speke in Devon was presented to the local Justices of the Peace for living at home with her alms-dependent widowed mother in 1635, while the habitation of other young people of modest means with parents went unnoticed.[43] A 1574 defamation dispute in the parish of Bromsberrow in Gloucestershire reveals the underlying tensions in assessing whether young people should reside at home. Responding to objections raised against witness John Guynell, husbandman John Ferne argued:

> he haith knowen him [John] sythence his infancye whoe was borne in Elsfield and is one honest yonge man lyvinge sometyme in service & sometyme with his mother a widowe & a thriftie yonge man of sufficient credite to beare witness in the saied cause.

The original objections raised against John Guynell were that he was allegedly very poor and reliant on parish alms. One witness added that he was lame. If we believe that he was the physically impaired son of a poor widow, it becomes a reasonable assumption that some allowances were made regarding his living situation and his labour. John described himself to the court as a husbandman and it appears that flexibility in the conditions of his labour was permitted; sometimes he worked as a day labourer and sometimes in service. He perhaps sporadically received relief when his disability prevented him from working or earning a sufficient income to support himself. His periodic residence at home with his widowed mother was tolerated by most.[44] It is likely, then, that the objection-raising witnesses in this case took advantage of his poverty and disability, presenting a hyperbolic and unsympathetic view of his status.

But being reliant on a parent was rarely referred to by objection-raising witnesses. Only three objectionable witnesses were negatively characterised as dependent on parents across the four courts. All three (one woman and two men) fell in the 'thirty and under' age bracket. In none of these cases was it explicitly stated that they ought to be in service *rather than* living at home. In fact, only one witness in each of the three cases made any reference to them living at home at all: Agnes Plumbley of Westbury in Somerset was described in 1604 by husbandman George Spiring as a 'very poore girle nowe dwelling

42   Wales, '"Living at their own Hands"', 29–30.
43   DHC, Chanter 866, Mary Flood vs Dorothea Tucker (1635). For a more detailed discussion of this case, see Mansell, 'Female Service and the Village Community', pp. 77–8.
44   GA, GDR/32, Elinore Grove vs John Bromadge (1574); GDR/32, John Bromadge vs Guy Grove (1574).

at home with her father'. The atypical production of her father as a witness in this case provides access to further information. His deposition reveals that he was fifty-six years old and got his living 'by hard labor & working at the myneryes [mines]'. He was worth, by his own estimation, just four shillings. He confirmed that his daughter was poor and had lived with him for three years, having formerly been employed as a servant.[45] In 1606, gentleman Alexander Walton of Moorlinch in the same county deposed that Jacob Allyn, who self-identified as a groom, 'liveth at daye labor with his father'.[46] The final example of dependence on parents being expressed in the exceptions was of a twenty-year-old yeoman, Thomas Powell, whose misbehaviour was clearly the issue rather than his residence in the familial home and is discussed in detail later in this chapter.[47]

Similarly, terms associated with being 'masterless' are also rarely found in the exceptions responses. Living without a master features as an accusation only four times in the sample: it is used three times in Somerset to refer to two men and one woman under thirty, and once in Devon to refer to a female witness also under thirty. Criticism of the witness Alice Hancock of Isle Brewers in Somerset represented the clearest articulation of service being perceived as a means of honest labour. She was described in 1613 as 'one that will staye with noe Master but is an idle wenche and ran awaye from Rabidge Labyes mother 6 or 7 yeeres since or therabouts'.[48] Yet, even here, perhaps running away and being idle were her true 'crimes', rather than failing to live in service. Thomas Fox of Westbury in Somerset was described as 'unmarryed and for the most part masterles' in 1604. Close reading of the case reveals that the issue raised by witnesses concerned trade and apprenticeship (another area of labour regulation that the Statute sought to reform) rather than living out of service. Thomas was a tailor, but witnesses deposed that he had served just two years of his apprenticeship. Their grievance, therefore, was that 'hee bee scarcely his crafts master, yett hath continewed a masterles man'. The labour laws sought to regulate access to crafts and trades that required formal training in the form of apprenticeship.[49] Thomas' failure to complete his training was the concern here, not his living outside service.[50] Here, laws on service and apprenticeship appear to have reinforced one another.

Despite the preoccupation of the Statute with forcing unmarried people to live under a master, the framework for what was permissible was much broader.

45   SHC, DDCd28, John Hardweech vs William Bowlting (1604).
46   SHC, DDCd30 and DDCd38, Margaret Huckbridge vs Agnes Salter (1606).
47   SHC, DDCd34, Marcus Taber vs Thomas Powle (1603).
48   SHC, DDCd45, Matilda Midleton vs Rabigia Labie (1613).
49   Chris Minns and Patrick Wallis, 'Rules and Reality: Quantifying the Practice of Apprenticeship in Early Modern England', *Economic History Review*, 65 (2012), 556–79.
50   SHC, DDCd28, John Hardweech vs William Bowlting (1604).

Rather than explicitly criticising young people for living without a master, objection-raising witnesses more frequently expressed their concerns about those who had no fixed place of residence or were vagrant. The expression of views on vagrancy was gender-related; female witnesses less frequently depicted objectionable witnesses as vagrant. Their contributions accounted for just four of the forty-seven references to vagrancy. This is low considering that 20 per cent of objection-raising witnesses were women. All four of the women who participated in this discourse were between the ages of eighteen and twenty-five and in service. The restrictions on their own freedoms may have made them particularly aggrieved at those who had no fixed abode and enjoyed living outside the control of a master. Perhaps litigant parties might deliberately showcase women in service as objection-raising witnesses to serve as a clear juxtaposition against the unruly self-governance and autonomous lifestyles of individuals brought in as witnesses on the opposing side.

Although fewer women participated in discourse around vagrancy, a higher proportion found themselves the target of it. They were the recipients of 48 per cent of vagrancy-related attacks on their character, and women aged thirty and below were a particular target. In 1607 broadweaver Hugo Salter of Uley in Gloucestershire objected to the testimony of Joanne Daingerfield, who he described as 'one that hath noe certen habitacion but worketh sometimes with one & sometimes with an other as she cann procure worke in anye place'.[51] The concern about Joanne was directly linked with work but, elsewhere, no clear connection with labour or lack of service was referred to. In 1578, twenty-five-year-old Richard Rogers was described as 'one who neyther hath any certeyne place of abode but is compted [counted] for a common renigate and a vagabond'.[52] In using these terms, objection-raising witnesses tapped into the language of settlement and vagrancy that was prevalent in the period. As Wales reminds us, it is important to consider the labour laws alongside other legislation on settlement and poverty.[53]

Service might help to pin down the vagrant, but it was not always a successful strategy. The Statute stipulated that service should be annual; however, this was not always the case.[54] A 1594 defamation dispute from Gloucestershire reveals tensions between holding a position in service and vagrancy. Three male witnesses – Maurice Earle (22), Thomas Baker (26) and Griffin George (22) – all self-identified as servants. Yet the six witnesses produced to discredit

---

51   GA, GDR/100, George Birche vs Thomas Payne (1607).
52   DHC, Chanter 860, John Morris vs John Sparcks (1578).
53   Wales, '"Living at their own Hands"', 22.
54   See Jane Whittle, 'A Different Pattern of Employment: Servants in Rural England c.1500–1660', in Jane Whitte (ed.), *Servants in Europe, 1400–1900* (Woodbridge, 2017), pp. 57–76; Mansell, 'Female Service and the Village Community', pp. 91–2; Mansell, 'The variety of women's experiences', 328–31.

their testimonies labelled them as vagrant. Many, including local minister Thomas Rocke, agreed that Thomas Baker 'was & yet is servannte' to Richard Oliffe, but his fellow objection-raising witness Thomas Hughes deposed that 'Thomas Baker ... is not worth tenne shillings & such a one as hath no certayne place of aboade but is accompted a wandering ydle fellow.' Another witness added that Thomas Baker's mother was poor and had never married, living by the relief of the parish while her son 'is not worth xx [20] s & is such a one as hath no certayne place of aboad'. Servant Joanna Estington described Maurice Earle as 'a vagrant person & such a one as hath no certayne place of habitacion'. While Maurice claimed to be a servant in nearby Prestbury, Thomas Rocke countered that he 'is at this instannte placed as he hath heard in London'.[55] It is likely that the periods that these men worked in service were short and did not provide the stability of residence that early modern parishioners considered important for young people. Evidence like this further demonstrates that the clause of the Statute that service should be annual was not strictly enforced.

Service as the Statute envisaged it was therefore a strategy for ensuring a stable residence for labouring young people that society understood and, in some cases, upheld. But the responses of objection-raising witnesses reveal a wider spectrum of what was deemed permissible: living at home offered young people the stability society sought for them and acceptability was assessed according to family finances and dynamics. Being masterless was referred to less frequently than having no fixed abode simply because stability was not conceived solely in terms of service. Service did not always offer stability: if young people were moving too frequently from master to master then eyebrows might be raised. Stability was an important social marker of belonging and individuals who remained in the same place could be held to account within their local community. Having the stability of a fixed abode represented economic security and some insurance against risk. The views that objection-raising witnesses articulated intersected with the aims and concerns of the Statute, but stability was conceived as achievable outside service.

Social policing

From the perspective of the young, the stability of service might offer the chance to gain wealth and skills to marry and earn their own living. But other forms of employment could offer higher remuneration.[56] Whittle found that a servant

55   GA, GDR/79, Joane Mare vs Joane Oliffe (1594).
56   Jane Humphries and Jacob Weisdorf, 'The Wages of Women in England, 1260–1850', *Journal of Economic History*, 75 (2015), 405–47.

couple who had worked for around five years each and had saved all their wages could together buy and stock only a cottage holding in early modern England. Service, she concludes, was 'not a route to social mobility' in and of itself.[57] The Statute of Artificers reinforced this idea by aligning service as a form of employment for those under a modest income threshold. Those with greater wealth were accorded more labour freedom.

But the 'exploited poor' that Hill talks of might benefit from service in another way.[58] Contemporary writings framed service as socially and morally beneficial to the young. Wales suggests that, from the mid-seventeenth century, calls for social and moral reform intersected with concerns about labour shortages. He cites a 1682 rebuke from the Kent justices of young people working in service for only part of the year and 'getting a habit of idleness, laziness and debauchery'.[59] The word 'debauchery' covers a multitude of immoralities, many of which were the subject of the objections raised to witnesses listed under the category 'criminal activity or antisocial behaviour' (Table 8.2). Theft and sex outside marriage were the two most common activities that witnesses objected to amongst those aged thirty and under and are the focus of this section.

Young male witnesses were much more frequently accused of theft than their female counterparts by opposing witnesses: two-thirds of the accused were men.[60] Theft was referred to in conjunction with being vagrant in five of the nine accusations. Again, explicit references to being without a master were largely absent. Only one direct link was made. Thomas Powell, a twenty-year-old witness from Bathampton in Somerset, described himself as a yeoman in his 1603 deposition. His status (and assumed wealth) would have spared him from forced service under the Statute. No objection-raising witness contested his wealth, acknowledging that he was maintained by his father, but this was not represented in a positive light. Thirty-year-old Susanne Cottle, a married woman, deposed that he 'doth live verie rudelye & idlye without a master'. Mason John Skryne added that he 'hath knowne him to steale som apples out of another man's orchard' within the last year. While the Statute imposed no requirement for Thomas Powell to be employed in service, each objection-raising witness in this case took exception with both his masterlessness and his criminal activities. What was permissible by Statute was not accepted by his neighbours, particularly in light of his proclivity for theft. The tension between

---

57   Jane Whittle, 'Servants in Rural England c. 1450–1650: Hired Work as a Means of Accumulating Wealth and Skills Before Marriage', in Maria Ågren and Amy Erickson (eds), *The Marital Economy in Scandinavia and Britain, 1400–1900* (Aldershot, 2005), p. 104.

58   Hill, 'Pottage for Freeborn Englishmen', pp. 345–6.

59   Wales, '"Living at their own Hands"', 29.

60   The gender pattern was even more pronounced among the older group of witnesses with whom exception was raised: men represented 93 per cent of those in this age bracket linked with theft.

Statute and popular opinion is clear in Agnes Jeffery's deposition: she deposed that he 'hath noe Master *but* liveth under his father', indicating that she saw a contradiction in his unruly lifestyle, social status and living situation.[61] While this may have been an exceptional case, it nonetheless reveals that Thomas Powell's stable residence did not offer the order and discipline that society sought for young people.

Social concerns expressed about young people by objection-raising witnesses could therefore transcend class divides. The perceived benefits of service as a means of social regulation extended to a wider group than the Statute set out. This maps onto evidence found elsewhere: in 1615 in Exeter, Marie Stone, the twenty-five-year-old wife of a baker, criticised Elizabeth Strachley, the daughter of a wealthy widow, saying 'it were [would be] good for you to be putt forthe to service, and not steye at home seeing you are no better hable to govern your self'.[62] However, the Statute presented living at home as a privilege to be accorded only to those meeting its wealth criteria. In the cases above, while the Statute assumed that young people like Thomas Powell and Elizabeth Strachley from wealthier households would be well governed without entering service, their neighbours sometimes disagreed. Conversely, the Statute assumed that young people from poorer households could not be well governed and therefore mandated that labouring young people should be placed in service.

If theft was more strongly associated with male objectionable witnesses, women aged thirty and below were much more likely to be identified by objection-raising witnesses as having engaged in sexual relations outside marriage. Unmarried women have been seen as the particular target of the Statute, appearing more frequently before the secular courts for non-compliance. Sex outside marriage and illegitimacy were of particular concern.[63] Wales indicates that 'presentments of young women do not overtly focus on matters of sexual behaviour, although it is more than possible that in many cases fears and assumptions were too commonplace to need articulating'.[64] Sexual misbehaviour has certainly been understood as gender-related; Laura Gowing found that the language of insult in the London consistory courts was almost always focused on sexual immorality in relation to women.[65] High female presentment rates could therefore be explained by fears of pre-marital sex.

---

61 SHC, Marcus Taber vs Thomas Powle (1603). Italics my own.

62 DHC, Chanter 867, Henry Cockram vs Bartholomew Jaquinto (1615).

63 For examples, see Wales, '"Living at their own Hands"', 19–39; McIntosh, *Controlling Misbehavior*, p. 160.

64 Wales, '"Living at their own Hands"', 35.

65 Gowing, *Domestic Dangers*, pp. 62–3. See also Keith Thomas, 'The Double Standard', *Journal of the History of Ideas*, 20 (1959), 195–216; Bernard Capp, 'The Double Standard Revisited: Plebeian Women and Male Sexual Reputation in Early Modern England', *Past and Present*, 162 (1999), 70–101.

The contemporary preoccupation with illegitimacy is nonetheless puzzling given that rates were quite low in early modern England; Macintosh found only 1.8 per cent of live births to be illegitimate in Romford between 1562 and 1619.[66] But the exceptions raised against female witnesses do support the idea that this was a public concern. Of seventeen witnesses under thirty who were described as living incontinently with another person or having had sex outside marriage, twelve were women. In 1629, tailor Francis Deswall of Yarpole in Herefordshire deposed that twenty-five-year-old servant Mary Maylard 'hath been suspected to be of lewd behavioure, and an incontinent person, and [he] hath heard John Cannop confes that he had the carnall use of her body about a yeare agoe'.[67] Scattered evidence confirms that parishioners were concerned about young women falling pregnant outside wedlock and there is some indication they considered service a solution to this. In 1601, cordwainer John Jellyborne of Glastonbury in Somerset voiced his concern about Alice Stone, his former servant. He noted she had had several masters and proceeded to name seven positions in service (once with himself) that she had held within the last twelve to fifteen months:

> First, with one John Raynolds of the Signe of the Hart in Glaston then with John Lane, or first with the said Lane, and then to the Hart. Then to the Pellycane, then to the Bell, then to the Hart againe, thease 3 places being severall Innes in Glaston aforesaid. Then shee came to this deponent and made covenant to dwell with him for a yeere.

In associating Alice with employment in inns and places of entertainment, John perhaps already hinted at her loose morals. He then continued that, while she was employed in his service,

> one Philipp Greene then constable of Glaston came to him & tould him of the said Alice, saying that shee was a light idle huswief, and one muche feared least shee would suffer her self to bee begotten with childe, and so charge the towne with a bastard.

Such frank expression of fear of illegitimacy is rare in the church courts, as a false allegation could lead to a defamation suit. But John Jellyborne was on relatively safe ground, as it transpired that he and other witnesses firmly suspected Alice to have had an illegitimate child.[68]

---

66   Marjorie K. McIntosh, *A Community Transformed: the Manor and Liberty of Havering, 1500–1620* (Cambridge, 1991), pp. 68–9. See also Roger A. P. Finlay, 'Population and Fertility in London, 1580–1650', *Journal of Family History*, 4 (1979), 26–38; Peter Laslett, *Family Life and Illicit Love in Earlier Generations: Essays in Historical Sociology* (Cambridge, 1977), pp. 137–41.
67   HARC, HD4/2/13, Jane Dirry vs Sibell Francke (1629).
68   SHC, DDCd32, Henry Sock vs Maria Barter (1601).

The chargeability of a fatherless child on the parish was of clear concern here. If a father could not be identified, poor rates levied on parishioners were used to maintain the mother and child. The focus on ensuring the sexual chastity of young unmarried women was therefore as much an economic concern as a moral one. The language of poverty mapped closely onto the vice of having a child out of wedlock.[69] The aims of the Statute and the poor laws intersected in this respect. Across the dataset, thirty-five individuals were identified as parenting an illegitimate child. Interestingly, almost equal numbers were men and women; but of the sixteen young people (aged thirty and under) associated with this perceived offence, ten were women and words associated with poverty were simultaneously used to describe seven of them. The economic implications of having a child out of wedlock were clearly perceived as much lesser for young men. Only one young man was described as poor or similar, indicating the wider range of choices available to men with illegitimate children to earn a living.

Nonetheless, there is little evidence in the depositions to suggest that illegitimacy and sex outside marriage could be avoided by placing young women under a master. John Jellyborne's deposition is unique in its coupling of illegitimacy and being masterless or living outside service. It is possible that his deposition deliberately played into the narrative that young women required the control of a master. In fact, it might be somewhat ironic that John Jellyborne saw Alice Stone's illegitimate pregnancy as connected to her lack of a secure position in service. Many masters appeared before this very same court for fathering their servants' children. Of the c.900 female servants who were recorded across all depositions of the four courts between 1550 and 1650, 114 had or were suspected to have had a child out of wedlock. In two-thirds of these cases, the master of the servant was implicated as the father.[70] In 1605, a defamation suit was raised in the Gloucester court, whereupon a master was accused of fathering the child of his servant (she herself had named her fellow servant as the father). The defamatory words were spoken by a young woman in the street who bemoaned the situation, reporting what may have been a familiar adage: 'the servant hath the name but the master had the game'.[71] Furthermore, given the number of witnesses who testified in court against predatory masters, it is reasonable to assume that service may not have been seen as a safe haven for young women. Authorities' attempts to curtail the vice of illegitimacy through service failed to recognise that masters' behaviour could fall short of their expectations. As a result, their means of addressing the problem of illegitimacy may have been out of step with popular concerns.

---

69   See Shepard, *Accounting for Oneself*, p. 138.
70   In the remaining third of cases, the father was either unidentified or a man who was not their employer was named.
71   GA, GDR/95, William Locksmithe vs Alice Butler (1605).

Few unmarried women who gave birth out of wedlock could remain in service. Employers were unlikely to house a newborn and unmarried new mothers would have little or no time to perform service. Returning to service was more likely if their child had died or was sent away. In 1587, a servant named Jane of Driffield in Gloucestershire gave birth to her master's child. Her master, a yeoman named William Hawkins, gave a 'poore man monye to carrye the same childe out of the conntrye', allowing Jane to remain in his service.[72] More typically, however, unmarried mothers performed forms of day labour in conjunction with childcare. Cicilia Frances alias Kempe, aged thirty, of Wedmore in Somerset, deposed in 1626 that she was worth nothing but her clothes and did charwork for Mr Robert Hole. She admitted that 'shee was never marryed, and that shee hath had two base children borne of her bodie the one of them aged seaven years old & upwards & the other dyed'.[73] Service was supposed to provide a secure labour framework for the unmarried. But unmarried mothers were rarely the beneficiaries of this system. The institution that promised to protect young women from the vice of pre-marital sex and illegitimacy simultaneously facilitated those 'vices' by placing them in a stranger's household where patriarchal power dynamics left them exposed to the sexual advances of their employers. When these women then fell pregnant, the institution turned them away.

Conclusion

Studying objections or exceptions to church court witnesses allows for a fine-grained analysis of popular conceptions of labour patterns and social behaviours of young people. The evidence analysed in this chapter demonstrates the advantages of studying this material. It has shown that popular attitudes towards young people and labour were more complex than those laid out in the 1563 Statute of Artificers. It also highlights dissonance between the Statute legislators and the populace in their conceptions of the state of the young and unmarried. The vocabulary used by objection-raising witnesses in discrediting the testimonies of young people expressed concerns of poverty, vagrancy, and lack of fixed abode, but service was not exclusively presented as the solution.

The labour laws gave parishioners a means by which to control the exceptionally poor or exceptionally unruly but not necessarily a framework by which to regulate the behaviour of *all* young unmarried people of modest means. Hill is right to suggest that the legislation accentuated the marginalisation and

---

72   GA, GDR/65, Thomas Iles vs Joanna Addams (1587).
73   SHC, DDCd51, Eleanor Hodges vs Nicholas Barker (1626).

exploitation of the very poorest in society, but for most young people its impact was probably much less.[74] Service was not conceived of as the only remedy to the vices of young people. Equally, it could be occasionally considered a solution for the unruly behaviour of those who did not fall under its remit (as the examples of wealthier young people indicate). There is tension between the presentation of service as an institution that regulated and controlled youth, and evidence that shows that the godly household free of vice and corruption was far from the reality of service for some. More than 10 per cent of all female servants recorded between 1550 and 1650 in the church courts had fallen pregnant.[75] This high proportion surely shaped popular conceptions of service. It is therefore unsurprising that service was considered only one form of labour available to young women.

Falling foul of the Statute did not leave a sufficient stain on one's character to form an effective objection to their testimony before the court. While in some isolated cases direct mention of a failure to be a yearly covenanted servant was lodged as an objection to a young person's deposition, objections typically invoked a broader range of social, economic and moral deficiencies. The economic concerns that the Statute focused on addressing through service and the social regulation that preoccupied enforcers were discussed much more loosely by witnesses in court. Ordinary people accepted a wider range of patterns of work among the young than were formally mandated by the Statute and its magistrates.

---

74   I am currently working on analysing consistory court depositions from the diocese of Norwich with a view to undertaking a comparative study of exceptions responses as prosecution rates for infringements have been found to be higher in East Anglia.

75   It is important to note the context for this high figure. Church courts were responsible for enforcing morality in early modern society and punishing those who had sex outside marriage fell within the remit of the court. Nonetheless, when coupled with the persistent trope of lecherous masters and vulnerable female servants in plays and other writings from the period, the figure surely indicates that service must have been perceived as a typical context in which sex outside marriage might occur.

9

Exposed Lives: Compulsory Service and 'Vagrancy' Practices in Sweden in the 1830s

THERESA JOHNSSON[1]

From the late Middle Ages until well into the nineteenth century, compulsory service constituted a central principle for regulating labour in large parts of north-western Europe. As A. L. Beier has pointed out, compulsory service formed the link between labour law and vagrancy law; and, in many places, failure to comply could lead to being legally considered a 'vagrant'.[2] Labour and vagrancy legislation were crucial elements of a complex system of interlocking regulations targeting the labouring poor, which included restrictive poor relief systems, bans on begging, and settlement and mobility restrictions.[3] The Servant Acts, combined with their legal sanctions – vagrancy laws – and other compounding laws and social practices, fixed the boundaries of 'free labour' and provided the elite with a means of coercion against weaker counterparts in, to borrow the words of Andy Wood, 'a profoundly unequal, and often cruel, class structure'.[4] The laws had many potential uses and broad, flexible scopes of application: regulating the labour markets, gearing the labouring poor's work efforts into legally recognised employment, suppressing wages, creating societal order, enforcing work discipline, upholding the sanctity of contract and preserving

---

1 I would like to thank Erik Lindberg of Uppsala University for valuable comments during the writing of this chapter and Maria Ågren of Uppsala University for fruitful discussions and advice.
2 A. L. Beier, '"A New Serfdom": Labor Laws, Vagrancy Statutes, and Labor Discipline in England, 1350–1800', in A. L. Beier and P. Ocoboc (eds), *Cast Out: Vagrancy and Homelessness in Global and Historical Perspective* (Athens, GA, 2008), p. 35.
3 C. Lis and H. Soly, *Worthy Efforts: Attitudes to Work and Workers in Pre-Industrial Europe* (Leiden, 2012), p. 435.
4 D. Hay and P. Craven, 'Introduction', in D. Hay and P. Craven (eds), *Masters, Servants, and Magistrates in Britain and the Empire, 1562–1955* (Chapel Hill, 2004), p. 1; A. Wood, 'Subordination, Solidarity, and the Limits of Popular Agency in a Yorkshire Valley, c.1596–1615', *Past and Present*, 193 (2006), 20.

unequal relations between the rich and the poor.[5] As Catharina Lis and Hugo Soly have emphasised, 'labour laws, poor laws, and criminal laws' became increasingly intertwined from the early modern period onwards in large parts of Western Europe.[6] Legal sanctions were an integral part of contract enforcement, and took many forms depending on judicial doctrine and social practices over the centuries. However, there is only limited knowledge of whether and how these sanctions were practised. One explanation for this, as Beier observed as late as 2008, is that 'the subject of compulsory service has largely been ignored' in recent (British) social historical research.[7]

Just as compulsory service cannot be analysed without placing it into the legal and institutional framework it was part of, the enforcement of compulsory service cannot be fully understood without taking vagrancy practices into account.[8] However, 'vagrancy' is another topic to which mainstream social history has long paid scant or predominantly prejudiced attention.[9] In his seminal study published in 1985, Beier argued for the need to move away from the narrow approach of studying the elite and their views on what they called 'vagrancy'.[10] Since then, several studies have normalised the 'vagrant' in history, turning the phantoms of 'work-shy' sturdy beggars into poor people trying to make a living, often in dire circumstances.[11] Anne Winter has written that 'vagrancy' is a penal, pejorative, vague and variable concept associated for centuries with antisocial behaviour, and that this very perspective has been retained in the historiography.[12] The treatment of the 'vagrant' in Swedish historiography is a case in point. Although thousands of arrests could be

5   Hay and Craven, 'Introduction', pp. 33–5; Lis and Soly, *Worthy Efforts*, p. 435.

6   Lis and Soly, *Worthy Efforts*, p. 444.

7   Beier, 'A New Serfdom', p. 56; cf. J. Bennett, 'Compulsory Service in Late Medieval England', *Past and Present*, 209 (2010), 9. For an exception, see J. Whittle, *The Development of Agrarian Capitalism: Land and Labour in Norfolk 1440–1580* (Oxford, 2000).

8   By the nineteenth century, the concepts of legal protection and 'vagrancy' had 'been united'. See A. Snare, *Work, War, Prison, and Welfare: Control of the Laboring Poor in Sweden* (Ann Arbor, 1977), p. 131.

9   When used on their own, 'vagrancy' and 'vagrants' are, in this chapter, placed within quotation marks to signal that these terms are derogatory or judicial constructions rather than meaningful descriptions of people's behaviour; cf. A. Winter, 'Vagrancy as an Adaptive Strategy: The Duchy of Brabant, 1767–1776', *International Review of Social History*, 49 (2004), 249–77.

10   A. L. Beier, *Masterless Men. The Vagrancy Problem in England, 1560–1640* (London, 1985), pp. 3–4.

11   N. Rogers, 'Policing the Poor in Eighteenth-Century London: The Vagrancy Laws and Their Administration', *Social History*, 24 (1991), 127–47; Winter, 'Vagrancy'; P. Fumerton, *Unsettled: The Culture of Mobility and the Working Poor in Early Modern England* (Chicago, 2006); T. Hitchcock, A. Crymble and L. Falcini, 'Loose, Idle and Disorderly: Vagrant Removal in Late Eighteenth-Century Middlesex', *Social History*, 39:4 (2014), 509–27.

12   Winter, 'Vagrancy', 249–50.

made each year for compulsory service and vagrancy offences in the 1800s, little attention has been paid to compulsory service and vagrancy policing.[13] Conversely, there is considerable knowledge of elite discussions on the same topics.[14] The labour and vagrancy laws of Sweden are also well known, and have been the subject of scholarly study since the nineteenth century. An older generation of Swedish social historians saw compulsory service as a cornerstone of labour legislation at the time, but their perspective was framed on the question of whether hard-working persons could be subject to legal sanctions, or if these mainly affected 'work-shy' persons who, perhaps deservingly so, were labelled 'vagrants'.[15] The 'vagrant' has been coupled with deviance, criminality and marginality, and with few exceptions has generally remained an outsider in Swedish historiography.[16]

This chapter argues for the continued need to bring 'vagrancy' into studies of labour law history. As mentioned, during recent years several valuable studies on 'vagrancy' have been published, usually with the focus on the migrating labouring poor. Following Judith Bennett, this chapter treats the uses of compulsory service and vagrancy laws as fundamental to labour legislation in general, and not limited to issues of mobility.[17] Legal sanctions could also place the settled labouring poor into the legal category of 'vagrants'.[18] The chapter deals with compulsory service and the particular institution of 'legal protection' (*laga försvar*) in Sweden in the 1830s. From 1664 the principle

13   Few systematic studies exist on the legal sanctions in relation to compulsory service before the 1850s. For an important analysis of the legislation and coercive measures, see Snare, *Work*. See also A. Montgomery, *Svensk socialpolitik under 1800-talet* (1951); V. Helgesson, 'Kontroll av underklassen. Försvarslöshetsfrågan 1825–53', in I. Hammarström (ed.), *Ideologi och socialpolitik i 1800-talets Sverige* (Uppsala, 1978); T. Magnusson, *Det militära proletariatet: Studier kring den värvade armén, arbetsmarknadens kommersialisering och urbaniseringen i frihetstidens västsvenska samhälle* (Gothenburg, 2005); Y. Svanström, *Policing Public Women: The Regulation of Prostitution in Stockholm 1812–1880* (Stockholm, 2000); and T. Johnsson, *Vårt fredliga samhälle: 'Lösdriveri' och försvarslöshet i Sverige under 1830-talet* (Uppsala, 2016).

14   For example, G. Hammarskjöld, *Om lösdrifvare och deras behandling, företrädesvis enligt svensk lag* (Lund, 1866); A. O. Winroth, *Om tjenstehjonsförhållandet enligt svensk rätt* (Uppsala, 1878); B. Harnesk, *Legofolk: Drängar, pigor och bönder i 1700- och 1800-talens Sverige* (Umeå, 1990); M. Kumlien, *Continuity and Contract: Historical Perspectives on the Employee's Duty of Obedience in Swedish Labour Law* (Stockholm, 2004). Legal scholars have shown great interest in the status crime of 'vagrancy' in Sweden as elsewhere.

15   G. Utterström, *Jordbrukets arbetare: Levnadsvillkor och arbetsliv på landsbygden från frihetstiden till mitten av 1800-talet*. Vol. 1 (Stockholm, 1957), p. 327.

16   Cf. E. Österberg, 'Vardagens sträva samförstånd: Bondepolitik i den svenska modellen från vasatid till frihetstid', in G. Broberg, U. Wikander and K. Åmark (eds), *Tänka, tycka, tro: Svensk historia underifrån* (Stockholm, 1993), p. 144.

17   For a similar perspective see Snare, *Work*.

18   Bennett, 'Compulsory Service', 12.

of compulsory service was codified in the initial paragraph of the Servant Acts, and constituted the backbone of Swedish labour law until its abolition in 1885. Legal protection was fundamental to compulsory service, and contemporaries talked about the system of legal protection.[19] The concept summarises the system's interlocking regulations and sets the boundaries for what was considered a legally recognised occupation. Being engaged in a 'lawful' occupation, possessing an independent farm, having burgher's rights, owning factories, practising craftsmanship or being employed or entering service according to the regulations for trade, manufactures and crafts or the Servant Acts gave legal protection from being exposed to prosecution for 'vagrancy'. Innumerable and changing acts and ordinances defined the occupations or living conditions that were considered legal. The Servant Acts must thus be placed into a broader dynamic legal framework of labour legislation. The existence of a law allowing authorities to order persons to enter service or find other means of legal protection means that involuntary unemployment was not a legally recognised status. Despite its wordiness, the legislation was vague – a hallmark of vagrancy laws – giving leeway for local actors in choosing whether or not to use it.[20] This makes it difficult to know whether compulsory service had any importance at a given place and time, such as a parish in Sweden in the 1830s.[21]

The main empirical focus of this chapter lies on a narrow but central aspect of the legal protection system: detainments in jail for 'vagrancy'. Using evidence predominantly from c.1,000 vagrancy cases handled by the county government in Västmanland in the years 1829–38, this chapter explores how the labouring poor could experience the system of legal protection.[22] Most vagrancy policing and, for example, bargaining between different actors in employment contract issues happened locally and has left few traces in the archives. Still, the detainments provide glimpses of how the labouring poor could experience the system of legal protection. The chapter is based on a combination of different sources, including official reports, interrogations, jail records and parish assembly minutes, which have been described elsewhere.[23]

19 C. Livijn, *Promemoria angående Sveriges försvarslöshetssystem* (Stockholm, 1844). Cf. Snare, *Work*.

20 A. Eccles, *Vagrancy in Law and Practice under the Old Poor Law* (Abingdon, 2012), p. 139; Johnsson, *Vårt fredliga*, p. 35.

21 Recent studies on 'vagrancy' in England have emphasised the local variations in definitions of 'vagrancy'. See Bennett, 'Compulsory Service', 12; Eccles, *Vagrancy*; C. Mansell, 'Female Service and the Village Community in South-West England, 1550–1650: The Labour Laws Reconsidered', in Jane Whittle (ed.), *Servants in Rural Europe 1400–1900* (Woodbridge, 2017), p. 80.

22 The chapter builds on parts of Johnsson, *Vårt fredliga*, chapters 2–3.

23 For details, see appendices 1–3 in Johnsson, *Vårt fredliga*.

The county of Västmanland is a most likely case for the enforcement of compulsory service. Vagrancy offences, the judicial processing of individuals, fell under the jurisdiction of the county governments or, in some towns, a so-called Police Chamber. The county governor of Västmanland was the wealthy landowner Count Fredric Ludvig Ridderstolpe, who once called cottagers 'corroding vermin' in the Diet and was a strong proponent of compulsory service. There were many potential conflicts regarding labour supply and forms of employment in the county, and the 1830s was a decade characterised by proletarianisation, polarisation, unemployment and poverty. In this particular time and place, compulsory labour should not be understood in a limited context of forcing idle men and women to work for particular employers. It was an institution with highly varied aims and functions.[24] As pointed out by Annika Snare, in the 1800s, when labour was no longer considered a scarcity, the system of legal protection was driven by other motives: it was a tool for policing the labouring poor.[25]

This chapter consists of four sections. The first gives an overview of the institutional framework in the 1830s, the second treats detainments on a national level, the third explores compulsory service and 'vagrancy' practices in Västmanland and the fourth concludes the chapter.

Compulsory service in the 1830s: an overview of the institutional framework

Sweden was still rural in the 1830s, with only 10 per cent of the population living in towns.[26] There was little industry aside from ironworking, and government policy had confined most trade and commerce to towns. Real wages for male agricultural day labourers were constant between 1800 and the 1820s, declining thereafter until the 1850s.[27] Tommy Bengtsson has shown a relationship between class and mortality in Sweden in times of harvest failures during the first half of the nineteenth century. The landless experienced increased mortality when real wages fell.[28] Since the mid-eighteenth century Sweden had undergone a process of proletarianisation, and by the 1830s Västmanland had become one of

24   Cf. Lis and Soly, *Worthy Efforts*, p. 436.

25   Snare, *Work*, p. 131.

26   *Historisk statistik för Sverige*, vol. 1 (Stockholm, 1969), pp. 50, 53.

27   J. Söderberg, 'Long-Term Trends in Real Wages of Labourers', in R. Edvinsson, T. Jacobson and D. Waldenström (eds), *Historical Monetary and Financial Statistics for Sweden: Exchange Rates, Prices and Wages, 1277–2008*, vol. 1 (Stockholm, 2010), p. 464.

28   T. Bengtsson, 'Mortality and Social Class in Four Scanian Parishes, 1766–1865', in T. Bengtsson, C. Campbell, J.Z. Lee *et al.*, *Life under Pressure: Mortality and Living Standards in Europe and Asia, 1700–1900* (Cambridge, 2004), pp. 163–70.

the most proletarianised counties.[29] Its county seat, Västerås, is located around 100 kilometres west of Stockholm. Measuring 6,740 square kilometres in total, Västmanland officially had 89,262 inhabitants in the year 1830, of whom 9 per cent lived in one of its four small towns. Västerås was the biggest town, with a little over than 3,000 inhabitants.[30] The countryside was divided into seventy parishes, administrative units with far-reaching self-governance.

In 1826 county governor Ridderstolpe wrote in response to a state commission investigating the vagrancy situation in Sweden that the legislation concerning 'vagrants' and legal protection was so vast that even to obtain an overview entailed tedious work. Not surprisingly, Ridderstolpe did not limit himself to the Servant Acts or vagrancy laws. In his listing, Ridderstolpe included the Poor Relief and Settlement Act of 1788, laws on passports, the County Governor Instruction of 1734, taxation laws, land laws, various labour laws concerning journeymen and retired soldiers, and many more.[31] Poor relief rates in Sweden around 1830 were at an absolute minimum in a comparative European perspective, with rates per capita around 6 per cent of the level of those in England and Wales.[32] Until the promulgation of a new national Poor Law in 1847, the parishes had great freedom to organise poor relief in any way they wanted, and so practices varied. Sometimes the only form of relief was to be allowed to beg within the parish; begging outside one's parish of belonging had been prohibited for centuries. Men considered able-bodied and married couples with or without children could not normally expect any kind of relief.[33] According to an ordinance of 1788, the parishes had the right to refuse legal settlement to masterless persons residing with others, so-called lodgers (*inhyse-shjon*). Lodgers often worked as day-labourers, and their legal status had been an issue for centuries.[34]

Many county governors looked at lodgers with the utmost suspicion, and Ridderstolpe once called 'the lodger class' a 'nursery' for 'vagrants'.[35] County governors were not to intervene with the work of the judicial powers, but the policing and judicial treatment of 'vagrants', 'idlers' and beggars fell under

29   C. J. Gadd, *Det svenska jordbrukets historia. Bd 3. Den agrara revolutionen: 1700–1870* (Stockholm, 2000), pp. 89, 228.

30   *Historisk statistik*, pp. 49, 61.

31   National Archives of Sweden (hereafter RA), 'Utlåtande av KB Västmanland. Kommittén angående lösdrivare och försvarslösa år 1825', ÄK-20.

32   P. Lindert, 'Poor Relief before the Welfare State: Britain versus the Continent, 1780–1880', *European Review of Economic History*, 2 (1998), 113.

33   E. Engberg, *I fattiga omständigheter: Fattigvårdens former och understödstagare i Skellefteå socken under 1800-talet* (Umeå, 2005).

34   The day-labourers' rights and duties were officially introduced in the 1723 Servant Act, §11. See Kumlien, *Continuity*, p. 46.

35   RA, 'Utlåtande'.

their jurisdiction.[36] This was a peculiar circumstance, as pointed out by contemporary observers, since the Swedish constitution of 1809 stipulated that no one's freedom should be removed unless they had been tried in court. In 1818, the so called Law Committee in the Diet ruled that it was incontestable that every member of society's personal freedom should be protected, but it was equally important that everyone used their capacities to fulfil their duty to work for the benefit of the rest of society.[37] The enforcement of already imprecise legislation thus took the shape of summary justice, which gave rise to legal uncertainty regarding, for example, the legal status of the masterless labouring poor.[38] Ridderstolpe once remarked that whether or not a lodger had legal protection depended on the mindset of the official who looked into the matter.[39] A clearer illustration of how the system of legal protection stood in opposition to the principle of legality is hard to find.

The reprisals for not complying with compulsory service were not elaborated in the Servant Acts. Instead, complementary legislation regulated the legal sanctions, and these were subject to considerable change during the 1800s. After some years of relaxations, the legal sanctions became stricter in 1833, when a Vagrancy Act was promulgated: the Ordinance Respecting the Treatment of Unprotected Persons (*försvarslöshetsstadgan*).[40] This might seem a paradox during a time of rapid proletarianisation, commercialisation and declining real wages for the labouring poor, but can be understood in the light of contemporary elite discussions and fears of the 'dangerous classes'.[41] The previous relaxation had only concerned the penal provisions for men. From 1819, men could be sentenced to hard labour for not complying only if they had committed theft or had begged. Moreover, in 1824 the impressment of 'vagrants' into the army – only relevant for men – was abolished. In so doing, the legislation was also stripped of the ethnonym 'Gypsies'. An ordinance of 1814 (also abolished in 1833) allowed previously unpunished women to be sentenced to a house of correction. Legal sanctions for men and women therefore differed until 1833. From 1833, it was again, as before 1819, possible to sentence men to hard labour without reference to any specific action (begging or theft).[42]

---

36 *Kungl. Maj:ts nådiga förordning, huru med försvarslösa personer förhållas bör. Given den 29 juni 1833*, Svensk författningssamling (SFS), 27:1833 (hereafter: Vagrancy Act). 'Vagrancy' was a crime of status and an administrative offence: Snare, *Work*, p. 129.

37 P. Eklund, *Rätten i klasskampen: En studie i rättens funktioner* (Stockholm, 1974), p. 210.

38 Cf. A. L. Seip, *Sosialhjelpstaten blir til: Norsk sosialpolitikk 1740–1920* (Oslo, 1984).

39 RA, 'Utlåtande'.

40 Vagrancy Act, SFS 27:1833

41 Cf. Snare, *Work*, pp. 132–5.

42 For an overview of the judicial framework, see e.g. Snare, *Work*.

The two Servant Acts in place in the nineteenth century (the acts of 1805 and 1833) prescribed compulsory service for one year (six months in Stockholm after 1833) for men and women from the age of fifteen, with no upper age limit.[43] Besides having a lawful occupation based on statute, or owning an independent farm, the act of 1805 allowed legal protection to be offered for married, settled couples with a fixed abode in the countryside, where they were committed to working and made an 'honest' living, as well as for caregivers (not gender-specific) for infants and old or disabled parents. After 1833, caregivers were no longer exempt and the category of married couples was omitted. Instead, persons who could prove they were provided for by someone else did not have to find legal protection. Another exception was made for all who supported themselves in 'an honest way'. However, this 'honesty' had to be approved by the parish assemblies. As suffrage to the parish assemblies was limited to landowners – the more property one owned, the more influence one potentially had – the state had given local elites considerable freedom to use the legislation according to local interests and needs.[44] The masterless labouring poor thus remained in a state of legal uncertainty and, with stricter legal sanctions introduced in 1833, the 'system of legal protection was fully reinstated'.[45]

Arrests and incarceration of 'vagrants' in contemporary national statistics

One of the harshest critics of the system of legal protection was the director-general of the State Prison Board, Clas Livijn, who wrote in 1844 that the Vagrancy Act of 1833 was barely enforceable.[46] It was simply impossible to incarcerate all unprotected people, not least because of lack of space in state correctional facilities. The majority of those sentenced to hard labour were sent to one of the state houses of correction or to the Pioneer Corps (men only in the latter case).[47] If not sent to the Pioneer Corps, people sentenced in

43 *Kongl. Maj:ts nådiga legostadga för husbönder och tjenstehjon. 15 May 1805,* Årstrycket; *Kongl. Maj:ts förnyade nådiga lego-stadga för husbönder och tjenstehjon. 23 Nov. 1833,* SFS 43:1833
44 Cf. Snare, *Work,* p. 161.
45 *Underdånigt förslag till förordning angående lösdrifveri, m.m.* (Stockholm, 1882), p. 28; Montgomery, *Svensk,* p. 63; Kumlien, *Continuity,* pp. 85–8. For a different opinion, see C. Uppenberg, 'The Servant Institution During the Swedish Agrarian Revolution: The Political Economy of Subservience', in Jane Whittle (ed.), *Servants in Rural Europe 1400–1900* (Woodbridge, 2017), p. 174.
46 Livijn, *Promemoria,* pp. 13–14.
47 Norrköping City Library (hereafter NSB), Styrelsen öfver Fängelserne och Arbetsinrättningarne till Kongl. Maj:t afgifna Berättelse angående Fångwården i Riket år 1835, fols 121–2, Kriminalvårdsstyrelsen i Norrköpings arkiv.

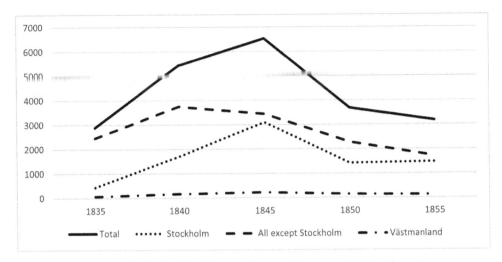

Figure 9.1. Arrests for lack of legal protection and 'vagrancy' in Sweden, 1835–55. Source: *Bidrag till Sveriges officiella statistik. Serie G. Fångvården. Fångvårdsstyrelsens underdåniga berättelse för år 1860* (Stockholm, 1862), p. 3.

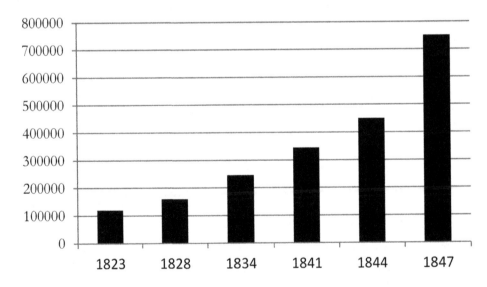

Figure 9.2. Costs for the Swedish state prison system according to the state budgets, 1823–47. Source: *Register till riksdagens protokoll med bihang, 1809–1866* (Stockholm, 1891–3), pp. 561–6. Note: nominal values in rix-dollars.

Västmanland were placed in one of two institutions in Stockholm: the Northern Correctional Facility for Women and the Southern Correctional Facility for Men. Men sentenced to a house of correction were to serve for an unlimited time or until they had obtained legal protection, both before and after 1833. Before 1833, women were to serve a sentence of one to three months. In reality, women could be imprisoned for much longer, as they also were supposed to have obtained legal protection before being released. After 1833, women were sentenced in the same way as men.[48] From 1835 to 1839 'vagrants', the largest prisoner category, comprised around 50 per cent of all prisoners in state institutions.[49] In 1838 501 people without a criminal record were being detained for 'vagrancy'.[50] The total number of arrests for lack of legal protection and 'vagrancy' increased in the decade after official statistics became available in 1835 (Figure 9.1).[51] Even if it had been possible to penalise unemployment for centuries, the trend now – in the words of Annika Snare – was towards institutionalisation.[52]

The detainment of thousands of people cost money, and the central government's costs for the prison system increased rapidly during the first half of the nineteenth century (Figure 9.2). The law could not be enforced by incarcerating everyone who could be labelled a 'vagrant' in legal terms. However, that does not mean that legal protection and compulsory service had no significance. Obviously, it mattered to the state budget and to all those thousands who were detained, for instance, in the county jail of Västmanland.

Detainments for 'vagrancy' in Västmanland

Detainments into the county jail for 'vagrancy' could result from several sets of circumstances, such as having one's passport checked in a tavern or on a road somewhere. Detainments could be used as a strategy in disputes over settlement, labour contract fulfilment and workplace evictions. Detainees were also handed over by local courts. The county government would examine the legal protection of previously punished or tried detainees. Far from all orders to obtain legal protection involved detention. For instance, as a direct consequence of the new Vagrancy Act of 1833, the county government issued a decree aiming at a stricter control of the legal protection of resident poor on a parish level. All town councils and bailiffs were ordered to send in lists of

---

48 Johnsson, *Vårt fredliga*, pp. 92–3.
49 *Styrelsens öfver Fängelserne [årsberättelse 1838–1839]* (Stockholm, 1842), p. 17.
50 *Styrelsens öfver Fängelserne [årsberättelse 1838–1839]* (Stockholm, 1842), litt. F.
51 The c.3,000 arrests made in 1845 in Stockholm account for half of the arrests in Sweden, whereas the population of Stockholm (88,000) represents only 3 per cent of the Swedish population.
52 Snare, *Work*, p. 162.

people lacking legal protection to the county government after the yearly
tax registrations, together with the opinion of the parish assembly.[53] The
immediate follow-up was also delegated to local authorities: town councils
and parish constables. In Västerås, for example, on two consecutive days in
1838 between thirty and forty people – including at least two fourteen-year-
olds – were called to the town council and ordered to find legal protection
within two weeks.[54] After 1833, the county constable in the nearby district
of Tuhundra would ask the parish assemblies about masterless labouring
poor in the parish and what should be done with them.[55] If the accused failed
to obtain legal protection within a stipulated time frame, they were interrogated by the county government. The use of tax registers for control of
protection was nothing new; the novelty was the creation of detailed administrative routines. An important stipulation in the law of 1833 was also linked
to the yearly tax registration, which again placed the labouring poor in a
position of dependence upon wealthier counterparts. In conjunction with
the registrations, masterless persons who did not have legal protection and
who were not approved by the parish assembly could avoid being treated as
a 'vagrant' if they had written proof of one or more trustworthy persons
acting as sureties.[56] The work the person performed should also be testified
in writing. Each guarantor was made responsible for up to fifty rix-dollars,
a considerable amount of money. There is evidence from several tax districts
that such sureties were required.[57] People with no approval from the parish
assembly and no guarantors could be ordered to find employment. Towns
and parishes could transgress the law and order people to leave before the
registrations because of alleged lack of protection.[58] The use of compulsory
service was fundamentally entwined with local settlement policies.

A medieval castle in Västerås constituted the physical heart of the county
administration. Fewer than five chancellery officials received thousands of
petitions, complaints, referrals and applications every year, and performed a
variety of tasks including issuing passports. The jail consisted of nine arrest
rooms scattered across the building, and had room for about thirty prisoners,
but occasionally as many as seventy detainees could be jailed at the same time.[59]

---

53 Uppsala State Archives (hereafter ULA), Västmanland länskungörelse 1833, no. 151.
Tax registers show that this was enforced: ULA, Mantalslängder Barkarö, Lundby, Dingtuna,
Lillhärad, EIc:263, Länsstyrelsen i Västmanland, landskontoret.
54 ULA, Dombok 15 January 1838, §15, AII:86. Västerås rådhusrätt och magistrat.
55 ULA, Brevdiarium 15 January 1834, no. 16, vol. 21, Kronofogden i Västerås fögderi.
56 Vagrancy Act, SFS 27:1833.
57 ULA, Inkomna skrivelser, diverse borgensförbindelser, vol. 239, Kronofogden i Kungsörs
fögderi; ULA, Sockenstämmoprotokoll, 16 March 1834, KI:3, Heds församling.
58 ULA, Sockenstämmoprotokoll, 3 December 1837, KI:4, Heds församling.
59 ULA, Slottspredikant Wallins skrivelse till Styrelsen över fängelser och arbetsin-
rättningar, 9 March 1838, AIa:127, Länsstyrelsen i Västmanland, landskontoret.

In the years 1829–38, 2,895 detainments were recorded, and in addition more than 2,000 prisoners in transit passed through the castle. Of these detentions, 1,066 were recorded for 'vagrancy' only, including the detainments of 121 children accompanied by parents or a close relative.[60] There were 851 arrests in Västmanland for 'vagrancy' as the sole offence and another sixty-three for 'vagrancy' combined with some other offence.[61] On 189 occasions, detainees who had stood trial for other offences were ordered to find legal protection. Furthermore, twenty-three released prisoners from state prisons were sent to Västerås county jail, only to be deemed unprotected by the county government. Around sixty detainments concerned runaway servants.[62] The everyday state-building performed in the castle was thus heavily influenced by vagrancy policing.

Delimiting the scope to only the 851 arrests for 'vagrancy' made in Västmanland, some factors that shaped the extent to which detainments were used as part of local vagrancy policing can be outlined. In the countryside, only around twenty bailiffs and county constables were at the disposal of the county government. Parish constables sometimes assisted the county constables. Police capacity was much greater in towns, especially in Västerås, where one district court judge, assisted by several men, was dedicated to police work including monitoring that no persons lacking legal protection were accommodated. They patrolled the town asking people for identity papers in streets and taverns, and they could search people's homes for alleged 'vagrants'.[63] Prosecutions for accommodating people who lacked legal protection or passports seem to have been more common in towns, with half of the arrests made in Västmanland occurring in a town.[64] Västerås stands out, with its 332 arrests representing 39 per cent of all arrests in the county.[65] Moreover, 39 per cent of all arrests in the countryside were made close to Västerås. Further away, there were more

60 'Vagrancy' is here employed as an analytical term covering various offences and descriptions of actions or states of being (lack of legal protection, roaming, begging, 'vagrancy', travelling without a passport, and many more), punishable only or in practice by the use of vagrancy legislation. The neat columns of the national statistics regarding detainments for lack of legal protection or 'vagrancy' (or roaming) do not mirror the source it was built upon: jail records. For an elaboration and deconstruction of the statistics, see Johnsson, *Vårt fredliga*, pp. 123–45.

61 The place of arrest for 215 detentions made in other counties are not discussed further here because of the difficulties in following up individuals who were transported to Västerås from other counties.

62 ULA, Fångjournaler 1829–38, D2b:7–D2b:12, Kriminalvårdsanstalten i Västerås. As in many other places, leaving service prematurely could lead to being labelled a 'vagrant'.

63 ULA, Instruction för Police Rådmannen i Westerås 1 January 1827, §2, EI:3, Västerås rådhusrätt och magistrat; ULA, Dombok, 10 June 1838, §2, A1:38, Västerås kämnärsrätt.

64 J. Sundin, *För Gud, staten och folket: Brott och rättskipning i Sverige 1600–1840* (Stockholm, 1992), pp. 216–17; Johnsson, *Vårt fredliga*, p. 328.

65 In the three other towns (Arboga, Köping, Sala) a total of 107 arrests was made.

cost-efficient ways to deal with unwanted people. For example, paupers who begged outside their home parish could be transported back home without state involvement; the cost of the transport was paid by the pauper's home parish or by withdrawing poor relief from the pauper.⁶⁶ The years 1837 and 1838, in which the harvests were poorer than usual, accounted for 34 per cent of all arrests between 1829 and 1838. Many people were reported to be on the move in the spring of 1838.⁶⁷ That year, more than half of the arrests were made in the county seat.

People were arrested in various constellations. The most common detention was of a single man (c.66 per cent). Single women constituted only 10 per cent of the detainees. However, single women with children constituted the second-largest constellation after single men. Around 20 per cent of the detainees were women. In the larger sample of 1,066 detainees, age can be estimated for 60 per cent of the male detainees and 73 per cent of the female. Most were under the age of fifty (87 per cent of the men and 84 per cent of the women). On average, however, women were older than men. For men, the biggest concentration of those detained was in the age group 22–29 (27 per cent), whereas for women the biggest concentration was in the age group 30–39 (29 per cent). If they did not belong to the county, most detainees came from or moved around in middle Sweden, in counties adjacent to Västmanland, although some moved across wider areas.

The detainees can with few exceptions be described as labouring poor. Most, but far from all, did not legally belong where they were arrested. Four main categories of detainees can be outlined roughly. First, people who doubtlessly belonged where they were arrested. Some had previously been accused of a crime, others had not. Some were homeless, others not. Local elites could use vagrancy law as a policing technique to deal with people whose presence was found disturbing. Second, people who were known and settled at the place of arrest. Sometimes they were registered in the tax registers as lacking legal protection, while sometimes they had been excluded or never included in any register. There were conflicts around their settlement, and the parish, or some other actor, wanted to get rid of them. Third, there were people who were more or less always on the move. Sometimes they were registered in a parish somewhere, sometimes not. This was a heterogeneous group including peddlers of both sexes and people engaged in ambulatory crafts such as chimney sweeping. Others were on the move for long periods trying to scrape by. Fourth, arrests were also made of people outside their parish for temporary

66   Arkiv Digital (AD), Dödbok no 18, 14 December 1837, F:1, Sevalla församling; AD, Dödbok, 19 July 1837, Västerfärnebo församling; AD, Dödbok, 24 May 1831, F:4. Harakers församling.
67   ULA, KB Västmanland skrivelse till länsman Lejdström, 17 April 1838, AIa:127, Länsstyrelsen i Västmanland, landskansliet.

reasons, such as looking for work or being on the way to visit someone or collect something. Sometimes they had not been able to convince a county constable of the legality of their movement; sometimes they had begged.

The archives reveal many snapshots of how orders to obtain legal protection served functions other than to force people into service. On the contrary, difficulties with obtaining legal protection provided an opportunity for parishes to get rid of people. In October 1830 the wealthy landowner Carl Ridderstolpe – brother of the county governor – ordered the county constable in the parish of Rytterne to arrest a woman named Brita Stina Åkerström for lack of legal protection.[68] She had been a servant of his for two years, but now Ridderstolpe wanted to have her removed. The main reason was that she was pregnant with her second child and no longer considered useful. Together with her eight-year-old daughter Maja, Åkerström was taken to the castle. On the second day of detainment, she was interrogated and subsequently released with a passport and ordered to find legal protection within two weeks. A week later, Åkerström and her daughter returned to the castle to ask whether residing as a lodger at a sexton's house could be considered legal protection. The official said yes, but that if the sexton did not get permission to house her from the landowner – none other than Ridderstolpe himself – she should go to the parish priest for advice, and get help until she had recovered from childbirth. If the sexton had housed her without permission, he could have been prosecuted and evicted, illustrating the potential price of giving shelter. One week later, the parish priest wrote a letter to the castle insisting on Åkerström being removed and sent to a house of correction. In this case, labour regulations intertwined with settlement and poor relief practices in a way that was contrary to the interests of the state. Irrespective of the fact that caring for an infant should have made her exempt, the constable tried to arrest Åkerström one week after childbirth. The midwife intervened, but some months later, in April, he was more successful. Together with her daughters, Åkerström spent over three weeks in the county jail with a note of being 'unprotected' in the records, before being released. She was ordered to find legal protection within four weeks and given boat tickets to the county of Stockholm.[69] Åkerström had tried to comply in different ways; and, in doing so, she essentially fought a class struggle to avoid being harassed and jailed, but most importantly to get a roof over her and her children's heads.[70] Trying to comply was Brita Stina Åkerström's way of resisting.

68   ULA, Fångjournal 1830 nos 328–9, D2b:7, Kriminalvårdsanstalten i Västerås; ULA, Protokoll med handlingar 31 October 1830, §1, AIIa:4, Länsstyrelsen i Västmanland, landskansliet; ULA, Intyg av barnmorskan Anna Wisel 21 November 1830, no. 36, DIII:210, Länsstyrelsen i Västmanland, landskansliet.
69   ULA, Fångjournal 1831 nos 140–2, D2b:8, Kriminalvårdsanstalten i Västerås.
70   Cf. S. Rockman, 'Class and the History of Working People in the Early Republic', *Journal of the Early Republic*, 25 (2005), 530.

Decisions by the county government

In the castle, the state officials interrogated 'vagrants' whose identities, places of belonging and legal protection were scrutinised. County governor Ridderstolpe was often present. Against the backdrop of extreme class disparities, these face-to-face encounters with the highest state officials were presumably unpleasant events. The experience of entering an overcrowded jail where different categories of prisoners of all ages and sexes could share the same arrest room hardly added to the attraction of being arrested. More than 90 per cent spent at least one night in jail, and around 60 per cent were held in custody for two to ten days (see Table 9.1) before being released from the castle.

Table 9.1. The period of detention for 'vagrancy' only: detainees arrested in Västmanland.

Days	Number of people	%
0	45	6
1	110	14
2–5	301	37
6–10	188	23
11–20	100	12
21–50	45	6
51–100	19	2
≥101	3	0
Total	811	100

Source: ULA, Fångjournaler 1829–38, D2b:7–D2b:12, Kriminalvårdsanstalten i Västerås. Note: Detainees who died in jail or were taken to hospital are excluded. Some release dates are missing in the records.

Over one-fifth of the detainees were kept in custody between eleven and 100 days. Lengthy detainments could follow difficulties establishing identities and belonging. Detainees' abilities to account for themselves credibly and avoid raising suspicion were crucial.[71] The officials could sometimes have an incentive to release people without establishing their identity, since the jail was often overcrowded and it took time and effort to investigate people.[72] On many occasions, people who showed their passport to the officials were

71   Johnsson, Vårt fredliga, pp. 430, 438.
72   E.g., ULA, Överståthållarämbetets skrivelse till KB Västmanland 17 December 1838, 'Jonas', DIII:252, Länsstyrelsen i Västmanland, landskansliet.

ordered to leave the county immediately without being detained. A warning with or without an order to obtain legal protection within a certain time could be written on the passport. Detainments could also be lengthy if the county government had ordered a detainee to find legal protection before they could be released, or if a sentenced detainee appealed to the National High Court. Only nine appeals were recorded, and only three of them had any sort of success; they were granted another respite.[73]

The most common way to leave the castle was to be transported on a prison cart somewhere (48 per cent out of the total of 1,066 detainments). Others were released with a passport (42 per cent) and some sort of decision (for example, on arrival the person was entitled to poor relief) or order (for example, the person should not beg or 'roam', or had to obtain legal protection). To be released, the detainees had to be considered fit enough to travel to where they were supposed to, mostly to their parish of belonging. The risk of people begging when released was a major concern. Not all survived detention, and ten detainees died in jail. Others were taken to hospital. Six per cent – fifty-nine adults, one minor, and two accompanying children – were sentenced to a house of correction or the Pioneer Corps. Most detainees were sent to other counties (52 per cent). Another 32 per cent were transported to a parish, authority or specific destination within the county of Västmanland (and sometimes also allowed to continue to another county).[74] The majority were thus considered non-residents of Västmanland county.

At least 28 per cent of all arrests were followed by a decision directly related to compulsory service and labour legislation; for example, an order to find legal protection or a sentence to a house of correction. A majority of cases involved some sort of coercive measure such as deportation, removal or various orders being given. As seen in the case of Åkerström, caring for infants did not always protect people, even before 1833. However, children did protect their carers from being sentenced to hard labour. Until the promulgation of the new Vagrancy Act of 1833, children could accompany their caregiver to a house of correction. This happened only once in Västmanland, in 1832, to a woman and her two children whose parish of belonging was unknown.[75] In this case, the sentence was at odds with the law, as one of the children was just a few weeks old. From 1833, children were to be cared for by their home parish. Parishes could thus have financial motives such as poor relief concerns, making them reluctant to have, for example, a single mother sentenced to a house of correction. However, that did not necessarily stop parishes from harassing and reporting people, as seen in the case of Åkerström. The state was responsible for

---

73   Johnsson, *Vårt fredliga*, p. 315.
74   The rest of the cases are unclear.
75   ULA, Fångjournaler no 388, 15 September 1832, 'Palm', D2b:7, Kriminalvårdsanstalten i Västerås.

providing for children without a known parish of belonging. When detainees were sentenced, they were examined by a doctor who decided if they were fit enough to be sent to hard labour. Disability or illness did not automatically make people exempt. For instance, on one occasion the doctor concluded that a sentenced detainee was not able-bodied as his arms were deformed. He was subsequently released, but still ordered to find legal protection.[76] A boy in his teens, of short stature, who had lost his work at a mine after having suffered from fever, was sentenced to a state house of correction in 1832. He had never been accused of anything except begging.[77]

Age should have protected all detainees under the age of fifteen, but two children were sentenced to a state house of correction. One died while still in custody in Västerås. A couple of other minors were not released until they had obtained legal protection. No one older than sixty-seven was ordered to do the same. In total, twenty-one people over the age of sixty were detained for 'vagrancy' only: one was sentenced to a house of correction, four others were ordered to find legal protection, and one was released after having obtained legal protection. If poor, masterless people were prosecuted, they ran the risk of being ordered to find legal protection. Far from all had a criminal record, but begging, earlier arrests for 'vagrancy' and previous convictions were aggravating circumstances.

Common respites given to obtain legal protection were for eight days, two weeks, three weeks or, most frequently, one month. In the Vagrancy Act of 1833 the accused person's own guilt for lacking legal protection – which was to be evaluated by the officials – along with any criminal record was central to how they should be treated with regard to respites and release.[78] While the paragraph in the Servant Act stipulated compulsory service for those lacking legal protection, the vagrancy legislation both before and after 1833 typically contained formulations such as entering service *or* another legal occupation. In practice, the county governments in interaction with local stakeholders decided what served as legal protection. Orders to enter 'proper' service could explicitly be given.[79]

If a person was subsequently released, they were in most cases given a passport or some other written document to show the legality of and conditions for their movement. In conjunction with issuing the Vagrancy Act of 1833,

76   ULA, KB Västmanland skrivelse till KB Värmland, 31 October 1837, 'Björklund', AIa:126, Länsstyrelsen i Västmanland, landskansliet.
77   ULA, Fångjournaler, no. 403, 20 September 1832, 'Löfving', D2b:7, Kriminalvårdsanstalten i Västerås.
78   Vagrancy Act, SFS 27:1833, §§ 5–7, 13.
79   ULA, Protokoll med handlingar, 9 June 1836, §1, 'Rundqvist', AIIa:7, Länsstyrelsen Västmanland, landskansliet.

these so-called vagrancy passports were pre-printed, and contained details about the carrier and the conditions for release. The internal passport system played a key role in vagrancy policing, which unsurprisingly aimed at control over the movements of these 'vagrants'. This was made even clearer in the Act of 1833, which explicitly stated that passports for unprotected people should be issued following an existing decree of 1824 containing rules for the issuing of passports to 'vagrants' and 'unsettled families belonging to the labouring classes'.[80] In adjacent Dalecarlia officials kept a separate register for vagrancy passports, containing information on aspects such as physical appearance.[81] In Västmanland, many vagrancy passports were only registered in the county jail records, and these generally lacked important individual data such as age and appearance until the early 1840s.

The state officials did, however, become more meticulous from 1833 onwards. More passports issued to 'vagrants' were registered in the regular passport register.[82] Upon arrival in a parish the passport should be shown to the county constable and the parish clergy. If the 'vagrant' could not find legal protection, the county constable could decide to lengthen the respite and allow the 'vagrant' to go somewhere else. Sometimes county constables were explicitly to decide if someone should be ordered to find legal protection or poor relief. People who were released also came back to the castle by choice, for instance to plead for another respite. County governor Ridderstolpe once wrote that the state could save money on prison transports. If people were only accused of lack of legal protection, they could be summoned to the castle. He claimed that they came voluntarily because it was shameful to be seen on a prison cart, because they were attached to their homes, and because the first time around they were just warned.[83] The obedience of ordinary people in a society plagued by brutal class disparities and extremely fragile living conditions should not be underestimated. The county government was flexible and could be pragmatic, but its dealings with 'vagrancy' were also unpredictable, and occasionally the officials did not seem to have been sure what legislation to use.[84]

Several times, detainees were required to obtain legal protection before being released. If this proved impossible, the detainee could be sentenced to

---

80   *Kungl. Maj:ts nådiga kungörelse, angående vad vid utfärdandet av pass åt lösdrivare [...], iakttagas bör. Given den 18 maj 1824*, Årstrycket.
81   ULA, Passjournaler, 1820–1841, CVI:2, Länsstyrelsen i Kopparberg.
82   Johnsson, *Vårt fredliga*, p. 419.
83   ULA, KB Västmanland skrivelse till Kongl. Maj:t 1831, no date, AIa:126, Länsstyrelsen i Västmanland, landskansliet.
84   ULA, Protokoll med handlingar 12 December 1834, 'Ekman', AIIa:6, Länsstyrelsen i Västmanland, landskansliet. ULA, Skrivelser från enskilda personer, Jan. 1831, 'Bolin', DIV:407, Länsstyrelsen i Västmanland, landskansliet.

public work, which might last forever.[85] A little more than forty times detainees managed to get legal protection from jail and were thereafter released. In all these cases the legal protection obtained was the entering of service, but the exact circumstances of these employments are difficult to unravel. On a couple of occasions close relatives gave protection. Once, a district judge organised legal protection for a young girl; the stated reason was that he feared the girl would be damaged by the conditions in jail.[86] One detainee obtained legal protection through Ridderstolpe himself.[87] Many of the released detainees were not registered in the parish records of the employer, which they should have been if they were live-in servants. There can be various reasons for this: they were never employed (for example, the contract was fictitious, which according to law rendered an alleged servant a 'vagrant'), they stayed elsewhere, or the clergy chose not to include them.

From state correctional facilities, there is evidence of individual employers who 'took out' unsuspecting or desperate detainees as they had difficulties hiring people. A Baron Duvall in Västmanland, for instance, who had a very bad reputation, employed a sentenced 'vagrant' from the Southern Correctional Facility in Stockholm. The servant soon ran away, but was caught and taken to the county jail. In a petition, he claimed that not only had he had been brutally beaten, Duvall had also, among much else, whipped a milkmaid according to martial law as a punishment for the cows giving too little milk.[88] The Servant Act – this 'yoke of bondage' as some journeymen in Västerås described it in 1838[89] – gave the right to castigate, but some employers were more brutal than others.

The ability to obtain legal protection mainly depended on social networks. For example, a woman who was arrested in Stockholm explained to her interrogators that she had no friends or relatives in Stockholm who could give her legal protection. Instead, she wanted to be sent to Västmanland, where she had lived most of her life.[90] The county officials in both Västmanland and Dalecarlia asked the detainees from whom, or where, they thought they could obtain legal protection, and thereafter the officials made inquiries. Following the Vagrancy Act of 1833, it became a standard procedure to write to the parish clergy, who in turn asked the parish assembly if the parish or anyone else could offer legal protection to a sentenced detainee. There is no evidence of parishes giving legal

85   Snare, *Work*, p. 156.
86   ULA, Inneliggande handlingar, no date, 'Holm', F:30, Kämnärsrätten i Västerås.
87   ULA, Fångjournal no 436, 4 December 1831, D2b:8, Kriminalvårdsanstalten i Västerås.
88   ULA, Skrivelser 16 May 1831, 'Hagman', DIV:411, Länsstyrelsen i Västmanland, landskansliet.
89   ULA, Dombok, 30 July 1838, §347, A1:38, Kämnärsrätten i Västerås.
90   ULA, Skrivelser från andra myndigheter, no 132, no date, 1837, 'Flinta', DIII:211, Länsstyrelsen i Västmanland, landskansliet.

protection to sentenced detainees in Västmanland in the 1830s. Judging from the parish assemblies' answers when asked, employing a detained person could look bad and lead to ill-feelings within the community.[91]

It was difficult for many to obtain legal protection, even if they were released. The sources show ten instances of people asking to be sentenced to a house of correction, as they saw no other way out. The labouring poor were not a homogeneous mass: people had varying resources and networks. While the Servant Act could be described as 'a yoke of bondage', poverty in itself is a yoke of bondage. Poverty shapes people's lives, health and bodies, and a strong, healthy body made it easier to obtain employment. To put it simply, not all poor people had the same bargaining power.

Around 100 times, detainees were sentenced to hard labour for not being able to comply with the laws of labour and vagrancy. Of these, sixty-two were kept in custody for 'vagrancy' only, and 20 per cent were women. The act of 1833 had no effect on the number of sentences, which depended on one crucial bottleneck: available space in state institutions. The year with the most sentences was 1830, when eighteen people were sent to state institutions. Pure coincidence could place someone in transport to a house of correction. On one occasion, a sentenced minor died in jail, and Ridderstolpe simply sent another detainee in his place. About 18 per cent of all sentenced persons were accused only of lack of legal protection, usually in combination with begging. The rest had some sort of criminal record, which could be a petty theft that had happened twenty years earlier. In a summary justice procedure, the labouring poor could thus be punished for their status and expect harsher treatment than others for the same offence.

Conclusion

This chapter has argued for the continued need to bring 'vagrancy' into labour law studies. The imprecise legislation and its enforcement placed the masterless labouring poor in a state of legal uncertainty; in a state of exception in relation to the constitution. Compulsory service, which was abolished in Sweden as late as 1885, had served many different functions over the centuries. In the 1830s, its main purpose was not to force people into the service of particular employers. Instead, legal protection could be given importance in innumerable situations, which had fundamental importance for the living conditions of the labouring poor: when people wanted to settle, when they applied for a passport, when they moved across the landscape, when they tried to end an employment contract

91   ULA, KB Västmanland skrivelse till KB Uppsala, 26 May 1834, 'H. Sundberg', AIa:123, Länsstyrelsen i Västmanland, landskansliet.

and so on. It constituted a flexible power technique deeply entwined with the criminal justice system.

The system of legal protection has been explored in this chapter through the narrow lens of detainments in jail. Notwithstanding the experiences of all those whose legal protection was questioned but who were not sentenced or even detained, the symbolic value of detentions and sentences to houses of corrections should not be undervalued. Being apprehended by state officials could cut deep into people's intimate lives. Children were separated from their caregivers and couples were split up and sent to different counties. People's survival strategies were affected. Encountering the highest police authorities, and spending time, sometimes weeks, in jail, the detainees were interrogated in the castle concerning their identities, belongings and legal protection. Vagrancy policing, and thus compulsory service practices, was central to everyday nation- and state-building.

Previous Swedish historical research has argued that 'law-abiding' and 'work-willing' people ran only a negligible risk of being sentenced. Was Brita Stina Åkerström aware of those odds, during her and her daughters' three weeks in jail, or did she not consider herself work-willing? To reduce the system of legal protection to its ultimate consequence is to silence central aspects of the workings of class politics in a time of mass poverty. Brita Stina Åkerström manoeuvred in the system, but she was constrained by her poverty, by her status in society and by being an unwed mother. In recent years the concept of 'agency' has won momentum to describe the room for tactical manoeuvre among the labouring poor.[92] While this perspective is laudable, a focus on 'agency' must not obscure the harsh class-based realities of compulsory service and the societies of which it was part. Otherwise, there is a risk that the 'vagrant' once again is transformed into the phantom of the work-shy sturdy beggar, who knowingly navigates between the systems of criminal justice and the laws of labour and vagrancy.

92   E.g., Hitchcock *et al.*, 'Loose', 511.

10

The Moral Economy of Compulsory Service: Labour Regulations in Law and Practice in Nineteenth-Century Iceland

VILHELM VILHELMSSON

'Were I to describe', wrote Sigurður Björnsson, an aging farmer and former district commissioner (*hreppstjóri*)[1] in 1839, 'the wayward self-righteousness of servants, their selfishness and sense of entitlement, their lack of loyalty, their laziness and unreliability in present times, the hairs would rise on the back of my head.'[2] He goes on to describe how peasant households suffered as a result of what he perceived as the excessive demands of servants and their general insubordination, which, he deemed, resulted from the fact that they 'separate their own well-being' from that of their masters. He claimed that the root cause of this unruliness among servants was the widespread tolerance of illicit casual labour, thereby raising wage levels and spreading vice and immorality as the masterless status of casual labourers supposedly fostered antisocial behaviour and beliefs.[3]

His arguments echo a common discursive theme in public discussions on household discipline and master–servant relations in early modern Iceland, where, as a rule, servants were described as lazy, disobedient and self-serving,

---

1 A *hreppstjóri* was an unsalaried official whose tasks included administering poor relief, assessing tax rolls and organizing various communal affairs, as well as performing several police functions. See Kristjana Kristinsdóttir, 'Hreppstjórar og skjalasöfn þeirra: Um hreppsbækur og þróun stjórnsýslu frá átjándu öld til upphafs tuttugustu og fyrstu aldar', *Saga*, 56 (2018), 122–48.

2 Sigurður Björnsson, 'Um hússtjórnina á Íslandi', *Búnaðarrit Suðuramtsins húss- og bústjórnarfélags*, 1 (1839), 94–138, here 110ff. All translations are mine unless otherwise noted.

3 See Vilhelm Vilhelmsson, 'Ett normalt undantag? Tillfälligt arbete i lag och praktik i 1800-talets Island', *Arbetarhistoria*, 41 (2017), 35.

and masterless day labourers were portrayed as 'a cancer' on the public body.[4]
Indeed, most contemporary observers in eighteenth- and nineteenth-century
Iceland, like so many of their European counterparts in the early modern era,
seem to have been obsessed with the perceived insolence and insubordination
of servants and the social and moral threat of the masterless labouring poor.[5]

Most Icelandic historians have either ignored such descriptions, portraying
compulsory service, rather, as an effective means of social control and master–
servant relations as mostly benevolent and shaped by the reciprocal interests
of servants and peasants, or have acknowledged and reiterated this particular
discourse only to dismiss its relevance.[6] But what if such descriptions were
taken at face value as a more or less accurate – if somewhat exaggerated –
portrayal of a common experience of master–servant relations? As German
historian Alf Lüdtke has proposed, when historians are faced with such descriptions and 'proceed by discounting their indignation' to rather view them as
evidence of everyday practices, the discourse takes on new meanings.[7] It can
thereby reveal what James C. Scott has called the 'infrapolitics' of subordinate
groups, the casual occurrences of 'unobtrusive' but insistent contestation over
everyday matters that are inherent to asymmetrical power relations such as
that between masters and servants.[8] This study explores the infrapolitics
of compulsory service through an analysis of the contentious practices and
interactions between servants and their masters as they appear in the archives

---

4 Sigmundur Sigmundsson, 'Til hvørs eru Kóngsbréfin um Betlara og Lausamenn, Okur
og Práng?', *Margvíslegt gaman og alvara*, 1 (1798), 62.

5 See Vilhelm Vilhelmsson, *Sjálfstætt fólk: Vistarband og íslenskt samfélag á 19. öld*
(Reykjavík, 2017), pp. 92–5, 187–96 for discussion and citations. For European concerns
see, for example, Hanne Østhus, 'Contested Authority: Master and Servant in Copenhagen
and Christiania 1750–1850', unpublished PhD dissertation (European University Institute
Florence, 2013), pp. 154–6; Robert Jütte, *Poverty and Deviance in Early Modern Europe*
(Cambridge, 1994), pp. 143–53; Catharina Lis and Hugo Soly, *Worthy Efforts: Attitudes to
Work and Workers in Pre-Industrial Europe* (Leiden, 2012), pp. 440–62; Raffaella Sarti, '"The
Purgatory of Servants": (In)subordination, Wages, Gender and Marital Status of Servants in
England and Italy in the Seventeenth and Eighteenth Centuries', *Journal of Early Modern
Studies*, 4 (2015), 347–72.

6 See, for example, Gísli Ágúst Gunnlaugsson, *Family and Household in Iceland 1801–1930:
Studies in the Relationship Between Demographic and Socio-Economic Development,
Social Legislation and Family and Household Structures* (Uppsala, 1988); Sigurður
Gylfi Magnússon, *Wasteland with Words: A Social History of Iceland* (London, 2010);
Guðmundur Jónsson, *Vinnuhjú á 19. öld* (Reykjavík, 1981); Guðmundur Hálfdanarson,
Íslenska þjóðríkið – uppruni og endimörk (Reykjavík, 2007), pp. 65–8.

7 Alf Lüdtke, 'Introduction: What is the History of Everyday Life and Who are its
Practitioners', in Alf Lüdtke (ed.), *The History of Everyday Life: Reconstructing Historical
Experiences and Ways of Life* (Princeton, 1995), p. 14.

8 James C. Scott, *Domination and the Arts of Resistance: Hidden Transcripts* (New Haven,
1990), pp. 183–201.

of county magistrates and the proceedings of arbitration courts in northern Iceland in the nineteenth century. By shifting the focus from the normative prescription of labour laws to their application and contestation in everyday practice, this chapter illustrates how servants navigated and made use of labour laws in order to improve their lot, to demand their legal and customary rights, to test the elasticity of legal provisions and to resist the coercion inherent to labour regulations in preindustrial Iceland.

Compulsory service and labour legislation in preindustrial Iceland

The origins of compulsory service in Iceland can be traced back to the Commonwealth period (930–1262). Its law code, called *Grágás*, included stipulations that landless people should become dependents (*griðfólk*) of established households and some, at least, had to perform any labour required of them. The distinction between servants, slaves, freedmen (*leysingjar*) and other dependents remains unclear, however, as does the status of casual day labourers.[9] Law codes from the later medieval period included similar requirements on settlement, dependency and service for the landless.[10] Indeed, it has been argued that a system of 'life-cycle service' had already been firmly established in Iceland by the late medieval period.[11] As in other European countries, the Reformation in Iceland brought forth a consolidation of household discipline and the discourse on service and the master–servant relationship became increasingly paternalist.[12] Servant laws nonetheless remained the same until 1685, when a police ordinance introduced more detailed and stringent regulations and firmly established compulsory service as the preferred form of labour relations in Iceland, as it was in the other Nordic countries, although this particular

---

9   Sverrir Jakobsson, 'From Reciprocity to Manorialism: On the Peasant Mode of Production in Medieval Iceland', *Scandinavian Journal of History*, 38 (2013), 274–8; Auður Magnúsdóttir, 'Fór ek einn saman', in Guðmundur J. Guðmundsson and Eiríkur K. Björnsson (eds), *Íslenska söguþingið 28.–31. maí 1997. Ráðstefnurit*, vol. 1 (Reykjavík, 1998), pp. 83–94; Guðbrandur Jónsson, *Frjálst verkafólk á Íslandi fram til siðaskipta og kjör þess* (Reykjavík, 1932–4).

10   Jónsson, *Frjálst verkafólk*, pp. 137–57.

11   Árni Daníel Júlíusson, 'Signs of Power: Manorial Demesnes in Medieval Iceland', *Viking and Medieval Scandinavia*, 6 (2010), 1–29.

12   Loftur Guttormsson, 'Frá siðaskiptum til upplýsingar', in Hjalti Hugason (ed.), *Kristni á Íslandi*, vol. 3 (Reykjavík, 2000), pp. 267–97; Vilhelmsson, *Sjálfstætt fólk*, pp. 52–5. For an overview of the European context see Pavla Miller, *Transformations of Patriarchy in the West, 1500–1900* (Bloomington, 1998), pp. 15–31.

ordinance was superseded by revised but similarly stringent servant legislation in the eighteenth century.[13]

Compulsory service was thus the primary form of labour management from the medieval era until the turn of the twentieth century, when restrictions on free labour and settlement were gradually lifted amid intense popular debate and significant economic and social changes.[14] Icelandic society in the eighteenth and nineteenth centuries was almost entirely a rural farming community with the household serving as the fundamental economic unit and site of production. The economy consisted primarily of pastoral farming (raising livestock) at a low technological level.[15] Between 90 and 95 per cent of peasants in the early eighteenth century were tenants on modest plots of land and tenancy remained the norm throughout the nineteenth century, although the level of owner-occupancy gradually increased.[16]

Labour power accessible throughout the year for a modest price (such as live-in servants) was essential to this near-subsistence pastoral economy. It was calculated in the late eighteenth century that the average-sized farming household needed at least three male farmhands and three maidservants in order to perform all of the labour such a household required. The author added, however, that due to poverty and labour scarcity most peasants tried to make do with fewer servants.[17] Indeed, labour shortage and the proclivity of workers to make a living independently as day labourers in spite of the law, earning higher wages but living with less material security, was a matter of constant complaint in the early modern era.[18] The increasingly stringent laws on compulsory service were in part meant to rectify this problem, amongst several other social concerns.[19] One of the aims of labour legislation was thus

---

13   Jón Sigurðsson and Oddgeir Stephensen (eds), *Lovsamling for Island*, vol. I–XXI (Copenhagen, 1853–89), here vol. I, pp. 428–37; Vilhelm Vilhelmsson, 'Siðspillandi lögbrot. Páll Briem og leysing vistarbands', in Sverrir Jakobsson and Ragnheiður Kristjánsdóttir (eds), *Hugmyndaheimur Páls Briem* (Reykjavík, 2019), pp. 165–93. On servant legislation in the Danish–Norwegian realm, see Østhus, this volume.

14   Vilhelmsson, 'Siðspillandi lögbrot'; Magnús S. Magnússon, *Iceland in Transition: Labour and Socio-Economic Change Before 1940* (Lund, 1985).

15   Guðmundur Jónsson, 'Institutional Change in Icelandic Agriculture, 1780–1940', *Scandinavian Economic History Review*, 41 (1993), 101–28; Magnússon, *Wasteland with Words*, pp. 18–32.

16   Jónsson, 'Institutional Change', 109–23.

17   Skúli Magnússon, 'Sveitabóndi', *Rit þess íslenzka lærdómslistafélags*, 4 (1783), 137–207, here at 147 and 171.

18   See discussion and citations in Guðný Hallgrímsdóttir, *A Tale of a Fool? A Microhistory of an 18th-Century Peasant Woman* (London, 2019), pp. 58ff.

19   The purpose and context of labour legislation and its evolution in early modern Iceland is of course a more complex matter where many factors were involved, including the importance of service for the socialization of youth, the cultural role of the master–servant relationship and the general economic policy of the Danish royal state. For a nuanced and informed discussion see Hrefna Róbertsdóttir, *Wool and Society: Manufacturing Policy,*

to enable an equitable redistribution of the workforce, evidenced for example by a decree from 1746 prohibiting peasants from keeping more than two children of working age at home.[20] An analysis of census records from six parishes in northern Iceland in the early nineteenth century shows that the proportion of households with servants ranged from 45 per cent up to 84 per cent, most of which had only one or two servants.[21] In most regions there were also a couple of larger manorial estates, occupied by wealthy upper officials and the land-owning elite, which employed greater numbers of servants and farmhands doing more specialised tasks, although the manorial economy had been in long-term decline in terms of both size and number of estates since the sixteenth century, a process which accelerated from the late eighteenth century onwards.[22]

As several historians have argued, social stratification in eighteenth- and nineteenth-century Iceland was minimal in comparison to other European countries. For the most part peasants and servants belonged to the same social class, commonly worked side by side, ate the same food, lived within the same single-room turf cottages and generally shared the same life experience.[23] There was also significant social mobility, where individuals would move back and forth between independence as tenant farmers and periods working as servants.[24] Life-cycle service was the perceived norm, however. It was the general expectation that all youths, except perhaps for the children of state officials and the land-owning elite, would spend some years as servants before marrying and becoming part of the peasantry.[25] Studies have shown that around 80 per cent of servants in Iceland became peasants themselves at some later date, although Icelanders seem generally to have remained servants much longer than in the other Nordic countries, and as much as 10 per cent of males and 20 per cent of women ended up as lifetime servants because they never married.[26]

Economic Thought and Local Production in 18th-Century Iceland (Gothenburg, 2008), pp. 157–69.

20 Sigurðsson and Stephensen, *Lovsamling for Island*, II, p. 612.

21 *Manntal á Íslandi 1801: Norður- og austuramt* (Reykjavík, 1980); *Manntal á Íslandi 1816*, vol. 5 (Reykjavík, 1973). The parishes analysed were: Staðarbakka- and Efranúpssókn, Melstaðarsókn, Víðidalstungusókn, Undirfellssókn, Holtastaðasókn and Höskuldsstaðasókn.

22 Árni Daníel Júlíusson, *Landbúnaðarsaga Íslands*, vol. 2 (Reykjavík, 2013), pp. 14–18.

23 Loftur Guttormsson, *Childhood, Youth and Upbringing in the Age of Absolutism: An Exercise in Socio-Demographic Analysis* (Reykjavík, 2017), pp. 276ff.; Guðmundur Hálfdanarson, 'Social Distinctions and National Unity: On Politics of Nationalism in Nineteenth-Century Iceland', *History of European Ideas*, 21 (1995), 768–70; Jónsson, 'Institutional Change', 103.

24 Gunnlaugsson, *Family and Household*, p. 61.

25 Hálfdanarson, 'Social Distinctions', 768–70.

26 Júlíusson, *Landbúnaðarsaga Íslands*, vol. 2, p. 50; Loftur Guttormsson, 'Il servizio come istituzione sociale in Islanda e nei paesi nordici', *Quaderni Storici*, 23 (1988), 355–79.

Despite the relative egalitarianism of Icelandic society the labour system in eighteenth- and nineteenth-century Iceland nonetheless had a high degree of legal compulsion and physical coercion. All persons (with only a few exceptions) above a certain age who did not run their own household were required by law to become servants in legal households. They were subject to the authority of their masters who, until 1866, had the right to physically punish disobedient or insolent servants. A decree from 1783 placed the power (and responsibility) of labour management more firmly in the hands of district commissioners and county magistrates, who were now required not only to stringently enforce compulsory service but also to procure for those who were unable to do so themselves a place in service or a farmstead to rent.[27] This highlights the fact that compulsory service in Iceland, as in several other countries in north-west Europe, was not only a matter of regulating labour but also one of moral and social order and was entwined with legislation on matters such as vagrancy, settlement and poor relief.[28] Numerous examples in court archives illustrate this, such as when magistrates or district commissioners forced peasants to take vagrants in as servants or forbade peasants to get rid of troublesome servants who would then become wards of the commune.[29] In lieu of poorhouses or other such solutions, annual service within established households thus remained an important measure against homelessness and similar social problems in nineteenth-century Iceland.[30]

Legally speaking, landless adults in eighteenth- and nineteenth-century Iceland had little choice but to become servants. In practice, however, the entire system was more flexible, as some managed through a variety of evasive tactics to avoid service for extended periods and work instead as casual labourers on the margins of the law.[31] The majority of labourers, however, probably entered service as the law required. As servants they were subject to regulations on master–servant relations as proscribed in a decree on domestic discipline from 1746. A part of a series of reform decrees inspired by the ideology of

---

27   Sigurðsson and Stephensen, *Lovsamling for Island*, IV, pp. 683–6.
28   Lis and Soly, *Worthy Efforts*, pp. 444–6; Raffaella Sarti, 'Freedom and Citizenship? The Legal Status of Servants and Domestic Workers in a Comparative Perspective (16th to 20th century)', in Suzy Pasleau and Isabelle Schopp (eds), *Proceedings of the Servant Project*, vol. 3 (Liège, 2006), pp. 134–7; Østhus, 'Contested Authority', p. 88; Carolyn Steedman, 'Lord Mansfield's Women', *Past and Present*, 176 (2002), pp. 114ff.
29   See examples and further discussion in Vilhelmsson, *Sjálfstætt fólk*, pp. 111, 159–62, 201ff.
30   Gísli Ágúst Gunnlaugsson, 'The Poor Laws and the Family in 19th Century Iceland', in John Rogers and Hans Norman (eds), *The Nordic Family: Perspectives on Family Research* (Uppsala, 1985), pp. 16–42.
31   Vilhelm Vilhelmsson, 'Tactics of Evasion: The Survival Strategies of Vagrants and Day Labourers in Eighteenth and Nineteenth Century Rural Iceland', *1700-tal: Nordic Journal of Eighteenth-Century Studies*, 17 (2020), 34–56; Vilhelmsson, 'Ett normalt undantag?' 32–40.

the Pietist movement influential in Denmark at the time, the decree was to instigate a general moral reform of households based on the Lutheran values of industriousness, obedience and submission to patriarchal authority.[32] The decree ordered that servants should work 'with utmost devotion and loyalty for their master's benefit and respond to any orders they are given with submission and obedience'. It also proscribed a number of rights and duties, including the right of masters to physically punish their servants for any oversight 'in the same manner as their own children'. Masters were in turn required to treat their servants fairly, feed and clothe them properly, avoid overburdening them with work and provide them with spare time to practise their Christian duties.[33] The decree was superseded by legislation on master–servant relations in 1866. While the new law removed the legal right of masters to physically punish servants above the age of sixteen it retained the prescriptions on servant submission and obedience, allowing masters to rescind contracts with servants who violated household discipline.[34] They would then be treated as vagrants according to the law unless they were at least twenty-five years old and able to purchase a licence to work as casual labourers for a fee, which amounted to a year's wages.[35] The legal requirement for youthful and landless people to become servants thus remained in full force until the end of the nineteenth century, when further changes were made to the law.

Other legislation directly impacted the everyday life of many servants. Household discipline from the mid-eighteenth century onwards was subject to regular inspection by the parish clergy, who were in turn required to report unruly servants to the authorities.[36] A decree on marriage from 1746 dictated that unwed parents should be forcibly separated and forbidden to live in the same parish in order to put an end to 'scandalous' living arrangements, leading many unwed servants to concoct schemes to be able to remain with their partners and their children.[37] The particular nature of the master–servant relationship also served to add a degree of severity to any crimes committed by servants within the boundaries of that relationship. Thus a decree from 1789 proscribed additional punishment for servants guilty of theft from their

32   Guttormsson, *Childhood*, pp. 81–3. On pietism and its influence, see Thomas Munck, *The Enlightenment: A Comparative Social History 1721–1794* (London, 2000), pp. 52, 169.

33   Sigurðsson and Stephensen, *Lovsamling for Island*, II, pp. 605–20. Citations are from p. 613.

34   Sigurðsson and Stephensen, *Lovsamling for Island*, XIX, pp. 383–95.

35   Vilhelmsson, 'Siðspillandi lögbrot', pp. 181–3; Sigurðsson and Stephensen, *Lovsamling for Island*, XVIII, pp. 544–53.

36   Guttormsson, *Childhood*, pp. 107ff; Vilhelmsson, *Sjálfstætt fólk*, pp. 62–4, 69. The decree is in Sigurðsson and Stephensen, *Lovsamling for Island*, II, pp. 566–78.

37   Sigurðsson and Stephensen, *Lovsamling for Island*, II, pp. 600–5. Pertinent examples can be found in Vilhelmsson, *Sjálfstætt fólk*, pp. 11–12, 160–1, 211–20.

masters, towards whom they 'owed special loyalty and care', as it was phrased in the revised criminal code of 1840.[38]

The special loyalty that servants owed to their masters refers to the role of service in the socialisation of youths and in regulating the morals of peasant society through clearly defined duties and responsibilities, and thereby maintaining social order.[39] This view was perfectly described by MP and later bishop Pétur Pétursson (1808–1891), who argued vehemently in defence of compulsory service in a speech in 1861 on the grounds that it served as a 'moral contract' within which the subservient learned to obey and respect their superiors while the latter took to heart the responsibilities which their status entailed, thereby reinforcing social order and harmony.[40] The master–servant relationship was thus defined by law as a moral relationship which encapsulated dominant ideas of social hierarchy and discipline, and was perceived and understood as such by contemporaries who wrote numerous treatises on the matter.[41] This paternalistic view of the master–servant relationship dominated public discourse in Iceland until the final decades of the nineteenth century, even though the same authors continually chastised servants for their insolence and peasants for their disregard of their paternal duties. These everyday practices and experiences are the subject of the remainder of this chapter.

Repertoire of resistant practices

When studying court records and arbitration proceedings for evidence of contentious labour relations some recurrent themes emerge which together form what one could call a repertoire of resistant practices, a leitmotif of the infrapolitics of servants that aimed at testing the elasticity of permissible behaviour, improving their lot or seeking retribution or justice. Foot-dragging, petty theft, insolence and flight appear as common tactics employed by servants to escape, evade, avoid, refute, resist or subvert coercion and the indignities of subordination. Some practices were 'tactics' employed, often intentionally antagonistic, to 'negotiate' the power relations between master and servant

38 Sigurðsson and Stephensen, *Lovsamling for Island*, V, p. 577; *ibid.*, XI, p. 544.
39 On 'moral regulation' as a subject of analysis in social history see Alan Hunt, *Governing Morals: A Social History of Moral Regulation* (Cambridge, 1999).
40 *Tíðindi frá alþingi Íslendinga 1861*, pp. 1127–8.
41 Some notable ones include Magnús Stephensen, *Ræður Hjálmars á Bargi fyrir börnum sínum um fremd, kosti og annmarka allra stétta, og um þeirra almennustu gjöld og tekjur* (Reykjavík, 1820/1999), pp. 72–6; Bjarni Einarsson, 'Um dyggð og elsku þjónustufólks og hvernig henni verði náð', *Rit þess íslenzka lærdómslistafélags*, 5 (1784), 33–65; n.a., 'Um hússtjórn á Íslandi', *Ársritið Húnvetningur*, 1 (1857), 29–48; [Baldvin Einarsson], *Ármann á alþingi, eða almennur fundur Íslendinga*, 1 (1829), 13–95.

(and/or the authorities), including the status of servants within the household, their chores and duties, their relationship with other household members or the degree of autonomy they enjoyed.[42] Other practices were more in line with Scott's 'weapons of the weak', acts of defiance that were purposefully hidden from sight.[43] Overall, they illustrate the inherent volatility of the master–servant relationship and its legal framework of compulsory service as well as contextualising the disregard of its assumed hierarchies, which social commentators such as Sigurður Björnsson so fervently complained of.

Negotiating the moral economy of service

The proceedings of arbitration courts include many complaints about servant misbehaviour. Yet since the law demanded the unconditional obedience of servants, the direct causes or nature of the complaints are rarely discussed in much detail. It was usually enough to establish that the insolent behaviour had taken place. Thus we find servants, both male and female, who were accused of 'wicked words and shameless taunts' against their masters,[44] of spreading 'innuendo' against their masters or mistresses,[45] of speaking 'with less respect than that which he owes his masters',[46] of absconding or taking leave of work without permission and so on. Since the expressed role of arbitration commissions, established in Norway, Denmark and Iceland in the end of the eighteenth century as part of broader judicial reform within the Danish–Norwegian kingdom, was not to pass judgement but to facilitate accord between the contested parties, most cases were concluded with some sort of agreement.[47] Servants could, and often did, manipulate this process to gain some form of advantage in their dealings with their masters.

---

42   For further discussion of power relations as the subject of negotiation, see Michael J. Braddick and John Walter (eds), *Negotiating Power in Early Modern Society: Order, Hierarchy and Subordination in Britain and Ireland* (Cambridge, 2001).

43   James C. Scott, *Weapons of the Weak: Everyday Forms of Peasant Resistance* (New Haven, 1985), pp. 290–303.

44   National Archives of Iceland (hereafter NAI). Arbitration court archives. XVI. Hún. G. Skagaströnd. Book 1 (1812–1857), pp. 11–13.

45   NAI, Arbitration court archives. XVI. Hún. A. Miðfjörður. Book 1 (1799–1865), pp. 181–2.

46   NAI, Arbitration court archives. XVI. Hún. G. Skagaströnd. Book 1 (1812–1857), pp. 45–6.

47   See Vilhelm Vilhelmsson, 'Inngangur: Sáttanefndarbækur sem sögulegar heimildir', in Vilhelm Vilhelmssson (ed.), *Sakir útkljáðar: Sáttabók Miðfjarðarumdæmis í Húnavatnssýslu 1798–1865* (Reykjavík, 2017), pp. 11–45; Eva Österberg, Malin Lennartsson and Hans Eyvind Næss, 'Social Control Outside or Combined with the Secular Judicial Arena', in Eva Österberg and Sølvi Sogner (eds), *People Meet the Law: Control and Conflict-handling in the Courts: The Nordic Countries in the Post-Reformation and Pre-Industrial Period* (Oslo, 2000), p. 245.

Thus in 1843 two servants in northern Iceland, a married couple, absconded, leaving their master without any servants. He had them brought before the local arbitration court for violating their service contract, where they in turn accused him of maltreatment, leading to an agreement where the servants agreed to return to their master as long as he apologised and promised to improve his conduct towards them.[48] In 1839 a farmhand used the opportunity to abscond when his master was ill and bedridden. When brought before the arbitration court the servant explained that he had absconded because he had been poorly fed and his wages not fully paid, nor were the wages of a maidservant in the same household. He eventually agreed to return, but only until a replacement had been found. From then on he was free to seek a servant position elsewhere if he so wished.[49] Another man had made an oral agreement in 1863 to become a servant but failed to show up at the traditional turnover date in the spring. When brought before the arbitration court a few months later he promised to fulfil the agreement and become a 'faithful and submissive servant' as promised only if his master agreed to pay him a certain amount of wages and to allow him to work on his own behalf during the profitable winter fishing season, conditions with which the peasant promptly agreed.[50]

The necessity of servants for the economy of peasant households combined with regular periods of labour scarcity, as well as the legal framework of arbitration, could thus be exploited by servants to improve their working conditions. Or to use analytical concepts originally developed by economist Alfred O. Hirschman but recently adapted to the historical study of desertion and runaways, strategies of 'exit' such as absconding from service could be seen as ways to 'voice' grievances from a safe distance and thus to negotiate working conditions or other aspects of the power relations of service upon return or otherwise to facilitate permanent exit.[51]

---

48   NAI, Arbitration court archives. XVI. Hún. A. Miðfjörður. Book 1 (1799–1865), pp. 172–3.

49   NAI, Arbitration court archives. XVI. Hún. B. Vesturhóp. Book 1 (1801–1872), pp. 139–42.

50   *Ibid.*, pp. 236–8. For a similar case see NAI, Arbitration court archives. XVII. Skag. B. Viðvík. Book 1 (1800–1903), p. 114. It was common for peasants to send their servants to the seaside to man fishing boats during the winter season, retaining their catch and the sometimes considerable profits thereof for the household. See Loftur Guttormsson, 'Population, Households and Fisheries in the Parish of Hvalsnes, Southwestern Iceland, 1750–1850', *Acta Borealia*, 28 (2011), 142–66.

51   Marcel van der Linden, 'Mass Exits: Who, Why, How?' in Matthias van Rossum and Jeannette Kamp (eds), *Desertion in the Early Modern World: Comparative Perspectives* (London, 2016), pp. 31–45; Leo Lucassen and Lex Heerma van Voss, 'Introduction: Flight as Fight', in Marcus Rediker, Titas Chakraborty and Matthias van Rossum (eds), *A Global History of Runaways: Workers, Mobility, and Capitalism 1600–1850* (Oakland, 2019), pp. 7–9. Hirschman's original work is Albert O. Hirschman, *Exit, Voice, and Loyalty: Responses to Decline in Firms, Organizations and States* (Cambridge, 1970).

This was, of course, always a gamble and such strategies could fail. One example is the case of the twenty-three-year-old farmhand Stefán Þorfinnsson, who in 1849 sued his mistress for what he claimed was unlawful termination of his contract.[52] One day, at mealtime, Stefán had begun arguing with the farm overseer. The mistress of the household ordered Stefán to cease his arguing or leave the room. He refused and said he would not leave unless he was to leave for good. She responded that he should leave if he so wished. He then gathered his belongings and left, assuming she had fired him, and went directly to the authorities to submit his complaint. Servants who were unlawfully dismissed were entitled to receive a full years' pay, which he must have known.[53] During the trial it became clear from witness depositions that Stefán had in fact made plans to leave beforehand, as he was unhappy with the workload and believed he was paid unfairly, and had tried to convince other servants to elope with him. Stefán also accused the overseer of having beaten him over the head, which the latter vehemently denied. Once the contrasting testimonies of who said what to whom began to emerge Stefán withdrew his complaint and the case disappears from court records. In the census of 1850 Stefán was still listed as a farmhand at the same farm (named *Friðriksgáfa*), suggesting that he had stayed on as a servant after all.[54]

While his attempt to voice his grievances in order to facilitate an exit from this particular service ultimately failed, Stefán's case still attests to the agency of servants and the ways in which the conditions of labour were contested and negotiated on the basis of perceived rights and duties according to labour laws. This is evident in his insistence that the overseer had beaten him over the head. The decree on domestic discipline from 1746 allowed masters (or their surrogates, such as overseers) to physically discipline unruly servants but explicitly forbade blows to the head, thus categorising such blows as abuse.[55] The overseer in turn vehemently denied the blow to the head, despite freely admitting to hitting Stefán for dragging his feet during the hay harvest, indicating that both were keenly aware of the subtle difference between legitimate and illegitimate violence within labour relations.[56] A study on the termination of

---

52   NAI, Magistrate's office of Eyjafjarðarsýsla. GA/8–2. Judicial proceedings (1849–1851), fols 36v–38v.

53   María Elísabet Guðsteinsdóttir, 'Sjaldan veldur einn þá tveir deila. Ástæður og fjöldi vistarrofsmála í dóma- og sáttabókum 1800–1920', unpublished BA thesis (University of Iceland, 2020), pp. 45, 49.

54   See online census database www.manntal.is.

55   Sigurðsson and Stephensen, *Lovsamling for Island*, II, pp. 609, 613. On the early modern understanding of the difference between the legitimate disciplinary role of restrained violence and unrestrained violence as disorderly abuse, see Susan D. Amussen, 'Punishment, Discipline, and Power: The Social Meanings of Violence in Early Modern England', *Journal of British Studies*, 34 (1995), 12–18.

56   For similar disputes between servants and their masters on whether or not particular punishments classified as abuse, see Østhus, 'Contested Authority', pp. 267–77.

service contracts in nineteenth-century Iceland also shows that servants and masters were acutely aware of how communication could be manipulated in this manner and would use similarly opaque language as Stefán and his mistress when voicing grievances in order to ensure their position were they to bring the matter to court.[57]

Judicial sources rarely provide direct evidence of how servants perceived their rights. An interesting exception is a maidservant who sued her master in 1868 after being dismissed from service for 'behaving intolerably'. She proclaimed to the court that she believed 'servants were not required to obey their masters unless their orders were kindly given'.[58] Though servants were rarely so outspoken about their perception of their legal rights in court, some common themes indicate several reasons that were perceived as being valid excuses for disrupting the everyday social order. Servants commonly refer, for example, to the bad temper of masters or undefined 'ill treatment' when asked to explain why they absconded.[59] Unpaid wages, poor or lacking provisions of food and clothing or other breaches of the legally required obligations of masters were also common reasons servants gave for absconding or otherwise rescinding contractual obligations.[60] Other sources, such as autobiographies of people who had spent their youth as servants, also describe how servants would sometimes abscond if they felt they were insufficiently fed or otherwise treated

---

57   Guðsteinsdóttir, 'Sjaldan veldur einn', pp. 48–50.

58   NAI, Magistrate's office of Eyjafjarðarsýsla. GA/10–2. Judicial proceedings (1865–1875), fols 93r–93v.

59   NAI, Arbitration court archives. XVIII. Eyj. A. Siglufjörður. Book 1 (1808–1874), fol. 6r; NAI, Arbitration court archives. XVI. Hún. A. Miðfjörður. Book 1 (1799–1865), pp. 172–3; NAI, Arbitration court archives. XVII. Skag. B. Viðvík. Book 1 (1800–1903), pp. 53–4; NAI, Magistrate's office in Eyjafjarðarsýsla. GA/7–1. Judicial proceedings (1838–1842), fols 134v–135r; NAI, Magistrate's office in Húnavatnssýsla. GA/8–1. Judicial proceedings (1830–1835), p. 124; NAI, Magistrate's office in Húnavatnssýsla. GA/8–2. Judicial proceedings (1835–1837), p. 521; Guðsteinsdóttir, 'Sjaldan veldur einn', pp. 41–4. In nineteenth-century Sweden cruelty and abuse by masters was also deemed a legitimate reason, recognized by the courts, for servants to abscond. See Carolina Uppenberg, 'The Servant Institution During the Swedish Agrarian Revolution: The Political Economy of Subservience', in Jane Whittle (ed.), *Servants in Rural Europe 1400–1900* (Woodbridge, 2017), p. 178. Similar provisions can be found in servant laws in Flanders in the sixteenth century. See Thijs Lambrecht, 'The Institution of Service in Rural Flanders in the Sixteenth Century: A Regional Perspective', in Whittle (ed.), *Servants in Rural Europe*, p. 51.

60   NAI, Arbitration court archives. XVI. Húnavatnssýsla A. Miðfjörður. Book 1 (1799–1865), pp. 109, 223; NAI, Arbitration court archives. XVI. Hún. B. Vesturhóp. Book 1 (1801–1872), pp. 64–6, 118–20, 139–42; NAI, Arbitration court archives. XVI: Hún. F. Engihlíð. Book 1 (1799–1890), pp. 135, 170–1, 207–9; Dalvík Regional Archive (Hsk.Svarf), H-1/40. Arbitration proceedings from Svarfaðardalur (1799–1902), pp. 11, 49–50; Már Jónsson (ed.), *Bréf Jóns Thoroddsens* (Reykjavík, 2016), pp. 282–3.

poorly.[61] The commonality of such complaints suggests not only that many servants were aware of their legal rights but also that master–servant relations were perceived, by some servants at least, as a particular moral economy where servants expected a degree of reciprocity and implicitly demanded that the paternalist obligations of masters should be observed.[62]

Labour regulations, it must be remembered, not only coerced workers into submission but also guaranteed them certain rights. These included provisions that masters should feed and clothe their servants 'according to … tradition', pay their wages on time and in full and refrain from verbally (or physically) abusing them.[63] Regulations stipulated the amount of labour the average worker should perform as well as the rations of food and number of clothing items servants should receive.[64] There were some regional variations in the provision of food and clothing for servants and such provisions were also dependent upon the state of the economy at any given time.[65] Some servants were nonetheless adamant in demanding their traditional provisions. That was the case with Halldór Þorkelsson, for example, who brought his master to arbitration court in 1810, during a particularly dire period in Icelandic economic history, because his master had provided him with less butter (a traditional currency in preindustrial Iceland) than he was due.[66] The cases discussed in this study suggest that this 'moral economy' of service was maintained through the practices of servants who were conscious of their rights and had the means to employ these tactics of contestation and negotiation.

Such tactics were not available to all, however, and absconding from service was also not always a tactic of negotiation or a way to voice grievances. Compulsory service remained a highly coercive regime of asymmetrical power relations that put a great deal of power and authority into the hands of masters

61 Hallgrímsdóttir, *A Tale of a Fool?* pp. 59ff.; Benjamín Sigvaldason, *Brautryðjandinn. Þættir úr æfisögu Jóhannesar Oddssonar, verkamanns á Seyðisfirði* (Akureyri, 1938), pp. 19–20; Elínborg Lárusdóttir, *Frá liðnum árum: Endurminningar Jóns Eiríkssonar frá Högnastöðum* (Reykjavík, 1941), pp. 102–12.

62 'Moral economy' tends to be a muddled concept. I use it here in the manner of E. P. Thompson and James C. Scott, referring to ideas and values attached to economic relationships that have developed over time through traditions of reciprocal obligations and are maintained and reproduced through practices of negotiation and claim-staking. See E. P. Thompson, 'The Moral Economy Revisited', in E. P. Thompson, *Customs in Common* (London, 1991), pp. 259–351, particularly pp. 341–50; James G. Carrier, 'Moral Economy: What's in a Name', *Anthropological Theory*, 18 (2018), 18–35.

63 Sigurðsson and Stephensen, *Lovsamling for Island*, II, pp. 614–15.

64 Guðmundur Jónsson, 'Changes in Food Consumption in Iceland, 1770–1940', *Scandinavian Economic History Review*, 46 (1998), 24–41, particularly 25–7.

65 Jónsson, *Vinnuhjú*, pp. 31–2.

66 NAI, Arbitration court archives. XVII. Skag. B. Viðvík. Book 1 (1800–1903), pp. 53–4.

and state officials. Some absconding servants were fleeing starvation[67] or violent abuse,[68] sometimes gaining a permanent exit from abusive situations, like a maidservant on the run from her master who was found by the local parish priest in 1812, half-starved, beaten and exhausted. He brought the master to arbitration court, where they came to an agreement that freed the servant from her abusive master.[69] Others – such as a sixteen-year-old farmhand who fled the violent temper of his master (who was also his uncle) – were caught by the authorities only to be returned to their masters following a public flogging for their crime of absconding.[70] Some servants left work simply to enjoy some temporary time off for their own leisure,[71] or because they were avoiding impending punishment for some oversight, returning once the fear (or threat) of a beating had subsided.[72] As Stephanie Camp has argued in her excellent study of everyday resistance of slaves in the southern United States, such acts of 'truancy' served not only to (temporarily) escape violence and terror but also to 'establish some limits to the amount and pace of their work'.[73] It was a way to reclaim some degree of personal autonomy and thus served to contest the control masters had over the time and body (or labour power) of their subordinates.

Undermining authority

Other contentious practices were less openly defiant and more in line with acts of 'everyday resistance' as elaborated by James C. Scott and many others.[74] Such activities were generally meant to stay hidden, but appear occasionally in court records or other sources when servants were caught or

---

67   NAI, Magistrate's office in Eyjafjarðarsýsla. GA/3–4. Judicial proceedings (1809–1813), fols 162v–164v.

68   NAI, Magistrate's office in Húnavatnssýsla. GA/8–1. Judicial proceedings (1830–1835), pp. 225–30.

69   NAI, Arbitration court archives XVI. Hún. B. Vesturhóp. Book 1 (1801–1872), pp. 38–9. There are many other documented cases where authority figures in local communities assist mistreated or abused servants in claiming legal restitution from their masters. See Vilhelmsson, *Sjálfstætt fólk*, pp. 96–7. This underscores Amussen's argument that, by doing so, they upheld the legitimacy of the patriarchal structure of authority in society. Amussen, 'Punishment, Discipline, and Power', 14.

70   NAI, Magistrate's office in Húnavatnssýsla. GA/8–1. Judicial proceedings (1830–1835), pp. 225–30.

71   NAI, Magistrate's office in Húnavatnssýsla. GA/10–2. Judicial proceedings (1864–1869), pp. 212–16; NAI, Magistrate's office in Húnavatnssýsla. GA/8–2. Judicial proceedings (1835–1837), pp. 413–16.

72   NAI, Magistrate's office in Húnavatnssýsla. GA/7–2. Judicial proceedings (1827–1830), pp. 157, 410–12.

73   Stephanie M. H. Camp, *Closer to Freedom: Enslaved Women and Everyday Resistance in the Plantation South* (Chapel Hill, 2004), pp. 35–59. Citation from p. 40.

74   Scott, *Weapons of the Weak* is the foundational text for studies on everyday resistance. A more recent and theoretically nuanced articulation, with a good overview of the field of

their antics were otherwise revealed. The subversive practices of shepherd Böðvar Jónsson, sentenced in 1829 to receive a flogging of twenty lashes for pilfering and absconding from service, are a case in point. He was arrested for vagrancy in 1827 at the age of eighteen and the magistrate forcibly placed him, in accordance with the stipulations of servant laws, in the service of an upstanding local farmer, where he was to be 'weaned off laziness and other vices', as the magistrate stated.[75] The disciplining that was the purpose of Böðvar's forced service was of minimal success, however. During his trial other household members described him as insidiously lazy, noting how he would work diligently when others were looking but stop as soon as they looked away. He was especially lazy, according to them, whenever the master was away from home.[76] As a shepherd, his primary task was tending the livestock as it grazed on nearby fields. A maidservant reported that he repeatedly failed to herd the livestock back home for milking on time, arriving only very late in the evening, much to the ire of the maidservants, whose tasks included milking the sheep on their return from the fields.[77] The fact that other servants testified against Böðvar illustrates the contingent nature of the resistant practices discussed in this study, as the status of servants and their relationship to their masters could differ immensely depending on the context, even within the same household.

Many similar descriptions of insidious foot-dragging behind the backs of masters can be found in court records and other sources, describing how servants would seize any opportunity to catch some sleep, tend to their own interests, get drunk or just muck about.[78] As servants living in peasant households that blurred any possible distinctions between work and non-work, where they were subordinate to the authority and whim of their masters within a cultural setting that venerated industriousness as virtue and perceived idleness as sin, seizing control – however temporarily – of the use of their own body, of work activities and tempos, was a way of reclaiming a sense of embodied personal autonomy.[79] It was a form of refusal of the complete control masters claimed over the body and labour power of servants and a limit to their authority. While such practices are impossible to measure with any degree of accuracy, their common occurrence was treated as general knowledge by contemporaries. Thus

---

'resistance studies', is Anna Johanson and Stellan Vinthagen, *Conceptualizing 'Everyday Resistance': A Transdisciplinary Approach* (London, 2020).

75   NAI, Magistrate's office in Húnavatnssýsla. GA/7–2. Judicial proceedings (1827–1830), p. 409.

76   *Ibid.*, pp. 419, 421.

77   *Ibid.*, p. 421.

78   See discussion and citations in Vilhelmsson, *Sjálfstætt fólk*, pp. 123, 130.

79   For a similar analysis within a different context see Alf Lüdtke, 'Organizational Order or *Eigensinn*? Workers' Privacy and Workers' Politics in Imperial Germany', in Sean Wilentz (ed.), *Rites of Power: Symbolism, Ritual and Politics Since the Middle Ages* (Philadelphia, 1999), pp. 311–12.

Jónas Jónasson (1856–1918), a priest and student of cultural history, wrote in his seminal volume on Icelandic customs and everyday life that, due to the long hours of constant labour, Icelandic servants were accustomed to 'shirking their duties, whenever the opportunity arises'.[80]

Petty theft, or pilfering, was another resistant practice where mistreated or otherwise disgruntled servants could simultaneously (but secretly) defy the values of a social order that legitimated their subordination and improve their own immediate material conditions. A noteworthy example is the case of a maidservant in the household of the county magistrate (sýslumaður) of Húnavatnssýsla who was sentenced in 1836 for petty theft.[81] Though not all accusations could be proven, she was strongly suspected of having stolen a variety of foodstuffs (including an assortment of biscuits and cakes, treats rarely available to the common Icelander), some candles and various types of cloth.[82] Most of these items she had delivered as gifts to her seven-year-old illegitimate son, who was living with his impoverished father in a cottage nearby. She eventually admitted to stealing a few items of food, a few pieces of cloth and some unprocessed wool, from both her current and her previous masters. She had been a servant for the magistrate prior to giving birth to her son in 1829, but had been dismissed from service once the boy was born and the scandal of illegitimacy became attached to the household.[83] A few years later she returned to work for the magistrate but was forced to leave the boy with his father. The trial proceedings betray her scorn towards her masters, as other servants describe her attempts to entice them into conspiring against the master.[84] She also defiantly proclaimed that she had stolen 'not from necessity but from longing to steal' and the presiding judge explicitly asked his scribe to write that she showed no signs of remorse.[85]

Interestingly, her extensive pilfering came to the attention of her master and the authorities only when she became embroiled in a more serious case of sheep-rustling (of which she was acquitted). Such instances, where pilfering is discovered by accident or is referred to casually in unrelated cases, occur again

---

80   Jónas Jónasson, Íslenzkir þjóðhættir (Reykjavík, 1934), p. 3.
81   NAI, Magistrate's office in Húnavatnssýsla. GA/8–2. Judicial proceedings (1835–1837), pp. 526–34.
82   Ibid., pp. 444–50.
83   Ibid., p. 390; NAI, Church archives. Undirfell. BA/2. Church register (1816–1875). The illegitimacy ratio in Iceland was high by European standards, and the majority of unwed mothers were servants. See Gísli Ágúst Gunnlaugsson, '"Everyone's Been Good To Me, Especially the Dogs": Foster-Children and Young Paupers in Nineteenth-Century Southern Iceland', Journal of Social History, 27 (1993), 345. On legislation and popular attitudes towards illegitimacy see Sigríður Ingibjörg Ingadóttir, 'Óegta börn', Sagnir, 14 (1993), 54–62.
84   NAI, Magistrate's office in Húnavatnssýsla. GA/8–2. Judicial proceedings (1835–1837), p. 394.
85   Ibid., pp. 394, 440.

and again in the court records.[86] It seems that it was mostly more serious cases of larceny, such as the theft of livestock, which were reported, or when servants stole from persons not belonging to the household itself.[87] In all likelihood, pilfering was seen to belong within the boundaries of household discipline, with masters meting out punishment themselves, as they sometimes declared that they had done when the magistrate inquired.[88] Pilfering was indeed viewed by many as mere youthful ignorance, a result of poor upbringing that could be corrected through discipline. Such arguments were, for example, sometimes put forward by the defence council when thieves were brought to court.[89]

Whether or not servants pilfering from their masters was a form of resistance remains an open question, as servants rarely articulated the reasoning behind their actions before the court. A few exceptions can be found, where it is explicitly stated that a case of pilfering was a response to particular grievances. Thus three young men conspired in 1811 to steal food from the pantry of the farm Torfalækur. One of the men, a day labourer living illegally at a nearby farm, had previously been a servant in Torfalækur and had somehow acquired a key to the pantry. He met the others, a troubled youngster being held prisoner at the farm while awaiting transportation to the workhouse and a twelve-year-old boy who was a foster child at the farm, in secret and gave them the keys, saying that now they would take their revenge against the 'folks at Torfalækur'. All had reason to bear a grudge towards the household at Torfalækur, as all had suffered beatings and other mistreatment during their stay there.[90]

Regardless of whether pilfering was purposefully performed as an act of resistance or not, the fact remains that, by stealing from their masters, servants were in breach of not only the law but also what MP Pétur Pétursson called the 'moral contract' of the master–servant relationship.[91] Their action was a violation of the submission and deference they should, by law as well as cultural expectation, show towards their master and his household order. Pilfering thus served to undermine the mirage of the orderly household as the

86   For further discussion with multiple examples see Vilhelmsson, *Sjálfstætt fólk*, pp. 141–3.
87   For a similar analysis see Susan Howard, 'Investigating Responses to Theft in Early Modern Wales: Communities, Thieves and the Courts', *Continuity and Change* 19 (2004), p. 413.
88   See, for example, NAI, Magistrate's office in Húnavatnssýsla. GA/7–2. Judicial proceedings (1827–1830), p. 410. Historian Sarah Maza has similarly concluded that the pilfering of domestic servants in eighteenth-century France was 'widespread' but rarely reported due to the exceedingly harsh punishment proscribed. See Sarah C. Maza, *Servants and Masters in Eighteenth-Century France: The Uses of Loyalty* (Princeton, 1983), p. 100.
89   Vilhelmsson, *Sjálfstætt fólk*, p. 140.
90   NAI, Magistrate's office in Húnavatnssýsla. GA/5–2. Judicial proceedings (1807–1812), pp. 238–57.
91   *Tíðindi frá alþingi Íslendinga 1861*, pp. 1127–8.

metaphorical foundation of social order and revealed the inherent volatility of compulsory service as a labour regime, no matter what the immediate reason was for any singular act. Many other documented subversive practices by servants – purposefully hidden from sight because they knew they were transgressing the boundaries of permissible behaviour – had similar effects, such as maidservants spreading gossip and sexual innuendo about their masters[92] or frustrated shepherds mistreating the livestock they were entrusted with.[93] By acting counter to how they were expected to act and consciously in opposition to their masters' interests or to the detriment of their masters' reputation, their practices were a contentious dispute of labour relations – as defined by law and cultural norms – in one form or another, regardless of whether or not they were explicitly articulated as such, and regardless of what motivated such acts.

Concluding remarks

It should be evident, from the discussion above, that court archives and other sources detailing the everyday lives of ordinary people can serve to verify the discourse on servant misbehaviour displayed in numerous accounts, such as that by Sigurður Björnsson cited in the introduction. Master–servant relations were fraught with tension and conflict and labour legislation was a matter of contention and strife over labour conditions, servant rights and duties, authority and discipline and the autonomy and dignity of those subject to the dictates of labour laws. To what extent the cases found in court archives and arbitration proceedings can be considered representative of labour relations in preindustrial Iceland is of course open to debate. Economic historian Guðmundur Jónsson, for example, has argued that a focus on the everyday resistance of servants may 'exaggerate the possibilities of the landless poor to manipulate the social system to their own advantage'.[94] He may well be correct. The 'dark figure of crime' notwithstanding,[95] the contentious labour relations found in court

---

92   NAI, Magistrate's office in Eyjafjarðarsýsla. GA/7–1. Judicial proceedings (1838–1842), fols 134v–135r; NAI, Arbitration court archives. XVI. Hún. A. Miðfjörður. Book 1 (1799–1865), p. 121.

93   NAI, Magistrate's office in Húnavatnssýsla. GA/5–3. Judicial proceedings (1819–1821), pp. 280–7; NAI, Magistrate's office in Húnavatnssýsla. GA/8–2. Judicial proceedings (1835–1837), p. 389; NAI, Magistrate's office in Húnavatnssýsla. GA/5–2. Judicial proceedings (1807–1812), p. 241.

94   Guðmundur Jónsson, 'Review of Vilhelm Vilhelmsson, Sjálfstætt fólk. Vistarband og íslenskt samfélag á 19. öld', *1700-tal: Nordic Yearbook of Eighteenth-Century Studies*, 15 (2018), 162–3.

95   For discussion see Pieter Spierenburg, 'Crime', in Peter N. Stearns (ed.), *Encyclopedia of European Social History from 1350 to 2000*, vol. 3 (Detroit, 2001), pp. 335–9.

archives might well be exceptions from otherwise harmonious relations or successful socialisation. Yet, the correlation between master–servant disputes as they appear in court archives and the prevalent discourse on disorderly servants is noteworthy and may be taken as an indication of how many people experienced master–servant relations in everyday practice. By that I do not mean that subversive practices, contestation and strife of the sort described in this chapter were everyday occurrences, but rather that disputes over labour relations took place within the confines of everyday life and were shaped by its particularities and contingencies.[96] The documented instances discussed in this chapter display a range of possibilities available to disgruntled servants to test the elasticity of permissible behaviour, to enforce perceived rights within the 'moral economy of service', to reclaim a personal sense of autonomy or simply to seek vengeance or vent frustrations. Although there are many indications that these possibilities were employed to a greater degree than previously assumed by historians, the extent of such practices are impossible to gauge as they elude any statistical analysis due to their 'everyday' and hidden nature. The agency of servants was, as with all other subalterns, 'contingent and ambivalent',[97] but it was there nonetheless as servants manoeuvred within and around the coercive legislation and cultural norms that governed their lives.

96 For further discussion on the complicated and ambiguous notion of 'everyday life' see Ben Highmore, 'Introduction: Questioning Everyday Life', in Ben Highmore (ed.), *The Everyday Life Reader* (London, 2002), pp. 1–34.
97 Gyan Prakash, 'Introduction', in Gyan Prakash (ed.), *After Colonialism: Imperial Histories and Postcolonial Displacements* (Princeton, 1995), p. 15.

Index

PEOPLE, MARKETS, GOODS:
ECONOMIES AND SOCIETIES IN HISTORY

ISSN: 2051-7467